THE
OF

MW01520958

The True Story of a Pearl Harbor Survivor
and his Nephew and Namesake

9/24/22

Best wishes to the entire
Bozich family and, espescially,
to Hayden, Brown Class
of 2026.

~~DM D. Dei~~

Don Deigan, '73 and '82

Donald D. Deignan

outskirts
press

THE SHADOW OF SACRIFICE
The True Story of a Pearl Harbor Survivor and his Nephew and Namesake
All Rights Reserved.
Copyright © 2017 Donald D. Deignan
v3.0

Outskirts Press, Inc.
http://www.outskirtspress.com

Paperback ISBN: 978-1-4787-7840-0
Hardback ISBN: 978-1-4787-8157-8

Outskirts Press and the "OP" logo are trademarks belonging to Outskirts Press, Inc.

PRINTED IN THE UNITED STATES OF AMERICA

DEDICATION

In loving memory of my parents, Dr. Frank J. Deignan and Margaret Donovan Deignan, and for Kathy Leonard and Kathy Bruso without whose help and support this book would never have been possible.

TABLE OF CONTENTS

PART III. THE LEGACY

ACKNOWLEDGEMENTS

Without the help and cooperation of many generous people in Ireland, Scotland and throughout the United States, the completion of this book would have been literally impossible.

Dr. Judy Barrett Litoff, Chairperson of the History Department at Bryant University, encouraged this undertaking from the outset. I wish also to thank President Barak H. Obama with whom I had a chance to discuss this project, briefly, during his visit to Providence Rhode Island on October 25, 2010. President Obama and I have in common the fact of having U.S. Army World War II veteran relatives buried in the National Memorial Cemetery of the Pacific in Honolulu Hawaii, and Mr. Obama was able to provide some valuable assistance. Congressman James R. Langevin (D-2-RI) and his staff have been completely supportive and helpful throughout the research process, as has United States Senator Jack Reed (D-RI) and his staff both in Rhode Island and in Washington D.C.

Jan Seymour-Ford, former Research Librarian at Perkins School for the Blind, and her successor, Jennifer Arnott, provided much valuable information with unfailing patience and good humor. Mr. Gary B. Wier, former Deputy Administrator at Rhode Island

State Services for the Blind and Visually Impaired, was instrumental in obtaining pertinent personal records for me as was Mr. Chris Underwood of Perkins School.

Ms. Carol Terry, Librarian at the Rhode Island School of Design and Mr. Douglas Doe, Assistant Archivist at the same institution, were helpful in obtaining copies of materials pertaining to my father's tenure as Dean of Students there.

The Leitrim Genealogical Society provided material essential to an understanding of the Deignan family's history in Ireland before and after the Great Famine of 1845-1851. Mr. Chris Atkinson, historian of old West Linton, kindly shed much valuable light on the Deignan family's long sojourn in Lowland Scotland.

Ms. Marie D'Auteuil of North High School in Worcester Massachusetts kindly provided me with a copy of my uncle's student records there.

My friend and college classmate, Ms. Susan Shea, did much useful research on my Uncle Donald's service in the Civilian Conservation Corps on Mt. Greylock in western Massachusetts in 1936. Mr. Barry Eager, former Secrctary of the Steamship Historical Society of America provided very useful information about American civilian shipping between the wars. Mr. Mike Mullins, Curator of the USS West Virginia Association, supplied me with vital data about Pearl Harbor attack casualty lists. My friend Pamela Dahlberg took many moving photographs for me of the National Memorial Cemetery of the Pacific when she visited Hawaii in 2008. Professor Richard Hauzinger read and commented insightfully on an early draft of Chapter Eight which lies at the heart of the matter. John Dineen, Esq. "fought the good fight" on my behalf with the often intransigent and impenetrable bureaucracy of the United States Army. Dr. Michael Burkart also read an early draft of Chapter Eight and made very helpful comments.

My debt of gratitude to Librarians and Archivists is particularly great. Robyn Christensen of the Worcester Historical Museum, Nancy Guadett and Joy Hennig of the Worcester Public Library, Mott Linn and Sandi Kane of the Clark University Library, Brendan McDermott of the Mugar Memorial Library at Boston University, Jane Gorjevsky of Columbia University Library, Linda Sueyoshi, Librarian, Hawaii & Pacific Section, Hawaii State Library in Honolulu, Mary Lee Dunn and Mr. Gus Hedden, Director of the Parsons Memorial Library in Alfred Maine and Mr. Charles Dinsmore of the Smathers Library at the University of Florida, Gainesville, were all most helpful in providing primary source research materials.

Mr. Shawn Smith and Mr. Richard Boylan of the National Archives and Records Administration facility in College Park Maryland made our two research visits enjoyable and productive. The staffs of the Military and Civilian Branches of the National Personnel Records Center in Saint Louis were all extremely helpful with various aspects of my extensive Civilian Conservation Corps and U.S. Army records research. Mr. Dave Keough, former Chief Archivist at the Military History Institute at Carlisle Barracks in Pennsylvania supplied me with much useful primary source material on the inner workings of the United States Army bureaucracy. Mr. Thomas Jones of the Army's Human Resources Command in Alexandria Virginia provided me with a copy of my uncle's "Individual Deceased Personnel File" (IDPF) which was absolutely essential to the understanding of Donald Joseph's sudden death in the line of duty during World War II on March 18, 1942. Deborah Cooney, a skilled, independent researcher, was especially helpful in tying up "loose ends" at the National Archives and Records Administration in College Park.

I need now to thank three American soldiers each of whom contributed in very special ways to the successful completion of this project. Brigadier General Richard Valente (U.S. Army Retired) served as a young Army Officer in the same Field Artillery Unit of which my uncle Donald Joseph had been a member during World War II. General Valente patiently read and commented extensively on Chapters Six and Eight, in draft form, and saved me thereby from making a great many factual and interpretive errors. He also introduced me to the inner workings of a Field Artillery Battalion from the point of view of a Commanding Officer. Sergeant-Major Edward Kane (U.S. Army Retired) and a "Hibernian Brother," into the bargain, took great interest in this project and made sure that I had a place of honor at any number of Pearl Harbor Day observances. The late Mr. Leo LeBrun, Pearl Harbor survivor and veteran of the 8th Field Artillery Battalion, generously granted me many telephone interviews in the course of which he gave me first-hand information and unique insights about the lives of ordinary soldiers in Hawaii, prior to, during and after the Pearl Harbor Attack, which I otherwise would not have had. I am deeply grateful to all three of these gentlemen for their service to our country and for the profoundly important help which they so generously gave to me.

I wish also to thank Mr. Will Cole, Military Reporter for the Honolulu Advertiser, for his assistance with Hawaiian aspects of this project and Ms. Mary Inada of the Honolulu County Medical Examiner's Office. The entire staff of the Hawaii Army Museum could not have been more welcoming and helpful. Mr. James Messner and Dr. Duane Vachon, Public Relations Specialists at the National Memorial Cemetery of the Pacific in Honolulu made our visit to my uncle's grave both moving and cathartic. At the same time and place, Father Dave Travers conducted an extraordinary graveside ceremony which brought spiritual healing, peace of mind and closure, equally, to me and to my "Uncle Donald." Mr. Marshall Uchida went out of his way to facilitate my visit to Waimea Bay on the north shore of Oahu and to help me find the very spot on which my uncle met his tragic death. Ken Dooley, John P. Cook and Douglas Still also deserve my thanks. I want to thank the entire Bruso family for their love and unfailing support. My cousin Kathy deserves special recognition as keeper of the "Family Archives." Finally, my wonderful wife, Kathy, deserves the most special thanks of all. Without her constant love and unstinting efforts as researcher, scribe, editor, proofreader and critic, this book would never have seen the light of day or possessed any such merit as it may have.

Finally, I need now only to say that any errors of fact or interpretation in the pages which follow are my responsibility, alone and entirely.

INTRODUCTION

Late on Wednesday evening March 18, 1942, barely one hundred days after Japan's devastating "surprise attack" on the bulk of the United States Navy's Pacific Fleet based at Pearl Harbor, a group of American soldiers were guarding a beautiful beach on the north shore of the Hawaiian island of Oahu against an expected Japanese amphibious invasion. The atmosphere was tense. Suddenly, a gunshot shattered the almost perfect silence of that tropical night. In its aftermath, one young American soldier lay dead not far from the beach he was guarding. But who was he? And what were the circumstances which had led to his tragic death? "The Shadow of Sacrifice" unravels these complex mysteries and, in the process, tells the compelling and poignant story of the way in which that single gunshot has echoed down through the generations of one typical American family. Here is a complex mystery, a tragedy, a kind of love-story, a tale of survival and transformation, and the unfolding record of promises made and kept.

My name is Don Deignan, and the young American soldier who died mysteriously on that Hawaiian beach so many years ago was my uncle, Donald Joseph John Deignan. Although he was the man I am named after, I have come only recently to know him more fully and accurately as a person. Since Donald and I share the same first name, to avoid confusion throughout the balance of this book, I will refer to him as "Donald" or "Donald Joseph" and to myself, unless specified otherwise, as "Don Deignan" or "the author" or in the first person singular. Our family name is pronounced **"DEGGNAN."** Over time, it has been spelled "Duignan," "Degnan," and "Deignan."

Joseph Deignan was born in Worcester Massachusetts on March 15, 1915. Less than a week later he was Baptized into the Roman Catholic Faith as "Donald" Joseph Deignan, the name which he used for the rest of his life and by which he was always known within his family. He grew up in Worcester, in central Massachusetts, a major New England industrial city, as part of a large Irish immigrant family. But in several important respects his family background was distinctive and it deviated significantly from the typical Irish immigrant norm except that he grew up under very difficult socio-economic circumstances. My Uncle Donald dropped out of high school in the midst of the Great Depression and in 1934, at the age of nineteen, unable to find other work, he joined the Civilian Conservation Corps. Then, in July 1939, he enlisted in the United States Army. On December 7, 1941 he was serving at Schofield Barracks as a Field Artilleryman on the island of Oahu, Territory of Hawaii, when the Japanese struck Pearl Harbor and its supporting military installations by surprise. Having survived that momentous event, he later received the gunshot wound from which he died just three days after his twenty- seventh birthday. He was buried in Hawaii with full military honors. He remains at rest there today.

This book is about the long, complex and evolving relationship between my late uncle, Donald, and me. Its pages are informed throughout, equally and unapologetically, by Irish-American sensibilities and Roman Catholic religious beliefs.

The narrative is divided into Three Parts and Nine Chapters. Part One (Chapters One, Two and Three) describe my changing perceptions of my "Uncle Donald" from the time when, as a little boy, I first learned about him, through my adolescence, and into my young adulthood. Part Two (Chapters Four, Five and Six) are a straightforward "Biography" of my uncle based on the scantlings of such available, historical sources as survive. Part Three (Chapters Seven, Eight and Nine) provide an interpretive analysis of his "Legacy" from my present point of view as an adult and a professional historian. In effect, the narrative contains and is advanced in turn by three distinct "voices": those of an impressionable child, a conventional biographer, and an adult analyst. Readers who may wish to focus on particular "themes" in this book can do so as follows: the spiritual aspect of of my relationship with Donald Joseph is dealt with in Chapters One and Nine; disability issues are discussed in Chapters Two and Seven; and cultural and military matters are addressed in Chapters Three, Six and Eight. The "NOTES" are intended to indicate the various sources from which information is drawn and, occasionally, also to provide specialized additional commentary on particular subjects. They need not necessarily be consulted by general readers, however, for, I believe, the story can stand on its own even without them.

Although its focus is primarily personal, this book treats in microcosm four great American historical themes of the Twentieth Century: the Immigrant Experience, the Great Depression, World War II, and changing national attitudes toward persons with physical disabilities. In addition, I hope that it may also serve as something of a "cautionary tale" for the Baby-Boom generation of which I am a part. For the time is rapidly passing when any of us will still be able to ask surviving World War II veterans about their particular, personal experiences in that momentous conflict. There are good reasons why our fathers, uncles and grandfathers were reluctant to talk in detail with many of us about what they did and saw during "The War." In the end, as I myself discovered, family investigators who delve into surviving "official records" may unintentionally learn things they never suspected and unearth uncomfortable historical details which they would really rather not have known. All this being said, at certain sublime moments in American history young men and women have stepped forward to defend our country in times of supreme crisis. Being the direct descendant and namesake of a "Pearl Harbor Attack survivor" has always been and remains for me a great privilege. Although I had no choice in the bequest of this legacy, I bear this personal and historical distinction willingly and proudly.

Whatever else the following narrative may be about, it deliberately takes no part in the continuing historical controversy surrounding the complex diplomatic, economic and military decisions and events leading up to the infamous Japanese attack on Pearl Harbor and its environs. I take that calamity as a given and view my uncle merely as one of its many thousands of stunned survivors and nothing more. What Franklin Roosevelt knew about Japan's supposed intensions, when he knew it, and what he did or did not do with any such foreknowledge is of no relevance in the context of this book.

From that time in the late 1950s when I first became aware of my special relationship with Donald J. J. Deignan until I began serious research on this project in the spring of 2005, I accepted largely without question certain "received truths" about my late uncle's life and death handed down to me by his family. Since beginning my systematic inquiry, however, I have come increasingly to realize that there is a widening gap between family lore and the emerging historical facts surrounding the life, death and legacy of my father's youngest brother. My growing awareness of these hitherto unknown facts has radically reshaped this project and compelled me to reconsider and seriously to revise many of the fundamental assumptions I held about Donald Joseph when I began my work. His individual saga, it turns out, was far more complicated than even I had supposed. I had set out, originally, merely to preserve my uncle's ostensibly heroic memory. Unexpectedly, and by virtue of the difficult conclusions to which my research has led me, it has become my task to tell his true story and, even perhaps, to help his troubled soul to attain at long last a measure of reconciliation and peace. In attempting to do so, I have sought to discharge "a Debt of Honor" which I could not in good conscience allow to go any longer unpaid.

PART I.

"A PEARL HARBOR HERO"

DECEMBER 7, 1959

December 7, 1959 fell on a Monday. All the events described in the pages which follow are either historically related to or flow directly from a single occurrence on that specific "Pearl Harbor Day" Anniversary.

On that particular December morning in 1959, shortly before 7:00 A.M., a small car made its way north along Massachusetts Route 128 toward metropolitan Boston. That automobile carried two people. Its driver was a short, fifty-two year old man; a College Dean at the height of his academic career. He had black hair, wore glasses and sported an elegant "salt and pepper" moustache of which he took great care. The passenger was a slightly built boy, small for his age, an only child, who had just recently celebrated his tenth birthday. Their destination was Perkins School for the Blind in Watertown, Massachusetts. The boy, a visually impaired and physically handicapped Perkins student, was returning to his residential school after a weekend at home with his parents in Barrington, Rhode Island.

The car radio was on and tuned to WNAC A.M., the flagship station of the "Yankee Radio Network" in Boston. The seven o'clock News was read that morning by Gus Saunders, the station's long-time anchorman. Mr. Saunders, who had a deep, sonorous voice, began the newscast by noting that this date, December 7, 1959, marked the eighteenth anniversary of what President Franklin D. Roosevelt had called "a date which will live in infamy"; December 7, 1941 when the Japanese launched their "sneak attack" on Pearl Harbor and propelled the United States into World War II. Mr. Saunders went on to remind his listeners that more than 2,400 American lives had been lost on that day.

There was a long silence in the car after the news finished. At last the driver, my father, said, almost as if to himself, "That was *terrible! Terrible!*"Then, after another pause, he added, "You know that your uncle Donald, for whom you were named, was killed at Pearl Harbor?" I said, "I know," because I already did. My father hardly had to ask that question because I had known vaguely about the general significance of my name for a couple of years already.

All of a sudden I was overcome by deep sadness. To my little boy's mind this feeling was something indescribable, inarticulate and yet very real. I began to sniffle quietly and to look out the misty car window at the passing late fall landscape. Perhaps concentrating diplomatically on his driving, my father took no notice. I recovered my composure quickly.

We were quiet for the rest of the trip. When we arrived at Perkins I said goodbye to my dad who patted me on the cheek, wished me "good luck," shook hands with me and said, "I'll see you on Friday." Then he drove away and I walked off on my Canadian crutches, which I then used because I have cerebral palsy as well as a visual impairment, to the first of my fourth grade classes for that week. For me this was not to be an ordinary Monday. The day had started badly and it was about to get much worse.

As a public relations event Perkins School for the Blind held a Christmas Concert in the middle of every December. The choruses of the Institution's Upper and Lower Schools (the equivalent of elementary and secondary grades in a public school setting) combined to present an array of musical numbers, both secular and religious, intended to entertain the general public which was invited to attend our performances free of charge. (Although, on its front cover, the "Christmas Music" Program noted that, **"The Perkins Choristers invite you to contribute to the FUND FOR BLIND CHILDREN OVERSEAS at the booth in the museum.."**)[1] The music we had to learn was often complex. To put on this annual show, we required several weeks of rehearsal. And this Monday was to be a rehearsal day. The first of our two concerts was to be held on the upcoming Sunday afternoon, December 13, 1959, with the second to follow two nights later. So we had less than a week to complete our preparations.

Around mid-morning we Lower School choral conscripts, all fifty of us, made our way across campus to the institution's Main Building. Arriving there, we trooped into Dwight Hall, its assembly area, where the concert was to be performed in a few days time. For the Concert itself, we and the Upper School Chorus would take the main stage, located at the front of the Hall, together. On this occasion, however, since the Lower School Chorus was rehearsing by itself we occupied the balcony at the rear of the room. So there I was in the front row of the balcony looking out on what seemed to me at the time to be the cavernous, whitewashed vastness of Dwight Hall. Its windows, high up on the auditorium's walls, let in the dim light of a gloomy, cloudy December day.

We started working our way through the musical program under the direction of our choral teacher, Miss Thayer. I was never much good in the musical performance department but I had no choice about being in the Christmas Concert Chorus and so my mind quickly began to wander.

Christmas was coming in a few weeks and as a ten year-old kid I was still a firm believer in Santa Claus. After the two upcoming public concert performances I also had a couple of weeks of vacation at home to look forward to. But at that moment I really didn't care about either of those things. Instead, my mind went back to the events of earlier that morning and to the fact that I knew this was the Pearl Harbor Day Anniversary.

My earlier sadness returned, this time as full-blown sorrow, and I began to cry softly and unashamedly. Then I was overwhelmed with grief, shaken by uncontrollable sobs. The kids in the rows beside and behind me were singing loudly as I wept alone:

"Jesus, Jesus, rest your head,
You have got a manger bed.
All the evil folk on earth
Sleep in feathers at their birth.
Jesus, Jesus, rest your head,
You have got a manger bed." [2]

One of the few good things about being a young, partially-sighted student in a school for the blind was that none of my classmates could see me crying. I kept my anguished sobs as quiet as I could so nobody could hear me either. I then experienced profound, solitary, inconsolable grief. For several minutes I just stood there, holding on to the balcony railing in front of me, while the tears streamed down my face. All the while, the music practice went on around me.

My uncle Donald had died long before I was born. I then knew nothing else about him except that he was my father's youngest brother who had been killed in World War II when "the Japs" surprise-attacked a place called Pearl Harbor in Hawaii. But, even so, I felt at that moment a profound sense of loss. Although the idea of death was still largely an abstraction to me at the time, I knew that, in this life at least, I would never get to know him. The awareness of that unfillable void in my future life moved me deeply. His death seemed terribly *"unfair"* to my child's mind. I couldn't change the past. I couldn't bring him back. In fact, there seemed to be nothing at all I could do to relieve my despair. I felt at once altogether helpless and totally alone in my gnawing, forlorn, irrational grief.

At first I saw no way out of my individual misery. But then a dawning realization about the way forward came to me. Young though I then was, I had already received the rudiments of a religious education in my Roman Catholic Faith. So I knew, therefore, about "the Communion of Saints": the Catholic doctrine which holds that the souls of our righteous departed dead live on in Heaven in the presence of God. [3] We have a vital reciprocal relationship with them. We can pray for them and to them for help and spiritual strength. They can see and hear us. Their prayers to God can intercede for us and can bring us help and blessing in time of need. Thus the living here on earth are bound by continuing ties of love, mutual devotion and support to those vibrant souls who have gone before us and who now live in glory and peace beyond the grave. They watch over us, praying and interceding constantly for us with Almighty God. We will all be reunited with them again in person in Heaven one day. In the meantime, however, they are actually with us in the spirit. They are a real presence, spiritually, not just a figment of our imagination or an expression of a psychic longing. [4]

In the depths of my solitary sorrow, this saving realization reached me and I suddenly knew what I should do. Silently I started to pray. First, for the repose of my Uncle Donald's soul, I said an "Our Father" followed by a "Hail Mary" and then "An Act of Contrition," the only formal prayers I then knew. Then I continued my prayer, shifting its emphasis, by saying, to myself,

"Uncle Donald, I love you and I honor your memory. Please help and comfort me. I know that you can hear me. I know that you are in Heaven with Our Lord and that you and He are watching over me and waiting for me to join you one day there. In the meantime, I will live my life so as to honor your memory and to make you proud that I share your name. I will try to live my life for both of us; a long and successful life you never had the chance to enjoy."

I knew that my prayers had been heard. But I did not know then whether or when they would be answered. Anyway, I felt better then; less hopeless and more focused, almost even uplifted.

Our concert rehearsal, which had begun with "JESUS, JESUS, REST YOUR HEAD" by John Jacob Niles, was coming to an end with Katherine K. Davis's "CAROL OF THE DRUM."[5] A few years later, this piece was to become a world famous Christmas staple, as "THE LITTLE DRUMMER BOY." Meanwhile, I had undergone a transforming experience. It had come out of a combination of deep spiritual belief and an acute psychological need. At one and the same time, though of course I did not understand the dynamics at work in my mind and soul at that moment, I had found my way out of a profound emotional crisis and discovered the start of a path which was to lead me on a long, complex, circuitous and rewarding intellectual journey for much of my life. Fyodor Dostoevsky, the Nineteenth Century Russian novelist and philosopher, once cogently observed that, "…some good sacred memory, preserved from childhood, is perhaps the best education."[6] In a very real sense, my "education" in life began on December 7, 1959.

I left the Dwight Assembly Hall that forenoon with a new-found sense of purpose and in the spiritual and psychological company of my own personal "Pearl Harbor Hero" and exemplar. Earlier that morning, after all, my father had reminded me that, "Your uncle Donald was killed at Pearl Harbor." So, under the psychological circumstances in which I then found myself, it was easy for me to elevate my uncle and namesake from a mere casualty into a genuine "Hero" of that event. I needed him to be so; a person above reproach, who, because he had himself suffered and sacrificed, could understand my trials and actually help me through them by virtue both of his life example and his ongoing spiritual support. Although I did not fully realize it then, I had been given a great gift. In the difficult years to come, thanks to my acute awareness of my Uncle Donald's real, personal and spiritual presence in my life, I would have an inexhaustible source of inner strength, distinction and inspiration to draw upon. The solace and direction he was to supply in my childhood would be augmented and then transmuted in me, as an adolescent and a young adult, into an insistent professional curiosity to learn ever more about the background, life, death and legacy of that mysterious young man whose heroic example and continuing involvement and support was to make all these positive changes possible.

CHAPTER TWO

"NEITHER FISH NOR FOWL"

Even before my birth, my name had been inextricably linked with that of Donald Joseph Deignan. As soon as my mother became pregnant my parents had decided that if their first child was a boy they would name him after "Donald," in memory of my father's youngest brother. That decision, like the life it was intended to honor, has cast a very long shadow indeed.

My beginnings were even less auspicious than were those of Donald Joseph himself. But, in many ways, I have been blessed to an extent that my young uncle never was.

My parents were part of that American generation whose lives were blighted by the Great Depression and put on hold by World War II. The children of impoverished, barely literate Irish immigrants, each of them had nonetheless managed to go to college during the "Great Depression," the terribly difficult decade of the 1930s. They met in the early 1940s as students at Clark University in Worcester, Massachusetts.

My mother, Margaret Donovan, had graduated from Boston University at the age of twenty in 1934. Immediately, she began teaching high school English in a small town just outside Worcester. She remained a teacher until after World War II when she married my father. At that point, as was customary in those days, she had to resign from her position as a teacher .

My father's academic odyssey was much more complicated. In 1929 Frank J. Deignan had been, at the age of twenty-two, a copy-writer at B.B.D. &.O. (Batten, Barton, Durstine & Osborn), one of the largest advertising agencies in the United States. Although he was originally from Worcester, he was then living and working in New York City. After the stock market crash in October, 1929, on the principle of "last hired, first fired," he had lost his job. For the next ten years he traveled around the United States and the world working at every possible menial job imaginable. For a time he washed dishes in a Salt Lake City whore-house. Another winter he lived in a log cabin and ran a trap-line in northern California. On yet another occasion, he was in charge of "a bunch of bums" clearing brush on the right-of-way of the Boston & Main Railroad. Throughout the entire Depression, no matter how bad the jobs were or how low his pay, as he used to say, "I was never on Relief!"

As the eldest boy in his family, Francis had dropped out of high school after the eighth grade to help to support them by working full time. He earned his High School Diploma in night school.

Poor as he was, throughout his ensuing Depression-era travels, he managed to take college courses wherever he went in the United States.

By 1939 Frank Deignan had returned home to Worcester and by the fall of 1942 he was well into his senior year at Clark University. Sometime after the attack on Pearl Harbor, probably in September or October 1942, a U.S. Army recruiter had visited the Clark campus. My future father, like virtually every other able-bodied male in his college class, volunteered on the spot. He and the other upperclassmen, at least, did so on the understanding that they would be allowed to graduate before being called-up and that they would be commissioned as Second Lieutenants upon entering the service. Nonetheless, he was ordered to report for duty within six months of his enlistment and he entered the Army of the United States as a Private. He never received the promised Officer's Commission. This breach of faith on the part of the military was a source of continuing bitterness for him for the remainder of his life.

Meanwhile he had met my mother, Margaret, in a statistics class the two of them had taken together at Clark. Apparently they had something of "an understanding" even before my father joined the Army. Before he left for basic training in Arkansas, in the spring of 1943, she gave him a leather shaving case with his initials stamped in gold-leaf on it. He carried it with him throughout the War and I have it to the present day. I don't know if my future parents corresponded during the war. Even if they did so, none of their letters have survived.

After his Honorable Discharge from the U.S. Army in December 1945, Sergeant Francis James Deignan returned to Worcester, took up where he had left off with my mother and completed his long interrupted undergraduate studies. He earned a Bachelor's Degree from Clark University in 1946 and received his Masters Degree in Psychology from that same institution in 1947 on the G.I. Bill. He then went off to continue graduate study at Harvard University. On October 16, 1948, he and my mother were married in her home town of Millbury Massachusetts. She was a smart, short, petite woman with curly, dark brown hair, a dazzling smile, a musical laugh and a wonderful sense of humor.

My mother's health had always been delicate. As a little girl she had Scarlet Fever which left her heart seriously and permanently damaged. This circumstance, together with her relatively advanced age, made her pregnancy problematic at best. Nonetheless she and my father very much wanted children despite the obvious risks to my mother's health.

On Sunday, November 20, 1949, my then-pregnant mother experienced a bad accidental fall. She was rushed to the Richardson House at the Boston Lying-in Hospital and I was delivered on an emergency basis there early the next morning.

I was born eleven weeks premature.[1] My birth weight was for those days an extraordinarily low 2lbs. 13ozs. The physician who delivered me, Dr. B.H. Nelson, thought that I would not long survive so he, himself, baptized me then and there. Shortly after my birth, my father called Dr. Nelson to ask how I was doing. He replied, "You have a son, but he's doing very poorly. If he survives at all, he will never be anything more than a vegetable. My advice to you is that you institutionalize him. You might just as well forget about him!"

Many years later my mother told me that my father—having learned that I would be severely disabled—had then replied to the Doctor's advice to forget all about me by saying, "No, no! I love him even more *because* he's handicapped. I can make something of him."

Because my birth weight was so low, and owing to my extreme prematurity, I was immediately placed in an incubator. In those days, premature infants like me were routinely put in incubators into which pure oxygen was then pumped. This pure oxygen diet caused hemorrhaging within the immature eyes of such infants to occur and led to the development of scar tissue on the retina, a condition called Retrolental Fibroplasia.[2] The effects of this condition could range from mere visual impairment, through "legal blindness" to total blindness itself. I fell on the cusp between being "legally blind," which I am, and visually impaired.[3]

But there was still more to complicate my case. As an additional result of prematurity, I was also soon diagnosed as having cerebral palsy; a neurological condition with a wide variety of possible, dire developmental consequences. Because cerebral palsy can have an adverse impact on different parts and functions of the brain, one person with it can be left nonverbal, confined to a wheelchair and unable to move many or any parts of the body while another individual might equally be able to walk, with a slight limp, speak clearly and perform many routine physical tasks without too much difficulty.[4]

Although I am by definition "severely disabled," my degree of vision loss and motor- impairment are in practical terms both fairly moderate. Sixty years ago, however, the combination of these disabling conditions placed me on the margins of American society. Paradoxically, although I had a good deal of useful vision, I was considered to be a "blind person" by rehabilitation professionals. And even though I had cerebral palsy, I could walk and was not confined to a wheelchair. Thus, almost from the start of my life, I was hard to categorize: I was "neither fish nor fowl."

For the first two and a half or three months of my life, although I was very well cared for in the physical sense, psychologically I was left profoundly isolated and alone. There, in my hospital incubator, I missed the necessary and natural opportunity "to bond," as a newborn infant, with any human being. Since this formative human experience, or lack of it, occurred long before I became verbal I have no words to articulate the visceral feelings of loss and loneliness which were so much a part of my life in early infancy.

In late January or early February, 1950, I came home from the hospital in Boston after my stint in the incubator as "an infant under glass." My parents, who were each teaching on the college level at the time, began their search for necessary developmental support services for me. The initial outlook was bleak.

Sixty years ago, support services for severely disabled premature infants who survived beyond the first few hours after birth
were rudimentary at best. Although the manifold physical and
developmental problems of such infants were beginning to be
recognized by medical professionals, the parents of these children were, often, their most effective and only advocates. My
parents were no exception. To the daunting challenge of my upbringing in the late 1940s and the early 1950s my father and
mother brought great energy and immense professional skill. In
my late parents I was exceedingly blessed. To them I owe more
than I can ever say or imagine. They were not only professional
psychologists but thoroughly decent, socially sensitive, compassionate people as well.

In 1951, when my father was named Dean of Students at the
Rhode Island School of Design in Providence, we moved to the
Lakewood section of Warwick, Rhode Island. Not long thereafter, thanks to a referral by Dr. Kenneth Burton, an orthopedic
surgeon in Providence, my parents had me evaluated at Meeting
Street School—then the Rhode Island affiliate of the National
Easter Seal Society—which specialized in the assessment and
education of "crippled children" like me.[5] The challenge of finding an appropriate educational placement for me had to be addressed. This was not done without difficulty or a little bit of
professional "buck-passing."

As early as January 24, 1952 Mrs. John Langdon, then Executive
Director at Meeting Street School, wrote to her opposite

number, Mrs. Leonore Gay, the Administrator at the Bureau for the Blind in Providence, and said:

> Recently we have had a patient here referred to us who is apparently legally blind. We have evaluated the child, and for your information are enclosing a summary of our findings.

In the "History" Mrs. Langdon provided, it was noted that, "... this two year old boy was referred to the Meeting Street School, the chief complaints being his inability to walk, and his refusal to stand."[6] But then Mrs. Langdon and her staff dug deeper into the matter and decided to punt:

> In discussing the case at staff meeting yesterday, we felt that the child's major problem was the blindness, and perhaps the parents might get help from your parents' group. We will talk with them about it, but thought you should have the information. Perhaps you already know about this child.[7]

In fact, I was one of seven children under the age of five who was referred to the Bureau for the Blind for services during its 1951-1952 reporting year.[8] Mrs. Langdon then succinctly summed up the dilemma of educating multiply handicapped youngsters in those days when she wrote:

> This boy is of good intelligence, and we feel that a plan should be made for him to attend

one of the schools for the blind. We understand
that Perkins does not take children with multiple handicaps. Do you have any information
on schools that do? I understand there is such
a school outside of Philadelphia. This family
needs help on what to do with a pre-school
blind child that will encourage development.
We would appreciate receiving information for
the future on facilities available for a child such
as this.[9]

I got off to a very good start thanks, again, to my parents. My
mother was able to stay home with me during my formative
years. She was my first and best teacher, but even my mother
could only do so much for me on her own. On March 10, 1954
a Social Worker at the Bureau for the Blind visited our home and
reported that:

Mrs. Deignan is interested in educational possibilities for Donald. She feels he has too much
vision to utilize Perkins Institution, and wondered about sight—saving classes. Worker explained that, at the present time, they were held
only in the city of Providence, and there would
be a question of tuition outside of Providence.
Suggested that the mother talk with the school
authorities in Providence about these, and also
with the school authorities in Warwick, as to
what provision they could make for attendance

at school in another city. It might be that with
special help in the schools, Donald would be
able to adjust in the regular school.[10]

But there was no real choice, for, as Mrs. Gay, the Administrator
at the Bureau for the Blind, pointed out in her Annual Report
for 1954:

> Rhode Island has no School for the Blind, and
> so far, no local schools have "Braille" classes.
> Providence alone has "sight conservation"
> classes designed for the visually handicapped,
> but not blind. An occasional blind child at-
> tends such a class. The State Department of
> Education provides scholarships whereby blind
> children of average intelligence traditionally
> receive their education at Perkins Institution in
> Watertown, Massachusetts, from kindergarten
> through senior high school, provided they can
> keep up to grade. (In spite of its name, this is a
> residential school, <u>not</u> an institution, and there
> is talk of changing its name.) Children spend all
> school vacations at home with their parents and
> usually come home on weekends."[11]

But my parents were determined to find appropriate educational services for me even if they had to start from scratch. In 1955
my mother returned to work as a high school English teacher in
Barrington, Rhode Island, an affluent suburban Providence community to which we had moved earlier that year. As professional

psychologists, my parents recognized the theoretical benefits of providing education for disabled children in integrated public school settings. In the mid 1950s, however, this advanced "theory" of what we would today call "mainstreaming" was far from standard practice. At least one experienced worker at the Bureau for the Blind had her doubts about the best course for my educational future to follow. As late as March 21, 1957, Mrs. Bertha Mitchell, the worker in question, reported:

> Home visit made on this date, by appointment....The matter of vision was discussed at some length, and the child demonstrated his manner of looking at things close to, and at a distance. He appears to recognize large objects at a distance, especially if they stand alone. In the matter of near vision, the problem appears to be more complicated.....The question arose in my mind as to whether or not a child with this much vision will accomplish very much with finger reading. I also wondered if he would be a suitable candidate for Perkins with his multiple handicaps.[12]

Being way ahead of their time, my parents had enrolled me in a regular kindergarten in the Barrington public schools. After surviving that experience, I entered first grade in the fall of 1956 where I vegetated for a year. At that time, no optometrist or ophthalmologist could or would prescribe eyeglasses for me even though I had a good deal of vision. The development of "low vision services" as a specialized subset of optometry was still several years in the future and so, in the meantime, I was left in a public school classroom unable to learn to read or write while my non-disabled peers were learning to do so. Without the professional support services for blind or visually-impaired children which are now mandatory and customary in public schools throughout the United States, the results of this educational experiment were entirely predictable. In late March 1957 the same Mrs. Mitchell, from the Bureau for the Blind, just quoted above, wrote to Perkins to inquire if, in spite of my multiple handicaps, they would admit me as a student. By way of background, she provided the following historical summary:

> Both parents found it very hard to accept Donald's eye condition. In the past, they both refused to acknowledge blindness. For the past two years, Donald has been attending public school—last year in kindergarten, and this year in first grade. The kindergarten teacher did not feel the child was ready for promotion in June, 1956, but mother insisted, and he entered first grade last September. He is unable to keep up with first grade reading, and his first grade teacher believes his failure in reading is due to low vision. The child's parents have gradually come to the same conclusion.... They are now ready to send Donald to a school for the blind, if the child with his multiple handicaps, is acceptable to such a school.[13]

Accordingly, I was tested and otherwise evaluated in May 1957 and found to be "...acceptable to such a school" as Perkins, on one condition. My parents were required before my admission to sign a waiver, "...releasing the school from any responsibility for possible injury which may occur to boy because of his crippled condition."[14]

My going off to that institution represented a personal and professional defeat for my parents. Their theory of beneficial education for a severely disabled child in an integrated public school setting had failed miserably, for its time had not yet come. For me, the prospect of leaving home and living in an utterly alien, residential, segregated environment would prove to be a major psychological blow. In a letter conveying the test results to my father, the Head of the Psychology and Guidance Department at Perkins told him that my intelligence and social development fell within normal limits for youngsters of my age. Mr. Carl Davis then concluded this same letter on a hopeful and mutually respectful note, although he had earlier addressed my father as "Mr. Deignan" rather than as "Dr. Deignan," which was his due, by saying, "If you are planning to have him attend Perkins in the Fall, I know that you will have him well prepared for the change to the residential living situation."[15]

"The Massachusetts Asylum for the Blind", the first such institution of its kind in the United States, was founded in Boston in March 1829 by Dr. John Dix Fisher. It received its first students in 1832. Dr. Samuel Gridley Howe, Fisher's Brown College classmate and fellow Harvard Medical School graduate, became the school's first Director. In 1840 the institution was renamed in honor of Colonel Thomas H. Perkins, a wealthy Boston merchant, who gave houses, land and a great deal of his own money to establish and sustain the School.[16] Dr. Howe served in the post of Perkins School Director for forty- five years. Along the way, he met and married Julia Ward who—as his wife—became famous as the author of "The Battle Hymn of the Republic." For the balance of the Nineteenth Century, Perkins School occupied several different locations in South Boston at various times. It became increasingly clear, as the number of students grew, that a new and more spacious campus would be needed to accommodate the institution's expanding population. Prominent architect R. Clifton Sturgis designed the new facility in the "English collegiate gothic" style. Construction on this new campus was begun in 1912 in Watertown, Massachusetts, eight miles outside of Boston, and the School opened in its new and present location in 1913.[17]

On September 15, 1957, a cloudy Sunday afternoon, I was not yet eight years old when my Second Grade school year was about to begin at Perkins. The Campus seemed huge to me. As my father drove through the entrance, I looked out the car window at the various red brick buildings, the green grass and the many big old trees scattered around the spacious grounds. It seemed to take forever to find the particular place where I was to go. Along the way, my father stopped the car and asked for directions from some older boys walking across the Campus. In the fifty plus years since then, I have often looked back with wry amusement at the irony of asking students at a school for the blind for directions to any place, but that's exactly what my father did. Eventually we found "Anagnos Cottage" and went inside, where we met its housemother, "Mrs. J."[18] After being taken upstairs to my room, my mother unpacked my clothes and put them neatly into the bureau which had been assigned to me. Then I was introduced to my roommate, Gerry DeFort, and his family, after which it was time for all the parents to go. Just before he left, my father pressed a small, toy metal car into my hand. He had written my name "Donnie" on the side of it in magic marker. I still have it. But I had little time to play with it in the school days ahead. From then on, the remainder of my "childhood" was to be largely a weekend thing.

Then I said "goodbye" to my mom and dad. Our parting was at least as hard on them as it was for me. But they left anyway and I then had a sinking feeling in the pit of my stomach. I don't remember whether I started to cry before my parents had gone or immediately afterwards. But I do know that the level of my anxiety increased markedly after they disappeared and soon enough I added vomit to my tears. I don't remember now if I cried myself to sleep that first night or not but I do recall that I dreamed vividly of home. In my dream I saw our big white house and I thought I heard my dog barking excitedly and out of sight in the distance. I was awakened early next morning by strange, sour smells and the unfamiliar clattering of large pots and pans and the clink of crockery coming from the kitchen downstairs. This was a rude awakening, indeed, to the reality of life in a residential school for the blind in America in the late 1950s.

The student population was divided by age into Lower School (kindergarten through sixth grade) and Upper School (seventh through twelfth grade) and further differentiated by intellectual ability level into "A," "B," and "U" (Ungraded) Divisions as well. Perkins, as I was soon to learn, was a place full of intricate and overlapping hierarchies: Upper and Lower School students; "partially sighted," "totally blind," and "deaf-blind" students; day-students and residential pupils; "smart kids," "not so smart kids" and "special ed kids." Additionally, I was to discover that one's status within at least some of these groups was to a great extent pre-determined by the degree and nature of an individual's disability. But "place" was also determined largely by the categorical labels put upon each of us at the start of our academic careers. Lastly, I was to find that—in this very small world—upward intellectual and social mobility was difficult to achieve and that acceptance by erstwhile "superiors" as a "peer" was even more problematic. Since, upon my entrance at Perkins, I was unable to read or write Braille—or anything else for that matter—I was placed in the General Studies or "B. Division" when I started Second Grade. The fact that I was one of a very small number of students who could not walk very well further set me apart from most of my fellows who only had varying degrees of visual impairment. In an attempt to lessen the effects of the cerebral palsy, in the late 1950s and the early 1960s, almost every summer, I had an orthopedic surgery to correct one thing or another. School would end in early June. The next week I would have a pre-operative physical exam. Then I would be operated on, usually during the third week of June, and remain immobilized in a cast up to the hip until the middle of August. On one occasion I had two operations at the same time and, in early August 1959, a worker from the Bureau for the Blind reported:

> Worker went to Client's home today, to intro-
> duce herself to Client, and to W., and to talk
> with W. about Client's progress in school, and
> his present physical condition....Worker was
> admitted to the home by W., and found both W.
> and Client present in the living-room. W. in-
> troduced Worker to Client, who had both legs
> in cast, and was seated on a couch, surrounded
> by his toys. W. explained to Worker that Donny
> had only recently had surgery done on his legs.
> According to W., the doctor feels that this op-
> eration was a success, and that there is a good
> possibility that Donald will be able to learn to
> walk. However, this will probably be very dif-
> ficult for him to achieve, and W. feels that it will
> take a long time and a great deal of effort be-
> fore he will be successful.[19]

In each instance, during these several years, the cast or casts would be off by mid-August and I would have a month or so before the start of school "to get back on my feet," literally, and have to learn to walk all over again, each time, with a new and slightly altered gait.

Thus I began my ten years at Perkins School on the outermost margins of a very small universe. I was an anomaly, seeing too much to be blind and walking so poorly as not to be able to keep up or to fit in. Added to these conditions, the social "stigma" of having started out in the "B. Division" was to remain with me for a long time, and its after effects were to linger into junior high school when I at last moved up into the "College Prep" or "A. Division."

The Lower School students lived in "Cottages" which housed 20 to 25 pupils each, together with a housemaster, housemother and several other staff people. First, second and third graders lived in and for the most part took their academic classes in their Cottages which had classrooms, a dining-room and a living- room on the ground floor and bedrooms upstairs. Blind or visually impaired children of a similar age and varying cognitive ability levels shared the same Cottage. In the lower grades boys and girls learned together but lived in separate parts of a given Cottage.

There were eight or ten students in my class that first year at Perkins. Our second grade teacher, Mrs. MacIntyre, got down to business with me right away. She gave me individualized instruction at the start of my first day even though she had to teach substantive lessons to several other students in her class at the same time. As I had said earlier, I entered Perkins unable either to read or write in print so I began to be taught Braille almost immediately. The Braille reading system is named for Louis Braille, the 19th Century French educator, himself blind, who invented it. The Braille alphabet is based on a system of six "dots" which, when combined in various complicated groups within small spaces called "cells", can be used to form individual letters, whole words or symbols signifying a number of words clumped together. After learning the idea that individual "dots" in combination could be used to form "letters", I was instructed to place my hands lightly on the page of Braille material before me with the tips of my forefingers touching gently together to form a kind of triangle whose bottom side was the margin of the page placed flat on the desk directly in front of me. Reading was accomplished by moving my hands horizontally across the page from left to right while holding my forefingers together, like a large inverted letter "V", in the way already described. My progress was painfully slow but eventually I got the hang of it and then letters, words, sentences and entire ideas made their way directly from the page, through my fingertips, and into my brain. From then on, I developed a love of reading, in whatever manner, which has remained with me to the present day.

The mechanics of learning to write Braille, a skill every bit as important as reading it, were far more difficult for me to master. Like everybody else in my class, I was taught how to use a "slate and stylus" with which to write. This process involved placing a heavy, blank piece of Braille paper between the two hinged metal halves of the slate. The top part of this device consisted of four or five horizontal rows of open-faced, evenly spaced small rectangles shaped exactly like standard Braille "cells." The back or bottom of the slate held solid, embossed spaces which corresponded exactly in size and shape to the openings opposite them on the front or top of the implement. When the two halves of the metal slate were closed on one another, the paper was held firmly in place between them. The stylus was a small instrument with a flat-topped wooden head which fit easily into the palm of my hand. Attached to this was a little metal shaft which ended in a sharp point. After placing the stylus point in the desired rectangle on the face of the slate, each individual "dot" in the Braille "cell" could be punched into the blank paper by pushing down hard and straight on the stylus, whose point was to be held and guided between the fore- and index fingers of one hand. For me this method of writing proved extremely difficult. My cerebral palsy prevented me from achieving the kind of "fine hand motion" necessary to use the slate and stylus effectively. I never developed any speed at writing with it. For me, writing with the slate and stylus was always a slow and literally painful process. I quickly came to regard its use as something akin to torture! Much later on, I was taught to use a "Perkins Brailler." This heavy metal machine, similar in concept to an old-fashioned manual typewriter, allows the user to roll "Braille paper" into it and then to emboss Braille symbols onto the page by pressing down simultaneously on one or more of its six keys in the desired combinations. This method of writing was much easier for me than the slate and stylus format had ever been. But my progress was only relative. My persistent slowness both in reading and writing Braille would continue to be a source of concern for teachers and administrators during most of my remaining years at Perkins.

After what felt like a terribly long, lonely time, the Friday of my first week at School finally came and I bounded down the sidewalk, on my wooden crutches, late on a sunny afternoon to meet my mother and father. I was going home again, at last! When we got there, my dog—a Collie and German Shepherd mix—stood up on her hind legs, put her front paws on my shoulders, licked my face vigorously with her long pink tongue which felt like sandpaper, and nearly knocked me down in her excitement and happiness to see me. But my weekend reprieve was all too brief. Sunday afternoon rolled around again before I knew it and I was headed back to Perkins once more. Although I soon came to enjoy my studies, I continued to be desperately homesick. Even though I began to make some friends in Anagnos Cottage, after each school day, I sank almost immediately into deep, searing, solitary misery. These feelings remained with me, off and on, for the next two and one half years. My revelatory experience on December 7, 1959, described in the previous Chapter, would begin to change all that.

From that day on, I discovered in myself the strength of character and focus, the "distinctiveness and sense of mission," which I had previously lacked. Going forward, my "Uncle Donald" and I formed a spiritual and a psychological team which, together, could overcome anything. I would pray for him and he would pray for me, giving me strength and "grace" from above. The example of his "heroic service" for our country inspired me and gave me a high standard of excellence to aim for and against which to measure my own day-to-day conduct. Seen against the backdrop of his suffering and death at Pearl Harbor, my own troubles paled and were put into a necessary perspective. I was able to invoke his very real "presence" whenever I needed it to help me to ward off loneliness and to stay strong in the face of any difficulty. While my parents were fifty miles away, Donald was always right there beside me. I knew that he was actually watching over me and that he genuinely cared about me. I was convinced that his strength and compassion would sustain me in times of trouble and see me through to the end of whatever work I had to do. With Donald in my corner, I no longer had any need or reason to feel sorry for myself.

Donald and I shared more than our name and a profound spiritual bond rooted in our Roman Catholic upbringing. We also had in common our Irish-American immigrant heritage. Surviving evidence of his life, such as it is, gives no indication how he felt about his ancestry or ethnicity. But such knowledge, and pride in it, certainly formed an important part of my childhood makeup and world view.

I must have been about four years old when my mother explained to me one day that our family names, hers and my father's, were "Irish!" She told me where Ireland was and that we, our family that is, had come to America from there a long time ago under difficult conditions. Her love for that place and her pride in being part of it came through loud and clear. To be "Irish" was something very special, she said, and a thing of which to be proud. So, while seated in the Lower School Assembly Hall late one Thursday afternoon in the fall of 1958 when I was well into my Third Grade year at Perkins, it came as no surprise to me when the Roman Catholic Nun who taught our "Religious Education" class read us a story with an Irish theme.

The great educational institution which would become Perkins School for the Blind had been founded in the early Nineteenth

Century by "Boston Brahmins." Most of them were easily identi-fiiable as Protestants. This being said, the School's Administration was scrupulous in seeing to the religious needs of all of its pupils. In my experience, on Holy Days of Obligation, for example, Catholic upper school students were taken by bus to Saint Patrick's Church in Watertown for early morning Mass. A large majority of Perkins students, reflecting the predominant population of New England from which most of us came, were Roman Catholics. "Religious Education" was provided weekly by appropriate outside represen-tatives of most of the denominations present in the School. (We Catholics were taught "Religion" in the Lower School by Nuns and in the Upper School by Seminarians studying for the Priesthood.) There were a fair number of generic "Protestants" in the School, too, and a smaller leaven of Jews. It should be said that we all got along very well together. Most of the Jewish kids, for instance, participated in the annual "Christmas Concert" without protest and with much the same sullen resignation that most of the rest of us "Christians" felt. In the Upper School, where daily "Chapel" was mandatory, we all robustly sang what were for the most part avowedly Protestant Hymns. There, too, Christian students of whatever stripe dutifully recited "The Lord's Prayer" together until we completed the phrase, "…but deliver us from evil" at which point the Catholic majority would fall conspicuously silent leaving the Protestant remnant to finish off with, "For Thine is the Kingdom and the Power and the Glory now and forever, Amen."

The last class period of every Thursday afternoon was set aside for Religious Education. On this particular Thursday afternoon in 1958, our fully-habited teaching Sister, whose name I don't remember, read us a pamphlet called, I think, "The Story of Duffy." "Duffy" was an aspiring Altar Boy serving in a castle chapel in an unnamed location in mid-Seventeenth-Century Ireland. I identified with him right from the start of the story. I did so, in the first place, because I knew that both he and I were "Irish" and "Catholic." But his story also moved me even more deeply and personally because I saw myself in him. He was described as being small for his age, clumsy and fairly slow-witted. He was always getting into trouble for unintentional mistakes he made or shortcomings he manifested. While I didn't think of myself as being especially "dumb" I certainly was small, even among my classmates, and I was undeniably clumsy too, owing to my cerebral palsy. "One day," so Duffy's story ran," a very bad man, named Oliver Cromwell," and his Protestant soldiers, came to the little boy's village. They burned the houses of the ordinary people and forced them to seek refuge in the half-ruined castle which dominated the town. Duffy joined his countrymen in entering the castle for safety's sake. Cromwell's men headed for the castle chapel intent on destroying it and on desecrating the consecrated "Blessed Sacrament" enshrined therein. But Duffy, now in the church, intervened. Clothed in his Altar Boy's garb, he seized the vessel containing the Consecrated Host and ran from the besieged building with Cromwell's men in hot pursuit. Duffy was chased by the soldiers up a flight of ruined stairs to the highest point of the fortress whose wall fronted on a lake. Being trapped by the Cromwellians, men who hated "the Faith" and would defile "the Body of Christ," Duffy jumped to his death in the lake below so as to save "The Blessed Sacrament" from God's enemies. Not surprisingly, under the circumstances, "The

Story of Duffy" had an immensely powerful and lasting impact on me. Combining as it did elements of my religious faith, ethnic heritage, and difficult physical circumstances, I said to myself, "he's just like me! That's who I am, too."

Try as I might, I have been unable to locate a copy of the pamphlet containing Duffy's story. It made such a powerful impression on me at the time it was read, and ever since, that I know my recollections of its narrative are altogether accurate. The validation and comfort that I took, personally and particularly, from "The Story of Duffy" in 1958 were to lay the psychological foundations for the acceptance of the "mission" I was to take up on December 7, 1959. By that date I already knew in a very and specific sense "who and what I was." I was very much like poor Duffy. His story brought tears to my eyes. I felt deeply sorry for him, even as I identified closely with him, but I was also very proud of him and of what he had done. Even so, I knew that he was merely a fictional character in a story and not a real person. My "Uncle Donald," by contrast, was very *real!* "Duffy" first taught me to feel interest in and sympathy for somebody beyond myself and he gave me a clearer idea of my own identity. Duffy's story also planted a seed in my mind, which, many years later, would flower into an interest in the systematic study of Irish History and launch me into my career as a professional historian. Looking back on it now I realize that, although Duffy's story was a superbly effective piece of religious propaganda, he prepared both my heart and my head for the appearance which "Donald" would soon make in my life.

Ironically, on December 8, 1959—the day after my Pearl Harbor Anniversary "encounter" with Donald—a conference concerning me took place at Perkins. On that date Miss Lydia Fletcher of the Bureau for the Blind wrote in her file:

> Donald discussed with Miss Whitelaw, Mr. Smith, and Mr. Davis of Perkins. Donald is in the B section of the 4th grade, and making satisfactory progress....He is a cerebral palsy case, and his physical condition may be a handicap. Has had surgery which affects his legs, and makes him less mobile than he was previously, although it may not affect his school work. His C.P. condition may, however, prevent him from doing as good work as his potential would suggest, and if it were not for this, he might be in the A division.[20]

None of the adults who took part in that conference had any idea of the psychological transformation which I had undergone just the day before. In retrospect, at least, early indications of that lasting change in me was arguably apparent just a couple of months later. On February 16, 1960 I was coincidentally given a battery of the psychological and intelligence tests which were administered periodically to all Perkins students. In light of my abject state of mind during my previous two and one half years at Perkins, the Examiner's findings on this occasion were both interesting and insightful:

Donald Deignan was tested with the Interim Hayes—Binet Intelligence test on February 16, 1960. The subject was spastic as a result of cerebral palsy. He rode in a wheelchair from his own cottage to the one in which the test was to take place. However, he managed himself quite well on crutches, walking from the outside of the cottage to the testing room and back again....Donald was an energetic, enthusiastic child, quite devoid of shyness. His actions and remarks quite constantly evinced a struggle toward self sufficiency and independence. He wished to impress upon Examiner that he was in complete control of the situation, "I can see, you know," he remarked to her. When K questioned him about the rather severe scratches on his face, Donald told her, "Oh, I was hit with a snowball. It didn't hurt," he added. During the test proper, the youngster utilized many devices in order to avoid a direct "I don't know answer."... Donald may quite possibly have difficulty establishing his independence and self-sufficiency. He gave frequent indications of a fear of failure and usually rationalized his feelings of insufficiency. Nevertheless, the results of the test and the Interview suggest that Donald definitely possesses both the intellectual ability and the required motivation for an intellectual performance, well above average.[21]

Toward the end of my Fourth Grade year, in the spring of 1960, my father announced that we would be moving to Rome, Italy, for the next academic year. In his capacity as Dean of Students at the Rhode Island School of Design, my father had applied for and been awarded a $75,000.00 grant from the Carnegie Foundation to establish a "Senior Honors Program" in Italy for the twenty most promising seniors at the Rhode Island School of Design. He made a preliminary trip to Rome in April of 1960 to find a headquarters facility for the new program. Late that summer my parents and I sailed for Europe on one of the ships of the Italian Line. By the middle of September 1960, we were established in a villa on the Janiculum Hill overlooking the Trastevere section of Rome. Shortly after that, I started Fifth Grade at the Notre Dame International School in Rome.

Notre Dame International School was an all boys facility run by the Christian Brothers, originally an Irish Roman Catholic teaching order, which by then administered similar institutions in the United States and throughout the world. The Administration at Notre Dame was far more receptive to my presence as a "handicapped student" than officials in the Barrington public schools had been a half dozen years earlier.

To the best of my knowledge, none of my classmates in Rome were in any way disabled. I was clearly "different" and at first some of them teased me a good deal. Soon, however, they accepted me as one of them and I had an enjoyable academic year in a very cosmopolitan setting. My fellow students were the sons of American military personnel, businessmen or diplomats accredited either to the Italian Government or to the Vatican. They were a pretty easy-going bunch and I learned that I could do fairly well, academically and socially, among them. The only concession made to my visual handicap was that I was given oral rather than written examinations. Oftentimes, these exams were administered to me in front of the whole class. Our teacher, Mr. Gillan, taught all of our subjects himself, save for Italian, as I remember. When the other students finished their written tests he would bring me up to the front of the room and ask me the same questions aloud. When I got one wrong, my classmates would maintain a sympathetic silence. When I answered correctly, sometimes they would cheer and applaud. Taking oral exams at this point in my educational career prepared me very well for what was to come later on. I learned to "think on my feet" and to perform well under pressure and in public. When, many years later in Graduate School, I was expected to do Oral Exams as part of my Doctoral Program in History, at Brown University, I thought nothing of it since I had been doing them since I was a child. For the rest, my year at school in Rome in 1960-1961 taught me that there was an entirely different world of "normal, non-disabled people" beyond the confines of Perkins School for the Blind from which I had been temporarily liberated. In Rome, for the first time, I learned that the world was full of other young people without physical disabilities with whom I could compete and even become friends. In the fall of 1961, however, it was back to Perkins again. But, in the meantime, I had been exposed to an array of alternate possibilities for my life so I never settled back fully or easily into the old institutional routine.

Sometimes, back at Perkins, my old sadness returned but never to the same degree to which it had afflicted me in earlier years. One exception, however, was Pearl Harbor Day in 1961. By that time I was a resident of Potter Cottage, the last stop before entrance into the Upper School. It was a rainy day so we could not go out onto the playground for Recess. There was, however, an indoor play area where we could gather between classes to let off pre-adolescent steam. Because it was Pearl Harbor Day I was feeling particularly low so I struck up a conversation with a schoolmate named Billy Barry. He had been born to American parents in the Panama Canal Zone and December 7th happened to be his birthday. I was delighted to find another kid to whom, coincidentally, Pearl Harbor Day meant something special. Just talking with Billy, about his Birthday, and my Uncle Donald, eased my melancholy quite a bit. He, at least, "understood," more than the rest of my school fellows did, why I was feeling downhearted that day.

Just as I started Seventh Grade and moved into Elliott Cottage in the Upper School, my parents insisted to the Director of Perkins, Dr. Edward Waterhouse, that I be promoted from the "B. Division" to the "A. Division" and given at least the chance to try and perform well among the higher functioning students. This class was as numerically small as my former academic cohort had been. I knew most of the "A. Division" students well because we had lived and played together for years. Nonetheless, they regarded me as "an outsider" and some of them at least let me know it! Coming as I had from "the B. Division" I was not their intellectual equal, or so they thought. Small classes, which were the norm at Perkins, led to the creation of very tightly-knit groups. Every time a new student came on the scene, the class dynamics were disrupted and each of us then had to find a new alignment within the transformed collective. Of course this situation was really not very different from that which obtains in any large private "prep school." The major difference, however, was that our world was much smaller. There were no more than perhaps two or three hundred students in all of Perkins School. The population of the Upper School into which I now moved was, of course, much smaller than this total. Thus the pool of potential friends and allies was very shallow. What is more, since most of us had lived and studied so closely together for many years, institutional memories were long and old patterns of thought and perception were hard to break. In this hothouse atmosphere, where small differences and petty incidents were long remembered and much magnified, I had to make a new place for myself within what was initially a fairly hostile environment. At first, it was not particularly easy to do so.

My academic record in junior high school, and indeed throughout most of the upper grades as well, was very uneven. I was, and am, a poor speller. Abysmal in mathematics, and in all of its incomprehensible variants, my performance in foreign languages and science was no more than adequate. But in English literature, civics, and history I excelled. The "Progress Report" Comments section written in the middle of my Eighth Grade year captured my mixed performance very well:

> Donald has made satisfactory progress in al-
> most all of his academic subjects this term. He
> has produced some of his best work in Social
> Studies. In the reading of literature in English
> class also, he is well able to understand the ma-
> terial and discuss intelligently what he has read.
> Since his Braille reading and writing skills are
> still weak, however, Donald should be encour-
> aged to practice to improve these important
> tools. He has shown a little improvement in
> Arithmetic but is still unable to keep up with
> his classmates. He will continue to receive tu-
> toring assistance in this subject.... He is cour-
> teous with the adults both in his classes and in
> the cottage. He does not participate in the so-
> cial activities of the school as freely as he might
> and should be encouraged along these lines....
> If he continues to apply himself seriously to his
> academic subjects, he should be ready in June
> for promotion to the Freshman class.[22]

Then, as now, Perkins housed the New England Regional
Library for the Blind and Physically Handicapped. Most Friday
afternoons, before heading home for the weekend, I would stop
into the Library and pick up a "Talking Book," available then on
old- fashioned long-playing phonograph records, to take with
me. During summer vacation I would arrange to have bunches
of recorded books sent home to me from Perkins. Thanks to
the Perkins Library and its fine staff of Librarians, I was first

introduced to historical novels which caught my imagination immediately. I read classic works of fiction such as <u>Treasure Island</u> and <u>Robin Hood</u> as well as <u>Les Miserables</u>, many of the travel books of John Gunther and <u>The Rise and Fall of the Third Reich</u>. Access to the Perkins Library stimulated my developing interest in history of all kinds and made me a lifelong auditory and multimedia learner.

Apart from the inherent benefits derived from very small classes of no more than ten to fifteen students, we had some excellent teachers. Anthony Ackerman and Marina Fairbanks Muldowney taught us English. Calvin Kennard, a colorful and eccentric Harvard graduate who taught history, recognized and encouraged my interest in that subject.

Slowly, I carved out a niche for myself among my new classmates. Over time I became the class "wordsmith," politician and history expert. Eventually I won all the prizes the School had to offer for English composition and History. In addition, I was twice elected President of the Boys' Student Council. My classmate, Jo-Anne King, accomplished the same electoral feat, simultaneously, among the Perkins girls. In the Upper School, boys and girls had most classes together in what was called 'The Howe Building" but our living arrangements were strictly segregated and the massive Main Building , another name for the Howe, kept us physically separated, except under tightly controlled conditions, after school hours.

For all the progress I may have made academically and socially in fitting into a new and highly competitive group of college-bound students, life at Perkins was largely isolated and rather insular. My personal sense of isolation was in many respects even greater than that of most of my classmates. Because of my limited physical mobility, I could only walk slowly and with difficulty. I could not engage in competitive sports such as football or baseball but I did captain my cottage's candlepin bowling team during the 1967 fall season and we won the school championship in that sport that year.

Once again, owing to my inability to walk what were for me long distances, I was even unable to take part, in Upper School, in occasional off-campus jaunts to the local burger joint. But my able-bodied classmates were always very good in bringing back for me whatever I wanted whenever they made such excursions.

The Perkins Endowment rivaled those of some of the best universities in the United States. In the early 1960s, when fear of Nuclear War with the Soviet Union was at its height, the School had actually excavated an entire hillside on our spacious campus and constructed a massive "Fallout Shelter" within it. In the event of a Nuclear exchange this structure was projected to house roughly 1000 people, students and staff combined, for, I think, six months. When the threat of all-out "hot war" lessened, some of the supplies from this emergency facility made their way into our food chain. Leaving aside the fact that Boston would almost certainly have been the prime target of multiple Soviet missiles, if war had broken out, in which case none of us would probably have survived anyway, I am deeply grateful for purely culinary reasons that no such conflict occurred.

Our real isolation from the outside world was brought home to me, with great force, on the evening of November, 9, 1965. While waiting to go downstairs for supper my roommate and I watched from our bedroom window as the lights of Watertown, Massachusetts, the community which surrounds the Perkins campus, all suddenly went out. The light in our room flickered briefly and then came back on as brightly as ever, as did the decorative lamps which ringed the perimeter of the campus. The School, of course, had its own massive emergency generator and so, as the entire Northeastern United States experienced one of the worst and longest power failures in American history, life went on for us as usual and without further interruption.

My long Perkins experience left me somewhat scarred, emotionally, but fully functional—psychologically if not physically—thanks to Donald's early and invisible but very real support. I eventually graduated from Perkins with an excellent all-round education, a lukewarm college recommendation and plans never to look back. On June 30, 1968 when I was formally "Discharged," Ben Smith, the School's Principal, summed up my high school career fairly when he wrote:

> After spending a year in Europe with his family Donald returned to Perkins in September of 1961 and entered the 6B grade. When Donald was promoted to the Upper School, he entered the A division of the 7th grade and remained in the A division throughout the remainder of his time at Perkins, graduating in June of 1968....

> Donald was a serious student and did well aca-
> demically in everything but math. Donald was
> well liked by his peers and was President of the
> Student Council in his senior year. He gradu-
> ated sixth in a class of fourteen college prepa-
> ratory students. After graduation Donald plans
> to spend a year in Europe studying and then
> continue his studies at a college in the United
> States.[23]

From my childhood into early adolescence, Donald had seen me
through! When I was a homesick, lonely little boy—unsure of
his own identity and his place in the world— Donald's presence
in my life had given me the spiritual solace and the psychological strength I had needed to survive in very difficult circumstances. He made a real, positive difference for me especially in
those pivotal years between 1959 and 1963. As I grew older, of
course, I progressively differentiated and distanced myself from
him and moved out from underneath his protective shadow. I
called on him less and less for "help" in times of trouble and consciously worked hard at school so that he would be proud of me
and of what I had been able to achieve in honor of his memory
and for the sake of both our names.

Since I was a boy, "Uncle Donald" had been my own personal
"Hero!" Growing up, there had been no other kids of my ac-
quaintance who could claim the special bond I had with a young
man who had died bravely while fighting for our country at Pearl
Harbor. Maturing among "mere teen-aged boys and girls," I came

deliberately to see myself as "a Man apart," immensely proud to bear a hero's name and deeply privileged to be the keeper of his memory. This unlooked-for bequest made me far stronger and tougher than I otherwise would have been or, in fact, than I probably needed to be. In all honesty, it should here be said that in my own imagination I made Donald into the "Pearl Harbor Hero" that I needed him to be. His family never said much about him apart from the fact that he had been killed at Pearl Harbor and that I had been named after him. But, given these scraps of information, my needy and wounded psyche not surprisingly did the rest. Since he had undeniably died while fighting for our country, of course he must have been "a hero."

For a very long time, I had wanted to visit Donald's grave in Hawaii. In the summer of 1968, my opportunity to do so was not too far off, although I did not know that then. At the time, I could not have imagined or predicted what the complex, life-changing consequences of that impending visit to the South Pacific would soon be.

CHAPTER THREE

"HE WAS JUST A KID!"

Sunday, August 30, 1970 was one of the toughest days in my father's entire life.

For me, too, the emotionally wrenching events of that long ago summer Sunday were terribly difficult. But they also marked another important milestone on my complex journey of discovery which had first begun with Donald on December 7, 1959.

Early that Sunday morning at the very end of August 1970 my father rented a car in Honolulu, where we had arrived from Japan via Hong Kong a few days before, and we drove out to the National Memorial Cemetery of the Pacific to visit my uncle's grave. In the afternoon of that same day, we took a Navy launch out to the U.S.S. Arizona Memorial at Pearl Harbor. On both those occasions I witnessed something I had rarely seen before, my father crying openly and unashamedly in public. Deeply moved, at the U.S.S. Arizona Memorial my father said audibly, "We should have bombed Tokyo back to the Stone Age."[1]

Dr. Frank Deignan was a genuinely kind and socially sensitive man. Witty and shy, he kept his innermost feelings and deepest emotions tightly in check and very much to himself. Only five feet four inches tall he nonetheless liked to think of himself as "a tough guy" and he had plenty of reasons to see himself as being so. He was raised in dire poverty and he came of age during the Great Depression, experiences which scarred him psychologically for life. As if this was not bad enough, during World War II he spent several years serving with the U.S. Army as an enlisted man in the miserable jungles of the Netherlands East Indies (Dutch New Guinea) where, as he once told me with that laconic stoicism so typical of a great many World War II combat veterans, "I saw a lot of death!" So my father's public tears, unexpected and uncharacteristic as they were, both at Donald's grave and again at Pearl Harbor, affected me deeply and disturbed me profoundly too.

During his entire adult life, my father loved to travel. In the early 1930s he had driven an automobile from the east coast to the Rocky Mountains, where it broke down, and then ridden the rails all the way across the rest of the country to California in search of work. Later in that same decade, under circumstances about which I have been able to learn nothing conclusive, he made his way as far as Lebanon. He had a friend at the time who was highly placed in the National Maritime Union. One of my father's many Depression-era jobs was a stint working behind the counter at the soda fountain at Penn Station in New York City. When his friend Jimmy Morrissey and his pals from the Merchant Seaman's Union were between ships and short on money, my father would feed them at the Penn Station soda fountain. So, to return this favor, it is quite possible that, through "Jimmy," my future father might have been able to obtain a Merchant Seaman's Card and thus work his way to the Mediterranean and the Middle East. Several surviving, labeled, black-and-white photographs, which I have in my possession, establish that Frank Deignan in fact visited the "Lebanese Republic" in May of 1937. He may also have visited the Rock of Gibraltar for many years later he let slip on one occasion, when I was writing a college term paper on the Spanish Civil War, that he had "considered going to fight in Spain," on the Republican side of course.

At any rate, one day in the spring of 1970 as he neared the end of his twenty-plus years in college teaching, my father announced to my mother and me that he wanted the three of us to visit the World's Fair, "Expo '70," to be held later that summer in Osaka Japan. Although he was given on occasion to somewhat impulsive behavior, my father's intention to visit Japan surprised me. Although he was not prone to emotional outbursts, I remembered several occasions during my childhood when—for whatever reason—my father ranted against "The Goddamned Japs who thought they were going to sleep in the White House."

I learned many years later that this imprecation against the Japanese had a solid historical basis in American popular culture during the early 1940s.[2]

For my part, I had no desire to go to Japan but I warmed to the idea when my father remarked, "And on the way home we can visit my brother's grave in Hawaii."

I was extremely ambivalent about the Japanese portion of our projected trip in the summer of 1970. I had harbored feelings of deep hostility toward all things Japanese since I was a small boy. I had been taught, after all, that "the Japs killed your uncle at Pearl Harbor!" As if that single circumstance was not enough to shape my hostile attitude, American popular culture in the 1950s and 1960s finished the job. We did not get a black and white TV, "an idiot box," my father called it, until 1957. Once we did have a TV, documentary series such as *Victory At Sea* (1952-1953) and *The Big Picture* (1951-1964), not to mention dramatic weekly shows such as "Combat" (1962-1967) and "The Silent Service" (1957), and "war movies" in general, became a staple of my weekend afternoon viewing. Most of the series and films just mentioned dealt primarily with our war against Japan. The major exception was of course the weekly show "Combat," which was set in Europe. At the time, I harbored far less dislike for the Germans portrayed there than for the Japanese. As a kid, I thought that the Germans had much "sharper uniforms" than did their "Jap" counterparts. What is more, I had known, from 1966 onward, that Imperial Germany had supported the cause of Irish Independence from Britain during World War I, so I was predisposed to give "the Krauts" something of a pass in my younger days.

Several films, in particular, made a lasting impression on me and powerfully reinforced my loathing of the bloodthirsty Japanese.

"Wake Island" (1942), "Bataan" (1943), "They Were Expendable" (1945) and "Run Silent, Run Deep" (1958) were the four films which most shaped my developing anti-Japanese sentiments as a boy growing up in America in the two decades immediately following World War II. In these films the Americans were always portrayed as being brave, resourceful and—even in the face of impossible odds and certain death—good humored and sometimes almost philosophical. The "Japs" or "Nips," by contrast, were habitually pictured as sneaky, bloodthirsty, brutal, unintelligible savages.

Some particular scenes from each of these films burned their way into my boyhood memory. In "Wake Island", after the Japanese assault troops have landed, one of their Officers, pistol in hand, makes his way to the door of the U.S. Marines' radio-shack. The young American radioman keeps sending his messages. Off-handedly he then swivels around in his office chair to half face the intruding and belligerent Jap Officer and says with the kind of bravado that only Hollywood could script:

"Do you guys have an appointment? I'll be with you in a minute."

The Japanese then snarls something unintelligible and shoots the radioman, who slumps over dead in his chair without having fired a shot in self-defense. In "Wake Island's" penultimate scene, the film's two American principals--a Marine Officer and a civilian construction boss--toast one another, with a hip flask, after establishing that one of them graduated from V.M.I. and the other from Notre Dame. A curtain of naval shellfire descends on both men just as they are finishing their mutual toast. The last scene comes up immediately after that as the camera focuses in on endless ranks of new Marines marching right off the screen and into the audience. The message of the film was crystal clear: all classes and sections of American society must unite to defeat the national enemy no matter how much personal sacrifice that might take. I cried openly when I first saw "Wake Island" as a kid and, once again much more quietly, when it was shown one night in the Student Union when I was a Junior in college.[3]

I found "Bataan" to be equally moving and memorable. In this film a beleaguered American patrol, led by Lloyd Nolan and Robert Taylor, is ordered to destroy a bridge and then to hold a remote position in the Philippine jungle during the early days of the war. Comprised of an utterly unrealistic cross-section of American society, the members of this gallant little band are picked-off, one-by-one, by Jap snipers who are almost always in hiding. In the picture's final scene the last surviving American soldier, a gaunt, unshaven "Sgt. Bill Dane" (Robert Taylor), tosses aside his now empty, useless sub-machinegun and crouches down behind his last remaining heavy caliber weapon. Traversing this machinegun he mows down the unseen, advancing Japanese. While doing so, he laughs maniacally at them and says, both to the oncoming enemy and to his American movie theater audience:

"We're still here! We'll always be here!"[4]

His death is not shown. Taylor's heroic image dissolves into a cloud of smoke, generated by his machinegun, as the credits almost immediately start to roll. "Bataan's" message was that brave American military professionals, like my Uncle Donald, were willingly dying "to buy time" so that the United States could mobilize sufficient manpower and resources to destroy the Japanese menace once and for all.

"Wake Island" (released in 1942) and "Bataan" (released in 1943) were made relatively soon after the events they depicted. Both of these films were intended as unabashed wartime propaganda. Their purpose was to unite the nation, maintain American home-front morale and boost Armed Forces recruitment. In all three aspects they succeeded brilliantly even though they were shamelessly manipulative and their depiction of actual events was wildly inaccurate.

"They Were Expendable," which was directed by John Ford, came much later in the war. It was somewhat more measured but no less poignant and memorable to me than were "Wake Island" and "Bataan." In this film, a P.T. Boat crew, led by John Wayne and Ward Bond, gallantly attempts to stave off the Japanese invasion of the Philippines in early 1942. Outgunned and outnumbered from the start, they nonetheless inflict considerable damage on enemy naval forces. In the end, however, they are worn down by hunger, fatigue and a lack of materiel support from the United States. In the final scene Wayne and his bedraggled, exhausted men—their P.T. Boat gone and their conventional fight all but over— march off into the distance and into what we know will be a long and terrible captivity at the hands of the cruel Japanese. Nonetheless, as the final scene ends, their fighting American spirit is unbroken and their heads are unbowed. They have done their duty and we should all be proud of them, or so was the clear implication of this film.

"Run Silent, Run Deep" came later still. The novel and film of this story, to both of which I was exposed as a boy, dealt with the exploits of a U.S. Navy submarine and her crew in the early days of the war. An early scene in this film shows the surviving members of another torpedoed U.S. Sub bobbing about in lifejackets amid the floating debris of their destroyed vessel. It turned out that this ship, and several others like her, were sunk owing to the particular treachery of one Japanese Commander. In the end, the featured American crew exacts completely satisfying vengeance on him and his underlings. The lesson was that the untrustworthy Japs could be beaten, in the end, by American courage and ingenuity.

While other contemporary films such as "The Sands of Iwo Jima" (1949) and "The Bridge On the River Kwai" (1957) had less of an impact on me than did the four pictures already mentioned, they too served to reinforce my deep dislike and low opinion of the Japanese. For some reason, I never happened to see "From Here To Eternity" (1953) when I was a boy. That film, and the novel upon which it was based, were to occupy a very special place in my psyche much later on in my adult life.

When my father informed us that we would be going to visit Japan during the summer of 1970, memories of "Wake Island," "Bataan," "They Were Expendable" and "Run Silent, Run Deep" came flooding back to me in vivid detail. I didn't really want to go to Japan. The war movies on which I had grown up, and the knowledge that "the Japs had killed my Uncle Donald," were all I felt I needed or wanted to know about *that country* and *those people!* Full at that time of the certainties of youth, I was, in fact, both surprised and disappointed that my father would "sell-out" his principles and the anti-Japanese sentiments of my upbringing by deliberately taking us to Nipon even for the briefest of visits. After all, I reasoned, not only had they murdered Donald in cold blood but the self-same aggressive militarists had been responsible for compelling my father to go and spend several tedious, dangerous, miserable years in "that stinking jungle in New Guinea."The only thing that made the prospect of a trip to Japan the least bit bearable to me was the knowledge that, after that "ordeal" was over, I would get to make the long desired pilgrimage to Donald's grave in Hawaii as my "reward"!

My lengthy exposure to American popular culture in the form of war movies, documentaries and dramatic series apart, my experience of real Japanese people, prior to the summer of 1970, was extremely limited. In my Fifth Grade class at Notre Dame International School in Rome there was a Japanese kid named T. T.Yamazaki. He had straight black hair. He was short and stocky and he wore thick glasses. He was very shy and his English seems to have been rather limited. He sat toward the back of the class while I was placed up front so I could follow the teacher and, maybe, even "see the blackboard." So I never had much if anything to do with young Mr.Yamazaki .[5]

One Sunday afternoon in the fall of 1962, just as I was starting junior high school back at Perkins, I had my second encounter with a Japanese fellow student. My parents drove me back to Perkins that day, after a weekend at home, as usual. Students were milling around the Elliott Cottage living-room waiting for supper to be served. On Sunday nights we typically had sandwiches and potato chips provided to us instead of the more formal sit-down meals in the dining-room which were standard during the rest of the week. Walking into the Cottage living-room with me, my father scanned the room and said in a perfectly audible tone—with a sharp, derisive edge in his voice—"I see you have *a Jap in your class!*" I was embarrassed, and a little self-conscious, at my father's coldly matter-of-fact remark. I said, "Dad, that's Junzo Segoshi. He's studying music." My father looked at Junzo once again and observed, equally audibly, "He's an Albino." This happened to be true but I didn't understand any such distinction at that time. Junzo, who was from Tokyo, was taking a post-graduate year at Perkins and studying piano, or perhaps piano tuning, while at the School. He was tall and thin with thick glasses and snow-white hair. He had some vision. Junzo made an effort to be friendly with all of us. I'm sure he was homesick, as I had been in earlier years, and one of my more musically inclined roommates once informed me that Junzo was "a cool guy." I don't know what became of him. In the many years since we met, I have occasionally wondered if his life as an adult back home in Japan may not have been especially difficult. As a person with a pronounced physical disability and a genetic mutation, what must his life have been like in a highly homogeneous society which seems to value social cohesion and similarity, among its members, above all else? I don't know if he heard or understood my father's hurtful characterizations of him, all those many years ago, but if I met Junzo, now, I would apologize to him in my father's name and in my own.[6]

But even my father's prejudices had their limits. In the Psychology Department at Rhode Island College, where my father was then teaching, he had a female Japanese colleague named Yutaka Kayama. Although neither she nor her family were Christians, she had received part of her education in Japan in Roman Catholic schools. She had gone on to earn her terminal degree at Boston College so she was thoroughly familiar with American academic culture. Towards my father, as a Professor and as an older man, Dr. Kayama was always respectful and even deferential. My father appreciated her attention and he found her attractive and fascinating in an exotic sort of a way. He invited her to have dinner with us in advance of our trip to Japan. She brought with her Japanese coins, with holes in the middle of some of them, and explained the various monetary denominations. After dinner, she gave us an origami demonstration in which she made delicate little birds out of ordinary pieces of paper. She said that her parents liked to entertain western visitors and she promised to write to them and to her friend, Miss Uchida, so that we could arrange to meet once our ship had arrived at Kobe Japan in August.[7]

In accordance with my father's plan, in mid-July, 1970 we took a bus from Providence to Montreal and thence, after a spectacular three day train trip on the Canadian Pacific Railroad, we arrived in Vancouver, British Columbia. From there we made our way by train to San Francisco. On the evening of July 22, 1970, we

sailed from that port, bound for Yokohama, Japan, aboard the
S.S. Oriental Pearl. American- built just before World War II,
our ship had more recently become part of the Orient Overseas
Line, which carried bulk cargo and a fair number of passengers
between the United States and various ports in the Far East.[8]
The Oriental Pearl sailed with a Taiwanese Captain and crew
under a Liberian "flag of convenience" but I doubt she had ever
seen Monrovia although that place was listed in giant letters as
her home port on the ship's stern. The day before we sailed,
my father had taken a long walk from our hotel down to the
docks to get an advance look at the ship. Upon his return he
described the vessel as, "an old rust-bucket," primarily, I think,
so as to tease my mother, who wasn't all that enthusiastic about
making a long trans-Pacific voyage on a combination passenger-
freighter which had seen better days. In the event, the Oriental
Pearl turned out to be a fine means by which to cross the vast
Pacific. Our outside cabin was spacious and air conditioned. Life
on board ship was pleasant and leisurely.

Before leaving home my father had checked out Ruth Benedict's
book The Chrysanthemum And The Sword from the Rhode Island
College Library. Deprived of his customary lecture hall full of at-
tentive students, my father was still a "Professor." After breakfast
each morning he spent our first few days at sea introducing my
mother and me to the nuances of Japanese culture as he was coming to understand it thanks to Ruth Benedict's insights. He would
stand seriously before us, dressed in shirt, tie, vest, slacks and
shoes, and "lecture" from the 3 by 5 cards he drew from his pock-
et. Apparently the two of us weren't enthusiastic or responsive

enough to suit his professorial expectations so after a while he gave up on the two of us, in disgust, as a cultural "lost cause" and retreated to his deckchair in the sunshine where he kept his further reading and his opinions to himself. After more than twenty years of marriage, my mother had successfully learned how to "tune him out" whenever my father started lecturing at her. For my part, I had no interest at all in learning about the psychological differences between those societies whose behavioral norms were based on "guilt," like the Puritanical United States of America, and those whose conduct was predicated on the avoidance of "shame," like Imperial Japan. The Oriental concept of "Face-saving" equally held no fascination for me.

The two things Japanese in which I was then interested were rice crackers and ice cold Kirin beer which I consumed with gusto in the Oriental Pearl's lounge in the course of many, long, lazy afternoons at sea. The rest of the time, during most days, I swam innumerable laps in the ship's small but perfectly adequate outdoor pool and conversed on deck in the sunshine with our fellow passengers.

Having recently finished my sophomore year at Rhode Island College, I had long since decided that I wanted to major in History with a view, some day, to teaching on the college level. After two years of studying history, I was already aware of the importance of collecting "evidence" and of the value in "documenting" my travels. This fact-gathering and impression-preserving impulse was especially strong on this occasion because I hoped to be able to obtain specific and useful information about

Donald Joseph Deignan when we visited his grave on the homeward leg of our journey. Accordingly, since cerebral palsy prevented me from writing rapidly or legibly with a pen or pencil, I carried a cassette tape-recorder constantly throughout the entire trip from Providence to the Far East and all the way back to Hawaii. In the course of six weeks, I made five or six audio cassette tapes of varying lengths and technical quality to chronicle our experiences. Listening to those tapes again, more than forty years after they were made, much of their content now seems shallow, self-important and affected. Nonetheless, they provide a raw and accurate narrative of most happenings and they recapture my frame of mind at the time when they were made. I will incorporate selected excerpts from these recorded recollections throughout the remainder of this chapter.

We arrived in Yokohama harbor on the evening of August 3, 1970. Monday, August 4th was a hazy, blazing hot day. That afternoon we disembarked and toured Yokohama's port area. The next afternoon, which was equally sweltering and humid, my parents went into Tokyo to do some serious shopping while I remained behind on our wonderfully air-conditioned ship. Ever since she learned that we were going to Japan, my mother had been hankering for a string of cultured pearls. My mom and dad walked for hours up and down "The Ginza," Tokyo's main shopping street, looking for what she wanted but not having any luck. In the late afternoon, they were approached by a polite, young "salary-man" (a term used in Japan to refer to an office worker) who asked if they needed help. Although he was on his way home from work, he changed his plans and spent the next several hours shepherding my parents from one expensive store to another until my mother found exactly what she wanted. He then negotiated a good price for her and resolutely refused to take anything from my father by way of a "thank-you" gift when they finally parted. My mother and father were deeply impressed with this nameless young man's spontaneous act of kindness and, when they told me about it later, I was too.

The Oriental Pearl having discharged much of her cargo of timber from the Pacific Northwest, we sailed from Yokohama late that same evening and reached the port of Kobe early the next morning. We disembarked, took a taxi to the railroad station, and set off for Okayama City to visit Mr. and Mrs. Kayama, the parents of our junior professor friend back home.

Back home, my father would rarely if ever stop and ask anybody for directions. Almost never would he ask for help! His behavior in Japan was no exception. When we reached the Kobe railroad station he purchased our tickets, motioned to my mother and me, and said "Come on!" He led us to the platform and we boarded the train. Instead of being conducted to comfortable seats in an air-conditioned coach compartment, which we expected, as the train pulled out of the station we found ourselves standing in the vestibule, over the coupling mechanism, between the regular passenger cars.

The space in which we were located, on this strictly local train, was small, cramped and narrow. The inside of this "compartment" was lined with burlap. Vertical metal struts, running from floor to ceiling, provided some stability for the walls against which we were soon leaning. Every time the train stopped at an intermediate station, which it did fairly often, more standees would crowd in with us. The right-of- way was rough. The train would sway and jolt every time we hit a bump in the roadbed. The floor, too, would flex and buck as we rocked from side-to-side along the rails. I was soon jammed tightly into a corner of this careening passageway on wheels. The main vertical support behind me kneaded my lower back. Every time the train would pitch or undulate I would be bounced forward, off the wall, and then as the carriage righted itself again, I would be slammed back into the adjoining subordinate support struts which I struck with my shoulder-blades. We were all packed in so tightly together that the bodies of my fellow passengers literally held me up. I could not have fallen down even if I had wanted to do so. All I could do was to stand up as straight as possible, bear down hard on the handles of my Canadian Crutches, lock my knees, and roll my upper body back and forth in unison with the uneven motion of the train. After about forty-five minutes of this, I became completely numb from the waist down.

Meanwhile, the sun beat down on the steel roof of the train and as the morning progressed the temperature and humidity, already very high outside, rose still further within our small confined space. We were all quickly drenched in sweat. There were no windows, as such, but there were vents up near the ceiling which let in some light and hot, humid, outside air.

After about an hour traveling like this, my mother piped up and said, "I feel like I'm in a cattle-car." Despite his many previous imprecations against "the Japs," my father was a man who knew when and where to pick his fights. In response to my mother's angry complaint, he merely said, philosophically, "What can you do?" I said nothing but concentrated, instead, on trying to keep my balance even though I still could not feel my feet.

Our fellow passengers, meanwhile, talked softly among themselves. Eventually, a young man made his way up beside me and bowed politely. I think he just wanted a chance to practice his English with a native-speaker. He asked me, "Where are you going?" I told him that we were traveling to Okayama City to visit some Japanese friends who lived there. He smiled and said, "Ah, yes, Okayama City, ah yes." But then either his nerve or his vocabulary—or both—must have failed him. He simply bowed, smiled once more, and retreated to his former spot among our fellow passengers.

Next, my mother sounded off again. She seemed to be on the verge of actually crying frustrated tears as she wailed, *"I feel I'm being treated like an animal in here!"* Neither my father nor I had any response to offer. The Japanese around us murmured to themselves.

Shortly after this point in our journey, something happened which I remember with absolute clarity even though the incident in question occurred more than forty years ago. I am only five feet tall, shorter even than my late father was. Suddenly, a little elderly Japanese lady far shorter even than I am made her way through the crush of people and stood directly in front of me. Even with my relatively poor vision, in the days before I had acquired highly specialized glasses for reading and distance viewing, she came so close to me that I can remember every detail about her vividly. She wore sandals. She had on a simple one- piece dress which ended about half way down her shins. It had short sleeves and was dark blue with solid white circles, perhaps the size of quarters, scattered throughout the garment. Her hair was curly and gray. Her wrinkled face was the color of a walnut. She bowed to me and when she then smiled, I noticed that most of her front teeth were missing. She extended her hand toward me and said something I couldn't understand. I put out my hand, in return, and she placed in it a small blue and white cotton handkerchief with a tiny checkerboard pattern on it. I took it, bowed, smiled at her and said, "Thank you! Thank you very much!" She bowed again and, still facing me, she walked backwards into the dense crowd behind her.

Immediately I began mopping my forehead and face from which the sweat was pouring. When I did so, for about ten or twenty seconds afterward, I felt the most delicious, cool breeze wafting over my dried face. Within a very few seconds, beads of sweat began to form again and started rolling down my face once more. I dabbed away, again, with much less satisfactory results than before. In no time, the little handkerchief was soaked through and practically useless for the purpose for which it had been originally offered. I tried, therefore, to return it to the lady who was still quite near me but she motioned that I should keep it and so I did. I still have that handkerchief.

Perhaps the lady, who I think had been in the compartment with us since the start of our trip from Kobe, admired my "pseudo-samurai spirit": my stoic, uncomplaining silent acceptance of a difficult situation. Or maybe she just felt sorry for the profusely perspiring, disabled, little foreigner jammed into the corner of a makeshift conveyance not fit even to carry livestock. Whatever her reasons, I have never forgotten her simple, extraordinary, spontaneous act of human kindness!

After about two hours, or so, we finally reached Okayama City. When the crowd in the vestibule began to disperse and I first tried to walk again, "pins and needles" shot throughout my entire body. From being bounced back and forth off the steel reinforced burlap-covered walls, my back and shoulders were bruised and sore.[9]

Once we got off the train my father quickly found a phone booth and called Miss Uchida, Dr. Kayama's school friend who was expecting us. She arrived in a very few minutes and drove us in her air- conditioned car to her home where we were to meet Mr. and Mrs. Kayama for lunch. Of them I said, at the time, that, "Mr. Kayama is an elderly but very distinguished looking man in his early seventies and his wife is a very spry and lively, intelligent woman perhaps in her late sixties."[10]

Reflecting on my experience, later that evening, I further re-called that:

> Miss Uchida's home is brand-new. It's very
> modern. We had western-style furniture and
> we were served by one of her nieces who, in
> good Japanese-fashion, knelt on the floor as she
> served us. And we had air-conditioning, which

was a blessing, since it was very hot and muggy with intermittent rain.[11]

Lunch was equally exotic and welcome. As I noted, shortly after the meal:

> We were served a delightful Japanese lunch which consisted of several courses; (the) first being dried seaweed in the form of crackers....And also candy-coated peanuts, similar to those you find in a box of Crackerjacks. Next came osushi,… a small rice cake which is delicious. Then came bean-curd soup which was very fine. It consisted of an almost clear broth… in which floated pure white blocks of bean-curd which was tasty, a very satisfying dish. When we finished that off, the highlight of the meal was watermelon which would melt in your mouth. It was pink and firm and altogether delightful. And to go with this, we had as a beverage "Kirin Beer," a very light and lively Japanese beer, of which Japan is justly proud.[12]

After lunch, our hosts took us to Okayama City's largest park, Korakuen Garden, which is reputed to be one of the three most famous and beautiful landscape gardens in Japan.[13] Young man that I was at the time, it impressed me as, "…a masterpiece of landscaping." Its lawns were "…beautifully manicured, and the park is dotted with .. Japanese houses, of all descriptions and for all purposes…. It's just a beautiful place around which you could wander for hours."[14]

As a parting gift, after our day together, Mr. and Mrs. Kayama gave us a box of local peaches, which turned out to be delicious.[15] When they learned the calamitous details of our train ride from Kobe to Okayama City that morning, they were horrified. Mr. Kayama, himself, escorted us to the train station, made sure we had the proper tickets for good seats on the fast afternoon train to Kobe and settled us into them before he said "Goodbye.". We made ourselves comfortable, enjoyed the efficient air-conditioning system and took in scenic views of the passing landscape through the large picture windows in our carriage. Before long, railroad staff people brought us refreshing cups of tea and steaming hot towels to press on our faces and necks.[16]

On the train trip back to Kobe, I reflected on the experiences of our day and recalled later that, "We were able to go into a real Japanese home and to meet very fine and friendly and gentle people; to be given the privilege of their hospitality."[17] In what seemed like a very short time we reached Kobe and boarded the Oriental Pearl once again.

Early the next morning we boarded a commuter train, this time with real seats, for the short journey from the port of Kobe to the site of the Worlds' Fair in Osaka. After buying our tickets for the Fair, my father rented a wheelchair for me and we entered the expansive grounds. He did fine, pushing me along briskly, until we found ourselves at the top of several flights of steep, concrete stairs with no obvious way for the wheelchair to get down them so that we could go in to the next Exhibit Pavilion. While we were pondering our dilemma, three young Japanese men wearing gray uniforms, plain baseball caps and white gloves approached us and offered their help. They obviously worked at the Fair assisting visitors to the Exposition who appeared as if they needed help. Looking from the wheelchair and me to my father their leader said to him, "Shrow!" My father, who was already beginning to suffer from the hereditary, progressive hearing loss which with advancing age increasingly afflicts male members of our family, thought the fellow was instructing him to *throw* the wheelchair down the stairs. So, to confirm this, my father said, "Throw it?" His voice had a quizzical tone but he sounded like he was seriously entertaining the idea. "Shrow!" the leader repeated more emphatically "Throw it?", my father said, again, with increasing enthusiasm in his voice. By this time I was scared. The awful thought flashed through my mind that these three, young, Japanese guys might actually be about to pick me and the wheelchair up, together, and fling the whole business down the many flights of stairs. So I said, "Hey, let me out, I'll walk!" Recognizing that we were getting into serious linguistic difficulty, another member of the Attendant trio volunteered, "Showry!" Just in time, the light went on in my father's head and he said, "Ah, slowly!" as if it had been his idea all the time. What the Attendants had wanted to do was to turn the wheelchair around backwards, tip it up on to its large rear wheels and guide it carefully down the steps to the bottom. So they tipped me back, gently, in the chair. Their leader got directly behind me, taking the chair by the handles, and each of his colleagues took charge of a wheel on either side. Together, they half carried, half rolled me in the chair down to the bottom of the steps. We thanked them and moved on to view the next Exhibit in which we were interested. But we did not stay too long at the Fair.

That evening, our ship weighed anchor and we left Japan behind us. As we did so, I reflected on my brief experience in the "Land of the Rising Sun" as follows:

> It's hard to believe…that this is the country which precipitated World War II for the United States; the country that launched the attack on Pearl Harbor, and that these people some thirty short years ago changed both the lives of so many Japanese and so many Americans as well. And it's a good time to reflect…this being the twenty-fifth anniversary of the dropping of the first Atom Bomb.…that the Japanese have renounced violence and war and militarism almost completely.[18]

We spent barely a week, altogether, in Japan. I expected to have been met by a superficial politeness which masked a cold, brusque xenophobia. I had arrived in the Land of the Rising Sun full of hostile preconceptions. Only reluctantly had I set foot in that same country whose people—a scant generation earlier—had deliberately devastated Pearl Harbor, overrun gallant American garrisons on Guam and Wake, bombarded "Fortress Corregidor" into submission and instigated the Bataan Death March while at the same time brutalizing and exploiting their neighbors on the Asian Mainland. "The Japs" had also, of course, killed my beloved uncle and namesake into the bargain.

Over and against my movie-fueled pre-conceptions and considerable knowledge of "historical facts," even I had to admit that,
without exception, the Japanese people whom we had met had
treated us with genuine kindness and real humanity. But our
long road home to Rhode Island did not run through Damascus.
Rather, it wound instead through South Korea, Taiwan, Macau
and Hong Kong. Nonetheless, my practical experiences on the
ground during that week in Japan forced me to begin to rethink
and at least in part to redefine my attitudes toward most things
Japanese. My opinion about the War-time Government of Japan
and the manifold atrocities which its armed forces committed in
the name of "The Emperor" has not changed one bit in the four
decades since my visit. In fact, in common with the dwindling
number of surviving World War II Pacific Campaign veterans, I
am still waiting for an unequivocal apology, for the "war crimes"
of its predecessor, from the present-day Japanese Government.
But, even as long ago as August 1970, I realized that intellectual
honesty together with my own recent experiences compelled
me to distinguish between the reprehensible World war II actions of the Imperial Government and the manifest decency of
the many ordinary Japanese people we had just met.

In the course of the Oriental Pearl's voyage from Yokohama to
Hong Kong, she discharged large quantities of general cargo:
raw lumber, huge bales of paper and many other American products in bulk. She replaced these stocks with other goods in each
port at which we called. In due course our good old ship would
carry these new cargos back to the United States, but we would
not make that trip with her.

We arrived in Hong Kong on August 22, 1970, after a month in transit from San Francisco. We flew out of Hong Kong on August 26 bound for Honolulu via Tokyo. On that long trans-Pacific flight aboard a 747 "Pan-Am Clipper," I had plenty of time to reflect and a great deal to think about.

I reflected further on my experiences in Japan and how different that country and her people turned out to be from what I had expected. Of course, I also thought with, growing excitement, about our impending visit to Donald's grave in Hawaii. I began to steel myself for the surreal prospect of seeing my own name in front of me on another man's grave marker. I began to worry, too, how my father might take the impact of standing at his youngest brother's final resting place. I thought about all these things, and much more, as the Pan-Am Clipper ploughed along through the multiple time-zones between Tokyo and Honolulu.

After thinking about Japan, and the rest of our eventful and interesting trip to the Far East, my thoughts turned again, too, to Donald and what I really knew about him, apart from the fragmentary information my father had given me since I was a boy. My thoughts turned to the one other source I had for what little, in total, I then knew about the young man I was named after.

My father's late mother, Anna Cross Deignan, had a sister named Louise. Louise Cross supplied the rest of what little I knew about my "Uncle Donald" before I visited his grave in Hawaii in 1970. My "Aunt Louise" was a real character. She was a typical "old-maid." She was short, with curly white hair, and she always wore the kind of green eye-shade associated in popular culture with book-keepers or Certified Public Accountants. She loved hard candy and she seemed to have an inexhaustible supply of it on or near her person at all times. She was deeply religious and a bit priggish. About her, lastly, there was always a vague and lingering "old peoples' smell," which was not unpleasant but distinctly strange all the same.

While I was growing up, she would visit us for an extended stay of a week or two every summer. She had known my father since his birth, and therefore she insisted on always addressing him as "Frannie." His Christian name was Francis but he liked to be called "Frank." Louise would always address him by his diminutive title, which drove him crazy, so soon after her arrival he would turn her care and feeding over to my mother, who waited on my aunt hand and foot. "Can I get you anything, Louise?" my mother would ask. "I'd love a cup of tea," she would reply and, after a long pause, "....a sandwich, if that wouldn't be too much trouble!" For my mother, it never was.

I looked forward to Aunt Louise's annual visits with great anticipation. Talking with her was like going into a time-machine. She had been born in Worcester around 1880 and her idioms were Nineteenth Century ones. She would talk about stores at which she "traded," for example. And she had very old-fashioned views on everything from "race" to "religion," all of which I found to be both quaint and fascinating. But I welcomed her appearances most because she would talk with me lovingly about "Donnie," my Uncle Donald, whom she had known very well from the time of his infancy to the occasion of his death.

He had been, she told me, her "favorite nephew." They had ex-
changed letters and post cards, regularly, when he was stationed
at Schofield Barracks before and immediately after the attack on
Pearl Harbor. Alas, Aunt Louise never brought any of this correspondence to share with me so all I have is her insistence that
it existed. She gave me some details about the circumstances of
Donald's death but the problem was that her stories or recollections always varied. Louise, not surprisingly, found it difficult
to talk about Donald's death. When she did so, she would start
to sniffle and wipe away tears. Once, she told me, he had been
wounded on December 7th while returning home from Mass.
Another time, according to her story, he had been badly burned
and lapsed into unconsciousness from which he never emerged
before his death. She even claimed, on one retelling, that she had
received a letter from the Roman Catholic priest who had attended him at the time of his demise. None of these renderings,
as I was to find out many years later in the course of my own
research, were accurate or reliable.

(I was able to tell Aunt Louise that I had visited Donald's grave
before she, herself, died suddenly in December 1970 in a public housing apartment in Worcester. Well-intentioned neighbors
cleaned out her apartment, after her death, before I could get
there to search for and retrieve the correspondence between
Donald and Aunt Louise so it is impossible to verify much of her
account of their relationship and his death.)

Following many hours in the air, we finally crossed the beautiful Hawaiian coast. After clearing customs, we took a taxi into

Honolulu and my father quickly found us a furnished bungalow to stay in for a few days. On Sunday morning he rented a car and we drove the few miles out of the city to the National Memorial Cemetery of the Pacific. My father had called ahead so we knew exactly where to go when we arrived there. We parked the car and walked up a gently sloping hill. On that quiet Sunday morning in late August, the three of us stood at last before the grave of the man whose legacy has done so much to shape my life.

I felt the need to express my feelings for posterity, so, using my tape-recorder, I said, "Now, on this very peaceful, lovely Sunday morning we are at the National Memorial Cemetery of the Pacific,… here among thousands and thousands of graves."

My father looked down at the gravestone and said quietly "I didn't remember that he was eight years younger than I am. *He was just a kid!*"

After that, he tried to read aloud the inscription on Donald's grave marker. It took him two tries to get it right because he was so overcome with emotion and because he had trouble seeing the abbreviations on it through his tears.

Then I said:

> Here, in this very lovely setting, the only sound is the occasional flapping of the flagstaff halyard in the breeze and the occasional car driving slowly by. But otherwise, it's very quiet, peaceful and altogether serene. An appropriate

setting for a cemetery of this kind. The stark symmetry of the graves is softened somewhat by the green hills and the many shade trees in the background.... And as I said earlier, this is a very lovely Sunday morning and many other visitors have come here. Numbers of the graves are freshly decorated with flowers of all kinds."[19]

It was difficult to maintain my own composure in light of my father's evident anguish. In fact, all three of us stood there and wept openly at that moment above Donald's grave.

His gravestone actually read:

> "B 100
> JOSEPH J. DEIGNAN
> MASSACHUSETTS
> PFC 13TH FIELD ARTILLERY BN 24TH INF DIV
> WORLD WAR II
> MARCH 15 1915 MARCH 18 1942"

As I looked down at it, I was emotionally overcome, confused, and intellectually troubled also. I had always been told that I had been named after my "Uncle Donald" but now I saw his name listed as "Joseph J. Deignan" on the grave marker. My first thought was that "The Army must have *screwed-up* somehow and gotten the name wrong." I had grown up with derisive comments from my father about the Army's inefficiency and stupidity during World War II and so I could conceive of the name problem on the grave marker as just such an example of those institutional traits in the American military.

Much more troubling, however, was the evident discrepancy between the supposed date of Donald's death—around or shortly after the Pearl Harbor Attack—and the March 18, 1942 date actually given on his gravestone. My mind raced at the gravesite to try to account for this fundamental, factual difference. Had the Army gotten the date of death wrong too, I wondered? Or, as I then almost immediately began to suppose, had Donald been wounded during the Pearl Harbor Attack and died in the following March of his injuries? This last conclusion is the one I carried in my mind until I actually started the research for this project.

So, then, standing there before Donald's grave, and in light of the new and profoundly troubling discoveries I had just arrived at, I made him a second promise. Back in December 1959, on that awful Pearl Harbor Day Anniversary when he had first come so forcefully into my life, I had promised him that I would always honor his memory and live my life so as to make him proud and to distinguish both our names. Now, seeing the discrepancies between what I had always believed and what was on the actual gravestone in front of me, I said, "Something is wrong here, Uncle Donald, and some day, when time and circumstances permit, I promise you I'll get to the bottom of this and set things right for you!"[20]

It has now been a little more than forty years since I made that second, tearful, heart-felt, additional promise to the man whose life story has meant so much to me. At that moment, there in the Cemetery, I had no idea how complicated and difficult the investigative, remedial task I was willingly undertaking would prove to be. The remainder of this book describes how I fulfilled my two pledges and what more I have discovered both about Donald and myself in the course of doing so.

PART II.

A SHORT LIFE

AT THE BOTTOM OF THE HEAP

The Deignan family was "at the bottom of the heap," socially and economically disadvantaged, in three countries: Ireland, Scotland and the United States of America. Extreme poverty was the common thread which bound these immigrant experiences together and marked those who underwent them for life.

Within his own generation of the Deignan family, Donald Joseph was in many respects destined to be different. Like his brothers and sisters he regarded himself as a Scottish Catholic rather than an Irish one even though the family traced their roots to Ireland. But, in addition, he was unique in that he would be the youngest son in a household dominated by women. In his own day he would also, paradoxically, be the least well-educated but the most widely traveled of all of them. Finally, he would be the only one among them to meet with an unexpected and violent death.

Donald Joseph Deignan never knew his grandfather, Francis, who died the year before he was born. But it was owing to the toughness, drive, initiative and good luck of that obscure, illiterate, Irish-speaking immigrant that Donald and his siblings had at least a chance to make something of their lives in the United States of America.[1]

"Francis Duignan" (1837-1914), Donald's grandfather, was born in County Leitrim, in northwestern Ireland, probably in 1837.[2] Ireland, an impoverished, northwest European island country slightly smaller than the state of Maine, was itself divided into four Provinces: Leinster, Munster, Ulster and Connaught. Within these larger provincial units it was further split into thirty-two Counties, the equivalent of our individual States. County Leitrim, located at the northern end of the westernmost Province of Connaught, along and slightly inland from the Atlantic seaboard, was among the most populous parts of the country but it was also reputed to be " ... the poorest county in Ireland."[3] Leitrim was itself subdivided into a hierarchy of lesser administrative entities the smallest of which were called "Townlands." There are 60,462 Townlands in Ireland.[4]

"Duignans" had inhabited the sprawling 15,000 acre Parish of Kiltubrid in south Leitrim for generations. The date of their arrival and the length of their residence in the Townland of Drumruekill, within the Parish of Kiltubrid, was however less certain. A local Leitrim commentator has observed that:

> Townland divisions have been handed down
> from ancient times. These land units vary in

size and each townland would have from four to a dozen houses or homesteads, each with land attached, scattered across its terrain. In Kiltubrid parish there are 82 such townlands.[5]

It was probably in Drumruekill, or in one of its neighboring Townlands, that Francis was born to Bernard Duignan and his wife Catherine (Nugent) Duignan sometime during 1837. The material circumstances into which Francis was born were dire, for, even during a period of relative prosperity:

> The housing was...miserable; the traditional cabin, one story high, one-roomed, mud-floored, mud-walled, with tiny windows, inadequate doors and grateless hearths, housed the majority of the population. This kind of dwelling was cheap, easily constructed and even more easily destroyed. It could be erected in a few weeks at a cost of about £6.[6]

It is certain that the newborn Francis was delivered in just such a setting, on a simple bed stuffed with straw placed on the floor of the "cabin" which his peasant parents occupied. The dim daylight the infant child first saw would have doubtless been filtered through a single, small window high up on one wall. A smoky turf fire burning in the open hearth along another wall would, at one and the same time, have provided heat, a means for cooking and, apart from a lamp, perhaps, the only source of feeble light in the house after dark.

Bernard Duignan (1800-1884), father of the infant Francis, was himself at the very bottom of pre-Famine Irish society. The record of his death in February 1884 lists his occupation as "Herd"[7], which suggests that he was at least a sometime drover of cattle or sheep. But he was also a "landless laborer" who paid high seasonal rent for a "conacre"--a tiny patch of agricultural ground—typically far less than an acre in size--on which he erected his mud house and grew the usually abundant crop of potatoes with which he fed his growing family.

Between 1750 and 1845 the population of Ireland more than doubled from approximately four million to an estimated 8.5 million people. This explosive population increase put immense pressure on the finite supply of suitable agricultural land and so, as Freeman put it:

> Subdivision of existing farms had led to the development of extremely small holdings; and in view of the steadily increasing population pressure, it was difficult to avoid this fragmentation, especially as thousands of labourers had no land at all but were obliged to pay high rents for conacre patches to grow their potatoes.[8]

Periodic famine was no stranger to the Irish people. Although the 1841 national census showed Ireland to be, for the moment, in a flourishing condition, the impression of relative prosperity would prove to be superficial and deceptive.

Between 1845 and 1851 a disease commonly called "the Blight" ravaged the potato crop on which the vast majority of Ireland's agricultural peasant population depended for their very survival. For seven terrible years in succession, the potato harvest failed each season, partially or completely, throughout the entire country. The result was prolonged mass hunger and suffering on an unprecedented scale. During this period at least one million Irish people succumbed either to outright starvation or to the epidemic diseases which accompanied it during "the Great Hunger."[9]

Given the precarious circumstances into which he was born around 1837, it is remarkable that Francis Duignan survived Ireland's "Great Famine" of 1845-1851 at all. What is more, he did so during childhood in County Leitrim in the Province of Connaught where that general national calamity was particularly severe.[10]

Ironically, had it not been for the Great Famine and its terrible consequences, Francis in his turn would probably have been condemned to eke out his own miserable existence in the same place and under the identical conditions of relentless poverty which had afflicted his forefathers. For young Francis, however, fate was to dictate otherwise. For he had a brother named Patrick. The surviving records pertaining to Patrick Duignan, and his relationship to Francis, are fairly imprecise and even contradictory. From them it is not clear either what the birth order of the two boys was or even Patrick's own age at the time of death. The County Leitrim Genealogist who "reconstructed" the family history says merely:

> We did not find the baptism of Patrick Deignan
> in Kiltubrid parish or any of the other Leitrim
> parishes. Patrick was aged 60 years in the 1901
> Census, yet he was aged 74 years at the time of
> his death in June 1901, therefore it is difficult
> to estimate a year of birth, however it appears
> that he was definitely born before 1841.[11]

Patrick's presence in the family and his survival to adulthood were to have an important impact on the future life and prospects of his brother, Francis.

Post-Famine landholding and demographic patterns were radically different from those in place prior to 1845. As a result of the Great Famine and the concomitant decline in population by virtue of death or emigration, the Irish people learned valuable, collective economic and psychological lessons. Land was henceforth no longer to be subdivided among multiple offspring. Small holdings were, rather, to be consolidated and kept intact at all costs so they could be passed on to one person as an inheritance. After the Famine, usually a single son would inherit "the farm" upon his father's death, with his siblings thus being compelled by the lack of traditional economic opportunity at home to emigrate. More than thirty years ago, F.S.L. Lyons captured both the profundity and the complexity of the change in the pattern of post-Famine landholding when he wrote:

….the farmer, with his eyes fixed on profit and in his memory the recollection of the terrible nemesis that had overtaken the pre-Famine fragmentation of holdings, had a powerful motive not only to add field to field but to bequeath the end result to his heir. To his heir — not necessarily to his family. If fragmentation was to be avoided there must be no division of the painfully acquired fields among all the children. Instead, one son (not necessarily the eldest) must be selected to succeed, and one daughter (perhaps) equipped with the dowry that would enable her to make a suitable dynastic alliance with a neighbour whose affairs were in a satisfactory condition. Upon the rest of the family this unifying, centralising tendency had of course the effect of presenting them with two bleak alternatives — either to emigrate or to remain at home as relatives assisting on the farm, with little hope of ever breaking out of the pattern of perpetual bachelordom or spinsterhood that had been devised for them. Even the son destined to marry was unlikely to marry young, for his father would seldom hand on the farm until obliged to do so by old age or infirmity, and sometimes not even then. Equally, the chosen daughter must remain single until her dowry had been painfully accumulated and her marriage elaborately negotiated, frequently by a professional match-maker.[12]

Even as late as 1857, with the typical post-Famine process of "consolidation" of land holdings well under way, the Duignan family appears still to have been in a marginal economic situation. In that year, surviving land records indicate that Patrick Duignan rented much less than an acre of "meadow" on one of Lord Southwell's Leitrim estates in the Townland of Moher in the Parish of Kiltubrid. For the 3 rods and 8 perches of land thus acquired, Patrick paid an annual rent of 10s.[13] This seems to have been about the average size of property and the standard rental rate for most of his neighbors as well. Since no mention of Bernard Duignan is made in the same record source as having rented land in his own right, it is reasonable to conclude that by 1857 Patrick had taken day-to-day responsibility for the management of the family "holding". At the time of his death in June 1901, Patrick's occupation, like that of his father, Bernard, before him, was listed as "Herd." But his eldest son and heir, also a Bernard, who died in a nursing home in the town of Carrick-on-Shannon on September 30, 1954 at age 77, was described as a "Farmer."[14] The same designation was listed for Bernard's younger brother, Peter, who also died in the same place on July 27, 1956 at 70 years of age.[15] Thus if Patrick Duignan's sons benefited from the phenomenon of "consolidation" and acquired additional land, so as to die as "Farmers," they did so much later in life and during the Twentieth Century. For all that, their material gains may have been relatively modest for, since the Famine, as T. W. Freeman cogently observed, in Leitrim, "Of all changes, by far the most significant has been the decline of population by two-thirds, which made possible the union of farms into holdings that still seem regrettably small."[16]

In the wake of the Great Famine, which Bernard Duignan, his wife Catherine and their two sons somehow survived while many of their neighbors starved to death in place or emigrated around them, Francis had no prospects for economic improvement or upward social mobility at home in County Leitrim. Francis eventually and reluctantly left Kiltubrid and County Leitrim behind him, but he was a long time going thence. His reluctance to leave home was deeply rooted in Irish cultural tradition and reinforced by transitory post-Famine economic circumstances.

No matter how difficult their day-to-day existence may have been, Irish peasants were deeply attached to the land and the locality from which they came. Significantly, the Irish language had within it no word for "immigrant." Its closest equivalent was "exile" to describe a person who had to leave Ireland, unwillingly, for whatever reason. Of the Irish, one observer remarked, "They are warmly attached to their native soil, to their cabins, their families, and to old customs and habits, ..."[17] Another commentator observed that their affection for "...their native land is wonderful, and in banishment or even emigration there is an air of romance thrown around every recollection of the country where they have toiled for mere subsistence."[18] As if strong cultural and psychological ties were not enough to prompt peasants like Francis to want to remain at home, if at all possible, the economic situation in Ireland improved markedly for many ordinary people in the decade following the Great Famine.[19] Nonetheless, at some point in the 1850s, Francis determined to emigrate to Scotland.

There is no record of Francis in the 1851 Scottish National Census. This is not surprising because at that date he would have been only fourteen or fifteen years of age. He was doubtless helping his father on the family farm in Kiltubrid with his brother, Patrick. Apart from his Death Certificate and Obituary, Francis seems to have left no written record behind. In any case, for the remainder of his working life Francis would be listed in official documents as an "agricultural labourer," a "general labourer," or, in the United States, simply as a "laborer."

By September 1860, however, Francis had reluctantly migrated to Scotland and settled in the small provincial town of Dalkeith in the southeastern corner of that country not far from the English border. There he had become a lodger in the home of Peter Merrin, another Irish immigrant. Francis married Merrin's daughter, Bridget, at the Roman Catholic Church of Saint David in Dalkeith on September 11, 1860.[20] By April 1861, when the next Scottish National Census was taken, the young Mr. and Mrs. "Degnan" had moved and were recorded as living in the town of West Linton, Peeblesshire, about five miles from Dalkeith.[21] Their eldest son, James, was born in West Linton, as were most of the rest of the Degnan children.[22]

The fact that Francis migrated initially to the Scottish Lowlands rather than to Canada or the United States was probably indicative of his precarious economic situation and even of his dire poverty. Had he been a few years older during and immediately after the Famine, he might have benefited either from "Assisted Emigration"—the practice whereby some overburdened Irish landlords cleared their estates of "excess tenants" by paying their passages to other parts of the British Empire—or by the heavily subsidized immigrant trade between Ireland and Canada which made travel to that country far cheaper than to the United States.[23]

As it was, Francis settled down with his new wife and infant son for what would prove to be a very long stay in the small village of West Linton, where he soon found work as an "agricultural labourer." A number of his older sons would subsequently follow him in that vocation. His eldest grandson, and namesake, who was born in Worcester Massachusetts in 1907, had only the vaguest childhood memories of his elderly immigrant grandfather. Francis Deignan (1907-1991) recalled his grandfather as being, "... an old man, named Patrick, who had a white beard and smoked a pipe." The little boy could be forgiven for confusing the first name of his grandfather with that of his great uncle, Patrick, who remained at home in Leitrim where, in due course, he inherited the family farm. Otherwise, the remaining photograph of old Francis, minus the supposed pipe, accurately reflects his young grandson's description of him.

In later life Frank Deignan, as young Francis as an adult was to call himself, once described his grandfather's occupation as that of "a Drainage Engineer." This received characterization may have been merely one more example of the Irish tendency—products as they were of an acutely status-conscious society—to inflate their own importance at the expense of others. In point of fact, until he came to the United States fairly late in life, Donald's grandfather was consistently characterized in official records as being nothing more than a hired hand on other men's farms. But he was not necessarily unskilled. The truth of his occupational status probably lay somewhere between that of a "Drainage Engineer" and a simple "agricultural labourer."

As a young boy working on the family holding with his father, Bernard, just prior to and during the Great Famine, Francis would have learned the rudiments of land management and even of "land reclamation," which involved turning waste ground or bog-land into productive acreage. Integral to this reclamation process was the practice of "Draining" excess water from boggy ground and then further preparing that same soil for systematic cultivation. For all its humble character, the long hard work which Francis Duignan did as a boy and a teenager in County Leitrim had a dignity and a practical value all its own.

That Francis as a young man sought refuge in nearby Lowland Scotland from the Great Famine and its aftermath in Ireland was not surprising given his acute poverty and lack of education or industrial skills. Whether by luck or by chance, however, he went there at a propitious moment when his newly acquired agrarian expertise would be in increasing demand.

There had been a well-established tradition of seasonal, temporary migration to Lowland Scotland from the Provinces of Connaught and Ulster to find work bringing in the annual agricultural harvest. This pattern long predated the Great Famine. During and after the Famine many thousands of hungry, destitute Irish people made their way to Scotland not as migrant laborers but as refugees and settlers. Apart from their desire for economic opportunity, what bound them to earlier generations of Hibernian seasonal migrants was the reception they received from the Scots.

Ever since John Knox had brought a particularly stringent version of the Protestant Reformation to Scotland in the middle of the Sixteenth Century, all Roman Catholics—whether at home or abroad--had been perceived as the great national enemy. In the opinion of most Scots Protestants, Irish Roman Catholics were little more than ignorant, superstitious, shiftless peasants prone to drunkenness, violence and political disloyalty to Britain. During and after the Famine, the Irish flooded into Lowland Scotland in their impoverished, disease-ridden tens of thousands. Once there these unwelcome newcomers were thought to lower wages and living standards simultaneously by working for less than Scotts laborers would and by creating instant urban slums akin to the rural hovels they had left behind in Ireland. Most of their Protestant neighbors despised them thoroughly. Even the relatively small number of indigenous Scots Catholics looked down on the new arrivals as uncouth "foreigners" who were giving loyal Caledonian adherents of "the Old Faith" a bad name. In the 1860s, in fact, tensions between native Scots Catholics and their Irish neighbors became so great that one student of the period has asserted that, "It is not overstating matters to say that near civil war broke out between the Irish and the Scots."[24]

Not surprisingly, then, two distinct parallel societies developed and existed side by side in mid- Nineteenth Century Lowland

Scotland. The Scots Protestant majority saw itself as the enlightened bulwark of Christian Civilization holding back the forces of foreign heathenism, superstition and rebellion. At best, the Irish Catholics or "Papists" among them were little better than beasts of burden fit only for menial labor and lives lived out in the squalor and deprivation of a permanent social and economic underclass.

In the face of such hostility and contempt, newly-immigrated Irish and their descendants in Scotland kept themselves deliberately apart. They became a close-knit community of sorrowful "exiles" longing to return to their beloved homeland. They were, like Zephania's ancient Israelites, "a people humble and lowly," a Godly remnant who had done "no wrong."[25] Nonetheless they found themselves reviled for their steadfast devotion to the Catholic Faith and vilified equally for their burning loyalty to "the Old Country" and for their devotion to the achievement of its political independence from the British Empire, of which Ireland was then an integral part, by whatever means necessary. So they built their own churches and schools and established social organizations to help them survive and endure in a profoundly alien and hostile environment. Knowing how unwelcome they were there, it is telling that only 8% of the total of some two million people who left Ireland between 1841 and 1921 chose to migrate to Scotland.[26]

Much about Francis Degnan's life and work was typical of the Irish immigrant experience in Scotland between 1860 and 1890. Like most of the rest of his countrymen there, his economic situation was always fairly precarious. Exclusively an Irish-speaker, like many others of the Famine generation who continued to use only "Gaelic," he never assimilated into the host society by learning English. But unlike many other migrants who quickly sought and found construction or factory jobs in expanding industrial cities such as Glasgow or Dundee, Francis continued to work on the land as an "Agricultural Labourer" just as he had done at home in County Leitrim. Especially if he had the kinds of occupational skills attributed to him by his grandson, there would have been plenty of familiar work for Francis to do, for:

> Enclosing land, draining marshy areas, planting trees for shelter, liming the ground, building farm houses, introducing turnips for winter feed and improving roads and bridges were all measures adopted locally by the new owners as part of…improvement.[27]

In fact, Francis found himself in West Linton just as the very skills which he possessed were in growing demand and local wages were rising to pay for them. One Scots newspaper noted the complexity of this phenomenon when it observed:

> …at no distant date the labourer had often considerable difficulty in obtaining work. Thorough draining followed by a higher system of cultivation and a consequently increased amount of manual labour have placed him in a different position; and his wages have advanced within the last ten years from 9s. and 10s. a week to

> 12s. and 15s. per week, or about 30%-50%.
> Even with this increase of rates, nearly the
> whole of the drainage operations are now exe-
> cuted, not by the native population, but by im-
> migrant Irish—the local labourers being nearly
> all absorbed by the demand for hired servants
> as ploughmen, cattle-keepers and barnmen.[28]

Irishmen had dominated the land drainage business even before Francis Degnan arrived in West Linton and they would continue to do so long after he and his family left Scotland.[29]

The Degnan family lived in Coalyburn, "…a hamlet about two miles from West Linton on the edge of Deepsyke Forest where there was at one time a number of coal pits."[30] The physical distance of the Hamlet of Coalyburn from the rest of West Linton was indicative of the psychological and cultural isolation of the Irish immigrant community residing there from its Scottish Protestant neighbors in the town proper.

Historically, there had been some coal mining done in the area but by 1860 the local mines appear to have "played out" and been abandoned. The erstwhile miners' "cottages" are shown on a map dating from 1860 and it appears that the Degnans took up residence in one of those recently vacated, sturdy structures.[31] If so, that simple, solid stone dwelling was a great improvement over the mud-walled, one-room "cabin" which Francis had so recently left behind in Ireland. But other aspects of his new Scottish surroundings must have been comfortingly familiar.

When Francis arrived in West Linton in 1861, and for a decade and a half thereafter, better quality thatch- roofed cottages still existed in the town. Patient horses pulled large carts through the small village streets which were lighted by gas lamps. Electricity would not supplant such lights until 1931. Meanwhile, the town featured several hotels and private guest houses for summer visitors. By 1875, the village had a public water supply system.

Immediately upon their arrival, Francis and Bridget settled down and started their family in West Linton. James, Peter, Francis, Mary and Charles came along in fairly rapid succession during the balance of the 1860s and the early 1870s.[32]

On August 8, 1877 Bernard Degnan, the next to youngest son of Francis and Bridget, was born into the distinctively Irish minority population in the "Hamlet Of Coabyburn" (sic) in the town of West Linton.[33] He was Baptized at Saint David Roman Catholic Church in Dalkeith on September 30, 1877.[34] Thus he joined his five older siblings, four brothers and one sister. The Degnan family would be completed soon thereafter by the birth of Bernard's younger brother William and another sister, Agnes.

Bernard's older brothers and sister appear to have attended elementary school in West Linton, for a time, after which they went off to work. Bernard too evidently went to school locally once he was old enough to do so.[35] As a young boy growing up in Lowland Scotland—only sixteen miles from Edinburgh, the country's national capital--he acquired a Scots "burr" and a taciturn, distant nature, neither of which he ever lost.

Railroad service came to the town in 1864 and, "...brought much prosperity to West Linton and was greatly responsible for its development."[36] Regular train service meant that West Linton's residents could reach Edinburgh in only 47 minutes and it is possible that Francis may have worked there for a time. The family may even have lived there for a period, since his daughter, Mary, is recorded as having been born in Scotland's capital, unlike the rest of her siblings whose birthplaces were uniformly listed as West Linton.

Apart from these scant details, nothing else can be said with any certainty about Bernard's early life and childhood growing up in Southeastern Scotland between 1877 and 1888. Equally mysterious is the reason which finally prompted Francis Degnan to uproot himself and his family, suddenly, after nearly thirty years of residence and hard work in West Linton.

Religious and economic tensions between indigenous Scots Protestants and Irish immigrant Roman Catholics were far from unknown between 1860 and 1890, but they were more commonly evident in Scotland's growing industrial cities—where competition for various urban jobs was keen—rather than in very small agricultural towns such as West Linton. Tom Gallagher, the historian of Irish Catholic Glasgow has noted that, "... a number of important local variations in Protestant-Catholic relations exist which make it unwise to generalise about the whole of central Lowland Scotland on the basis of what is the norm in its largest city."[37]

When Francis arrived in West Linton in 1861 the town's population was only 1,534.[38] It is unlikely that this figure increased much if at all over the next thirty years. There is no evidence of communal trouble within the village between native Scots and Irish newcomers during that same interval. So long as the Irish did jobs that Scots did not want, the immigrants seem to have been accepted and even to some extent accommodated by their indigenous neighbors.[39] So if religious tensions and ethnic rivalries were absent, or at least largely so, another explanation for the Degnan family's decision to quit Scotland in 1888 must be sought.

Temporary cyclical changes for the worse in the economic situation in Scotland in the years just before their departure may have contributed to the decision which Francis and Bridget made to emigrate to America in 1888. In 1886, only two years before the Degnans left West Linton for good, "Scotland, like the rest of the capitalist world, was in the midst of a severe recession…".[40] This discouraging development ran counter to the general economic trend of the previous three decades. Francis, as we have already seen, came to Scotland, originally, at a time when agricultural wages were rising, especially for Irish "Drainers" like himself. What is more, his growing family which had once represented "more mouths to feed" had over time turned into "more hands to work." The 1881 Scottish National Census listed both old Francis and his eldest son, James, working as "General Labourers." Another son, Peter, was categorized as a "General Servant" at that same time. Peter's immediate younger brother, Francis, was about to leave school and join the work force too. Finally, the Census also listed a "Lodger"—Peter Magbohan, a 54 year old, unmarried "General Labourer" from County Leitrim—as living with the Degnans.[41] Thus, even as early as 1881, the family had several different sources of income on which to rely. Since their needs and expectations were modest, they probably managed to live well enough during good economic times. But when economic conditions deteriorated, as they seem to have done during the middle part of the 1880s, the family's living standard would have been threatened severely by the possible loss of one or more jobs. Perhaps they feared a prolonged economic downturn and decided that emigration to America, where opportunities would supposedly be much greater, was in order.

Even during the best of times, most working-class wages in late Nineteenth Century Scotland—whether in industry or agriculture—were low. There was great disparity in the distribution of wealth among the upper, middle and lower classes. The 70% of the Scottish population at the bottom of society shared among themselves 1/3 of the nation's wealth while the top 8% of the people retained fully 25% of it for themselves.[42] For that part of the population who were immigrants or Scots-born children of Irish extraction, the economic situation was even worse.

Owing to limited education and rampant ethnic discrimination and religious prejudice against them, generally, upward socio-economic mobility for Irish Catholic immigrants and their Scottish-born children was all but impossible. And so, as the 1880s progressed, it is likely that James, Peter and even young Francis, too, recognized that if they stayed where they were they would never rise above the level of "General Labourers" or "General Servants," in which occupations they then found themselves stuck. All three of them may well therefore have imported their father to take the whole family to America where, even if the streets weren't exactly paved with gold, neither were they populated by grasping Scottish landowners, greedy middle-class industrialists or titled aristocrats who—among themselves—controlled most of the wealth of their homeland.

When, for whatever reason, the Degnan family finally decided to leave Scotland for America, they were but a very small part of a much larger number of fellow Scots who made an identical decision at the very same time. In the 1880s, a quarter of a million Scots left their homeland to start new lives somewhere overseas. Most of those emigrants, like the Degnans themselves, set off for the United States of America. [43] In the following decade an equal number of Scots migrants followed them to the same place.[44]

The Degnans of West Linton were in once sense typical Scottish emigrants in that they left Scotland together as a cohesive family unit and not as individuals, in stages. As one student of Scottish migration has noted:

> The family, in fact, was the common unit of planning and it is a particular characteristic of Scottish emigration that families were held together. Emigrant parties would contain representatives from all age groups from the young to the elderly. The assembly of such groups was in the hands of individuals, heads of families, making their bargains with private shipping interests. Thus the typical emigrant emerges as a person of

some means, independent in thought and action,
or the member of the family of such a person.
Emigration for such persons required sustained
effort, a consciousness of purpose, and personal
force to gather the necessary funds.[45]

The economic downturn of 1886 may have alarmed them and triggered their ultimate decision to leave Lowland Scotland for America. But even though they had several incomes to rely upon, it may have taken the Degnan family two years or more to accumulate the funds necessary for them to emigrate. Even though they were part of a flood of Scottish migrants heading for the United States during the late 1880s, the departure of the Degnans was at variance with the action, or inaction, of much of the rest of the Irish community in Caledonia. For, in the late 1880s, as James E. Handley has observed, Irish emigration from Scotland was decreasing steadily:

In the seven years from 1870 to 1876 inclusive
the annual average of Irish emigration from the
Clyde was over 700, the total being 5073. From
1877 to 1884 the total number was 6,677, or
an annual average of 835. These were the peak
years. Thereafter the number declined rapidly.
From 1885 to 1890, for example, the annual
average was only 255, the total for the six years
being 5,290.[46]

So it seems that the Degnan family was always destined to be part of one minority group or another. They had been part of the Irish Roman Catholic immigrant minority community in Scotland. But their children, at least, had denied that association and distanced themselves from that population by deliberately identifying themselves as "Scottish," not Irish, Catholics. The particular timing of their departure from Scotland placed them among a flood of outgoing native Scots but within that tide they were—as has just been shown—a tiny Irish-extracted emigrant droplet. When they reached America they would stubbornly retain their distinctive minority status within the tremendous Irish immigrant throng among which they would find themselves.

Sometime in early October 1888, Bridget Degnan and at least six of her children boarded the S.S. Corean—an emigrant ship of the English-owned Allan Line—for their voyage from Glasgow to Boston. They appear to have done so with only two suitcases among them.[47] Interestingly, old Francis and his eldest son James, who would have been twenty-seven or twenty-eight years of age at the time, did not appear on the Corean's Passenger List for that voyage, but, since the destination of Bridget and her family was listed as being "Worcester, Massachusetts," it is probable that her husband and eldest son had already gone ahead to that place to prepare for their arrival.[48] The Corean had made at least three prior trips between Glasgow and North America in 1888 before Bridget and her family did so. Therefore it is quite likely that old Francis and James were on one of the Corean's voyages earlier that same year. The voyage usually took between ten days and two weeks and it may have been interrupted by intermediate stops at Quebec and Montreal.[49]

Even though the younger men in the Degnan family may have longed for better economic and social opportunities both for themselves—and for their future children—in America, they did not leave Scotland behind them with entirely unmixed feelings. It was, after all, the only home any of them had ever known even though Scotland had never particularly welcomed or wanted them as its children. Their parents, Francis and Bridget, had been and always would remain unassimilated Irish peasants for whom West Linton was from start to finish an alien place. In its turn, America would be to them as foreign as Scotland ever was. But their children, all of whom had been born in "Caledonia," were, by contrast, "cultural Scots" of a very distinctive kind. For, "... Scottish Catholics drew a strong sense of identity from their religious faith, and significantly it was their religion and not their ethnic Irish identity which defined the community."[50] Thus when the Scots-born members of the Degnan family finally arrived in Worcester, Massachusetts, they found themselves to be part of a tiny ethnic minority surrounded by an immense Irish immigrant population with whom they did not particularly identify. Apart from their common religious faith, which was very important to all of them, the Scottish Degnans of Worcester would always take pains to distinguish themselves, deliberately, from their Irish neighbors. In their cultural outlook, economic attitudes and social sensibilities the Degnans would always see themselves as different and "distinct from their Irish and Irish-American neighbors. What is more, they would pass this peculiar, pugnacious, isolating self-identity along—unalloyed—to their American-born children. They would describe themselves as "Americans" first, but then, if pressed, as "Scots" too. These idiosyncratic Scottish family traits, behaviors and attitudes, whether inherited or learned, certainly influenced and may even in part account for Donald's personal conduct and individual choices both in his childhood and in his all-too-short adult life.

Bridget Degnan and her children reached Boston on October 18, 1888. Exactly when old Francis and James had landed there is unknown as is the precise moment when they arrived in Worcester, Massachusetts and arranged to receive the rest of their family therein. What is certain is that Francis Degnan "laborer" first appeared in the "Worcester Directory" in 1889 and was listed as living at 2 Sigourney Street.[51] That substantial, multi-family dwelling is still standing and in residential use at the present time.

For the second time in his life old Francis Degnan was an immigrant. In America, though, there were similarities to and differences from his earlier Scottish immigrant experience. In 1860, Francis had been a single, young man with no responsibility for anyone but himself. In 1889, by contrast, he was an aging man with a large family to look after if not entirely to support by himself. Once again, in Worcester, he found himself surrounded by large numbers of recent Irish immigrants. He and they were part of the third and last great wave of Irish immigration to the United States. But that tide was already beginning to ebb, somewhat, by the time that old Francis and his cohort arrived in Worcester. As Timothy Meagher, the pre-eminent historian of Worcester's Irish community noted, "If Irish immigration into Worcester slowed in the late nineteenth century…it did not stop. At the beginning of the twentieth century, half of all the Irish immigrants in Worcester had emigrated to America after 1880."[52]

Equally familiar to Francis was his usual work as a "laborer" but now he did it in an urban setting rather than in a rural environment or in a small-town locale. But even though old Francis still found himself among the type of people he well knew, there were significant differences, all the same, between him and many of his new Irish neighbors. Unlike him, they were bilingual or entirely English-speaking and most of them were literate besides.[53]

Old Francis and his bilingual, literate eldest son James seem to have decided before October 1888 that the rest of the Degnan family should leave Scotland and settle permanently in Worcester, Massachusetts. This conclusion is supported by the entry on the S.S. Corean's October 1888 Passenger List which gave Worcester as the final American destination of Bridget Degnan and her children. But why did the elder Degnans choose Worcester as their family's ultimate place of settlement? The most likely answer to this question is that Francis and James had learned beforehand that there was plenty of unskilled or semi-skilled work for them and the other male members of their family to do in that growing American industrial city.

Worcester, probably named after the city of that same name in southwestern England, is located about halfway between the cities of Boston and Springfield in the center of the Commonwealth of Massachusetts. It is situated near the head of the Blackstone River. Worcester was permanently settled in 1713, after two unsuccessful prior attempts to do so in the late Seventeenth

Century, and incorporated in 1722. In 1731, it became the seat of Worcester County.[54]

The local soil proved to be rocky, thin and unfit for anything but subsistence agriculture so the town's first inhabitants soon turned to other occupations to supplement basic farming. Sawmills, gristmills, potash production, shoemaking papermaking and textile manufacturing were begun and came to flourish.[55] In 1824, construction was begun on the Blackstone Canal which was completed in 1828. This inland waterway linked Worcester with Providence, Rhode Island at the head of Narragansett Bay. Thus Worcester acquired a trading link to the sea and an outlet for its first manufactured products in the wider world. Between 1835 and 1847 the city's standing was further enhanced when its central location made Worcester a hub for several new railroads which were completed during that period.[56] Booming railroad traffic soon eclipsed the Blackstone Canal as a commercially viable means of carrying freight. Meanwhile, as the Nineteenth Century progressed, Worcester became a major manufacturing city with a diversified industrial economy. In 1919, Charles G. Washburn, a member of one of the city's most important manufacturing families assessed Worcester's dramatic transformation when he wrote that:

> Worcester has developed from a country town
> to a great manufacturing city in less than ninety
> years. The population in 1830 was a little over
> four thousand and today is probably one hun-
> dred and sixty thousand. Within that time the

> steam-engine, the railroad, telegraph and tele-
> phone and commercial use of electricity have
> enormously increased the productive power of
> labor.[57]

Washburn attributed the city's growth and commercial success
to the dynamic spirit and inherent thrift of the Yankee business and banking elite which tightly controlled every aspect of
Worcester's public life.[58] But even though by 1890, shortly after
old Francis and his family arrived there, Worcester was undeniably the thirteenth largest manufacturing city in America, with
a population of 85,000, However, Washburn's opinion of its ac-
complishments may have been somewhat overblown, for, as a
more recent authority has written:

> ...visitors from more cosmopolitan cities
> like Boston or New York might have found
> Worcester little more than an overgrown
> small town then. The downtown was undis-
> tinguished, an embarrassment to its boosters,
> who lamented its rutted streets and the absence
> of first-class hotels. The city was also small in
> area, densely packed into a circle with a diam-
> eter of less than four miles through the 1880s
> and 1890s. There were still many farms in the
> city of Worcester in those days, and open fields
> and woods abounded within the official city
> limits outside that tight circle of settlement.[59]

Worcester, which as late as 1880 had only two miles of paved streets, was, "an average industrial city by American standards, dynamic and earnest but small and provincial."[60]

In spite of its small size and relative social backwardness, Worcester, by 1890, had become a manufacturing powerhouse increasingly capable of competing successfully for business in growing national and international markets.[61] But, interestingly, as Meagher has observed:

> The city's economy was, however, atypical of New England cities in many respects. In a region where many cities were devoted almost exclusively to the manufacture of a single item, such as textiles, paper, or shoes, Worcester's economy was diverse, producing everything from leather belts and barbed wire to corsets and breakfast cereal. The largest industries by the late nineteenth century were wire-making and machinery manufacture, but Worcester was never a single- industry town.[62]

For all its evident diversity, Worcester's industrial economy was becoming increasingly dominated by a single firm at the time when the Degnan family arrived in the city in 1889. In that year, the various "mills" or "works" of the Washburn & Moen Manufacturing Company occupied no less than 25 acres of prime Worcester real estate and the firm employed some 3,000 "operatives" of many different nationalities.[63] The direct successor to Washburn & Moen—the American Steel and Wire

Company— was to play a central part in the lives of the male members of the Degnan family from one generation to the next.

The manufacture of many different kinds of wire products gave the Washburn & Moen Company its reason for being. Ichabod Washburn and Benjamin Goddard began making wire in Worcester in 1831. In 1850, Philip Moen—Washburn's son-in-law—joined him in the business as his partner. In 1876, recognizing the profit potential in barbed-wire fencing—as an expanding American population moved westward to homestead and farm—Washburn & Moen acquired numerous patents covering all aspects of the production of that specialized type of wire. By 1889, the year of the Degnan family's first appearance in Worcester, Washburn & Moen were turning out two hundred and forty-five tons of wire daily and producing four hundred and eighteen different products.[64]

Although the manufacture of wire was to play a central role in Bernard's adult life and in the working lives of several of his older brothers, the Degnan family's initial entry into the American labor force came in the form of manual labor instead of industrial work. The elder Francis and his son James soon found employment in Worcester as "laborers." Little had they supposed that they would be trading spades in Lowland Scotland for picks and shovels in America but that, initially at least, is just what happened to them. In 1892 both men got jobs on the Fitchburg Railroad, Francis still as a laborer and James as a "wiper."[65] But then they learned a hard lesson in the "boom-and-bust" economics of the day. Each of them lost his railroad job in the Depression of 1893-1894 and both men found themselves as common laborers once again. The 1900 United States Census would list Francis as a retired, illiterate, Irish- speaking laborer.

The rest of the males in the Degnan family fared little better economically, as they reached maturity in America, than did their aging father or their eldest brother. Except for the two who married and moved out on their own, the rest all lived together for many years at 34 Prescott Street in Worcester's overwhelmingly Irish North End neighborhood. Charles (1874-1916) served honorably as an Officer in the Spanish-American War. After that, he became a successful bartender. On the occasion of his funeral in September 1916, his very young nieces and nephews sent him an elaborate floral tribute marked "Dear Uncle" with their names, "Mary, Anna, Francis, Robert and Donald Deignan" all included.[66] Thus, Donald's name almost certainly appeared in the newspaper for the first time in connection with the Obituary of his Uncle Charles which appeared on September 23, 1916. Peter, (1868-1936), may have been a wireworker and a roofer but there is no mention of these or any other occupations in his very brief Obituary.[67] Not much more is known about his eldest brother, James, (1861-1939) except that he married and had a large family.[68]

Tragically, much more is known about the life of William Deignan (1879-1941), because of the circumstances under which his death occurred. **"Roofer Killed in Fall From House: William F. Deignan, 62, Tumbles 40 Feet From Top of Three-Decker"** the <u>Worcester Daily Telegram</u> informed its readers on October 1, 1941.[69] William thus became the second child of Francis and Bridget Degnan to die a violent death within the space of thirteen months. The life and death of his brother, Bernard, will be dealt with presently, in detail, and in their own right. Francis Deignan (1867-1942) became a Bricklayer and his funeral Mass was attended by representatives from both the Bricklayers and Plasters Union and the Board of Labor and Industry.[70] The two girls in the family were even less conspicuous than their brothers had been. Mary C. Deignan (1872-1938), was listed on the S.S. Corean's Passenger list in 1888 as being 16 years of age and a "Domestic." But her "Obituary" if such it can be called, listed neither her occupation nor even her age at the time of her death.[71] Her last surviving sibling, Agnes T. Deignan, (1890-1947), received no better treatment at the time of her death. She was at least described as having been "a saleswoman at Pic 'N Pac"—presumably a neighborhood market or "convenience store"—but beyond that, the paper got its facts badly wrong, "She was born in Scotland, daughter of the late Francis J. and Bridget (Marrin) Deignan, and lived here many years."[72]

So from the foregoing paragraph it may be seen that the occupational prospects and performances of the Deignan children in America turned out to be only slightly better than they would have been if the family had remained in West Linton, as adults, for the rest of their lives. With the exception of Charles, whose service as a Military Officer followed by his job as a bartender represented steps up in American life, the rest of the family continued to find themselves in physically demanding, laboring or service occupations toward the bottom of the turn-of-the- century pay-scale in Worcester. For whatever reason, apart from James and Bernard, none of them appear ever to have married. Perhaps they were too poor, too economically downtrodden and too socially introverted—by virtue of their Scottish upbringing—to contemplate even the possibility of matrimony. In any case, most of them left no lasting legacy in their adopted city, state and nation.

While their older brothers and sister were making the gradual transition from the realm of immigrant adolescence into the world of American labor, it is reasonable to suppose that Bernard, William and Agnes were dutifully attending public school somewhere in Worcester's North End. As they, in turn became teenagers, it is also likely that each of them acquired casual, part-time jobs to help the family, financially, but there is no surviving documentary evidence to support this supposition.

Between 1894 and 1904 most of the Degnan family lived at 59 Prescott Street, a two story, wood-framed "dwelling," and it was at that address in 1902 that Bernard was first listed, under his own name, as being a "wireworker."[73] On February 12, 1901, at the age of 23, Bernard Deignan became a Naturalized American Citizen. Erroneously, however, the handwritten original of his Naturalization Certificate listed his birthplace as "Ireland" and not Scotland. More than twenty years later, he obtained a typewritten, corrected copy which listed his place of birth as "Peebles, Scotland". [74] Something more than a desire for mere legal accuracy may have prompted Bernard to take steps to rectify the original clerical error. It is clear, as has already been established, that throughout his life, Bernard Deignan identified himself as a Scot and not as an Irishman. Pride in his homeland aside, the likely reason for his lifelong identification with his Scottish ethnicity will be discussed in detail below.

Long before Bernard began working at the American Steel and Wire Company's North Works on Grove Street in Worcester in 1902, important changes had taken place at and around that venerable plant. As one historian of the Irish in Worcester has noted:

> In the middle of the nineteenth century, two new Irish neighborhoods developed on the north and south sides of the city. The northern neighborhood was called variously Messenger Hill, Fairmount Hill, or, most often, just the North End. Dominated by the massive red brick complex of the Washburn Moen Wire Company's North Works and cut off from the rest of the city by a railroad on the east and a pond and park to the west, the North End seemed like an isolated mill village.[75]

Since at least the early 1890s the Irish immigrant and Irish-American workers at the Washburn & Moen Manufacturing Company's several plants in Worcester had found themselves having to compete ever more fiercely for unskilled and semi-skilled jobs with a growing host of "foreigners" including French- Canadians, Lithuanians and Armenians. But by far the greatest threat to the economic security of established Irish workers came from the newly-arrived Swedes. Among the three thousand "operatives" employed by Washburn & Moen in 1889, there were one thousand Irish; nine hundred Swedes; five hundred Americans; two hundred and thirty-six Armenians; forty-five Germans; and three hundred and nineteen men of other nationalities.[76] Worcester's Protestant Yankee manufacturing elite played Irish and Swedish workers off against each other to its great advantage:

> It seems clear…that a number of Worcester manufacturers preferred to employ Swedish workers over Irish ones.…the Washburn Moen Wire Manufacturing Company…openly favored Swedish workers. It was Worcester's Swedes not its Irish, then, who established the kinds of links with factory owners and managers that provided a consistent flow of jobs for friends and family.[77]

Monumental changes in the American corporate landscape at the very end of the Nineteenth Century did nothing to lessen competition and tension between different immigrant groups at the bottom of the industrial heap. On March 11, 1899, the Washburn & Moen Manufacturing Company was bought by the American Steel & Wire Company. On April 1, 1901, American Steel & Wire was itself acquired by the United States Steel Corporation. Even so, American Steel & Wire continued thereafter to do business under its own iconic brand name.[78] Meanwhile, the number of Swedish workers at American Steel & Wire continued to increase.

Under these circumstances, when the newly-minted American Citizen Bernard Deignan started working at American Steel & Wire in 1902 he needed whatever advantages he could get. The most natural and obvious of these was his distinctive ethnicity. He was, after all, proudly a Scot and emphatically not an Irishman. One historian has called the Scots "invisible ethnics" who were, "… predominantly Protestant and eager to assimilate".[79] Of Scots, in Worcester, in particular, another commentator observed that they, "have been absorbed as rapidly as they have come."[80] It is probable, therefore, that Bernard emphasized his genuine "Scottishness" to distinguish himself from the Irish working masses around him and also to fit in more easily among the increasing numbers of his Swedish, Protestant co-workers. For Scots were found, "… in all organizations and churches."[81] Most Swedes, and quite probably their Yankee plant Foremen, too, would have naturally assumed that Bernard—Scot that he was—came from staunchly Protestant stock like themselves. So long as he did not divulge his Roman Catholicism in that discriminatory workplace, Bernard may well have hoped that he could not only "get by" but perhaps even "get ahead" at American Steel & Wire.

Some degree of upward economic mobility was not out of the question in Bernard's day. In fact, "Most men moved up to better jobs than their immigrant fathers had or than the new immigrant men arriving from Ireland found, but anti-Catholic prejudice…prevented the men of the new generation from entering the highest circles of Worcester's industrial hierarchy."[82] It was certainly true that young Bernard, unlike his father, Francis, did not have to do manual labor to earn a living. His pay at American Steel & Wire was certainly much better than anything that old Francis had taken home as an agricultural laborer either in Ireland or in Scotland. But Bernard's working conditions were far from ideal. Hours of work, at least until the First World War, were very long—the twelve hour day was standard—and wages were relatively low. In Worcester, in 1913, the annual wage of the typical workingman averaged only $625.38 per year. [83] And for those paltry wages, "Workers accepted exhausting labor, heat, fumes and danger as part of the job."[84]

By any standard, the American Steel and Wire Company was an immense industrial operation, of great economic importance, both in Worcester and nationwide. In 1919, Charles G. Washburn, the euphoric chronicler of all things industrial in his native city declared triumphantly that, "It is merely referring to a long established fact to mention that in no other city in the world are so many different kinds of wire and wire products manufactured as are produced in Worcester by the American Steel & Wire Company." He further informed his readers that the Company produced two hundred thousand tons of wire in an average year.[85] Much later in the Twentieth Century, long after both Bernard and Donald were dead, American Steel & Wire itself produced a pamphlet called "The Story of Wire" whose self-congratulatory tone might have made even Mr. Washburn blush. Its introductory paragraph said in part:

> If we but stop and think, we then realize just
> how important wire and wire products are to

> our way of life. As the world progresses and
> the need for new and better things arises and is
> fulfilled, wire in many shapes, forms and types
> will continue to play a very vital role.[86]

The closing sentence of this booklet's opening paragraph was extraordinary even for an "in-house" publication: "It is interesting, then, this romantic story of wire from raw mined ore to finished product, and that is the purpose of this book—to tell you the Story of Wire."[87]

In 1902 if Bernard Deignan thought that his distinctive Scottish character and self-conscious Caledonian identity would give him any advantages in his new workplace, he was sadly mistaken. For he was to do the same job, day in and day out—year in and year out—for more than three decades. Furthermore, even in the unlikely event that his imagination might have been captured, initially, by the "romantic story of wire," the "Romance" would not last; in fact it would end in disillusionment, drunkenness and violent death.

Between 1902 and 1935, Bernard Deignan worked as a "wire-drawer" at the North Works of the American Steel and Wire Company on Grove Street in the North End of Worcester. The industrial work of wire-drawing came at the end of several production steps and processes which turned newly extracted iron ore—after mining, shipping, purifying, heating, cooling and combining with additional elements in just the right quantities—into finished steel and wire products of all kinds. According to Mr. Washburn:

> The process of wire-drawing consists in taking a coarse wire rod and drawing it through a hole of less diameter than the rod, in an iron or steel plate, and repeating the operation until the rod is reduced to wire of the required size. The reduction is effected by stretching the wire, and not by removing the metal.[88]

Washburn may have gotten the basics of the wire-drawing process right but he left out important technical details.[89] What is more, he altogether neglected to consider its human costs and the inevitable toll— both physical and psychological—which the work took on the men who performed it under difficult conditions and for very low pay. Individual workmen had to stand in front of their wire-drawing machines for long periods of time, enduring loud, constant noise, while concentrating intently on every aspect of the mechanical operations of the devices which they tended.

Even the anonymous apologist for American Steel & Wire, already quoted, implicitly recognized the complexity of the work which he extolled. But, like Washburn before him, he did not take into account the more damaging human aspects of the undertaking:

> The manufacture of steel entails much more than just a big operation processing ore into iron and steel. Behind the huge installations that belch forth smoke and flame are years of experience, unrelenting supervision of seemingly

> unimportant details, and the ever present de-
> sire to produce at lower cost better wire and
> higher quality steel for your products.[90]

This same spokesman concluded his panegyric of American steel-making on a typically self-satisfied note:

> The net results of this endless parade of quality
> materials, close supervision of production de-
> tail, and over a century of steel making "know
> how,' is a finer, higher quality steel—a product
> that the American Steel and Wire Company and
> the United States Steel Corporation are proud
> to present to American Industry."[91]

In speaking of "over a century of steel making "know how," the author of "The Story of Wire" no doubt had in mind the numerous executives, chemists, engineers and metallurgists whose vision and technical expertise helped to make production of a vast array of fine finished steel and wire products possible. But he seems to have given not a moment's thought to the tens of thousands of ordinary workers whose hard labor brought those same products into being.

From 1902 until 1935, Bernard Deignan never once brought his work at American Steel & Wire home <u>with</u> him. But, instead, on every one of those exhausting days during which he labored there, *Bernard Deignan brought his work home <u>in</u> him!* Its incessant noise was in his head. Its diluted acidic fumes and chemical residues were in his lungs and bloodstream. Its heat sapped his energy and stamina and its deadening monotony dulled and eventually blunted his otherwise naturally sharp senses. Under such unrelenting circumstances and conditions, it is surprising that he ever mustered the courage and the optimism to marry at all. But, somehow, he did so.

Sometime in 1904 the Degnan family vacated 59 Prescott Street and moved a few doors away to 57 Prescott .[92] Bernard took the opportunity to strike out on his own, and by 1905 he was living at 1 Otis Street as a boarder.[93] At about the same time, or perhaps a few months earlier, he met Anna Cross. The precise circumstances under which Bernard and Anna first met are unknown. What is certain is that when Bernard left home and started life on his own, Worcester was full of young, attractive, single Irish-born or Irish-American working-class girls who would have been potential marriage partners for him. Once again, however, Bernard's *"otherness"* asserted itself strongly. His eventual choice of a wife was to prove to be an excellent one but it was also, literally, "egregious" or "outside the herd." Perhaps he simply wanted to make a clean break from his parents, marking his own maturity, as many young men are wont to do. But he may also have been deliberately rejecting the foreign, peasant, Irish-speaking culture which they so persistently personified. A match with an Irish-born "colleen" or an Irish-American woman would have perpetuated many of the very same customs and traditions which he may have been consciously seeking to escape. After all, as has been noted above, Scottish-born Catholics of Irish extraction—like Bernard—identified with their universal religious Faith rather than with their parents' country of origin.

The population of Scots in Worcester of any description was small, anyway, and the number of Scottish-Catholic girls would have been negligible if not nonexistent altogether. So, in the end, Bernard resolved his marital dilemma in the only way he could; by looking beyond his own national and ethnic groups—but still within the Roman Catholic community—for a wife. In doing so he was part of a broader trend, for, "the only non-Irish group of substantial size to share their Catholic faith, communal values, and working-class status were the French Canadians…".[94] Anna Cross was an American-born, English-speaking member of precisely that ethnic group. Anna, too, may have been attracted to Bernard, among other things, for much the same reason. Her father, John Cross, was born in Canada and his first language was almost certainly French. Her mother, Catherine Hurley, had been born in Ireland. Her parents, like Bernard's mother and father, came from poor, rural backgrounds and Anna may have seen her marital union with Bernard—a Naturalized American workingman with a relatively good paying factory job—as a step up the socio-economic ladder.

Bernard Deignan and Anna Cecelia Cross were married at St. Anne's Church, the second oldest Roman Catholic Church in Worcester, on June 21, 1905.[95] They made a handsome couple. She was short, shy and pretty. He was tall, serious and good looking.[96] The Deignans—Bernard adopted the standard American spelling of the family name at the time of his marriage—were typical working-class newlyweds except in one respect. Both of them were considerably younger than the average age for marriage at that time.[97] He was just 28 and she was only 22.

They started their married life at 9 Liberty Street not far from Bernard's place of work at the American Steel & Wire Company in the North End of Worcester.[98]

Their first "home" was on the second floor of a modest "three-decker," "… .a building of three floors, all floors of the same area, and each floor occupied by one family, with no spare room in the attic."[99] Such sturdy three-family or three-tenement residences, like the one which Anna and Bernard occupied at 9 Liberty Street, " … "formed like calcium deposits along the 'spines' which radiated from the city's industrial plants and manufacturing shops during the last quarter of the nineteenth century and the first quarter of the twentieth."[100] Between 1855 and 1930, some 6000 three-deckers were built in Worcester.[101] There was a pre-eminently practical reason for the widespread construction of such housing within the closely packed confines of industrial Worcester since, "… industry was localized, a pedestrian journey to work was the rule and some form of multi-family dwelling units on restricted lots of land was the optimal residential solution."[102] Despite their avowedly utilitarian purpose and character, an April 1905 "Report" found that most three-deckers had "adequate light and ventilation." Rents, too, were reasonable, averaging $7.59 a month in 1905.[103] The house at 9 Liberty Street, which Anna, Bernard, and their growing family occupied for nearly ten years, is still in residential use today.

The Deignans started their family quickly. Their first child, Mary, was born in April 1906. She may have been named for Bernard's older sister or, equally, for the Blessed Virgin Mary;

"Our Lady," in Catholic parlance. Francis came next, in August 1907. In so naming his first son, Bernard was clearly following the long established Deignan family tradition—observed by generation after generation in County Leitrim—of calling the first-born male child after his grandfather. But with the naming of his eldest son after his own father, Bernard's adherence to Irish family customs ended. Bernard and Anna were self-consciously ethnic minority swimmers in an Irish cultural sea. The Church to which they belonged, and in which they dutifully raised their numerous offspring, insisted that children should be named after Saints. But in this matter, Mr. and Mrs. Deignan were in step with evolving Catholic practice, in general, rather than with old country Irish traditions. As Timothy Meagher has perceptively noted:

> The vast majority of second-generation Irish in Worcester carried names such as John, Mary, James, Katherine, or Margaret....Such names might not have been so obviously Irish as Patrick or Bridget, but they were clearly sound Catholic names, names of the church's most hallowed saints, and appropriately emblematic of the kind of culture these second-generation Irish would create for themselves in Worcester.[104]

As usual, Bernard and Anna went their own way—within broadly established customary limits—in selecting names for their remaining children. Robert was born in June, 1910. His name probably reflected the influence of Anna's originally "French" or French-Canadian heritage more than anything else. Anna was born in December, 1912 and was doubtless named after her own mother. At unknown points in the birth sequence sons named Bernard and Paul were also born but each of them died either in infancy or in early childhood. There was also a daughter of uncertain name who did not live long and several more miscarriages or still-births as well. Deignan children seemed to come along every year and a half, or so, on average. Joseph, soon to be Baptized as "Donald," was born at home "on the kitchen table," like the rest of his siblings, in March 1915. In choosing their youngest son's two names, Bernard and Anna were together making particularly emphatic statements about the boy's distinctive religious and ethnic identities. His legal name, "Joseph"—whose Feast Day is March Nineteenth—was intended to honor the "foster father of Jesus," who, by virtue of that office, was and is one of the most important Saints in the Roman Catholic Faith. The choice of "Joseph" was almost certainly Anna's doing. The Baptismal Name "Donald," by contrast, was Bernard's deliberate choice. It represented yet another affirmation of his determinedly Scottish identity. "Donald" was evidently named for *"Saint Donald"* of Ogilvy in Scotland, the land of Bernard's birth. The Irish Gaelic variant of the name is "Donal." So by using the Scottish Gaelic version of the name Bernard was forcefully informing his Hibernian neighbors in Worcester that his youngest son, **"Donald"** was not to be mistaken by them for an Irishman! In any case, "Donald,"-- or "Donnie,"—as he was always to be known within the family—had two younger sisters. Eunice was born in April, 1919 and Catherine—named perhaps for Anna Cross's mother—was born in December, 1920. With her birth, Anna and Bernard had completed their family. In naming their children as they did, Mr. and Mrs. Deignan had both adhered to and to some extent defied the customs and the expectations of the times in which they lived.

Mary, Francis, Robert, Anna and Donald Joseph were all born on Liberty Street. But his available "Record of Birth" lists no specific address for Donald other than "Worcester, Massachusetts" as his "Place of Residence"[105] The confusion over Donald's place of birth stems from the fact that sometime in 1915 the Deignans moved from 9 Liberty Street to 15 Rodney Street, a few blocks away but still in the same part of Worcester. But because the 1915 Worcester Directory lists the family as living at 9 Liberty Street, and since Donald was born early in that year, it is highly probable that his mother gave birth to him at that location.[106]

Some months before Bernard and Anna moved their growing family from Liberty Street to Rodney Street, other changes were taking place within the older generation of the extended Deignan family. On August 12, 1914, little more than a week after the start of "The Great War" in Europe, old Francis Degnan died of cancer in Worcester, supposedly at age 70.[107] In the broader context of tens of millions of American immigrant stories, his particular saga was nothing special. But in retrospect and in microcosm, his achievements in life were remarkable. As a mere, illiterate, peasant boy, he survived Ireland's Great Famine. As a young man he migrated to Lowland Scotland where, friendless, alone and unable either to speak or to understand the local language, he nonetheless toiled, married, raised a family and attained a small measure of economic success. Much later in life, when the naturally complacent tendencies of most men his age would have been to" stay put" where they were, he again uprooted himself—and his family too—and sailed to America. There, at last, Francis and his wife and children struck permanent roots in the nourishing soil of the United States. One photograph of old Francis has survived. In it, he is impeccably dressed and flanked proudly by two tall, handsome sons.[108] But, for all that, his passing went virtually unnoticed, even in Irish Worcester. Because of its brevity, his Death Notice/"Obituary" is worth quoting in its entirety to illustrate this point:

> DEIGNAN—In this city. August 12, Francis
> Deignan, aged 70 years. Funeral from his late
> home, 34 Prescott Street, Friday morning
> with a high mass of requiem in the Church of
> the Immaculate Conception, hour to be an-
> nounced later. Relatives and friends are invited
> to attend.[109]

Although there was nothing wrong with their working-class accommodations on Liberty Street, the move of the younger Deignans to 15 Rodney represented an improvement in several material respects in the family's living conditions. For one thing the two-story Rodney Street house was much newer than the building in which their Liberty Street "flat" was located. On 1910 Insurance Maps of Worcester, 15 Rodney Street was not listed.[110] This means that the Rodney Street dwelling had to have been constructed sometime between 1911 and 1915. In addition, their new "flat" on Rodney Street was on the first floor and not the second as had been the case back at Liberty Street .[111] The ground-floor location must have been a welcome convenience for Anna, who had to stow large amounts of groceries within and had to shepherd growing numbers of children in and out of her home. Her relative respite from domestic drudgery was, however, to be fairly short-lived.

In May 1915 the American Steel & Wire Company's Worcester workforce was more than ever dominated by Swedes or Swedish-Americans who, together, comprised nearly 24 % of its total. By contrast, Irish or Irish-American workers accounted for only about 18% of the labor pool. Scots or Scottish-Americans, like Bernard, made up only 8.9% of the total.[112] Even though the Company had several thousand workers, it had almost more work than it could handle. When America entered World War I in April 1917 production demands increased still further and a labor shortage set in. Accordingly, wages rose sharply during the war years and the 8-hour day was introduced by the Company in 1918.[113] But once the war ended, demand for steel and wire products decreased greatly and 1919-1921 were years of severe economic depression in Worcester. The bad economic situation was made even worse by a simultaneous, severe housing shortage and a concomitant rise in rents throughout the city.[114] In reaction to decreased demand for their products, factory owners cut wages dramatically. By 1921, American Steel & Wire had reduced hourly wages for many of its workers from 37cents per hour to 30cents. By the end of the year, wages had fallen by

59.2%. from wartime levels.[115] Even before the worst effects of the post-war economic downturn took hold, rising rents and declining wages forced the Deignan family to move again.

In 1918, the Deignans relocated to yet another three-decker this time on Keefe Place—a thoroughly blue- collar section of town—off Lincoln Street in the northwest corner of Worcester. They would remain there, first at #2 (1918-1921), and then at #5 (1922-1936), for the next eighteen years.

Keefe Place first became a listed street in 1898. It disappeared from the Worcester Housing Directory in 1974, when it fell victim equally and finally to urban renewal and to the construction of Interstate Highway 290, which obliterated many working-class neighborhoods within the city.[116] Frank Deignan, as Bernard's eldest son liked to style himself in adulthood, had nothing but bad memories of his many long years as a teenager and a young man living on Keefe Place. He consistently described it as "a slum." But Frank's judgment, which was likely colored by increasing family problems in the home (to be dealt with below) may have been too harsh. A 1911 photograph in "Worcester's Three-Deckers," a booklet published by the Worcester Bicentennial Commission in 1977, shows Keefe Place as a residential street lined with neat rows of that quintessentially urban New England type of multi-family tenement house. But the buildings thus shown do not appear to be in any state of disrepair.[117] Indeed, the earliest surviving photograph of Donald seems to support the conclusion that the three-deckers on Keefe Place were plain, sturdy, serviceable three-family homes. The picture in question shows Donald—grinning broadly as a toddler of three or four—standing on a strip of grass with a small section of his neatly shingled and well- painted house in the background behind him.[118] So Donald and the rest of his large family grew up—for better or for worse—on Keefe Place in Worcester's grimy North End. When Donald left Keefe Place for good, in 1934 in the depths of the Great Depression, it would be to join the Civilian Conservation Corps so as to better himself and to help his mother and sisters, but not his father, financially. Their Worcester was, as his older brothers—Frank and Robert—were to demonstrate, a city to get away from as soon as possible without looking back. And that, in due course, is precisely what Anna and Bernard Deignan's three boys did, each in his own way.

This then is a glimpse into the world of urban Worcester Massachusetts into which Donald was born on March 15, 1915: a world of tightly-packed, immigrant tenements set hard by immense factories "belching smoke and flames" almost all of the time. It was a place of poverty, disease, malnutrition and high infant mortality. It was also a place of deep religious faith and of increasingly sharp sectarian and political tensions. Far away, on Worcester's affluent west side, a small group of Yankee, Protestant plutocrats— factory owners, business executives and bankers—kept wary eyes on the teeming and diverse population of "the City of Three-deckers" whose wealth they controlled with an unrelenting iron grip.

Growing up in such adverse circumstances as those just described certainly presented young Donald with numerous external challenges. But at home he, his older brothers Frank and Robert, his sisters and his mother all had to confront a problem as serious and daunting as any eventuality which the wider world might present to them. Their domestic challenge was the reality and the ramifications of their father's chronic alcohol abuse. For, at bottom, Bernard Deignan was a poor man worn out by drudgery, demography and drink. His father Francis had given him and his brothers and sisters the chance for a new start in America. But for Bernard, at least, everything eventually went wrong.

Not much was ever said about the home life of the Deignan family. They did not share either their "business" or their "secrets," even with their own children. They were a small, tightly-knit, closed-mouthed band of introverts. In their later lives, Bernard's adult children rarely spoke about their father and whenever they did so, it was not without prompting from younger people in the family. When they spoke about Bernard at all, it was only in cryptic conversational fragments and never with any sentiment or warmth. It is revealing, as has been mentioned, that Francis, Robert and Donald all left home as soon as they could. The girls who were left behind never had much to say about their father.

What has been said of the cautious native Catholics in Scotland could be equally well applied to the small number of their co-religionists in early Twentieth Century Worcester. In comparison to the hordes of outgoing Irish immigrants around them, on both sides of the Atlantic, "The Scots were less demonstrative, tight-fisted where money was concerned and, above all constantly fearful of provoking a Protestant backlash…".[119] It has already been suggested that, by emphasizing his Scottish background, Bernard had deliberately tried to "blend in" as a survival strategy at American Steel & Wire. He appears to have been no less guarded, canny and calculating at home than he was in the workplace.

His job as a "wire drawer" was dirty, dangerous and numbingly repetitive. It was also poorly paid. He started working at the massive American Steel & Wire Company at the beginning of the Twentieth Century, during the heyday of raw industrial capitalism in the United States . He left the same job, after nearly thirty five years of unrelenting toil with little to show for his efforts except a small pension.[120] His eldest son Francis, who did not love him, once described his father as being "very bright but frustrated." Little wonder! For between 1906 and 1920, every two years or so there was a new mouth to feed in the Deignan household. In Bernard's nonunion shop, however, there was no predictable, corresponding pay increase to keep pace with the expanding material needs of his growing family. Ever more children and a stagnant rate of pay placed Bernard in an economic vise which squeezed tighter and tighter as the years passed. Eventually the triple, constant pressures of work, family and poverty wore Bernard down and broke him completely.

Little direct evidence of Bernard Deignan, as a person, has survived. When in the early 1930s he wrote to West Linton to obtain a copy of his Birth Certificate for some unknown purpose, the Town Clerk there sent the requested document to him but chided Bernard in a cover letter for not having included sufficient return postage with his original correspondence. His family was certainly poor but Bernard may have been a stereo-typically "parsimonious Scot" into the bargain. Or, perhaps, his omission of sufficient return postage may have been nothing more than an innocent mistake.[121]

Three of his father's favorite sayings were handed down by his eldest son, Francis, but without any explanation or interpretation. One was, "Keep your feet warm and your head cool!" If taken at face value, the meaning of this advice was fairly transparent: "take care of your own basic needs and don't lose your temper." The meaning of the second one, "Run away laughing," was more obscure. Did it mean "be happy and optimistic no matter what life throws at you"? Or, more darkly, did it suggest that in any physical fight or verbal confrontation you should always be sure to leave your opponent "down and out" while you walked away contemptuously as a derisive victor? The third and final one of his sayings, "Every man to his last", was particularly pertinent and interesting. On one level it simply meant "Find out what you're good at and stick to it." But, for the Deignan family, this aphorism had a much more practical meaning too. They were so poor that Bernard, literally, made and repaired the shoes which his numerous children wore and all too frequently wore out. This practice, born as it doubtless was of extreme poverty, nonetheless confirmed that Bernard possessed the innate talent and native intelligence which his son Francis attributed to him. Personal experience, as well as economic necessity, may well have contributed to Bernard's talent for making and repairing his children's shoes. For, as Christopher Atkinson, West Linton's historian, has pointed out, "There had been a long tradition of making boots in West Linton, indeed the village produced a style of shepherd's boot, with a distinct up-turned toe, which was very popular."[122] It may well be that, as a boy, Bernard had watched the cobblers at work in his home town and brought that knowledge with him to America where it came in handy. In fact, family lore had it that Bernard's kids would often get "new shoes" at Christmas, made by their father. Such gifts would have been completely in keeping with Bernard's Scottish character and values since new shoes, made at home, were practical, useful and inexpensive all at the same time.

When Bernard Deignan started drinking inappropriately is not known. But the "*why*" of it is easier to grasp. His particular problem was an all too general one as well:

> Mired at the bottom of the economic hierarchy, most of Worcester's Irish workers earned too little to meet the needs of their families.... Since they could not support their families even with steady work, the problems for laboring men and women were severely compounded when they lost their jobs even for brief periods. Their jobs at the bottom of the economic hierarchy were not only the worst-paying but often the most dangerous positions available in Worcester's economy. Machine belts and gears in shoe shops, furnaces and rivers of molten metal in the wire mills, and wool or cotton dust in the textile mills all took their toll on the Irish and other workers."[123]

Throughout his adult life, both for cultural and occupational reasons, Bernard sought to distance himself from the masses of Irish workingmen around him. The Worcester Irish, particularly those of the immigrant generation, were notorious for their drinking.[124] But Caledonians were not far behind their Hibernian rivals, for, in Scotland itself, "On average, Scots drank five times as much spirits as the English so this shared weakness did not make the Irish nearly as conspicuous as they were in other centres of the diaspora where their fondness for alcohol became a key element of their stereotype."[125] A combination of cultural predilections and the crushing burdens of work, family and poverty eventually led Bernard to seek temporary comfort in alcohol consumption; and its use at some point apparently turned into abuse. Here again, the problem which Anna Deignan increasingly had to face was a fairly typical one for the wives of far too many workingmen, for "... if their ... husbands did not die, then they might be overwhelmed by their burdens, become addicted to alcohol, and grow violent...."[126]

Detailed accounts of Bernard's drinking patterns have not survived. But, in typically laconic Deignan fashion, his eldest son once said of him, with a hard and angry edge in his voice, "He was an alcoholic!" In the end, there is no knowing how much of his meager take-home pay and eventual pension Bernard regularly drank up or how he acted toward his wife and children when he had been drinking. When he was sober it appears that Bernard was cold and distant toward his children, none of whom ever remembered him with any evident affection. In any case, Bernard's bleak and difficult life ended violently late on the evening of August 31, 1940 when, while crossing the railroad tracks near his home, he was struck and killed instantly by a freight train. He died at age sixty three.

Although the manifold and cumulative effects of Bernard's progressively heavy drinking upon his wife and children can only have been negative, they did not occur in a moral or practical vacuum. Even if she never worked outside the home, Anna Deignan provided the foundation on which her family's stability and wellbeing rested. What her surviving children lacked in regard for their dissolute father, they more than made up in love for their mother. They demonstrated deep affection and respect toward her on both public and private occasions. No better proof of their feelings for her can be given than the fact that her eldest son, Frank, and her youngest daughter, Catherine—then pregnant with her first child—drove through a blizzard to be with Anna when she lay on her deathbed on March 18, 1956; coincidentally the fourteenth anniversary of Donald's own death in Hawaii. Nor was respect and admiration for Anna, as a person and a homemaker, confined to her own children. One of her daughters-in-law once said, "You could arrive unexpectedly at her door and within five minutes she'd have a meal on the table for you."

As has been previously noted, the North End of Worcester where Donald was born had been a solidly Irish immigrant neighborhood since the middle of the Nineteenth Century. But, even before his birth in 1915, things had begun to change. As early as 1907, the character of St. Ann's parish where he was

Baptized on March 21, 1915 was being transformed by the arrival of Italian, Lithuanian and Polish immigrants.[127] Like the Irish and French-Canadians before them, the newcomers were drawn to Worcester by the prospect of finding work in the city's numerous factories and mills and they did so in large numbers.

The arrival of large numbers of new immigrants in Worcester in the first two decades of the Twentieth Century served to exacerbate still further ethnic and religious tensions which had been on the rise since the 1890s. At that time, street brawls between gangs of Irish and Swedish youths had been commonplace. [128] In Donald's early years they still were. His oldest brother recalled, later in life, that Swedish Protestant kids sometimes supported by Finns would often confront Irish Catholic youths supported by French-Canadians and Italians in fierce street battles for "neighborhood turf ." Apart from endemic ethnic and religious rivalries, industrial tensions were rising too. In 1915, the year of Donald's birth, there was a prolonged and bitter machinists strike in Worcester which split the city along class and occupational lines. [129] The prolonged machinists strike ended in failure and taught the non-unionized men at American Steel & Wire an object lesson in industrial relations which they would not soon forget. In its light, Bernard Deignan and his coworkers plodded quietly along and took only what they could get with a spirit of grim resignation.

Meanwhile Donald began to receive the basics of an education in Roman Catholicism from his mother and older sisters, Mary and Anne. Its theological tone and character were, perforce, strongly

Irish. The Church in Worcester was then completely dominated either by Irish-born or Irish-American priests. Like the Irish immigrants in Scotland some fifty or seventy five years earlier, who had resented the administrative and cultural monopoly of native Scottish priests, ethnic Catholic newcomers to Worcester could do little or nothing about the structure and character of the American church in which they then found themselves. For their part the Irish in Worcester, both clerical and lay, enjoyed their triumph. In 1915, one Irish priest in Worcester declared, "It is a special blessing of the church in this country that it has been founded along the lines of the Irish church and no matter how great the flood of immigrants may be in the years to come, the tradition and custom has been established and it will continue along the lines of the dear church of Ireland."[130] Apart from its Triumphalist spirit, "Irish Catholicism in turn of the century Worcester was still a demanding, sometimes harsh, faith."[131]

In view of the frequent "harshness"of priests of the time, Donald, as a small boy, was probably afraid of many of the priests with whom he had to deal. He made his "First Holy Communion" at the recently established Saint Bernard's Church in the northeast corner of Worcester on June 3, 1923.[132] Prior to doing so, Donald would have had to make his first "Confession." "Confession" is now often called "The Sacrament of Penance and Reconciliation."[133] It is intended to do exactly what the title of the Rite suggests: to bring penitent sinners back into God's Grace and friendship by allowing people to discuss their failings and wrongdoings, to which they admit, and for which they formally ask forgiveness and express sorrow, in the presence of a sympathetic and compassionate priest who exercises the power of absolution given to the priesthood by Christ himself. Today, the "Sacrament of Reconciliation" most often takes place in an informal, well-lit, face-to-face setting. But during Donald's youth, and indeed well into the 1970s, old-style "Confession" could be a scary experience for a young child and an off-putting one even for a teenager. The "Confessional" was a heavily curtained, dimly-lit wooden booth with a floor-to-ceiling, carpeted partition down the middle. The penitent "sinner" knelt on one side of the partition, and the priest sat opposite him/her on the other. They communicated through a screen placed at eyelevel within the Confessional. A sliding piece of wood covered the grating on the priest's side of the booth. When he was ready to hear the Confession, he would slide the piece of wood to one side of the screen and wait for the person to begin by saying, "Bless me, Father, for I have sinned." If young Donald mumbled, or was nervous, or forgot something in the way of a prayer he was supposed to recite on such occasions he would likely hear, "Speak up!" or "How many times did you…?" or "Continue!" and so forth. For many young people, dealing with old priests who could not hear well and who often spoke with hard to understand Irish accents, "Going to Confession" was frequently neither a healing nor a pleasant experience. In any case, Donald also received the Sacrament of "Confirmation" at Saint Bernard's Church on May 19, 1926.[134] "Confirmation," administered by a Bishop, is the Sacrament which recognizes the person receiving it as a fully-fledged adult Christian within the Catholic Church.[135] Although it is beyond doubt that Donald was born, Baptized and Confirmed in the Roman Catholic Faith, the degree to which he practiced it as an adult is, at this point, unknown and unknowable. Chapters Eight and Nine, below, will, for reasons which will then become clear, discuss this matter more fully .

Donald's elementary school records have apparently not survived. But he probably started school, in his neighborhood, in the fall of 1921 at the age of six and one half years.

By the time Donald started elementary school, his two older brothers had already begun working, at least on a part-time basis. Frank had started bagging and delivering groceries for neighborhood markets by the time he was nine years old. Bob soon followed in his footsteps. Both boys turned their meager earnings over to their mother directly. Frank dropped out of school after eighth grade to go to work full time to help support the family. Bob graduated from high school in 1927 and soon left for greener pastures. He was followed shortly thereafter by Frank, who found a good job in New York City in 1929. He lost it, later that year, when the stock market crashed.

So as a young boy Donald was exposed to an example of "service" by the actions of his two older brothers. They worked, he saw, to support their mother and his sisters because they had to. This early lesson Donald never forgot. Once Frank and Bob had gone, during his crucial teenage years, Donald was left essentially alone in a household full of women. His father was nearing the end of his working life. A thoroughly besotted Bernard, by then, may well have lacked either the energy or the inclination to "mentor" his youngest son. One or both of Donald's older brothers could have fulfilled this vital role more than adequately but both of them had already left home during the critical years when he could have most used their guidance and discipline. By the time that both Frank and Bob returned to live in Worcester just before World War II, Donald had already left there for good and joined the Army. So any benefit which he might have derived from positive interactions with one or both of his older brothers never materialized. Under these circumstances, what happened to Donald next should not be surprising.

The origins from which he came and the environment in which he grew to young manhood created the underlying difficulties against which Donald had to struggle. But he also made a number of problematic personal decisions in the course of his life which served only to worsen the difficult original conditions in which he had found himself through no fault of his own. His individual choices made an already bad personal situation even worse than it might otherwise have been.

In the fall of 1931 he entered North High School. His surviving academic records from that institution show Donald to have been an indifferent and mediocre student. Whatever else he may have received from the direct example or overt guidance of his two older brothers, he did not acquire from them a notion of the practical importance of education. At least twice during his brief high school career he was recorded as being "Truant." Lacking either guidance or discipline from his psychologically distant, broken father Donald may simply have been bored with school. In addition, however, he may also have felt that it was time to go out and work to support his family as his older brothers before him had done. In any case, he dropped out of North High School for good on November 29, 1933, when the Great Depression was at its worst. What made this impetuous decision particularly tragic was the fact that his two prior prolonged periods of Truancy put Donald well behind his classmates at North High School. Ironically, if he had stayed in school and performed even marginally there, Donald could have graduated with a High School Diploma, which would have improved his work prospects significantly. Instead, he left North High School at age 18 with nothing at all to show for his indifferent efforts.[136]

Donald's decision to leave school early was not an entirely individual or an idiosyncratic one. To some extent, it may have been influenced by Scottish, Catholic working-class tradition. Writing of educational attitudes among Scots of Irish extraction—in Scotland—at this time, one authority has observed that, "Throughout the late nineteenth and early twentieth century, the children of Irish emigrants had a tradition of leaving school and going into unskilled occupations to eke out the family income."[137] But, in Worcester at least, the tradition of leaving school early to help the family economically was coming under increasing challenge at the very time when Donald voluntarily left high school. More and more Irish-American families were finding the financial resources to keep their children in school as long as possible because they had come to recognize the social and monetary benefits of education.[138] It is probable that the Deignan family was not financially secure enough to do this, however, even if they had been inclined to do so. Bernard's low wages and drinking, combined with the absence of his two oldest sons, meant that the family needed every penny it could earn just to survive. They could probably not have afforded to keep the adolescent Donald in school, and out of the work force, even if he had wanted his parents to do that. Frank and Robert were exceptional, within the family, in their commitment to higher education. In general, the Deignans were literate but not literary people. Apart from Frank, who achieved great things educationally, and his middle brother, Bob, who attended college for several years and was later very successful in life, the most ambitious among the rest of the Deignans finished high school. As a rule they did not read much beyond the daily newspaper. And the bulk of them left behind no personal written records which have survived. So much about their family life in general, and Donald's childhood and youth in particular, can only be inferred from scant, indirect, evidence. Finally, it is probably true that Donald was bored with school and that he did not see any point to it. If this was so, his attitude reflected the outlook of a large segment of the American working-class generation from which he came. Writing of them, one authority on the Civilian Conservation Corps, which Donald joined only eight months after leaving high school, said:

> As a result of their public school experience, many enrollees had a negative view of education. Their biggest criticism seemed to have been that the intellectual demands of the classroom were unrelated to the practical needs of the job market. A large number pictured formalized schooling as sitting in classes, studying

> things that did not interest them, listening
> to a teacher, conforming to rules, and all the
> rest of it—with dislike, for some even with
> abhorrence."[139]

As will be seen in the next Chapter, even when he knew better from personal experience and when he had ample opportunities to do otherwise, Donald did not choose to avail himself of further education. Education did not interest him and, in any case, he apparently lacked the ambition to pursue it.

His youthful self-image was probably always negative. In later life he would once describe himself as being best suited to do only the work of a "laborer." As a boy, Donald was shy, slightly-built, buck- toothed and extremely self-conscious about his personal appearance. Praise and encouragement were in short supply both in his household and from his Church. "Pride," he was taught, was the greatest of all sins and self-promotion was a particularly insidious form of that terrible transgression. "Don't be too full of yourself or you'll get a swelled head," was the constant warning from his strict Catholic parents. His Church too had at the very least an ambivalent attitude toward individualism, materialism and even "success" itself.[140] All in all, personal uncertainty seems to have shaped his developing personality.

For his first nineteen years of life, all of it spent in inner-city Worcester, pervasive tension was Donald's constant and unwelcome companion. At home it stemmed, equally, from poverty rooted in the economic callousness of the capitalist industrial system and in his father's addictive drinking. In the outside world it arose from old and continuing ethnic rivalries sharpened by increasing sectarian divisions which together found expression in political polarization. As a poorly educated youth, Donald was not at all well-equipped either to understand or to cope with such multifaceted and immense personal and societal stresses.

At first glance, during those deeply troubled times, Donald was so ordinary and anonymous as to be unworthy of notice. He had grown up in poverty and gone unmentored for most of the time. Along the way he made poor choices for which he, and he alone, was ultimately responsible. In the early 1930s, Donald Joseph John Deignan was one of several million short, scrawny kids with no real skills to offer prospective employers. Like the rest of them, Donald found himself competing for work with hundreds of thousands of unemployed well-educated, mature men who had families to feed. In that fearsome economic environment he drifted aimlessly around Worcester and apparently found nothing of substance to do. "Experience is the best teacher," or so the old saying goes. Donald, at this point, had a little less than a decade to live. During this time, his "best teacher" would impose many hard lessons upon him. To his credit he learned them increasingly well, or so it seemed.

IN THE "CCC" AND AFTERWARDS

Having made the decision to drop out of North High School in Worcester in the early 1930s, as the Great Depression gathered strength, Donald must have soon discovered the hard truth that he was an immature, unskilled teenager competing with hordes of experienced, adult men with compelling family obligations to meet. He may have found menial, casual jobs from time to time, but even if he did so, none of them lasted for long.

By early July 1934, his family likely was growing financially desperate. His older brothers, Francis and Robert, had long since left home and Donald's father, Bernard, was nearing the end of his working life. So some means had to be found to support the Deignan family and to spare it from utter destitution. For Donald and more than two million other young, unemployed American men like him, the newly established Civilian Conservation Corps or "CCC" provided an opportunity to achieve this objective.

Surviving records do not indicate when Donald first began to consider joining the CCC in order to help his family and to secure his own employment prospects. But he may have thought about doing so in the early spring of 1934. Formal "Enrollment" in the CCC was the last step in a drawn-out bureaucratic undertaking. As one of the organization's leading historians has written:

> For the typical CCC enrollee, actual arrival at camp was the culmination of a fairly lengthy selection process. Some months earlier he had taken the initial step toward entrance by applying to his local selection agency for consideration as an enrollee. He then waited patiently for a period of up to two months until his application had been processed.[1]

Thus, although he may have considered doing so sometime earlier, it is clear that on July 8, 1934, Donald filed an "Application for enrollment, for the period of six months, in Federal Emergency Conservation Work," with the Board of Public Welfare in Worcester Massachusetts.[2] At the time, he was far from alone in doing so, and competition for places in the CCC was keen. During its first few years, there were five applicants for each available slot.[3] At least 100,000 other men from Massachusetts enrolled in the CCC between 1933 and 1942.

In a message to Congress on March 21, 1933, President Franklin D. Roosevelt proposed the creation of what he called a "Civilian Conservation Corps." Only ten days later, on March 31, "The

Emergency Conservation Work Act," which provided the initial legal authority for what later became known formally as the Civilian Conservation Corps, became law. It was one of the most important pieces of remedial social legislation introduced by President Roosevelt, as part of his "New Deal," during the first one hundred days of his initial administration. The purpose of the Emergency Conservation Work Act was, "… the relief of unemployment through the performance of useful public work, and for other purposes."[4] In its preamble the Emergency Conservation Work legislation recognized the need to relieve, "… the acute condition of widespread distress and unemployment now existing in the United States…."[5] The nation's depleted natural resources had to be restored, and the President was authorized to undertake this task by coordinating and overseeing the efforts of the several Federal Departments and Agencies involved in carrying out this mandate. A list of the "useful public works" required by the Act included "… the construction, maintenance, and carrying on of works of a public nature in connection with the forestation of lands belonging to the United States or to the several States which are suitable for timber production, the prevention of forest fires, floods, and soil erosion, plant pest and disease control, the construction, maintenance or repair of paths, trails and fire lanes in the national parks and national forests, and such other work on the public domain, national and state, and government reservations incidental to or necessary in connection with any projects of the character enumerated, as the President may determine to be desirable…."[6] "The Emergency Conservation Work Act" not only set forth the kinds of useful projects to be undertaken in the public interest but it also established most of the administrative underpinnings which were to characterize the CCC, itself, later on. "The name CCC had been used by the president in his message to Congress on March 21, and it quickly caught on and replaced the original title."[7] The Act gave the President the regulatory authority to provide financially for the housing, clothing, feeding, medical care, hospitalization, transportation and cash allowance payment of all enrollees in the program.[8] But for all the latitude which a pliant Congress was prepared to give him at the start, the House and Senate deliberately circumscribed Mr. Roosevelt's power noting in the final section of the Act that, "The authority of the President under this act shall continue for the period of two years next after the date of the passage hereof and no longer."[9] The CCC program proved to be so politically popular that the President's authority under the Emergency Work Act was eventually extended until March 31, 1937.[10] Shortly after that a new piece of Federal Legislation, "The Civilian Conservation Corps Act" was passed by Congress which extended the life of the organization for another three years.[11]

From the start, the CCC program was intended to serve as a model for interagency governmental cooperation. At a Washington DC meeting in early April, 1933:

> Specific   functions   were   assigned…the
> Department of Labor was directed to select
> the men for enrollment; the War Department
> was to enroll the men, feed, clothe, house,

and condition them, and transport them to the camps; the Departments of Agriculture and Interior, through their various bureaus, were to select work projects, to supervise the work, and to administer the camps. Apart from the almost immediate extension of the Army's role, these divisions remained relatively stable until the CCC came to an end in 1942. [12]

So, by the time Donald joined up in the summer of 1934, the CCC was a well-established and effective organization with a little more than a year of complex administrative and practical work experience to its credit.

Donald's Application for Emergency Conservation Work was completed in the offices of the Board of Public Welfare at Worcester City Hall. His acceptance into the CCC may have taken place more rapidly than was usual, for his paperwork had been submitted on July 8, 1934 and his formal Enrollment occurred only two days later. His Application, which is included within the "DISCHARGE PAPERS" from the Civilian Conservation Corps, reveals much about young Donald as a person and it also sheds light, albeit indirectly, on his socio-economic circumstances at that time as well.

On the first page of his paperwork, called an "Application Memorandum," he gave his full name as "Donald Joseph John Deignan" although he merely signed that same document as *"Donald J.J. Deignan"*. Clearly, he referred to himself, ordinarily, as "Donald"—his Baptismal Name—rather than as "Joseph," his legal name. In addition, his use of the middle name "John" establishes that he had been Confirmed, as a teenager, in the Roman Catholic Church. Upon receiving the Sacrament of Confirmation, it was customary for the person being so confirmed to take a Saint's name and add this to his/her own given names. It is ironic that, later on, the United States Army would record him throughout his military service as "Joseph J. Deignan" rather than as "Donald J.J. Deignan," which style he evidently preferred.

He further described himself, in response to another question on the Application Memorandum, as a "citizen of the United States by birth..." He gave his date and place of birth as "March 15, 1915 at Worcester Mass." For "My usual trade or occupation," he listed "None." He left the space for "I have been unemployed since...." blank. He stated further that he had never been either a member of the Civilian Conservation Corps or of the Boy Scouts. He listed "My education...(as)...1 year high school"[13]

Apart from offering real jobs to hundreds of thousands of young, unemployed men for practical purposes, another important aim of the Emergency Conservation Work program was to provide their families back home with a steady if meager source of income. For this purpose, Donald stated on his Enrollment Application that, "The dependent relatives to whom I wish to allot parts of my cash allowance and the sums that I desire each one to receive are as follows:....Mrs. Anna Deignan....Mother....5 Keefe Place....$25.00 a month....".[14] Since Emergency Conservation

Workers were only paid a total of thirty dollars per month, this allocation of his wages to his mother, and sisters, was significant. Following the example of responsibility and support set by his elder brothers, Donald too demonstrated his deep affection and concern for his mother and female siblings. There was a second space provided on the same form for the inclusion of an additional beneficiary. Donald, pointedly, left this space blank. Many young men would naturally have directed their allotments to be paid to their fathers as the head of the household. But Donald did not do so. He chose, instead, explicitly to send his money home exclusively to his responsible mother. From him, by implication, Donald's worn-out, feckless father, Bernard, should expect nothing.

Enrollment in "Emergency Conservation Work" was serious business entered into resolutely. "I agree to abide faithfully by the rules and regulations governing the work and the camps in which I desire to be employed," Donald read, just before signing his name to the Application Memorandum. By signing on the dotted line, he had become a member of what would be known to history as "the CCC."[15]

The initial portion of the application process had been overseen by the Board of Public Welfare, an agency of the City of Worcester. Henceforth, during his terms of CCC service, Donald's future was to be regulated by a number of Federal Agencies, with overlapping responsibilities, including the Department of Labor, the War Department—with which he was to have much more to do in later life—and the Departments of Agriculture and of the Interior. If, after signing it, he had glanced at the bottom of the first page of his Application he would have had an inkling of the complex bureaucratic web into which he was willingly entering. He would have read that, "The UNITED STATES DEPARTMENT OF LABOR certifies that Donald Joseph John Deignan of 5 Keefe Place, Worcester, Mass. has been selected for enrollment in the Emergency Conservation Work under the Provisions of Act of Congress, approved March 31, 1933 and has been directed to report to U.S. Army authorities at Fort Devens Massachusetts for completion of his enrollment."[16]

The following pages of Donald's file were equally informative and contained even more information specific to him. They were entitled: **"INDIVIDUAL RECORD—CIVILIAN CONSERVATION CORPS."** Several of them were taken up by the results of a "Physical Examination." From this particular document we learn that Donald J.J. Deignan was five feet four and one half inches tall; that he had blue eyes and brown hair, together with a "Medium complexion"; and that his eyesight, hearing and lung function were all normal. Although his general health was good, there were subtle indications of prior problems and privations too. Even though he was only nineteen years of age, several of his teeth were already missing, and he was diagnosed with "moderate Gingivitis." Most telling of all, he weighed a scant one hundred and six pounds when he first entered the CCC.[17] While heredity certainly had a good deal to do with his short stature, his small size—characteristic of the Deignan family—also reflected the generations of grinding poverty and the marginalized peasant life in Ireland from which they had so recently escaped. For Donald and his siblings material conditions in urban America had not been all that much better than those which their ancestors had endured in rural Ireland and small-town Scotland. Donald's poor dental health and low weight suggest a very bad diet during childhood and perhaps even outright malnutrition coincident with extreme poverty. Thanks to the CCC, Donald was to benefit from excellent medical and dental care, as well as a good diet, for the first time in his life.

During parts of the next four years Donald would travel around the United States but his first assignment did not take him too far from home. He was sent, initially, from urban Massachusetts to the pine forests of southern Maine. "It was the Corps' original intention to locate all youths about two hundred miles from their home districts, too far for weekly visits, yet close enough for monthly trips, but this provision was frequently neglected."[18] Established theoretical policy notwithstanding, Donald's first assignment so close to home was somewhat unusual. For, at the time, a substantial amount of help was needed much farther away than Maine.

In July, 1934 Donald was a very small part of a massive wave of new CCC enrollees nationwide. During that month, the Midwestern United Sates was suffering from severe drought conditions. To combat this natural disaster, President Roosevelt issued an Executive Order authorizing 50,000 more men mostly from 22 draught-stricken states to enroll in the CCC.[19]

Almost immediately after his enrollment and processing at Fort Devens, Donald was sent by train on July 10 to Millinocket,

Maine for "conditioning." By July 15, he had reached Alfred, Maine and become a member of CCC Company 130 there. The longest portion of Donald's entire CCC service was to be spent in Alfred.

Established in 1794, the town of Alfred—located 30 miles southwest of Portland and 13 miles west of Saco in York County Maine at the southern end of the state—was, for most of its history, an agricultural village.[20] According to the 1930 United States Census it then had a population of 833. By 1940 that number had risen to1039.[21] So, during Donald's stay there in 1934 and 1935, the population was probably between 900 and 1000 people.

CCC Company 130, which Donald joined in July 1934, was organized at Fort Devens on June 1, 1933 and transferred by train on June 21 to land leased from Senator Emory S. Littlefield on the outskirts of the village of Alfred. Housed initially in tents, by December 1933 permanent wooden Barracks for the Company's officers, men and civilian "technical service" employees were completed. Eventually, the Camp featured ten different buildings.[22]

The Camp in which Company 130 was housed was, from Donald's point of view, to prove unusual in at least two respects. First, it was located in the outskirts of Alfred itself along Route 4, "across from our current County Jail…".[23] Second, it was out of the ordinary because, "Nine Alfred citizens served in Company 130…".[24] As has been noted above, CCC policy dictated that most enrollees should be assigned to camps about 200 miles from their homes so as to make visits on "Leave" possible but also to discourage too frequent absences from camp to be with family or friends. Although he did not address Alfred's recruitment anomaly in Company 130 directly, Mr. John P. Cook, an Alfred historian, further noted that, "…most of the company personnel were from out of town or from out of state."[25] Their closeness to town meant that, after a short walk or ride, "the boys" could enjoy themselves in Alfred almost whenever they wished to do so, either after the day's work or on weekends. The proximity of Donald's first Camp to town was at variance with his subsequent CCC experiences in both Massachusetts and Oregon. In those places, towns were many miles from Camp and transportation to them was often hard to come by.

Between July 10, 1934 and September 30, 1935, while he was serving in Company 130, Donald's work record is extremely cryptic. Next to the item **"Type of work"** is the simple notation **"Forestry"** and the performance evaluation, **"Satisfactory."**[26] Nothing is said either about his life or personal conduct in Camp or about what he and his fellow Corpsmen might have done in their off hours. However, thanks to the preserved work of Mary Carpenter Kelley—an Alfred native and local journalist—a good deal of general information about the life and work of Company 130 has come to light. Their Camp, a short distance outside of Alfred proper, was situated near a "cold, damp, swampy and rocky place…"[27]

The kinds of work which the men did varied greatly from time to time and from season to season. In June, 1934, for example,

Company 130 was moved from Alfred to Baxter State Park on Mt. Katahdin—Maine's highest point at 5276 feet—"for a summer's work." [28] So Donald joined his new CCC colleagues there in mid-July. For him, the cool breezes blowing atop Mt. Katahdin must have come as a pleasant surprise and a welcome relief. Life on Katahdin was in sharp contrast to conditions in the sweltering tenement on Keefe Place in Worcester which he had so recently left behind. While on the mountain, Donald and his fellow Corpsmen constructed camp sites, trails, dams and cabins, "which have been in use by campers ever since."[29] During the balance of 1934 and 1935, Donald's first CCC Company completed a significant number of similar public works projects in and around Alfred itself and throughout the Counties of York and Cumberland in southernmost Maine. "Between 1934 and 1935 the men of Company 130 built five public camp sites. Four of them were in York County and the fifth was in neighboring Cumberland County. One was built on Mt. Ossipee and another on Mt. Agementious, the two highest points in southern Maine."[30] Wherever they went, while completing public works projects, the men of Company 130 were good and careful stewards of nature:

> The type of camp ground furnished by the C.C.C. gives the motorist the use of a place in which to build his fire without danger of starting a conflagration, assures him of laboratory-tested spring water, and provides in almost all cases, adequate toilet facilities.[31]

Furthermore, according to the Camp's Chief Foreman, Mr. Delbert L. Moody, the boys of Company 130 derived great satisfaction from their work and took real pride in its results.[32]

But the primary purpose of the original "Emergency Conservation Work" Act had been the protection, preservation and revitalization of America's natural resources, most especially its forests. So **"Forestry"** work of all kinds was primarily what Donald and his transplanted urban comrades, virtually all of them men from Massachusetts like himself, mostly did in the pine woods around Alfred.

From the start, woodland pest control and disease eradication was Company 130's most important mission. As early as June 26, 1933—very shortly after its arrival in Alfred—"the boys" of Company 130 set to work with, "…the placement of white pine blister rust control crews in the field in Dayton and in Newfield."[33] White Pine Blister Rust was a deadly disease transmitted to healthy trees in close proximity to infected, wild currant and gooseberry bushes. Suppression and eradication of this forest plague was of great importance to Maine's timber-based economy. Writing in May, 1936, Mary Carpenter Kelley noted the crucial contribution which the CCC had already made to protecting one of the state's most important industries when she observed, "As York County has extensive stands of White Pine, which form a large part of its wealth, the importance of the Pine Blister control cannot be overestimated and the total of 81,854 man-hours that have already been put in by the men of the C.C.C. have been of untold value to the county."[34] White-Pine

Blister Rust eradication teams consisted of six or seven CCC enrollees under the supervision of a leader or "straw-boss." [35] "Blister Rust" was a serious disease threat exclusive to White-Pine trees. But there were additional, equally potent natural dangers in the Maine woods which Donald and the other young men of Company 130 also had to combat. Gypsy Moth and Brown-tail Moth infestations could be as lethal to many other types of trees as Blister Rust was to White-Pines alone. Taken together, all of these threats kept "the CCC boys" busy year round:

> Insect pest control is another project. This includes for winter work the swabbing of Gypsy Moth egg clusters with iodine to make them infertile, and the removal of nests of the Brown-tail Moth…. Blister Rust eradication is summer work and comprises the destruction of wild currant and gooseberry bushes. [36]

Pine Blister Rust and periodic insect infestations may have been frequent problems in the deep woods but in June, 1935, Donald and his fellow Corpsmen faced a new and looming challenge on the quiet streets of Alfred itself. The so-called "Dutch Elm Disease," imported accidentally from Europe, had first appeared in the United States, in Ohio, in 1933 where it had begun to ravage "American Elm Trees." Since then, it had spread east and was already in evidence in Connecticut in the summer of 1935. The spread of Dutch Elm Disease to Maine was greatly feared so in June Company 130 began a meticulous survey of all of the elm trees in sixteen designated towns throughout the southern part of the state. Twelve-man CCC "squads," led by an experienced Forester, carefully inspected each at-risk elm and noted its location. Dutch Elm Disease first manifested itself in the upper-most branches of the tallest and oldest trees. So CCC volunteers would climb into the treetops, aided by ropes, to determine the health of each individual Elm. They would take twig and leaf samples, from each plant, which would then be sent off for laboratory analysis. If "Disease" was actually found in a tree, the "boys" were to cut out the "dead wood" on the spot and then, perhaps, to cut down the entire elm as a precaution. The matter was regarded as being of such seriousness that the entire Dutch Elm survey project was overseen, personally, by Maine's State Entomologist Dr. Henry B. Pierson.[37] In the event, the June 1935 "American Elm" survey then found no evidence of Dutch Elm Disease in southern Maine.

When they were not engaged on public works projects or in woodland pest control, for good measure, the hard-working young men of Company 130 fought forest fires in summer and shoveled out the public roads in Alfred and in surrounding communities after winter blizzards which sometimes created snow-drifts twenty feet high.[38]

In light of the great variety of construction projects and reclamation activities in which Company 130 was involved while Donald served with it, the designation of his "type of work" as **"Forestry"** was far too simplistic. Clearly he acquired a number of new skills and had many novel experiences which served to broaden his outlook on life during the fifteen months he spent in Maine between July 1934 and September 1935.[39]

Much less evidence pertaining to the Camp life of Company 130 has survived than that relating to the actual work which its members did for the CCC. Nonetheless, and thanks largely once again to the surviving work of Mary Carpenter Kelley, some insights into the living conditions and the private lives of "the boys" are still to be had.

From its establishment in June 1933 until mid-April 1934—not long before Donald's arrival in Camp #2108—CCC Company 130 was commanded by Captain Henry F. Mulloy of the United States Navy. This circumstance was in itself somewhat unusual in that most CCC Camps were administered either by Regular Army or Army Reserve Officers. Given his Naval association, it is not surprising that Captain Mulloy obtained many of his supplies and much of the necessary equipment for Company 130 from Navy and Marine Corps surplus stocks.[40] When Captain Mulloy moved on to his next assignment, he may have been succeeded in Command of Company 130, temporarily at least, by one of his subordinates, Lieutenant G. Herbert Olson, another Navy Officer.[41] Even though the U.S. Navy was in administrative charge of the Camp at Alfred, it cooperated with the U.S. Army when a pair of its Infantry Officers conducted a two-day "Inspection" of Company 130 in December 1933.[42]

Once the permanent Barracks buildings were completed in December 1933, living conditions for "the boys" were described as being "very comfortable." Each man had "five warm blankets and a complete outfit of heavy winter clothing, so that with plenty of good food" and a "well-equipped recreation building they seem to have everything to make them contented."[43]

Although everybody in Camp had electricity and access to hot running water, "the boys" continued to eat out of their mess-kits throughout the duration of their Alfred service. By contrast, Company 107 on Mt. Greylock—which Donald joined in April 1936—provided real dishes and tableware for its men. Meanwhile, in Alfred, the administrative Military Officers and civilian Project Supervisors—who shared their own, exclusive "Barracks"—had it much better. They enjoyed fine quarters which featured "a huge chimney and fireplace in the officers' living-room." This had been constructed from "fine stones brought down from Mt. Ossipee in Waterboro" by "the boys." [44]

Although there were some disparities in material living conditions between the Officers and Supervisors on the one hand and the ordinary Enrollees in Company 130 on the other, "the boys" were grateful for the food, shelter, clothing, work and money which their CCC service brought them. Association with the Corps also provided less tangible benefits. Local clergymen and professors often gave lectures on various subjects in Camp in the evening or on Sundays. A Company basketball team was organized and it played teams from surrounding communities. Hiking, skiing and snow-shoeing were equally popular recreational activities available to the men during their leisure time.[45]

The spiritual and intellectual needs of the Company were also addressed. U.S. Army trucks assigned to the Camp transported

Enrollees to the church of their choice each Sunday in Sanford, a large mill-town neighboring Alfred.[46] During winter nights, Sanford High School opened its doors and offered evening classes to interested CCC Enrollees. In the winter of 1933-1934 80 men from Company 130 took advantage of this opportunity for intellectual enrichment at Government expense.[47] This attendance figure represented some what less than half of the Company's 200 man complement but it was nonetheless impressive because in its early years the CCC did not stress formal education as part of its mission. There is every reason to suppose that Sanford High School continued to offer evening classes to CCC men during Donald's term of service in Alfred. But there is no evidence in his surviving record to indicate that he ever availed himself of the opportunity offered at that time.[48] His evident lack of interest in further schooling was not untypical among his peers. But the persistence of this attitude over time was to place him in a minority among other CCC men.

There is no mention of Leave being requested or granted during the fifteen months of Donald's CCC service in Maine. All that is known from the official record about this period, in addition to the foregoing information, is that at the time of his Discharge on September 30, 1935 he owed the United States **"Nothing for Lost Clothing or Lost Equipment";** and that the "Work" for which he was **"best fitted"** was **"Forestry."**[49]

Even though he was never mentioned by name in any of Company 130's records, the fact that Donald's work in Alfred was altogether typical of that performed by CCC Company's throughout the United States is largely confirmed by the following general statement:

> Enrollees in a forestry camp might find themselves working in small groups under an enrollee leader, clearing dead wood, planting trees, digging out rocks, or building trails. Some might be clearing strips for firebreaks, others building lookout towers, telephone lines, small dams, or bridges.[50]

From its inauguration in April 1933 until its dissolution in June 1942, the CCC was organized along quasi-military lines. As we have seen, the United States Navy had been in charge of the Camp which Donald entered in July 1934. But this administrative circumstance had been somewhat anomalous and the Army played a dominant role, in most places, throughout the Civilian Conservation Corps's nine-year existence. The United States Army had been instrumental, albeit reluctantly, in mobilizing the CCC's first 250,000 enrollees between May and July 1933.[51] So it should not be altogether surprising that much of the CCC's organization and terminology were of a military character. For example, its basic unit was the "Company" which consisted of 200 young CCC enrollees between the ages of 18 and 25 who were known as "juniors" or "boys."[52] They lived in "Barracks" which housed forty to sixty men each. "Upon arrival at camp, enrollees were usually given two sets of clothing, a blue denim work or fatigue suit and a renovated Army olive drab uniform for dress purposes."[53] In most places United States Army Officers, usually Captains in the Regular Army or in the Reserve, were in overall charge of each large camp and their powers were broad:

> The commanding officer's functions included the complete charge of the camp, the personnel administration, and the welfare of the men. He was responsible for all matters of discipline and was authorized to implement a range of punishments from simple admonition for minor offenses to dishonorable discharge for more serious misdemeanors such as refusal to work, desertion, or unwillingness to abide by camp rules. The second in command had a variety of duties to perform, frequently combining the functions of finance officer, motor transport officer, quartermaster, and, before the educational advisers were appointed, welfare officer. There was also a medical officer, again usually taken from the Regular Army or the Army Reserve, for every two or more camps; he was assisted by two first-aid men selected from the enrollees.[54]

Serving directly under the Army Officers for administrative purposes were Enrollee "Leaders" or "Assistant Leaders" who were drawn in specific proportions from the Company in which they served. There were twenty-six such young men, who carried out a number of different assigned tasks, in each camp. Owing to their increased responsibility, Leaders and Assistant

Leaders earned considerably higher monthly pay than did ordinary Enrollees in the Company.[55]

The day-to-day work of "the boys" was supervised in each camp by eight "woodsmen" designated "Local Experienced Men" or "L.E.M.s"[56] While the particular work of various Companies may have been carried out under the jurisdiction of different Federal Agencies, the daily routine of camp life was the same throughout the entire United States.

A bugle sounded Reveille at 6 AM. Enrollees had to be washed and dressed and in their work clothes by 6:30 AM., ready for physical training. After physical training ended, the men moved off for breakfast in the Mess Hall. There six to twelve men sat at long mess-hall tables. Food was plentiful, plain but nourishing. A typical breakfast could consist of stewed prunes, cereal, ham, eggs, milk and coffee. After breakfast, platoon roll-call and inspection took place with the work day beginning at 7:45 AM. The men walked or rode to work. Work stopped at Noon and the enrollees were given an hour for lunch which usually consisted of sandwiches, pie and coffee served on the job site. The work day ended at 4:00 PM. The men returned to camp, either by truck or on foot, depending on their distance from the day's work site to home. Once back in camp they showered and changed clothes. Supper was served after 5:30 PM. Army-style Dress uniforms were worn at dinner. Substantial quantities of meat and vegetables were available with fruit and dessert to follow. Classes or recreation—such as table tennis or pool—were available in camp. Free time could also be enjoyed after the evening meal according to the wishes of the individual enrollee. They could even go into the nearest town if they wished to do so but they had to be back before 10:00 when "lights-out" occurred. Taps was blown at 10:15. The Camp Commander made a bed check at 11:00 PM at which point the Company's day ended.[57]

Donald left the Civilian Conservation Corps in Maine owing to **"Termination of Enrollment."** The starkness of this phrase should not be misconstrued. His legally allotted time had simply run out and Corpsman Deignan's "Discharge" was **"HONORABLE."** His last pay on the date of his Discharge was $5.00, a not inconsiderable sum in those days of the Great Depression. Upon his release, he was provided with transportation at Government expense from North Berwick, Maine back to Worcester, Massachusetts.[58]

As Donald left the Corps for the first time at the end of September 1935, the CCC was entering what might be called its "Golden Age." At that point the program was at the height of its popularity with both Congress and the general public. The House and Senate supported it on a strong bipartisan basis because of the economic benefits to local businesses which CCC Camps brought to Congressional Districts and the general public appreciated the reliable stream of extra money which enrollees sent home in monthly allotments. The "Emergency Relief Appropriation Act of 1935," which reauthorized the Corps until March 31,1937, increased the maximum term of service allowed from one year to eighteen months and it raised the upper age limit for eligibility to 28 years.[59] Donald's personal economic "Day of Reckoning" was thus postponed by the likelihood that he would be able to rejoin the CCC, in future, if that course of action proved to be necessary.

In the spring of 1936, President Roosevelt—in order to save money—proposed to downsize the CCC and close many of its camps. This idea was met with a firestorm of bipartisan Congressional criticism fueled by constituent discontent at the grassroots level. Thus, Donald "dodged an economic bullet," at least for a while.[60]

When he returned home to Worcester in early October 1935 Donald did so as something of a changed man. In the pine woods of southern Maine, over the previous fifteen months, he had for the first time experienced the discipline and rewards of hard, systematic work. He had provided deliberately and consistently for the financial support of his family. He may even have managed to save a little of his take-home pay although there is no direct evidence of his having done so. Meanwhile, his diet and his physical health had improved. His outlook on life was now mature and serious. In short, Donald had "grown up" and learned the meaning of the word "responsibility." But for all these gains, in a very real sense, he now found himself literally back where he had started from. The Great Depression was still ongoing. What was he to do? First, he went back home and then he found a job.

During Donald's absence in the CCC, in Maine, Bernard and Anna Deignan had moved from Keefe Place—where they had lived since 1918—to 53 Lincoln Street, a short distance away, in Worcester.[61] Whether Donald's monthly financial support allowed his family to move into better accommodations is not known but it is certain that his brother, Francis, always described Keefe Place as "a slum". Significantly, Frank never cast such aspersions on the two Lincoln Street locations at which his parents subsequently lived. It is clear that, upon his return from Maine, Donald moved back in with his parents since he gave their 53 Lincoln Street address as his own when he enrolled in the CCC, once again, in April 1936.

On the occasion of his second enrollment, Donald again went through the process of providing the CCC with general information. From this second "Application" we learn that he had been employed—after returning home from Maine—as a "milkman," and that by April 9, 1936 he had been unemployed for two months.[62] How and when he obtained the job as a milkman is unknown. But the implication of this statement is that he had held the position for quite some time, perhaps even as far back as the fall of 1935, although this assumption is admittedly speculative.

Why Donald left his employment as a milkman in February 1936 is equally uncertain. But it may well be that his employer simply cut his labor force for purely economic reasons. Since Donald's job performance in Maine had been officially characterized as **"Satisfactory"** and because his first CCC Discharge had been **"Honorable"** it appears that he developed and maintained an equally good work ethic during the 1934-1935 period. His subsequence performance record in the CCC was to be equally unblemished and so it is likely that he lost his interim job in Worcester through no fault of his own.

Donald's frame of mind when he first joined the CCC in July 1934 can only be guessed at. He had told them then, it will be recalled, that he had never worked.[63] In 1934 an employment opportunity under the aegis of the Federal Government had been his economic and personal salvation. The loss of his job in Worcester doubtless hit him hard both financially and psychologically.

By early April 1936 there was, once again, an unmistakable air of desperation evident in Donald's second CCC Enrollment Application. He made it this time at the "Army Base Boston Mass." He signed himself on that occasion as *"Donald John Deignan"* and his application was taken by *"Lauretta C. Bresnahan, State Selecting Agent CCC, 666 Summer Street, Boston, Massachusetts".*[64] He enrolled, formally, at Fort Devens on April 9, 1936, signing himself as *""Donald J. Deignan"* on that occasion. He informed military authorities that he had dutifully **"....registered for work with the nearest public employment office."** After listing his most recent job as "milkman", he responded to the question **"Work best qualified for...."** simply as **"laborer."** As a milkman he would have driven a truck on a daily basis. Doing so would have required a certain level of skill, expertise and personal responsibility. But now, by listing his qualifications as those of an ordinary **"laborer"** he was admitting a kind of defeat and opening himself up to the very real possibility of having to dig ditches for a living. Most poignant and telling of all was his response to a subsequent question. Donald left virtually no personal records behind him which could give an insight into his interior life or mental landscape. Sometimes, however, a single remaining word can be as powerful and illuminating as a lightning bolt across a pitch black sky. In April 1936, his intake interviewer asked, **"What kind of job do you hope to find after completion of C.C.C. enrollment?"** In answer to this query Donald replied with the simple, plaintive word, *"anything."!* [65]

A black and white photograph of Donald, taken at about this time, has survived. It shows him sitting on the steps of an unidentified Federal Building. He is wearing his CCC work uniform and holding a plain baseball cap in his right hand as if in salute of the unseen photographer. He is, characteristically, serious and unsmiling as he looks straight into the camera. Throughout his life, Donald was very sensitive about his appearance. His brother Frank remembered him as "….being very shy and having buck teeth." On the back of this particular picture is the hand-written inscription in ink,

> *"Donald Joseph Deignan*
> *21 yrs (sic) old March 15th"* **(1936).** [66]

Who took this photograph is unknown as is the geographical location and the exact date at which it was taken. One thing is, however, more certain. Donald J.J. Deignan attained his majority in March 1936 with few if any remaining illusions either about himself or about the wider world around him and his place in it. Gone was the scrawny kid who, a few years earlier, had dropped out of high school believing that any employer would be eager and lucky to hire him! That naive youth had been replaced by a mature young man who had learned the hard way from his previous mistakes. He had worked hard and successfully in the CCC in Maine but then he had found and lost work in the private sector and he now understood full well just how precarious his personal economic situation, and that of his immediate family, then was. His father had retired sometime in the previous year, after more than thirty years of continuous service at American Steel and Wire, with a small pension that could not by itself support the family. So now the financial burden of maintaining his family fell almost exclusively on Donald's small and narrow shoulders. No wonder his demeanor in the photograph just described appears at least resigned if not altogether sullen.

By this time Donald was thoroughly familiar with the CCC and he must have appreciated the additional opportunities which it could offer him should he choose to enroll in its ranks for a second time. But his decision finally to do so must have been taken reluctantly and as an expedient last resort. Another "hitch" in the Corps would provide him with a second chance at economic survival but, after its completion, he knew that he would have to look for further employment beyond its familiar and supportive confines, since enrollees were limited to two terms in the CCC. Meanwhile, it was off to Camp, once again, for him.

Between April 9 and April 11, 1936, he went through "processing" at Fort Devens.[67] Then on April 12 he was sent to Berkshire County in the western part of the state where he joined CCC Company 107 in Camp "SP-7"on Mt. Greylock—at 3,491 feet, the highest point in Massachusetts—twenty miles outside the town of Pittsfield. Donald was typical of the kind of enrollees the CCC was attracting in Massachusetts in the Winter and Spring of 1936. George E. O'Hearn, the Project Superintendent on Mt. Greylock, could have been speaking about Donald when he observed:

> For the most part of smaller stature, these recent arrivals have more nervous energy and it's not unusual to see the little chaps turn in a better day's work than the bigger fellows.... It is obvious likewise, that, when disciplined for breaking camp regulations, they take their medicine without undue grouching.[68]

Superintendent O'Hearn's general observation about his newest class of enrollees applied particularly well to Donald both in terms of his personal characteristics and his individual performance on Mt. Greylock. The Company which Donald thus joined was at the time a close-knit and highly motivated group of young men of whom Mr. O'Hearn further wrote approvingly, "When appealed to where esprit de corps is the key—note, they do not fail."[69] Already a CCC veteran of Company 130 in Alfred Maine, Donald fit right in, immediately, with the other "boys" in Company 107 on Mt. Greylock.

Company 107 had been transferred to Mt. Greylock on November 1, 1933 from its original location in Savoy, Massachusetts.[70] On January 30, 1934, some years before Donald's arrival on Mt.

Greylock, a somewhat confused itinerant CCC official reported to Headquarters in Washington, upon inspection, that, "This camp sets [sic] well up toward the top of Mt. Mansfield, the highest point in Mass."[71] In fact, Mt. Mansfield is the highest point in Vermont. A 1937 report sent to Washington about the Mt. Greylock installation was much more accurate:

> The camp itself sits at an elevation of 2,500 feet but is a good two miles below the summit by road. On all of the roads which the company is working on and all of the roads over which the boys of the company are transported to work there are long stretches of narrow road inadequately guarded with guard rails. Along the greater part of these stretches the ground falls away abruptly on the low side making it practically a certainty that an accident at any of these points would result most seriously if not fatally. I desire to strongly recommend that a project be approved for the construction of adequate guard rails ... at all of the most dangerous of these points.[72]

The Mt. Greylock State Reservation, consisting of 8,611 acres in area, had been established as the first state park in Massachusetts as long ago as 1898. Between 1933 and 1941, members of CCC Company 107 preserved its natural beauty and created or enhanced Mt. Greylock's tourist facilities. They improved the park's roads and carved out hiking trails and ski runs on its steep, forested slopes. In his monthly "Narrative Report" for August, 1934, Superintendent George E. O'Hearn, the civilian in charge of all CCC work projects on Mt. Greylock, called particular attention to work being done by Company 107 on a "fast run" one and three quarter miles long ski trail on the mountain's northeastern slope.[73]

Even in the midst of the Great Depression, there were still significant numbers of rich, young fellows and middle-aged men from Boston and New York who flocked to enjoy the diversions of winter sports which Company 107's work made possible on Mt. Greylock. One such person was Mr. Andrew B. Jones, an Executive at the Hudson Valley Paper Company in Albany New York. Prior to the 1935-1936 winter season on "Greylock," the CCC Company had completed work on "The Thunderbolt" Ski Trail, the aforementioned "fast run." On Christmas Eve, 1935 Mr. Jones wrote an appreciative letter to Mr. O'Hearn. Mr. Jones said in part:

> My dear Mr. O'Hearn: I spent last Sunday afternoon on the Thunderbolt. In spite of the earliness of the season, there was plenty of snow for some first-class skiing and I can say in all sincerity that it was one of the best days I have ever had skiing. Coming from me, this means a good day because, of all the skiers with whom I was associated during my four years at Williams College, I pride myself on being one of the most enthusiastic. I have done

> lots of skiing in the Berkshires, but have never
> done more skiing in so short a time, as I did on
> Sunday afternoon....It is a most exciting trail,
> if not <u>the</u> most exciting I have ever skied and
> you should know that I have had the pleasure
> of skiing on dozens of first-class downhill ski
> runs in the White Mountains and Adirondacks.
> There is no question about its being an exciting
> and first-class run for those who can take it,
> but I am inclined to believe that it is a run that
> can be appreciated adequately only by so-called
> experts, who are skillful enough skiers to break
> their speed by stemming and zig-zagging down
> the trail on the steep parts. Anyone who runs
> the trail straight is crazy unless he is of the
> championship fibre.[74]

The "expert assessment" which Mr. Jones gave of "Thunderbolt" was prophetic. On February 23, 1936—about the same time that Donald lost his milkman's job in Worcester because his boss could not afford to keep him on—the Mt. Greylock Ski Club sponsored the **"MASS. STATE DOWNHILL CHAMPIONSHIP ON THE THUNDERBOLT"**.[75]

Those affluent kids who took part in the "MASS. STATE DOWNHILL CHAMPIONSHIP," in February 1936, had nothing but *time* on their hands. By contrast, underneath their winter gloves, the "boys" of Company 107, whose labor created the precipitous ski trail on which that competition took place, *sported calluses on their hands*; calluses put there by poverty and hard work. It is true that, in later years, many of those same college students and/or erstwhile dilettantes who raced down the Thunderbolt, or other mountain trails like it, would go on to serve with distinction during World war II in the U.S. Army's 10th Mountain Division in Italy where they would put their skiing skills to good combat use against the Germans. But in the late winter of 1936 the socio-economic and intellectual gulf between the two disparate groups of youths then on "Greylock" could not have been wider.

Company 107's crowning achievement, both literally and figuratively, was their construction, also in 1936, of the impressive stone and timber structure known as Bascom Lodge on the mountain's summit. But Donald's first assignment on the heavily forested slopes of Mt. Greylock, carried out between mid-April and early November 1936, was more mundane than building a substantial mountaintop dwelling like Bascom Lodge where wealthy tourists and less affluent hikers could vacation or just spend the night.

The CCC Camp on Mt. Greylock had an active Forestry program. Since Donald had already done "Forestry" work while he was a member of Company 130 in Alfred, Maine, it would have made sense to place him in the same kind of familiar work when he reached his new station in western Massachusetts. But, as has been seen, there were plenty of other jobs to do on Mt. Greylock and he was assigned to take on one to which he had not been previously exposed in the Corps.

When he joined Company 107, Donald was immediately put to work on "Road Construction," which was defined as, "loading trucks w/gravel."[76] When he described himself as being best suited only to work as a "laborer," apparently the CCC took him seriously although elsewhere on the same APPLICATION he noted that in high school his "Subject of Specialization" had been the *"College Course."* But even though his work was physically demanding and intellectually unchallenging, his performance of it was uniformly "Satisfactory." Thus when he had said that he would do *"....anything"* in the way of work, Donald evidently meant it.

When Donald arrived on "Greylock" in mid-April 1936, Company 107 was still recovering from the particularly difficult winter season which it had just experienced on the mountain. The Camp's Forestry chief, J.T. Bankus led off Superintendent O'Hern's bi-monthly "NARRATIVE REPORT" for February— March, 1936 by noting that:

> There being a rather exceptional amount of snow on Greylock this past winter, efficiency in woods work suffered to a certain extent as did other projects. The depth of the snow hampered the men in getting to the projects, as well as making it necessary to dig 2 or 3 feet of snow away from the base of a tree before cutting in order to leave a less unsightly stump.[77]

The mountain's roads, with which Donald was about to become thoroughly familiar, had suffered equally severe damage as a

result of the last winter's ravages. R.G. North, Greylock's Camp
Engineer, reported to O'Hearn that:

> The two months making up this period are in
> many respects the worst two months of the year
> on our approach roads; first because February
> usually brings our worst blizzards blocking
> the road with drifts after every snow fall and
> second, because during March, the frost starts
> coming out, causing deep ruts which requires
> constant attention. These ruts were filled with
> stone and covered with gravel or cinders, only
> as such work was necessary to keep the truck
> housings above ground. The work of remov-
> ing snow and sanding icy slopes required la-
> bor to about the same extent as the work cited
> above…. One stretch of the New Ashford Road
> about 250 feet long was in such poor shape af-
> ter the flood storm of March 17th that it was
> necessary to rebuild it with a rock base and
> gravel surface, requiring 108 cubic yards of
> rock and 60 cubic yards of gravel. The storm of
> March 17th also washed out a number of short
> stretches on the New Ashford Road and the
> Sperry Road, the repairing of which required
> about 120 cubic yards of stone and gravel.[78]

So his new job loading and leveling massive amounts of gravel
in Camp trucks was a tedious but an essential task if necessary

highway repairs were to be completed on schedule. Throughout the summer of 1936 he continued doing this hard but important work as an aid to "Road Construction."

On Thursday, October 29, 1936 at about 1:45 PM, however, Corpsman Deignan's vital term of manual labor came to an unexpected end. He told the story himself by way of an "Injury Report" contained in his own CCC records: "While I was standing on a stopped truck spreading a load of gravel my foot slipped and I fell to the ground landing on my shoulder." In the course of his fall Donald sustained an "Injury of my left shoulder" which was judged by medical officials to be "moderately severe."[79] Fellow CCC witnesses to this accident, together with the military doctors who treated him, attested that Donald's injury was incurred through no fault of his own so this incident did not blemish his work record. He was taken initially to the Camp Infirmary for treatment and then transferred to the "Station Hospital" at Fort Devens where he remained as a patient from November 3 through November 10, 1936.[80] After leaving the Station Hospital in early November, Donald was assigned to different, less physically strenuous duty in the CCC. Between November 11, 1936 and April 1, 1937 he served as a "Gas Station Attendant" in Company 107. This next job entailed much more than pumping gas, changing oil and filling tires with air. In fact, according to one historical researcher:

> [Donald] serving as a Gas Station Attendant
> would have been a form of light duty, after his
> injury. It was a recordkeeping position. The

> CCC, the Army and others filled their gas tanks
> there and [Donald] would have been respon-
> sible for keeping track of the actual gallons dis-
> tributed to each entity.[81]

In contrast to his time in Alfred, at least twice during his term of
service on Mt, Greylock Donald was granted Leave from Camp.
He was "Absent With Permission" first from October 5 through
9, 1936 and again from February 15 through 21, 1937. Although
there is no indication in the Record of what he did or where he
went, Worcester was only a short train ride away so he may just
have gone back home for a few days with his family.[82]

Even when he was unable to leave Camp, Holidays and Sundays
were periods for relaxation and time off. In the "Greylock Camp
Report" there is an unsigned, undated brief document which
states that:

> Thirty-five men are sent to Pittsfield each
> Sunday to attend mass at St. Joseph's Church.
> Occasional Protestant services held in camp,
> last time January 14th.[83]

Given that the Company at full strength consisted of 200 men,
and taking into account the large proportion of unemployed
Roman Catholic youth in New England in the CCC, the figure
of thirty-five men from Company 107 attending Sunday Mass
in Pittsfield each week seems low. But the town was twenty
miles from Camp and especially in wintertime obtaining reliable transportation onto and off of the Mountain was a chronic

problem. The Company had only a very small number of State Parks and U.S. Army trucks at its disposal and they often broke down. So it is possible that, given these limitations, the men took turns in traveling to Pittsfield to attend Mass. But, in any case, since no evidence of Donald's religious practices or outlook have survived from Alfred, his time on Greylock or from later on in his life, it is impossible to say whether or how regularly he may have practiced his religion.

Since various "Work Projects" of the Corps were administered by several different Federal Agencies including the Departments of Labor, Agriculture and Interior—as well as by state agencies too--it is not surprising that most Companies compiled "Camp Reports," like those prepared by Superintendent O'Hearn, which were sent ultimately to the appropriate authorities in Washington D.C. for review and approval. Once again, Donald does not appear either individually or by name in the surviving "Camp Report" for Company 107 on Mt. Greylock. But this lengthy compendium, which contains various documents generated between 1933 and 1940, provides much useful information about Camp life during that extended period.

It appears that George O'Hearn, in his role as Project Superintendent, began compiling and submitting monthly or bi-monthly "Narrative Reports" about Company 107 on "Greylock," as he called it, as early as August 31, 1934. The last of these, already referenced above, dates from the February/ March 1936 time period, just before Donald's arrival on the mountain. O'Hearn's regular Reports dealt with everything

from "Weather" through "Projects" to "Plans and Ideas" as well
as "Public Reaction" to the CCC's efforts and "Morale" within
Company 107. Along the way, Mr. O'Hearn commented on
such other things as the varying quality of Enrollees from year
to year and the rise and fall in tension between military and
civilian authorities within the Mt. Greylock Camp. Although
the bi-monthly Reports uniformly predate Donald's April 1936
arrival on "Greylock," they provide an informative picture of
the life and atmosphere into which he entered when he arrived
there. Other documents within the larger "Greylock Camp
Report" file also suggest what happened within Company 107
after Donald's departure for Company 2110 in Canyon Creek
Oregon in April 1937.

From the start, it is evident that Company 107 led a difficult
and isolated existence in the rustic Camp which they built for
themselves just below Mt. Greylock's imposing summit. Even
though initially "the boys" lived in primitive conditions—using
Army mess kits, coping with intermittent electricity shortages,
and lacking both running water for the Infirmary and an adequate number of pairs of service shoes—"Morale" was surprisingly good even though the "state trucks" assigned to the Camp
for basic transportation and occasional recreational outings to
Pittsfield were usually unreliable. At the end of August, 1934,
O'Hearn commented approvingly:

> The general attitude of the enrollees toward
> their work in the field is commendable. I re-
> gret that the condition of our trucks is such

> that we do not believe it advisable to send them
> to town, as such recreational trips are desired
> from a camp as isolated as this one.[84]

The Greylock Camp was 5.3 miles from the nearest State Highway and it was well back in the woods. The "boys" had to maintain their vital, rudimentary road link to the outside world by themselves in all kinds of weather. Bitter cold and heavy snows in the winter months together with deep mud occasioned by the "spring thaw" which followed, continually threatened to cut Company 107 off from fresh food supplies, mail and outside entertainment. The last seasonal visit to Camp by a professional vaudeville troupe occurred in December 1934 and the showing of movies on Greylock ended at the same time.

In the isolating depths of a mountaintop winter, "the boys" had to be self-reliant. During the day, when they were not otherwise working, they snow-shoed and skied on the runs and trails which they themselves had built. At night they played cards, checkers and chess or shot pool and entertained each other with 'stunts" and talent-shows. Often, they simply listened to the radio in the Recreation Hall or in the Barracks. At the end of the winter of 1934-1935, in his bi-monthly Narrative Report for February-March, as he reflected on the past few difficult months, Superintendent O'Hearn mused, "I really wonder how our morale was up and remained where it did."[85] The explanation to Mr. O'Hearn's query is that, at bottom, the expectations of the CCC "boys" were modest and their needs were simple. O'Hearn, himself, recognized this reality when, some months later, he wrote, "Give them a break and give them good food. and they always "kick thru."[86]

By late spring 1935 the bad weather had broken, the vaudevillians had returned and monthly train trips from Pittsfield to Boston, on the Boston & Albany Railroad, were scheduled for the men from Company 107 and their colleagues in surrounding Camps.[87] "Morale," always high in those days, skyrocketed then. High-spirited and ingenious, some of "the boys" found their own way off the mountain, by unconventional means, to seek outside entertainment. Some of the young men had a "proclivity for descending the wire cut on the eastern side of the mountain to their favorite Adams speakeasy and then scrambling back up again, a demanding nine-mile evening excursion."[88] Less athletically inclined members of Company 107 found a local man with an automobile who "…for 50 cents, round trip…would take men down to Adams, or for $1, round trip, to the red-light district of Troy.[89]

It would be a mistake to conclude that all was idyllic on that mountaintop populated supposedly by hard-working, physically-fit young men, in harmony, equally, with nature and with the civilian and military authorities who supervised them there. Desertion from the CCC, on Mt. Greylock and elsewhere, was not uncommon.[90] What was more, every time a new Army Officer assumed command of the Camp, the civilian "Technical Services Personnel," like George O'Hearn, and the enrollees too, had to adjust to his unfamiliar administrative style and his particular performance expectations. Tensions between civilian and military authorities rose and fell each time such a leadership change occurred.

Donald spent almost exactly one year in Company 107 on Mt. Greylock. Surviving records show that during that time trouble was brewing in Camp between civilian and military officials. On July 6, 1937 a report to Washington from the field suggested retrospective administrative problems on Mt. Greylock by noting that:

> The two officers at this camp both came on duty on May, 6, 1935. Lieut. Reynolds is now relieved from duty as of July 19th with accrued leave beyond that date. He expresses himself as being severely disappointed and that he had hoped to be retained. Captain Fenton expects to be retained until late in the year before being ordered out but is resigned to the fact that he has but a few months more of service ahead of him at the most.[91]

Meanwhile, Donald had already departed for his next work assignment amid the tall, old-growth timber managed by Company 2110 in northeastern Oregon, where he would put in his last few months in the CCC. During his temporary absence from Massachusetts, as the CCC Program became more administratively troubled nationally and the quality of Enrollees declined, the leadership problems on Mt. Greylock went from bad to worse until, by late July 1939, one exasperated official was compelled to declare that:

> This camp has had an unfavorable reputation in recent years. For some unaccountable cause it

seems that officers in recent years have been a type that, for one cause or another, have been unable to give the desired service and administration. The consequence has been that several officers have been removed from service and others failed to maintain the level of morale that should prevail at all camps at this date.[92]

Although well-established CCC policy dictated that enrollees should be assigned to Camps not too far from their homes, all Corpsmen were essentially mere cogs in a giant, national "Public Works" machine. Donald was, of course, no exception to this rule. Accordingly, in the spring of 1937, when the CCC found itself with a large surplus of manpower in the eastern United States where it was no longer needed, many of those same young men were shifted at that time to work on projects in the far western part of the country.[93] Donald was one of several hundred thousand such transfers.[94]

Between April 2 and 6, 1937 Donald went through "Processing," at Fort Devens, once again. He was then in transit, by train, between April the 7th and the 10th. On April 11th, 1937 he officially joined Company 2110 of the CCC at Canyon Creek Oregon.

Donald's short stay in two National Forest Service Camps in northeastern Oregon, on the "dry side" of the Cascade Mountain Range, is the least fully documented of his three postings in the CCC.[95] He found himself in the heavily forested Blue Mountains of Grant County where Ponderosa and Lodge-pole pines, instead of the White-Pines he was used to in Maine, predominated.[96]

The nearest towns were John Day, which was then the County Seat, [97] and Canyon City, both situated along Canyon Creek, which had earlier enjoyed the same distinction.[98]

For the balance of the month of April he was assigned to "Forestry Project " Camp F-31 where he worked in a National Forest facility as a "Woodsman" apparently "Clearing" and "trimming brush on fire trails" with an axe.[99] This assignment, involving as it did hard physical work out of doors, would suggest that his earlier shoulder injury had healed completely or at least sufficiently enough to allow him to do such labor. For the remainder of his time in Company 2110, from May 1st through September 13, 1937, Donald continued to work as a "Woodsman. "[100]

In retrospect, at least three things stand out in regard to Donald's career in the CCC. The first is that his work record and personal conduct for the whole of his interrupted service between 1934 and 1937 were never less than "Satisfactory" and indeed both of them appear to have been entirely unblemished. In fact, in a handwritten note in his record, Donald's supervisor on Mt. Greylock wrote approvingly in the space entitled "estimate of member," "Satisfactory worker, satisfactory conduct, adaptable, a favorable attitude."[101] But if his work ethic and character were above reproach, his evident lack of initiative and personal ambition were far less laudable. One of his CCC contemporaries— a man who never actually served with Donald—observed in general that, "...boys who show ability are made leaders."[102] Although the selection criteria for Leaders or Assistant Leaders within Companies are not entirely clear, it is certain that Donald never attained any such post. As a practical matter, his family could have used the extra money which leadership status would have brought with it. The second aspect of his service to note is that he never stood out from his fellow Corpsmen in any manner at all. He always was "just one of the boys!" Even if advancement within any of his three Companies actually lay open to him as a possibility, Donald may have just been too "shy" to take advantage of any such chance. Allowing for his natural diffidence, a personality trait which his eldest brother, Frank, identified early on in Donald, there is still another aspect of his CCC career which is most disturbing of all: he was part of that sizable minority of men who never took advantage of the educational opportunities offered to all enrollees in the CCC.

The 1933 "Emergency Conservation Work Act" never mentioned education as one of the benefits or purposes of enrollment in the Corps. But almost from the start, increased educational opportunities "for the boys" were on the minds of most of the organization's civilian administrators. As early as November 22, 1933, Washington directed that education programs should be instituted nationwide.[103] They were in operation throughout all the CCC camps by June 1934.[104] In 1934 and 1935 thousands of classes of all kinds, frequently taught by Camp Advisors, were available to enrollees. In 1935, 57 percent of Corpsmen were taking part in these educational activities.[105] And every CCC Camp had at least a modest library for the boys to use after work each day.[106] On Mt. Greylock and at Canyon Creek, too, he could have taken advantage of these facilities but he did not do so. What is more, in Alfred, not only did the High School offer formal classes but "the boys" built their own log-cabin library in Camp as well.

Even though Donald had pointed out, during his intake interview for his first CCC Enrollment, that he had been in the *"College Course"* in high school, he was not "an intellectual" by any standard. Nonetheless, some anonymous teacher in the Worcester public school system had recognized his potential for learning. What is more, in the CCC:

> Within each camp the courses offered were extraordinarily varied and could range from wood chopping to empirical philosophy. More than half were vocational in nature; the rest were academic courses.[107]

In June, 1935, a little less than a year before Donald arrived there, the Educational Advisor on Mt. Greylock—Mr. Maurice F. Whalen—had established a varied program for the members of Company 107. He told Superintendent O'Hearn that:

> The educational program is designed to meet the needs of every man that is enrolled at the 107th Company C.C.C. It is constructed to enable every man to develop his powers of self-expression, self-entertainment, or self-culture; to develop pride in co-operative endeavor; to develop, as far as is possible, an understanding of the prevailing social and economic conditions;

and to preserve and strengthen good. habits of
health and mental development.[108]

Under these circumstances, it is a kind of secular "sorrowful mystery" why Donald seems never to have taken any advantage, whatsoever, of the wide variety of educational or vocational opportunities offered to him and his fellow Corpsmen. Guy B. Arthur, supervisor of project training for the Civilian Conservation Corps as a whole, once perceptively observed:

> To a great extent the CCC exists because boys cannot get jobs. Because many of them wanted jobs, rather than more schooling, they left school of their own volition, convinced that there was little or nothing to be gained by going. This train of reasoning is recognized by many authorities in the CCC." [109]

Mr. Arthur's foregoing insight certainly reflected Donald's frame of mind when he left North High School in the early 1930s. His negative attitude toward formal education may have remained with him throughout his entire CCC service. But, if this was indeed so, his particular outlook and conduct in rejecting any kind of further education ran counter to the example set by the rest of his immediate family. As early as 1934 his elder brothers, Francis and Robert, each had several years of successful college experience behind them. Donald's four sisters all attended high school and most of them graduated.

All this being said, the growing institutional belief that education of some type should be made an integral part of the CCC experience was not an idea universally held within the organization itself. For example Colonel Duncan Major, the War Department's long-serving representative on the CCC's National Advisory Council, once inveighed against what he saw as burdensome and potentially subversive book learning by saying:

> I have constantly fought the attempts of long-haired men and short-haired women to get in our camps . . . we are going to be hounded to death by all sorts of educators. Instead of teaching the boys how to do an honest day's work we are going to be forced to accede to the wishes of the long-haired men and short-haired women and spend most of the time on some kind of an educational course.[110]

Colonel Major's concerns about the propriety of some educational offerings may not have been altogether unfounded. For among the course offerings made available at the secondary level to enrollees on Mt. Greylock by Mr. Whalen were: Geometry, Journalism, History, Debating and Public Speaking, Algebra and Greek. But it should be pointed out that more practical classes in Forestry, Shorthand and Auto-Mechanics were also available. Colonel Major was also anxious about the "political indoctrination" of enrollees at the hands of supposedly left-leaning intellectuals and so course offerings such as "Current Events and Economics" could have done nothing to diminish his unease.[111]

Colonel Major and Corpsman Deignan never met. But if they had done so, the Colonel would have been pleased to learn that Donald was an obdurate member of that sizable minority of young men within the CCC who were immune to any such blandishments from supposedly "liberal" or even "left-wing" educators. Had they in fact conversed, Colonel Major might well have said to Donald, "Son, the United States Army is the place for you!" For, his poor personal choices notwithstanding, Donald had considerable innate talent. As will be seen in the next Chapter, when he did eventually join the Army Donald was promoted from Private to Private First Class well ahead of many of his buddies. Furthermore, his future military designation as a "Basic Soldier"—an Army generalist who could do any job as required without additional specialized training or close supervision—testified to his raw intelligence and psychological adaptability.

But for his part, and unlike all of his siblings, as a purely practical matter Donald never made the obvious link between *education of any kind* and upward socio-economic mobility in the future. He had been several times unemployed and the CCC was more than willing to augment his existing skills and even to teach him "a trade" which he could fall back on once his enrollment in the Corps ended. But, perversely, Donald wanted none of that. His failure to obtain further, self-improving education in the CCC was, for Donald, a life-changing opportunity sadly and unnecessarily missed. Even within the context of his own impoverished and struggling family, Donald—by willful choice—placed himself "at the bottom of the heap" where he was to remain for the rest of his all too short life.

On September 13, 1937 Donald was "Honorably Discharged" from the CCC for the second and last time. Informed at the time that he was "ineligible to re-enlist," Donald was provided with transportation from Enterprise, Oregon to Boston, Massachusetts. The last page of his record stated, optimistically, that Donald was leaving the CCC "TO ACCEPT EMPLOYMENT," but this statement, in all capitalized black letter type, appears to have been more a hope than a reality.[112] So, for the third and last time in his life, Donald once again joined the ranks of the long-term unemployed or underemployed.

For all the training opportunities he neglected, there can be no doubt that Donald's two stints in the CCC were nonetheless positive and beneficial both for him and for his family too. The bulk of his monthly pay allotment had supported his mother and still unmarried sisters through continuing hard times, supplementing their individual, meager and sporadic earnings. In the CCC Donald had matured physically and psychologically. Typical of most enrollees, he had even gained weight.[113] By the time he left the Corps in September 1937 he had gone from a scant 106 pounds—which is what he had weighed in July 1934—to a more substantial 115 and ½ pounds.[114]

The change which his CCC service had wrought in Donald was more than physical; it was attitudinal too. In a speech to the National Vocational Rehabilitation Association, Mr. L.S. Taber expatiated on the value of the CCC experience for the young men who enrolled in the Corps. For dramatic effect, Taber addressed the Association's members as if they, themselves, were CCC veterans:

> When you came in here you had been treated as a child at home. You had no work, and your folks were satisfied that you could not get any. They supported you. But the day you landed here, you became a man. You walked into a man's estate…. You will never be taken as a dependent again. You have earned your own way, and you will be expected to continue to do that. Not only that, you may be expected to continue to help support your family. You will continue in a man's estate, and you can never go back again to irresponsible boyhood.[115]

Since Donald was never particularly inclined to commit his personal reflections to paper, it is impossible to know with certainty how he assessed his own CCC experiences. But he would have quite probably endorsed the opinion of an Enrollee named Victor Pesek who wrote of his time in the Corps:

> I have learned how to think.
>
> I have learned patience, obedience, and attention to duty.

> I have learned to know and love mother nature,
> the trees, the flowers and all living things in the
> forests.
>
> Above all I have learned to obey orders of those in
> constituted authority, a lesson, if learned and prac-
> ticed by all of us, would make us better citizens,
> true Americans.... I thank my government.[116]

Corpsman Pesek, and perhaps Corpsman Deignan too, may have regarded the self- discipline, obedience to authority and sense of patriotic duty which they learned in the CCC as civic virtues. But what they may have seen as character-building traits profoundly worried and even appalled millions of other Americans of a more politically liberal bent. To such people, the United States Army's significant degree of administrative control over the CCC promoted "Militarism" and even smacked of "Fascism." Many of them believed that the "public works" aspect of the Corps' activity was little more than a thin disguise for out-and-out military training and the indoctrination of America's most disadvantaged youths for war. Liberal and leftist critics of the CCC often compared it to the German Labor Service which had begun as a work- relief program, like the Corps itself, but had then evolved into an avowedly military training organization once Adolf Hitler had come to power. In short:

> For many liberal Americans the Army connec-
> tion was something to be regarded with the
> gravest suspicion, and for some it was sufficient
> to render the CCC completely unacceptable.

There were, of course, unpleasant sides to the Army's control of the camps. Interference with education programs, suppression of radical ideas, ambivalence on the question of Negro enrollment — all these charges can validly be laid at the military's door. In addition, some of the Corps area commanders were too fond of treating the CCC as a reservoir for the Regular Army.... Effective contact was made principally at the camp level, and here the Army's role was much more positive. By 1936 only 3 per cent of the camp commanders were Regulars; the rest were from the Reserves. The majority of these had been through civilian colleges and were often non-military in their points of view. Not a few had themselves been unemployed, and their sympathies often lay more with the enrollees than with their superior officers. As camp commanders they effectively muted the harsher aspects of Army discipline and control. The attitude of the military is one of the reasons why close comparisons cannot be drawn between the CCC and the German Labor Service as it was modified under Hitler. By 1935 enrolment in the German agency was compulsory for all young men between the ages of eighteen and twenty-six, regardless of their economic situation, Its function had also broadened. No longer simply involved

with relief and conservation, it was now concerned with the molding of character along
Nazi lines through massive indoctrination and
with preliminary military instruction. The
martial caste of Hitler's camps was frankly admitted and thoroughly emphasized. The CCC
did not develop similar characteristics; to have
done so would have meant opposing the whole
course of American history. The Corps always
remained a voluntary organization concerned
primarily with relief and conservation, with its
wider functions never clarified. Despite close
military participation in its organization, it was
essentially nonmilitary in concept when it began, and, in keeping with the basic beliefs of the
Army officers themselves, it always remained
so.[117]

It is undeniably true that at least during Donald's years in the
CCC no type of military training was permitted within the
organization. Corpsmen never marched to and from meals or
work. Rather, they walked in uncoordinated groups to their destination in camp and its environs. But the question remains; to
what degree did the quasi-military organization of the camps—
to which they were all accustomed—predispose Corpsmen, like
Donald, to consider voluntary enlistment in the United States
Army as an attractive employment option once their CCC terms
had finally ended? It is clear that Donald enlisted in the Regular
United States Army in July 1939. But did he do so just because

it was a familiar and perhaps even a congenial environment to him? Or did he join up simply because, during the Recessionary years of 1937-1939, he could not find any work to do in the civilian world? At this distance and in light of the poor quality of the surviving records from the period, it is impossible to answer either of these fundamental historical questions with any degree of certainty.

It is interesting to note that those same American liberals who so deeply suspected and vigorously criticized the Army-influenced CCC also identified a critical underlying problem within the larger society itself. They:

> correctly claimed that there was little use in re-
> habilitating a boy permanently, even giving him
> new skills, if all that could be done in the end
> was to return him to the environment from
> which he came. [118]

Alas, that was precisely Donald's predicament when he returned to Worcester once more in the Fall of 1937. Some years earlier his civilian boss on "Greylock," Superintendent O'Hearn, had asserted on behalf of his "boys" that:

> "Honorably discharged after six months or
> more is a proof that they have responded to
> camp discipline, have become regular in habits,
> have learned to work, have had a tremendous
> build- up physically -- all in all excellent timber
> to train for various types of labor."[119]

But upon going home again, Donald soon understood all too well that the self-discipline and "Forestry skills" he had learned in the CCC did not translate into reliable, gainful employment opportunities in the urban work environment to which he had been forced, by dire circumstances, to return. What Donald did to keep body and soul together between October 1937 and June 1939 is not known. It appears that he did not move back in with his parents again as he had done in 1935 when he returned from Maine. In fact Donald evidently disappeared, altogether, from the historical record from the time when he finally left the CCC until he joined the Army.

During this unrecorded period he knew very well that he could not look to the CCC for yet another rescue. Perhaps, he must have thought, the United States Army with its familiar discipline and structure—not to mention its predictable rules and material rewards—might be for him the next best thing and a "safe haven" at last. In any case, as one historian of the CCC later observed, "its members made excellent soldier material".[120] Donald was to prove him right.

CHAPTER SIX

LIFE IN "C" BATTERY, 13TH F.A.:
1939-1942

In the course of his life, Donald Joseph John Deignan made at least three important decisions. The first was to drop out of high school. The second was twice to enroll in the Civilian Conservation Corps. And the third was to enlist, voluntarily, in the Regular United States Army during peace-time. As we have seen in Chapter Four, the first of these three crucial decisions—that to drop out of North High School in Worcester—was likely motivated by a combination of poor academic performance, boredom, and, perhaps, a genuine desire to contribute, through work, to the financial support of his struggling family. Whatever the complexities of his decision to leave school early may have been, that choice had proven to be disastrous. Uneducated and unskilled, Donald unwittingly joined the multitudinous ranks of the unemployed during the depths of the Great Depression. He soon learned, the hard way, that his "services" were emphatically not in demand. In Chapter Five it was also suggested that his experience of prolonged unemployment, twice during the 1930s, chastened Donald and profoundly shaped his largely negative self-image for the remainder of his life. If his initial decision to leave school was impulsive, by contrast, his second and third important choices, to enroll in the CCC and then to join the Army, were prompted by real-world experience and a keen awareness of the difficult and even desperate economic realities of the times in which he lived as a maturing young man.

But, even in the CCC where he met and worked closely with hundreds of other young men much like himself, Donald's self-doubt and lingering lack of ambition still haunted and hampered him. When he left the CCC in 1937, Donald found himself once again looking for work in a distinctly recessionary economy. Furthermore, his lack of self-improving initiative while in the Corps served to diminish his employment prospects in the stringent economic environment in evidence between 1937 and 1939. By failing completely to take advantage of the wide variety of educational and vocational opportunities available to him in the CCC, Donald made himself less attractive to prospective employers in the private sector than he otherwise might have been. So without steady civilian work for almost two years, in the end, he concluded grimly that voluntary military service was his last resort.

On Tuesday July 6, 1939, Donald—using only his legal name "Joseph J. Deignan"—enlisted in the United States Army. In doing so he must have thought that he had no other realistic choice if he was to survive and perhaps even to improve his difficult material circumstances. For, historically and even toward the end of the Great Depression, "… the army continued to be a haven for men who could not make a living in the civilian world."[1]

He joined up at Fort Devens, not far from Worcester, Massachusetts.[2] That place, and its bureaucratic routine, was already thoroughly familiar to him. He had passed through Fort Devens twice before; first in 1934 and again in 1936, when he had entered and then reentered the CCC. Owing to those prior experiences, he already knew about the completion of intake paperwork, the undergoing of physical examinations and the acquisition of a uniform. He was no stranger, either, to "Military Discipline" for, while in the CCC, he had served in three different "Companies" which were commanded by Reserve Army or Navy Officers. So he well knew that he was expected to obey orders, to keep himself fit and ready for duty, and to maintain his equipment and immediate surroundings in a neat and clean condition.

Either on the day before he formally joined the Army or in the course of "processing," shortly thereafter, Private Deignan would have had had a conversation, probably with a grizzled, old Sergeant, who asked him for what branch of the Army he wanted to volunteer. Doubtless this same old soldier advised him that the Field Artillery was preferable for practical reasons to either the Infantry or the Cavalry. As one of Donald's contemporaries was told in the exact same situation, "If you're in the Field Artillery, most of the time you'd be riding in the truck. If you're in the Infantry, you'll have to walk."[3] Donald was small in stature, being only five-feet, four-and-one-half inches tall, and if he had time to think about it at all, the prospect of endless marching with a full Infantry pack, a loaded rifle, a bayonet, a full ammunition belt and a steel helmet would not have appealed to him. Similarly, as a very poor boy, his knowledge of horses had been limited to the occasional Saturday Matinee "Westerns" he had seen as a kid. The Cavalry would not have been a realistic choice for him. So, for Donald, the Field Artillery was an easy decision which the Army made even simpler.

In 1898, in the wake of its easy victory in the Spanish-American War, the United States had acquired extensive overseas territorial possessions; some people even called them "colonies." Guam, Puerto Rico and the Philippine Islands had all been seized from Spain as "spoils of war" and the Hawaiian Islands had been "Annexed" after a pro-American planter faction there had overthrown the hereditary Monarchy.[4] In 1912, the War Department had established a "Colonial Army" to garrison and defend America's newly acquired Pacific Territories. Although it was an integral part of the Regular United States Army, the so-called "Pacific Army," made up of American military units permanently stationed overseas, was a distinctive organization.

As its leading historian has observed:

> … the enlisted men who filled the ranks of the Pacific Army were volunteers who had signed up either for two years in the Philippines or for three years in Hawaii. In the peacetime army,

they enlisted to fill a vacancy in a particular branch...and quite often to fill a specific slot. A recruit could thus select, from a limited number of choices, the regiment or battery or squadron in which he would serve and where he would be stationed. Once he had joined his "outfit," he usually remained there for the rest of his service."[5]

No doubt that same anonymous Recruiting Sergeant asked Donald in which of the Army's overseas "Departments" — Hawaii, the Philippines, the Panama Canal Zone, Alaska or Puerto Rico—he would like to serve. Several of those places had obvious drawbacks. Alaska was cold and remote. The Panama Canal Zone was hot and humid. Puerto Rico was a subtropical backwater. So, as for his potential overseas posting, it was almost certainly a toss-up for Donald between Hawaii and the Philippines. Both places were equally exotic and it is doubtful whether he, like most other Americans at that time, could have even found either Honolulu or Manila on a world map without some difficulty. Here again, perhaps that veteran non-commissioned officer who shepherded him through the intake process suggested Hawaii as being better than the Philippines because it was "more like America." If Donald had chosen a Philippine assignment the circumstances of his later life and death, together with his ultimate fate, might have been even less well understood than they now are. He might have ended up with the 24th Field Artillery Battalion on the Bataan Peninsula or, perhaps, in "Battery Boston" (an ironically appropriate placement for a Massachusetts man) on the small island known as "Fortress Corregidor." He might then have ended his days on the "Bataan Death March" or in one of the horrific Prison Camps in the Philippines or, worse still, on one of the "Hell ships" bound for Japan itself.

Fortunately, for whatever reason, Donald selected and was enlisted for and assigned to the Hawaiian Department. Stability and predictability of the kind he had found in the CCC were once again what Donald was looking for, and in the Hawaiian Department of the "Pacific Army" that is just what he was to find.

Once he had been Inducted into the Army and completed his initial processing at Fort Devens, he was sent to Fort Slocum in New Rochelle, New York, just outside New York City for a little more than a month of very "Basic Training." At Fort Slocum Donald found himself among hundreds of other Inductees. Thanks again to the CCC, much of what he was exposed to at Fort Slocum was already familiar to him. He knew how to wear and to care for an ordinary military uniform. He knew all about Barracks life and its individual and collective responsibilities. Lessons in "Military Courtesy" and non-fraternization within the ranks would have come easily to him. Whether Donald received any weapons training at that time is not known. While at Fort Slocum, Donald sent home to his mother a black-and-white photograph of himself and an unidentified "buddy" in their everyday uniforms which consisted of shoes and pants, a belt, a shirt, a tie and a "garrison cap." He wrote on the back of this picture, *"Fort Slocum New York July 1939.* [6]

On or just before August 15, 1939 Donald and a select group of his newly minted fellow Privates traveled from Fort Slocum to New York Harbor where they boarded the U.S. Army Transport Ship "Republic" bound for Honolulu, Territory of Hawaii, by way of the Panama Canal and San Francisco California. In the 1930s, the Army had its own fleet of four troop transport ships and two freighters which shuttled regularly between the mainland United States, Hawaii and the Far East. [7] One of these was the *"Republic."*

The ship which was to become the U.S.A.T. (U.S. Army Transport) "Republic" had been built in the Harland and Wolfe Shipyard in Belfast, Ireland, in 1907. Originally, she had been destined for service on the North Atlantic as a passenger liner for a German steamship company. She had been interned in 1914, in New York Harbor, at the outbreak of "The Great War" and taken into American service toward the end of that conflict in 1917 when the United States had declared War on Imperial Germany and its allies. She carried American troops to Europe and Czechoslovak soldiers home, by way of Siberia, after that conflict ended. A stint as an American passenger ship, called the "President Grant," followed until she was taken over by the U.S. Army in 1931 as the "Republic" and placed in service on the New York-Hawaii run. [8]

In late Summer 1939, life on board the U.S.A.T. Republic was evidently fairly pleasant even for the common soldiers. The ship carried officers and their families, as well as enlisted men, to their overseas stations. Even the enlisted personnel "dined four to a table" on the outward voyage from New York and their accommodations, otherwise, must not have been especially uncomfortable. During those long, leisurely days at sea en route to Hawaii, Donald must have thought that he had procured a ticket to Paradise. Ironically, he would turn out to be right about entering Paradise, in more than one sense of the word.

As Donald and his comrades set sail from New York on August 15[th,] 1939, war—in Europe, at least,—was in the offing. The Republic entered Panamanian waters on August 21st and transited the Panama Canal on August, 22nd, 1939.[9] Even then, while peace was still in force, U.S. Army armed guards from the Panama Canal Department boarded the vessel to see the ship safely through her Isthmian passage. Less than a week after the Republic passed through the Canal, security measures were to become much more stringent as World War II broke out in Europe and the United States strove to maintain her "Neutrality" in that conflict.

Meanwhile, Donald and some of his fellow soldiers were allowed to disembark in the Republic of Panama for a few hours of recreation and relaxation as their ship went through the Canal without them.[10] Private Deignan and his friends had some time to take in the local sights before they rejoined their ship on the Pacific side of the Panamanian Isthmus to complete their journey to Hawaii. Someone in their shore party took a picture of the group which Donald laconically labeled, **"*Panama City Horse Taxi.*"** Once again, he sent that photo home to his mother.[11]

As it happened, the U.S.A.T. Republic arrived in San Francisco on September 1st, 1939 just as Hitler's Army and Air Force were smashing their way into Poland. On that same day, as General George C. Marshall became Army Chief of Staff, the total strength of the establishment he commanded stood at 174,000 men.[12] The Republic remained in the port of San Francisco for a week to pick up additional passengers and military cargo bound for Hawaii. If Donald had a chance to leave the ship during this time, he must have glanced at some point either at the San Francisco Chronicle or at the Examiner. In either case, he would have read about the heroic, albeit hopeless, struggle of the gallant Poles against Nazi aggression. He also probably knew something about the long-standing depredations of the Japanese Imperial Army in Manchuria and China but whether any such vague general knowledge translated into particular anxiety about his own personal future prospects for safety and even survival is not known. What is certain is that while he was still at sea, en route to Hawaii, the international situation became markedly more tense. On September 8th, President Roosevelt proclaimed "a limited emergency" and ordered America's armed forces to enhance their training and preparedness for any eventuality.[13]

Departing from San Francisco on September 7th, the U.S.A.T. Republic arrived in Honolulu Harbor fairly early on the morning of September 14th, 1939. Donald and his fellow soldiers disembarked immediately and were taken by "the Pineapple Train" from the port of Honolulu to their duty station at Schofield Barracks some 20 miles inland on the Hawaiian island of Oahu.[14] Then:

> After three days of quarantine, the new soldiers joined recruit squads for their basic training. Once this was complete, they joined their "outfit" and remained with it for the rest of their tour unless they…were transferred."[15]

Because the Hawaiian and Philippine Divisions which comprised the Pacific Army were permanently based overseas, new recruits from the United States Mainland were constantly joining the ranks. Thus, "the…controversial practice…of rotating individuals rather than units," constituted a "challenge to troop cohesion, discipline and efficiency [which] continued throughout the Pacific Army's existence."[16] So Donald and his fellow, newly-arrived Privates would have had to adjust not only to a strange physical environment but to the psychological challenges inherent in fitting into a long-established, hierarchical organization as well.

The mission of the Hawaiian Division, which those new arrivals had just joined, was to protect the U.S. Navy's vital base at Pearl Harbor and to repel any possible invasion of the Hawaiian Islands by foreign military forces.

Schofield Barracks was then, as it is now, the largest U.S. Army installation in the Hawaiian Islands. The Post was named in honor of Major General John M. Schofield, a distinguished U.S. Army veteran of the Civil War, who first recognized the strategic importance of Pearl Harbor as an American naval base when he visited the Hawaiian Islands in 1873.[17] Its name notwithstanding, Schofield Barracks encompassed thousands of acres of tropical land; pineapple fields, sugarcane plantations, mountains, jungles and beaches, apart from the several massive "Quadrangles" where soldiers were actually housed.[18]

After disembarkation at Honolulu and his subsequent arrival on Post, Donald was assigned to Battery C of the 13th Field Artillery Regiment, which was then part of the Hawaiian Division. Affectionately dubbed "the Pineapple Army," the various elements of what was to become the Hawaiian Division had arrived in the Islands in 1921. From time to time, various sub-units had augmented the several Infantry Regiments which constituted the Division's core fighting force. Among these lesser Units had been the 13th Field Artillery Regiment which traced its "military lineage" all the way back to a gun battery commanded by Alexander Hamilton during the Revolutionary War.[19] More recently the 13th Field Artillery Regiment, which had been organized in Texas in late 1916, had distinguished itself in France during some of the hardest fighting of the American Expeditionary Force near the end of the First World War.[20]

From September 14th, 1939 onwards, Donald--and the nine other Privates who arrived with him on the Republic--were assigned to Battery C of the 13th F.A., which was itself a small part of "the Pineapple Army."

As it happened, Donald and the other men who arrived with him all joined the old Pacific Army in the very twilight of its rather short but distinctive existence. One of its earlier veterans paid his comrades the following, moving tribute:

> [They] were a lean sharp lot—their canvas
> gaiters scrubbed white, fitted over brilliantly
> shined shoes without a wrinkle, their uniforms
> made by Chinese tailors, at their expense, fitted
> their trim athletic bodies and bore no relation
> to the ill-shaped travesties of uniforms then is-
> sued to stateside garrisons. They could shoot
> well. Their drill was precise....These men were
> not intellectuals, probably a sixth grade educa-
> tion was their limit, but they were tough and
> they were loyal and they loved soldiering.[21]

So Donald and his newly arrived fellow Privates faced the immediate challenges of adjusting to an entirely new physical environment and of fitting into a long-established, hierarchical
military organization with its own customs and standards of
conduct. Although he was carried on the Unit's Roster from
the time of his arrival in the Hawaiian Islands, Donald may have
spent some weeks of orientation at what the troops called "tent
city" at Schofield Barracks before actually joining Battery C of
the 13th F.A. During this initial period he would have undergone
various kinds of aptitude testing and received what was called
"Individualized Instruction" after which he would have been
given a specific job within Battery C of the larger Field Artillery
Regiment of which it was a part.

The Regiment itself then consisted of several "Batteries" of artillery pieces. At the time when Donald arrived in 1939, 75mm
truck-drawn guns would have predominated. Later on, around

the time of the Pearl Harbor Attack, these would have been re-placed, theoretically at least, by 105mm Howitzers which would in turn have been supplanted by 155mm crew-served weapons.[22]

The combat role of "Divisional Artillery," of which the 13th F.A. was a part, was to provide close support in battle to the Infantry Regiment or Regiments to which it was assigned. In practice, the 13th F.A. and several other Units like it, served as Divisional Artillery for the Hawaiian Division and its successor military organization, the 24th Infantry Division. Field Artillery organiza-tion, employment and doctrine had been perfected in France by the American Expeditionary Force (A.E.F.) during the First World War. [23]

In offensive operations, the Field Artillery's job was rapidly to fire large numbers of high explosive shells into opposing posi-tions so as to suppress enemy resistance and to clear the way for the advance of the Infantry Regiment (formation of foot soldiers) which it was supporting. In defensive situations, the Field Artillery's task was to cover the retreat of friendly Infantry by dropping a curtain of well-aimed "ordnance" [shells] on ad-vancing enemy soldiers. When Field Artillerymen could actually see the target(s) at which they were aiming, they provided what was called "direct fire". When, by contrast, their target was sev-eral miles away over the horizon they provided "indirect fire." Whenever they engaged enemy artillery directly, whether seen or unseen, Field Artillerymen supplied "counter-battery fire."

At the start of Donald's military service in the fall of 1939, Battery C contained four heavy guns each of which was served in combat by a crew of six field artillerymen. Moving from place to place, "on the march" each man in the Battery had a specific job to do. Once the guns were actually deployed, lined up side-by-side in battle formation, each soldier in the Battery had a specific function or functions to perform. Each "Section Chief," under the supervision of the Battery's Commanding Officer, determined, in direct communication with his superiors, how to position the piece under his command so as to target and destroy the objective he was assigned. Equally, each soldier under his command had a particular job to do. Some soldiers would load shells into the weapon while others would be responsible for elevating or lowering the gun, depending on the distance which the individual projectile was required to travel, while other crewmen would adjust the angle of deflection, moving their gun from side to side as required. Once shells were fired, either by individual guns in the battery in sequence or simultaneously as necessary, shell-casings would be retrieved and removed by the gun crew.

But, although the gunners assigned to an individual artillery piece performed as a team, they did not work alone. They coordinated their efforts with those of fellow soldiers serving other guns in the Battery. In battle, the several Batteries in the Battalion worked in unison to place a constant stream of shell fire onto specific targets as they were identified. Behind the massed guns themselves, other soldiers in Battery C performed various supporting roles. Some men prepared ammunition and kept it flowing from ordnance stores to the guns for which it was intended. Other soldiers manned telephones or radios which allowed officers in the rear to communicate directly with the gun crews at the front. Yet more Field Artillerymen plotted the position of "targets" on maps and relayed their coordinates on the grid to Battery Commanders who in turn passed this information along to Section Chiefs on the battle-line. Altogether, then, the efficient and harmonious operation of an individual heavy gun, a battery, or an entire battalion was a complex business which required consistent, effective teamwork.[24]

Battery C alone had more than one hundred officers and men serving in it, in various capacities, at any one time. The specific jobs which many of them did could be determined by interpreting the various Army code numbers assigned to each soldier on the Battery C "Unit Roster," the master list of the officers and enlisted men serving within that organization. While many soldiers had specific, clearly defined jobs to do, other men were generalists rather than specialists within Battery C. These men, whose Military designation was "521" (Basic), demonstrated such intellectual and practical abilities that they were not assigned to particular jobs within the Battery. They could be ordered, as needed, to perform whatever task or tasks were required to be carried out at any given moment within the Battery. Throughout his Military career on the Hawaiian island of Oahu, Donald was among the 10% of personnel in the Battery classified as a "521" (Basic soldier). Although such a designation was a tribute to his intelligence, maturity, physical ability and psychological flexibility it makes it impossible to know with certainty what Donald's usual "job" within Battery C. was during that time.

Donald arrived on Oahu a little more than two years before the Japanese attack on Pearl Harbor. During the long peacetime interval between September 1939 and December 1941, he adjusted well to life in the 13ᵗʰ F.A., doing his duty conscientiously and beginning, slowly, to rise through the ranks in Battery C.

Sometime during May, 1940 he was one of four soldiers in that original group of ten with whom he had arrived in 1939 to be promoted from "Private," the Army's lowest rank, to "Private First Class" or "PFC." [25] The fact that Donald was one of a small group of new men to be promoted less than a year after his assignment to the Hawaiian Department suggests that his superiors saw in him a capacity for further professional development and perhaps even leadership potential within the enlisted ranks of Battery C. With this promotion came a small increase in monthly pay and slightly more professional responsibility. Shortly after being promoted, while wearing his dress uniform with the single stripe on its sleeve signifying his new rank, Donald persuaded a buddy to take his picture which, as usual, he sent home in a letter to his mother. In this black-and-white photograph he was characteristically serious and unsmiling, standing stiffly at "Attention." On the back of this undated picture somebody, probably Donald himself, wrote, *"Private First Class Donald J. Deignan."* [26] At that moment Donald had no inkling of what was to come. But, without realizing it, he had then reached the high point of his military service and accomplished the most significant achievement of his entire adult life.

Coincidentally, toward the end of that summer—late on the evening of August 31, 1940—Donald's father, Bernard, died a sudden and violent death. He was struck and killed instantly by a freight train as he was crossing railroad tracks while on his way home to 195 Lincoln Street in Worcester. Among his survivors, his Obituary listed three sons, "…Francis J., Robert T. of Worcester and Donald J. Deignan of Hawaii…." [27] Interestingly, for whatever reason, no mention was made of Donald's current military service in that Territory. Although relations between the Deignan boys and their father had always been strained, Donald listed Bernard as his "next of kin" on his military paperwork and he neglected to change that designation even after his father's death. That lapse was particularly surprising especially in light of the care which Donald had earlier taken to insure that his CCC pay had gone home to his mother rather than to his father. As will be seen presently, Donald's failure to correct his Army paperwork in September 1940 would cause his mother a great deal of practical difficulty, and no little anguish, after his own sudden and unexpected death in March 1942.

In most respects, Donald was a typical member of Battery C. Like him, many of his enlisted comrades came from blue-collar immigrant stock—Irish, Italians, French-Canadians and Poles—all drawn either from New England or the Middle-Atlantic states. Their numbers were augmented, considerably, by a fairly large group of working-class white Southerners. A smattering of Midwesterners together with a handful of recruits from the far west rounded out the Battery's personnel roster. All of them, like Donald, needed the steady jobs and the low if reliable pay which the peacetime U.S. Army then provided. The only significant difference between Donald and the majority of the men with whom he served from September 1939 until March 1942 appears to have been the slightly higher than average age at which he joined the Army. When he enlisted in July 1939, Donald was 24 years of age. Most of his colleagues, by contrast, were still teenagers or young adults in their very early twenties. The educational level of the enlisted men ranged from Grammar School all the way through four years of College but most of them, like Donald himself, had some years of High School to their credit.[28]

Construction at Schofield Barracks began in 1909. For many years thereafter living conditions on the Post were difficult and even primitive by Mainland standards. Soldiers often lived in tents for long periods of time while officers and their families survived in poorly constructed, temporary buildings. By the late 1930s, however, as the Great Depression ended and America began to rearm, to increase military spending and to expand its armed forces in preparation for war, life at Schofield Barracks started to improve rapidly. By the late 1930s, Schofield Barracks had newly constructed concrete buildings and modern amenities including a large, well-stocked Post Exchange, restaurants, a movie theater and a variety of new athletic facilities including a swimming pool.[29]

While Officers and their families enjoyed active social lives either on Post or in Honolulu, itself, ordinary soldiers were also in need of activities to occupy their time. "The army's answer to morale problems was activity, most notably in its emphasis on sports."[30] Regiments had to have boxing, football, baseball, track and basketball teams, and rivalries among the various Units stationed at Schofield Barracks were keen.[31] The very afternoon before Pearl Harbor was bombed, it is estimated that 12,000 members of Oahu's 43,000 man military garrison packed the Post football stadium to watch the climactic game between opposing teams from the 24th Division's 19th and 21st Infantry Regiments. Private William Cobb, who was serving in Battery C with Donald at that time, later said of their comrades at that organization, "All that those men used to do was eat, sleep, dream and live sports!"[32] It is uncertain whether Donald was merely a spectator or an active participant in one or more of his Battery's several athletic teams.

Opportunities for individual diversion were easy to come by and plentiful, too, in the years before the outbreak of World War II. With the end of Prohibition, "Beer Gardens" opened up on Post for the enlisted men and a beer could then be had for a nickel a can.[33] Soldiers could get day passes into Honolulu by simply asking for them from their "outfits" and the city was an inexpensive bus trip or shared taxi ride away. During off-duty visits to Honolulu soldiers were encouraged to wear civilian clothes so as to blend in more easily with the general population.[34] Once in Hawaii's Territorial Capital, the young men could eat, drink, brawl or engage in some of the less reputable pleasures which the city had to offer. In the 1930s there were a dozen brothels approved and inspected by the Army where soldiers could have sex for $3 with white prostitutes. Those establishments were concentrated along Hotel Street in downtown Honolulu.[35] The men of the Hawaiian Division could be a fractious lot. Fighting, gambling, alcohol and drug abuse, visits to brothels and even homosexual encounters—some consensual and others forced—were fairly common problems within its ranks.[36]

Surviving photographic evidence establishes that Donald himself made at least one visit to Honolulu for recreational purposes. A black and white photograph dated "October 8th 1941," possibly endorsed in his own handwriting, shows him and an unidentified fellow soldier—both dressed in civilian clothing—walking down a Honolulu street while carrying what appears to be cardboard dishes of ice cream.[37] The printed information on the back of this snapshot indicates that the picture was developed at "Smith's Drugstore" on Hotel Street. From that fact, alone, it should not necessarily be inferred that Donald and his buddies were in that vicinity for the common three-fold purposes of getting, "Stewed, Screwed and Tattooed."[38] But, at the same time, Kipling's famous admonition that, "...single men in barracks don't grow into plaster saints" should also be kept in mind.[39]

During most of the 1930s, the United States Army was—like the nation which it served—an institution under great stress owing to the financial ravages of the Great Depression. Army budgets were slashed year after year between 1930 and 1938. The Army's Hawaiian and Philippine Departments suffered from these cutbacks along with the rest of the American military establishment. The cumulative material and psychological effects of continuing financial reductions were dire:

> Lacking the means, and therefore perhaps the
> desire, for preparing for real war, the con-
> tingents of the Pacific army came to devote

much of their attention to spit-and polish, immaculate appearance, and frequent parades and ceremonies. The Schofield reviews, with the Hawaiian Division marching past, … were the delight of visitors. Only a few noticed that as late as 1931 nearly all its equipment was of World War I vintage.[40]

After 1938, although Army manpower increased steadily and modern equipment became available in increasing quantities, the lackadaisical spirit of the interwar years continued to pervade at least the lower ranks of the Hawaiian Division. Between September 1939, when Donald arrived in the Hawaiian Department, and September 1941, Battery C's training regimen was neither particularly strenuous nor especially intensive. On October 1st, 1941, however, the relaxed, pre-war atmosphere began to change dramatically. On that date, the old Hawaiian Division which had been recently "deactivated" was split in two and formally "reorganized," respectively, into the new 24th and 25th Infantry Divisions within the Regular Army. The traditional "square" Hawaiian Division had been built around four Infantry Regiments together with supporting Field Artillery, Engineer, Signal Corps, Quartermaster, Military Police and Medical Corps units. The new "triangular" Divisional configuration featured only three Infantry Regiments in each formation backed by a number of Field Artillery and other support elements. Battery C., and with it the entire 13th Field Artillery Battalion, and its sister organization, the 11th F.A., together with the 52nd and the 63rd F.A. Battalions, became part of the 24th Infantry Division.

For the sake of historical continuity, the 24th Infantry took as its official emblem and shoulder patch the green "Taro Leaf" to pay tribute to its organizational origin in the former Hawaiian Division.[41] In addition, its members proudly called themselves the "Taro Men."[42] After December 7th, 1941, they claimed the distinction within the U.S. Army of being "first to fight" at Pearl Harbor. Later on in the War they adopted the additional sobriquet of the "Victory Division". But, for the moment, all these honors and accolades lay in the future.

Brigadier General Durward S. Wilson assumed Command of the newly designated 24th Infantry Division on its "Organization Day," October 1st, 1941.[43] General Wilson, a North Carolina native and a 1910 graduate of West Point, immediately and energetically set about preparing his Division, with relentless efficiency, for combat.[44] The same day he took Command, Wilson published a list of his "Division Staff Officers."[45] He was intent on molding the 24th Infantry Division according to his expectations without delay. On October 10, 1941 he issued a four-page, single-spaced, typewritten "Staff Memorandum" dealing in detail with "Administrative Procedure." Its **"PURPOSE"** was, "…to incorporate in a single publication, current general instructions of a probable permanent nature pertaining to the administrative procedure, business methods, and general conduct of this headquarters, not specifically covered in Army Regulations or other directives of higher authority."[46] In the body of this Memorandum the Commanding General covered such topics as "Correspondence," "Recording of Important Telephonic Communications," "Radiograms," "Messenger

Service," "Solicitors," "Notification to G-4," "Allotment of Funds," and "Military Publications." The section entitled "Office Hours" made it clear that General Wilson expected to oversee a hard-working, professionally responsible Headquarters Staff. He wrote:

> The normal office hours for this headquarters are as follows:
>
> (1) Mondays, Tuesdays, Thursdays and Fridays: 8:00 AM to 4:00 PM.
>
> (One hour will be allowed for lunch, the time for lunch to be determined by chiefs of staff sections. An office force sufficient to transact any business that may arise will be present in each office during lunch hours.)
>
> (2.) Wednesdays and Saturdays: 8:00 AM to 12:00 Noon.
>
> (3.) Chiefs of staff sections are authorized to retain any or all of their personnel for duty on Wednesday afternoons if the status of their work demands it. The personnel so retained will be given another afternoon during the week, other than Saturday, for exercise.[47]

Thus, toward his subordinates, the Brigadier appears to have been a fair and sensible man rather than a taskmaster or a martinet. But he was also a reflective and conscientious administrator who did not expect or welcome "surprises" from his subordinates during the performance of his official duty. In section (3)(<u>b.</u>) of his paragraph on "Office Hours" he further wrote:

> All officers responsible for the submission of reports and recommendations to the War Department, which are made over the Commanding General's signature, will insure that they are on the Chief of Staff's desk in ample time to permit reasonable consideration thereof prior to their timely dispatch.[48]

Although the foregoing document provides valuable insight into General Wilson's temperament and professionalism, his primary concern was not the organization of Divisional Headquarters Staff. Rather, it was to oversee the training and "readiness" of all of his subordinate officers—and the many thousands of enlisted men under their command—for imminent warfare. Accordingly, on October 21, 1941 he produced and circulated a **"ROSTER OF OFFICERS"** of the 24th Infantry Division. On that date, Wilson's Command consisted of Division Headquarters, a Headquarters and Military Police Company, the 24th Medical Battalion, the 24th Signal Company, the 11th Quartermaster Battalion, the 3rd Engineer Battalion, the 19th Infantry Regiment, the 21st Infantry Regiment, the Headquarters & Headquarters Battery 24th Division Artillery, the 11th Field Artillery Battalion, the 13th Field Artillery Battalion, the 52nd Field Artillery Battalion and the 63rd Field Artillery Battalion.[49] Wilson's October 1941

"Divisional Roster" did not include the soldiers of the 34th Infantry Regiment who arrived in Hawaii on December 21st, 1941. They did not join the 24th Division until June 1943. Meantime, they were tasked with defending Schofield Barracks when, after December 7, 1941, the 24th and 25th Divisions were stationed in defensive positions elsewhere on Oahu.[50]

For its part, the 13th F.A. did not get off to an auspicious start within the new 24th Infantry Division. On October 1st, 1941— according to a brief **"HISTORY OF [THE] 13TH FIELD ARTILLERY BATTALION"** dated November 11, 1942—"… the battalion was designated as Division Reserve and was not assigned a mission in life, which was a great disappointment to the Commanding Officer."[51] Interestingly, the foregoing, un-attributed editorial comment was later lined through but not entirely crossed out so it may have reflected both the "original feelings" and the subsequent "second thoughts" of the Battalion's new Commanding Officer, Lieutenant Colonel Stanley Bacon. In any case, the Battalion's designation as "Division Reserve" can have done nothing to elevate its morale in the early Fall of 1941.

Meanwhile, the Division as a whole had begun intensifying its regular training schedule. So, for example, during the week of October 6 to 11, the Nineteenth Infantry Regiment marched to Waimea Bay on the North Shore of Oahu and practiced "water-borne firing." At the same time, the 13th F.A. spent that week on the Artillery Range engaged in "Service Practice."[52]

In the weeks which followed, however, individual Battery partici-pation in "Principal Training Activities" varied greatly. During the week of October 13 to October 18, Batteries B and A took part in "Road Marches" while Battery C, Donald's "outfit," appears to have remained at Schofield Barracks.[53] Not until October 24th did Batteries A and C conduct a joint Road March with Kaena Point as its destination. They left the Barracks at 7:15 in the morning and returned there at 3:20 in the afternoon.[54] Three days later, the entire Battalion with the exception of its Service Battery marched a total of 44 miles from Schofield Barracks to Puu Palailai and back again. The Battalion's Diarist noted "Roads good, weather dry and clear."[55] On October 30, 1941 the entire Battalion—save for its Service Battery—undertook a 47 mile March "From Schofield to Ewa Dump and return."[56]

During the first two weeks in November, Battery C, either in concert with the Battalion's Headquarters Battery, or in combination with its sister "Firing Batteries," A and B, took part in two more Road March practice sessions. Early on, however, this routine was interrupted by a more significant and ironically prophetic event. On November 4, 1941, General Wilson ordered a "Communication Exercise" to be held for all the combat arms of the entire Division. The purpose of the Exercise was to test various types of communications equipment, including "[carrier] pigeon," under field conditions to see how well "Messages" could be sent and received within the 24th Infantry Division. The 13th F.A. was to establish its Command Post in the "Vicinity Salt Lake." Under "General Instructions" to all the participants in the Exercise, General Wilson ordered that, "In order to avoid possible misunderstanding, each message or call (except those which it is desired be actually acted upon) will be preceded by the words, "This is a drill" (message) (call)."[57] Little more than a month after General Wilson issued this practical, cautionary Order to his troops—as Japanese bombs and bullets began falling on Pearl Harbor and Schofield Barracks—sirens would wail and the Public Address system would blare, *"AIR RAID! THIS IS NOT A DRILL!"*

If the enlisted men of the 24th Infantry Division, and especially those among them who were veterans of the old Hawaiian Division, thought that their new Commander was driving them harder than they were used to in October 1941, they had no idea what plans he had in mind for them during the balance of the year and well into 1942.

On October 30, 1941, General Wilson promulgated a "Training Memorandum" which was to apply to the entire 24th Infantry Division. The ambitious "Training Program" which it detailed was to run from "November 1, 1941 to May 23, 1942." Characteristically, his plan's "Introduction" consisted of one concise sentence: "Units of this command will be trained primarily for the defense of OAHU."[58] Under the heading, "TRAINING OBJECTIVE," the General wrote:

> This Division will be prepared, at all times, to carry out its war missions as indicated in current defense plans. The fighting efficiency of combat units must be based on thoroughly trained individual soldiers, confident in their knowledge of their weapons, and confident of their ability to use these weapons. The development of team-work, coordination, and the utilization of combined

> weapon power necessary in combat teams must
> follow the development of efficiency in the indi-
> vidual members of its subordinate parts.[59]

The Training Program called for "Divisional Field Maneuvers" to be conducted in Mid-January and again in early March 1942. These large-scale exercises were to be repeated and integrated into Hawaiian Department Field Maneuvers to be carried out between May 11 and May 23, 1942.[60]

In the interim, Wilson detailed "Training to be conducted by Subordinate Commanders." For defense purposes the island of Oahu had been divided by the Hawaiian Department's Commander, Lieutenant General Walter Short, into Southern and Northern Sectors. Responsibility for defense of the Southern Sector, which included the City and Port of Honolulu together with the Pearl Harbor Naval Base and the Pacific Fleet anchored there, had been given to the 25th Infantry Division. Protection of the less populous but strategically important Northern Sector, including especially the North Shore of Oahu, had been assigned to the 24th Infantry Division. So, from the outset of the Training Program, Wilson's priority was effective North Shore defense. Integral to the success of his defensive plan was the performance of the Division's 19th and 21st Infantry Regiments. Wilson expected a great deal from them. The combined "Objective" of their training was:

> To be prepared at all times to defend assigned
> sub-sectors or to carry out other war mis-
> sions. The training to prepare for this (sic) to
> stress such types of action as are most likely

to be used in war, particularly in the respective sub-sectors of the North Shore, including
beach defense, flexibility and defense in depth,
day and night withdrawals, delaying action,
defense against incendiary and other types of
bombing, defense against air-borne troops,
automatic counter attack, anti-sabotage, and
mobility. The major part of the North Shore
troops to be prepared to use any or all of these
types of action in the South Sector when the
situation demands it. All enlisted men of these
regiments, regardless of grade, rating or duty
to receive sufficient instruction with the rifle,
machine gun, .30 cal., and the automatic rifle
to enable each individual to use these weapons
in emergencies.[61]

Clearly the Brigadier General anticipated that *all* the men of the
19th and the 21st Infantry Regiments would be compelled to fight
a pitched battle with invading Japanese forces on and just behind
the North Shore beaches of Oahu. If and when such an assault
came, and if it was to be successfully beaten back, his Divisional
Artillery would play a crucial role in closely supporting their
hard-pressed infantry colleagues. So the next facet of his Training
Program focused on the work of the Field Artillerymen. The
"Objective" they were given was:

To be prepared at all times to support the mo-
bile land defense of regularly assigned sectors

with both organic and non-organic weapons
and to support with organic weapons the mo-
bile land defense of the island as a whole. To
be prepared with dossiers and other means to
assist all possible re-enforcing artillery for the
North Sector in rendering efficient support for
that sector. Special emphasis to be placed upon
that training which is necessary to provide adequate organic support for those types of action
mentioned in Par. 3 b (1) (a) above, especially
counter-attack and defense, including defensive fires on or near the beaches. Careful study
to be given the dual assignment problem of the
11th FA Battalion in its defense mission in dividing its training time between seacoast training
and training in divisional support missions.[62]

The possible lessened availability of the 11th F.A. in time of crisis may have caused General Wilson concern about the additional
strain which their potential absence would place on his remaining Field Artillery: the 13th, 52nd and 63rd Battalions. But whatever
anxiety he may have felt about the possibility of reduced resources
and manpower did not prompt him to upgrade the 13th F.A. from
"Divisional Reserve" to frontline status. Indeed he made no direct
mention of the Battalion in his Training Program's section on the
role of "Department and Division Reserve Units."[63]

In any case, General Wilson's carefully designed Training
Program was about to be dramatically altered and given an added

sense of urgency by unforeseen and catastrophic events which were just then inexorably unfolding. Meanwhile, much, much farther down the "Chain of Command," where P.F.C. Joseph J. Deignan was located, life in the peacetime Pacific Army at Schofield Barracks went on more or less as usual. Even as late as November 1941, as its historian wrote, if a soldier, "…had a good character, he could reenlist to fill his own position…".[64] And that is exactly what Donald did during that last full month of peace.[65] He "re-upped" for another three years.

In October 1941 it was clear that the Army's radical reorganization of the Hawaiian Division into two new fighting formations was an urgent effort to prepare for war in the Pacific region by stretching available military resources so as to do more with less. In September 1940, President Roosevelt had signed the "Selective Service and Training Act"—which instituted a peace-time Draft—and insured that eventually millions of American civilians would enter the military services of the United States. But it would take some time to recruit, train, equip and deploy those legions of new citizen soldiers, sailors, aviators, marines and coastguardsmen. Meantime, in the event of war, young "professionals," like Donald, would have to hold the line against the enemy in distant outposts such as Guam, Wake, the Philippines and Hawaii, Panama and Alaska. They would have to do so with inadequate resources and without the prospect of immediate material support from home.

Even though the inactivation of the Hawaiian Division, and its reorganization into two new, distinct fighting forces, heralded a significant change in War Department policy and expectations, life on the ground in Battery C still followed a predictable routine in the few months between the creation of the 24th Infantry Division and the outbreak of war with Japan. Soldiers and Officers transferred in and out of Battery C on a regular basis. In November, 1941, for example, Captain David W. Hiester moved from leadership of the 63rd F.A.'s Battery B to take Command of Battery C in the 13th F.A. [66] But sometimes Unit Roster changes were more temporary and owing to hospitalization for illness or injury. Men also left on and returned from "Furloughs." On occasion members of Battery C would leave for similar positions in other Batteries within the 13th F.A. or in different Army units altogether. All of these comings and goings were recorded on the daily "Morning Reports" produced by Battery C's clerks and signed by its Commanding Officer or one of his subordinates. In short, one day in Hawaii seemed very much like those which had come before it and those which would follow it. Each of them was to be marked by its own predictable, if no longer indolent, routine. Or so, perhaps, most common soldiers thought.

This Pacific calm was abruptly shattered in the early morning of Sunday, December 7th, 1941 when massive numbers of Japanese Naval aircraft and a far smaller contingent of "midget submarines" came out of nowhere to attack the Hawaiian Islands and their defenders "by surprise."

Exactly what Donald was doing at that historic moment is not clear. His self-described "favorite aunt," Miss Louise Cross, later insisted that he was returning from Sunday Mass when the Japanese struck. Although there was a regular Chapel at

Schofield Barracks, it appears that most enlisted men attended Mass at a large movie theater also located on the Post. So Aunt Louise's claim may well have been accurate, as far as it went. But her equally vehement assertion that "Donnie," as she called him, had been "wounded" or "burned" in the course of the Japanese Attack was without foundation. She also claimed that a Roman Catholic priest who had attended Donald during his last days had subsequently written to her with details of her nephew's death, but because none of her correspondence has survived it is impossible to verify this story. Nonetheless, Louise Cross and her sister, Anna Deignan after her, contributed to the creation of the "family myth" surrounding Donald's heroic death at Pearl Harbor.

In retrospect what is now clear is that Donald survived the Pearl Harbor Attack without sustaining any *physical* injury. Schofield Barracks was attractive to the marauding Japanese pilots only incidentally because of its close proximity to Wheeler Army Airfield. That installation which housed most of the Army's "Pursuit Planes" on Oahu was a primary target. Only after hitting Wheeler Field and its Army Air Corps "Fighter Squadrons" hard did enemy planes with bombs or bullets still on board expend their remaining "ordnance" on Schofield Barracks and its defenders. It is certainly true that some soldiers were in fact killed or wounded there by strafing Japanese planes and the climatic aerial attack scene in James Jones's autobiographical novel "From Here to Eternity" was actually filmed in C Quadrangle at Schofield Barracks when the book was adapted for the silver screen. "Purple Heart Award Citations," now held in the

National archives and Records Administration facility at College Park Maryland, establish that several soldiers from the 63rd, 52nd and 11th Field Artillery Battalions were wounded by Japanese air attacks on December 7, 1941. But, ironically, it appears that no one from the 13th F.A. was wounded or killed on that same occasion. Thus, although he was quite literally in the middle of the Japanese onslaught, Donald escaped injury or death during the Pearl Harbor attack just by the luck of random chance.

Although the U.S. Army, like the rest of the American military establishment on Oahu, had been caught unawares by Japan's "sneak attack," its response to it was rapid and effective. According to the Army's own "Official History":

> The 24th Division had a battalion of infantry on the road from Schofield Barracks to its assigned battle position by 9:00 a.m., and thereafter other divisional units left Schofield as soon as they had drawn and loaded their ammunition and otherwise prepared for action. By late afternoon, all divisional elements were digging in at their assigned field positions, with all weapons except heavy howitzers at hand and ready to fire. As General Short put it, in the deployment "everything clicked," one of his junior officers explaining: "We had gone so many times to our war positions that it just seemed like drill when they were firing at us." The deployment showed clearly enough that the Hawaiian

Department was thoroughly prepared to resist invasion, however unready it was against the peril of surprise air attack.[67]

A more informal history of the "Victory Division" added that:

The division immediately moved out and set up an elaborate system of coastal defenses on the north side of Oahu. From this side of history, that action might seem to have been a mere exercise, but in the hours and days immediately following the 7 December attack, there was ample reason to believe the Japanese might attempt an amphibious landing, and if that had happened, it would have been up to the 24th Division to stop them.[68]

What traumatic scenes, or personal losses, if any, Donald *may have witnessed or suffered* during the "Pearl Harbor Attack," itself, is not known. But present-day experts in Post Traumatic Stress Disorder, "P.T.S.D.," agree that a single, awful incident may be enough to trigger this destructive condition later on. The several months of extreme stress which certainly followed his experiences on December 7, 1941, can have done nothing to bolster Donald's psychological well-being.

Donald's sudden death late on March 18, 1942—just three days after his twenty-seventh birthday—came as a great shock to his entire family. In July, 1939, while completing his Enlistment paperwork for the Army, under "person to be notified in case of emergency," Donald had written "Mr. Bernard Deignan, 195 Lincoln Street, Worcester, Mass"[69] He may have thought at the time that if anything serious happened to him while he was serving in the Army, his father—with all his faults—might nonetheless be better able to handle any such event than his mother would be. After his father's death on August 31, 1940, however, Donald had, for whatever reason, forgotten or neglected to change this item in his Personnel File. Accordingly, the telegram from the War Department notifying the family of Donald's death had been addressed, inappropriately, to his late father rather than to his mother. The news of her youngest son's death left Anna Deignan devastated for the remainder of her life. And the fact that word of it was directed by the Army to her late husband, rather than to herself, was to cause no end of trouble in years to come.

At about 4:20 PM, Hawaiian War Time, on Friday, March 20, 1942, P.F.C. Joseph J. Deignan was buried with full military honors in Plot 2. Row L. Grave 16 in the Post Cemetery at Schofield Barracks, Territory of Hawaii.[70] Earlier that same day, allowing for the difference in time between the east coast of the United States and the Hawaiian Islands, Donald's death while serving his country had been front page news in **The Worcester Evening Gazette**, one of the city's two daily newspapers. The story, which amounted to his Obituary, was brief but crucially important and it is worth quoting in its entirety here:

Dies In Hawaii

 Private First Class Joseph J. Deignan, 25, died in service in Hawaii yesterday according to a telegram received by his mother, Mrs. Anna C. Deignan, of 195 Lincoln Street.

"Notified of Death Of Soldier Son

Mrs. Anna C. Deignan of 195 Lincoln Street, today was notified by the War Department that her son, Pvt. First Class Joseph J. Deignan, 25, died yesterday in Schofield Barracks, Hawaii, of a gunshot wound.

Deignan had been in the Army three years, and had re-enlisted just before the Japanese attack on Pearl Harbor for an additional six months, his mother said.

The War Department telegram failed to state when or how the wound was suffered, but Mrs. Deignan believes he was wounded during the Japanese raid, even though he corresponded with his family regularly since then. "He had not told (sic) he was wounded.

> Besides his mother he leaves two broth-
> ers, Francis J. of Worcester and Robert T. of
> Washington, D.C. and four sisters, Ann R.,
> wife of Biago B. Peluso and the Misses Mary
> K., Eunice V., and Catherine, all of Worcester.

> The telegram stated that "the body could not be
> sent home until after the war."[71]

With the publication of this piece in **The Worcester Evening
Gazette**, on March 20, 1942, the foundation of the "family
myth" of Donald's supposedly heroic death as a result of the
Pearl Harbor Attack had been laid. Unwittingly, Donald himself had contributed to its construction by writing to his family
after December 7th and assuring them that he was "all right."
After his death, Donald's mother drew the not unreasonable, if
circumstantial, conclusion that her son—not wanting to worry
her—had deliberately failed to mention the combat wounds he
had received on Pearl Harbor Day. After that, it remained only
for Louise Cross to embellish the story still further for posterity.
For its part, the United States Army did nothing to dispel "the
myth" surrounding Donald's death, even augmenting it considerably, albeit indirectly, in the decade following that event.

Almost immediately after P.F.C. Deignan's death late on the evening of March 18, 1942 the Army began compiling his "Individual
Deceased Personnel File" (or, "IDPF") . This File contained more
than thirty pages of miscellaneous documents which dealt with
everything from the physical circumstances of his demise and the
reporting of that event both to the War Department and to his

family, to his initial burial in March 1942 through his final interment in February 1949. In addition, the IDPF included copies of correspondence on various subjects which passed, sporadically, between the Army and Anna Deignan in the decade and more from 1942 through 1953. These letters were intended to comfort and console Donald's family for their loss. They were uplifting and even reverential in tone. Their purpose was to honor the "supreme sacrifice" which "P.F.C. Joseph J. Deignan" (Donald) had made for his country and, usually, they did so.

Section II, Paragraph 8. of Army Regulation 600-550 entitled "DECEASED PERSONNEL", in effect at the time of Donald's death, stated under the heading, "Letter of sympathy to nearest relative or other person designated to be notified in case of emergency" that:

> Upon receipt of notification of death from the surgeon of any person subject to military law, a letter of sympathy will be prepared by the Immediate commanding officer and mailed to the nearest relative or other person designated to be notified in case of emergency. The letter of sympathy will include a statement of the date, place, and cause of death, and if addressed to the widow or legal representative of the deceased, or other person designated in the one hundred and twelfth article of war, will contain Information relative to the following:

(1) Shipment of effects.

> (2) The names, official designations, and post-office addresses of the officers and officials to whom applications should be made for—
>
> (a) The effects.
>
> (b) Settlement of accounts. See paragraph 41.
>
> In the cases referred to in paragraph 5b, the letter of sympathy 'will be prepared by the officer making the report to The Adjutant General.[72]

There is no reason to suppose that such a "Letter of Sympathy" was not prepared and sent, inadvertently, to Donald's late father, Bernard Deignan, either by the Commanding Officer of Battery C or even by the commander of the entire 13th Field Artillery Battalion. But, in any case, no such correspondence has survived. The earliest extant communication to his family to be found in the IDPF dated from July 21, 1942. It informed Mr. Bernard Deignan of 195 Lincoln Street, Worcester Massachusetts, that the remains of his son had been buried in Plot 2, Row L, Grave 16 of the Post Cemetery at Schofield Barracks in the Territory of Hawaii on March 20, 1942. The letter went on to say:

> You may have the assurance that the burial was reverently and properly conducted, and that the grave has been so marked and registered as to insure so far as is humanly possible,…that the remains of your son may be, if possible, disinterred and returned to the United States

for final interment after the cessation of hostilities, if so desired by you. At that time, the
Quartermaster General will contact you as to
your wishes relative to the disposition of the
remains of your son.

For all his bureaucratic and even coldly clinical tone, the author
of this particular letter took pains at its end to soften the blow by
adding, somewhat stiffly, "This office expresses its sincere sympathy to you in your bereavement."[73]

The foregoing letter, written during some of the darkest days of
World War II, did nothing more than to adhere to standard practice
at the time. In fact, on December 11, 1941, less then a week after
the attack on Pearl Harbor, the War Department in Washington,
D.C. had issued a Directive which stated that the remains of deceased Personnel who died while serving overseas would not be
returned to the United States Mainland for burial until after the
end of World War II. So, for the next several years, Anna Deignan
could put off making the painful decision about the final resting
place for the mortal remains of her youngest son.

When the War finally ended, in the aftermath of the decisive and
complete Allied victory over the Axis Powers, the United States
Army could at last afford to turn its solicitous attention to the
families of America's hundreds of thousands of military dead.
Accordingly, on February 26, 1947, Brigadier General G.A.
Horon—an Assistant to the Army's Quartermaster General—
wrote a letter to the Deignan family. With it General Horon enclosed a photograph of the Schofield Barracks Cemetery where

Donald had been buried back in 1942. The Brigadier wrote in part:

> It is my sincere hope that you may gain some solace from this view of the surroundings in which your loved one rests. As you can see, this is a place of simple dignity, neat and well cared for. Here, assured of continuous care, now rest the remains of a few of those heroic dead who fell together in the service of our country.[74]

Although the tone of this letter was a marked improvement over that of the initial Quartermaster General's July 1942 correspondence, some things had not changed. Thanks to Donald's seeming inattention to administrative details in 1939 and especially in 1940, after his father's death, General Horon's 1947 communication was once again addressed to Mr. Bernard Deignan rather than to his widow. Speaking of the Schofield Barracks facility, in the final paragraph of his letter General Horon noted that, "This cemetery will be maintained as a temporary resting place until, in accordance with the wishes of the next of kin, all remains are either placed. in permanent American cemeteries overseas or returned to the Homeland for final burial."[75]

As the winter of 1947 gave way to spring, the pace of administrative events at the War Department in Washington D.C. began to quicken. On April 22, 1947, Anna Deignan received yet another letter from the Army addressed, mistakenly as before, to her late husband. It began sympathetically enough:

The people of the United States, through the Congress have authorized the disinterment and final burial of the heroic dead of World War II. The Quartermaster General of the Army has been entrusted with this sacred responsibility to the honored dead.

But very quickly this lofty tone changed and the letter's language descended into the kind of imprecise, insensitive "military bureaucratese" for which the Army had long been notorious:

The records of the War Department indicate that you may be the nearest relative of the above-named deceased, who gave his life in. the service of his country.

The enclosed pamphlets, "Disposition of World War II Armed Forces Dead," and "American Cemeteries," explain the disposition, options and services made available to you by your Government. If you are the next of kin according to the line of kinship as set forth in the enclosed pamphlet, "Disposition of World War II. Armed Forces Dead," you are invited to express your wishes as to the disposition of the remains of the deceased by completing Part I of the enclosed "Request for Disposition of Remains." Should you desire to relinquish your rights to the next in line of kinship, please complete Part II of the enclosed form. If you are

> not the next of kin, please complete Part III of
> the enclosed form.

In closing, the sender entreated,

> Will you please complete the enclosed "Request
> for Disposition of Remains" and mail in the en-
> closed self-addressed envelope, which requires no
> postage, within 30 days after its receipt by you? Its
> prompt return will avoid unnecessary delays.
>
> Sincerely,
> THOMAS B. LARKIN
> Major General
> The Quartermaster General".
> Incls.[76]

Being a good citizen and a very conscientious person, Donald's
mother completed the necessary forms and returned them to
the War Department in the postage-paid envelope provided.
The letter requesting her to do so had been signed, ostensibly,
by the "Quartermaster General of the United States Army". But
despite her prompt compliance with his request, worse was to
come for Mrs. Bernard Deignan.

At this point in 1947, the Army's records still listed Bernard
Deignan as Donald's legal "next of kin." And since, per established military procedure, Bernard had not formally "relinquished the right" of kinship, a serious problem had arisen.
Therefore the Quartermaster General assigned a subordinate,

one Major Richard B. Coombs by name, to sort things out. In doing so, Major Coombs made clear that he would brook no nonsense, even from a man who happened to be dead. On June 13, 1947 he wrote on behalf of the Quartermaster General to Bernard in the following peremptory terms:

Dear Mr. Deignan:

Reference is made to the inclosed *(sic)* form "Request for Disposition of Remains" signed by someone other than yourself.

This form was originally sent to you because according to the records of the War Department you are the legal next of kin of the above-named deceased and are therefore the only person authorized to direct the final disposition of his remains by signing this form. There is inclosed *(sic)* for your convenience another copy of the form "Request for Disposition of Remains". Will you therefore, please complete this form in accordance with your desires concerning the disposition of the above-named deceased, sign it yourself, and mail it in the inclosed self- addressed envelope, which requires no postage. Its prompt return will avoid further delay.

Sincerely,
3 Incls. RICHARD B. COOMBS
Major, QMC, Memorial Division.[77]

The Major's letter caused consternation and anger when it was received in the Deignan household on "Flag Day," June 14, 1947. On the very day of its arrival, the Deignan family crafted a blistering response. Anna Cross Deignan had married young. She had borne twelve children, seven of whom had survived to adulthood. She was a devoted "Gold Star Mother" and a very capable housewife who had not had the benefit of much formal education. Yet she appears to have been an innately talented person as witnessed by her long tenure as Secretary of a Branch of the Ladies Catholic Benevolent Association in Worcester. Instead of responding to poor Major Coombs, who was merely doing his job after all, she went straight to the top. She wrote directly to the Quartermaster General of the United States Army. She made perfectly clear how she felt and she told him exactly what she wanted by way of redress:

> 195 Lincoln Street, Worcester 5, Mass., June 14, 1947
>
> The Commanding General, Quartermaster Corps, Army of the United States, Washington 25, D. C.
>
> My dear General:
>
> On April 22, 1947 I received a letter from your department requesting that the next of kin of my deceased son, Pfc. Joseph J. Deignan 6 141 841, fill out an enclosed "Disposition of Remains" form and return it to your office. As I am certain you realize, it was a rather painful

task for me to agree to have my boy's body permanently interred in Hawaii. However, I completed the form and returned it promptly.

Today I received what I consider an unnecessarily callous letter from a subordinate of yours, one Richard B. Coombs, Major. Bernard Deignan, Joseph's father, was already dead seventeen months when my son met his death in March, 1942. As Joseph's mother I am certainly next of kin. I request that Major Coombs be officially reprimanded for the tone of his letter and for his failure to determine me as next of kin by a perusal of records in the office of the Adjutant General, and that I be furnished a copy of the letter of reprimand.

I am returning the original "Request for Disposition of Remains" form which I made out two months ago.

Very truly yours,
(Mrs.) Anna C. Deignan

Enclosures:

1. Completed 'Request for Disposition of Remains" form

2. Letter from Coombs.[78]

Whether this scorching letter was the product of individual or collective effort on the part of Donald's family is not entirely clear. His mother certainly had both the intellectual ability and the heart-felt motive to compose it all by herself. But certain aspects of it strongly suggest that it was the work of more than one author.

Anna's eldest son, Sergeant Francis James Deignan, had just recently returned from nearly three years of service in the United States Army. He had just finished a year of Graduate study and earned a Master's Degree in Psychology at Clark University. In the Fall of 1947 he would be off to Harvard on the G.I. Bill to continue his post-graduate work in a Doctoral Program there. Sergeant Frank Deignan came home from World War II bitterly resentful of his perceived mistreatment at the hands of the military. In 1942 they had promised him that he would be able to finish college before being "called-up" and that he would then be "Commissioned" as an Officer. The Army had broken both of those promises made to him years before. What was more, most of his time overseas had been served in what he later described as, "the stinking jungles of New Guinea."There, Sergeant Deignan had served in the Southwest Pacific Area Command of General Douglas MacArthur. Many of the American troops in New Guinea blamed MacArthur, wrongly, for "abandoning his Command" on Corregidor in March 1942. As if to confirm the suspicions of many men serving under him in New Guinea that he was both "a coward" and "a glory-hound," he left them behind, too, in October 1944 when he went off "to Liberate the Philippines."

That Anna's letter to the Quartermaster General called for Major Coombs to be "officially reprimanded" and that she be supplied with a copy of that document smacks of Sergeant Deignan's desire for "revenge" against the Army. After all, he knew Army "jargon" and administrative procedures intimately and he was well aware that an "Official Letter of Reprimand" would probably end Major Coombs's military career. Lastly, Francis idolized his mother and he certainly shared the terrible pain over Donald's death, which the entire incident resurfaced for the whole family. So even if Frank did not write Anna's letter for her, he most probably had a major part in composing it.

The Army's official response to "the Coombs incident" was fairly quick, very sensitive and quite conciliatory. On August 21, 1947, Lt. Colonel B.M. Baukhight of the Quartermaster Corps wrote as follows to Donald's mother:

> 21 August 1947
>
> Mrs. Anna C. Deignan
> 195 Lincoln Street
> Worcester , Massachusetts
>
> Dear Mrs. Deignan
>
> I have received your communication concerning a letter received by you from this office in regard to your son, the late Private First Class Joseph J. Deignan.

I deeply regret that the letter in question appeared abrupt in its manner and that the content caused you added distress.

Please be assured that the War Department is extremely aware of the deep feelings of the near relatives of those who gave their lives for their country, and it is our desire to be of the utmost assistance in every way.

Unfortunately, the information on file in this office did not reflect that Private First Class Deignan's father had also passed away. However, our records have been amended to give the proper information. I am certain you understand that Major Coombs did not intend in any way to offend you or to add to your painful task.

I am pleased to be able to inform you that we will comply with your desires concerning the final disposition of your son's remains as specified in the Request for Disposition of Remains form.

Please allow me to express my deepest sympathy in the tragic loss you have sustained, and if I may be of further service to you, please do not hesitate to call upon me at your convenience.

Sincerely yours,
B.M. Baukhight, QMC
Lt. Colonel, Memorial Division.[79]

While Lt. Colonel Baukhight's letter gave Mrs. Deignan almost everything she had demanded, it is interesting to note that no "official reprimand" for Major Coombs was mentioned in it nor was any such letter included in the Colonel's reply to her June 14th correspondence. Thus it appears that the Army's compassion had its limits and that, in the end, the military protected its own even from a justifiably wrathful civilian "Gold Star Mother" who had lost one of her three sons in the service of his country.

In her June 14th letter to the Quartermaster General, Anna had pointed out:

> As I am certain you realize, it was a rather painful task for me to agree to have my boy's body permanently interred in Hawaii. However, I completed the form and returned it promptly.[80]

But "painful" to his mother as any aspect of Donald's death and burial must surely have been, she was here being uncharacteristically disingenuous. The **"REQUEST FOR DISPOSITION OF REMAINS"** Form which Mrs. Deignan had indeed completed on April 22, 1947 had given her four options. She could have elected to have her son's body "RETURNED TO THE UNITED STATES OR ANY POSSESSION OR TERRITORY THEREOF FOR INTERMENT BY NEXT OF KIN IN A PRIVATE CEMETERY." Equally his remains could have been repatriated "TO THE UNITED STATES FOR FINAL INTERMENT IN A NATIONAL CEMETERY" or even sent to any selected foreign country for "INTERMENT BY NEXT OF KIN IN A PRIVATE CEMETERY" located there. Instead, she had chosen the first Option on the list, which was to have Donald buried in "A PERMANENT AMERICAN MILITARY CEMETERY OVERSEAS.[81] In discussing this decision many years later, Anna Deignan's adult children agreed that bringing Donald home for reburial in Worcester would have been "simply too painful for her to bear."

On September 2, 1949, the fourth anniversary of Japan's unconditional surrender to the United States and her Allies in World War II, the National Memorial Cemetery of the Pacific in Honolulu Hawaii was dedicated and opened to the public.[82] Burials had begun taking place there in January 1949, several months before the facility even opened officially. On February 4, 1949, Donald was among the first military personnel to be interred at the new National Cemetery in Section B, Grave 100.[83] At first, amidst much controversy, only temporary grave markers were used. For the most part, these were white, wooden crosses. Meanwhile, Anna Deignan had requested that a "Latin Cross" should adorn her son's permanent, flat gravestone.[84] On April 27, 1949, the Army informed her that this request had finally been fulfilled. She was further assured by the Quartermaster General, himself, that:

> The remains of your loved one have been permanently interred as recorded above among comrades who also gave their lives for their country. Customary military services were conducted over the grave at the time of burial.... You may be assured that this final interment

was conducted with fitting dignity and solem-
nity and that the gravesite will be carefully and
conscientiously maintained in perpetuity by
the United. States Government."[85]

The long, intermittent relationship between Donald's grief-
stricken mother and the United States Army had not been an
easy one. Army officials had tried to do the right thing but all
too often their words and actions had been insensitive and inept.
But, happily, the many exchanges between the Deignan family
and the Army ended on a Grace-note. On January 9, 1953, more
than a decade after Donald's sudden and unexplained death, his
mother received the following communication from the Chief
of the Quartermaster Corps's Memorial Division:

> Dear Mrs. Deignan:
>
> A photograph of the grave of your loved one,
> Private First Class Joseph J. Deignan, 6141481,
> in the National Memorial Cemetery of the
> Pacific, Honolulu, Territory of Hawaii, and a
> descriptive folder containing a brief history of
> the cemetery are inclosed. *(sic)*
>
> The National Memorial Cemetery of the
> Pacific is one of the most beautiful of our na-
> tional cemeteries. Provision has been made to
> assure that it will be maintained and cared for
> in a manner befitting the last resting place of
> our honored dead.

> These small tokens are sent as evidence of the
> respect and gratitude of your government for
> the sacrifices made by the members of the
> armed forces and their families.
>
> Sincerely yours,
> JAMES B. CLEARWATER,
> Colonel, QMC
> Chief', Memorial Division.[86]

As far as his family knew, Donald had died an American hero in World War II. In its various official communications with his parents, the Army had done everything it reasonably could to enhance and nothing to undermine this comforting and even uplifting assumption. In all of its public portrayals of him the Army had made of Donald, at the very least, "a generic hero" who rested at peace among "those heroic dead who fell together in the service of our country." But his family felt justified in going much further and they were prepared to do so. For they well knew that Donald, or "Donnie," as they persisted in calling him, had died while fighting bravely "at Pearl Harbor"! On America's darkest day he had come forward, gallantly, to defend our country against Japan's perfidious "Sneak Attack" and he had lost his life in the process. This fact in itself made him, for all of them, a very special kind of hero, "A Pearl Harbor Hero". This shining image was dutifully passed down, undimmed, untarnished and unquestioned, from one generation to the next for more than sixty years. Only recently has its historical accuracy been systematically scrutinized and called into serious question.

Donald's Obituary, Louise Cross's sentimental "recollections" in old age and some of the Army's own documents—when taken together—served to create the picture of Donald as a "Pearl Harbor Hero." But that "picture," upon closer inspection, is much more nuanced, more shadowy and gray, than it is "black and white."

For, in effect, the IDPF—on which so much of it is based—contains double and parallel, if not conflicting, narratives of the events surrounding the Army life and service-related death of Private First Class Joseph J. Deignan while he was serving with Battery C of the 13th Field Artillery Battalion of the 24th Infantry Division in the Territory of Hawaii in the months between December 7th, 1941 and March 18th, 1942. Extensive use has already been made in this Chapter of the correspondence which might be called the "public documents" preserved within the IDPF. These external records were intended, by the Army, for the aid and comfort of Donald's family. But at the same time his Individual Deceased Personnel File contained another set of strictly internal Army documents which constituted an altogether different record of the events pertaining to his death and actual legacy. It is now time, after a necessary detour of some length, to examine this second, internal narrative in detail and to evaluate the meaning of Donald's life, death and legacy, critically, in light of the additional information which it provides.

PART III.

THE LEGACY

CHAPTER SEVEN

"A CITIZEN OF IRELAND"

Although it is personally difficult for me to say so—since as an Irish-American I had always been warned to "never become too full of yourself"—Donald's most important legacy may well be the life which I have deliberately lived so as to honor his memory and to make him proud of the name which we continue to share. I am deeply indebted to Donald for the real spiritual and psychological help which he gave me when I was a boy and a young man. The ways in which I have attempted as an adult to "repay that debt," at least in an earthly manner, are discussed in the balance of this Chapter. The spiritual dimension of our relationship, and how I have tried to reconcile that part of our "accounts," will be left until the very last Chapter, where such consideration rightly belongs.

Donald's difficult life was cut short before he had a proper chance to make something of it. By contrast, my life has been long, full and—owing in part at least to his early influence—purposeful and rewarding.

When long ago, as a small boy, I promised my beloved Uncle Donald that I would do something worthwhile with my own life so as to honor his memory I did not then know how I would keep that pledge. To start with, however, it was inevitable that, in order to honor him somehow through my own life's work, I would have to move at some point out of Donald's psychological shadow and establish my own distinct identity as a person independent of him. This process of necessary differentiation had certainly begun by the time I started high school. It has continued and gathered momentum ever since.

Readers who have reached this point in the narrative will have long since recognized that, apart from the bequest of a name and with it an implicit life story, at least three additional, powerful influences have shaped my personality and character. The fact of congenital physical disabilities, a deep sense of personal identity rooted in my proud Irish-American ancestry and the sincere and sustaining practice of Roman Catholicism have all molded me into the adult I have become. Accidents at birth and of ethnicity were and are circumstances entirely beyond my control. For many years now I have increasingly accepted the one and altogether delighted in the other. Similarly, I have long since internalized the precepts and values inherent in the faith of my fathers. Donald's overarching presence throughout my life has been the unifying thread which has bound these elements together and given them coherence and meaning. In this Chapter,

I will deal specifically with the impact which physical disabilities and my Irish heritage have had on my adult life. I will also here address my development as a professional historian and consider the issues of "objectivity" and "evidence" in writing a biography and in interpreting the legacy of a person who was so necessarily close to me. I will leave an extended consideration of the influence of Roman Catholicism in my adult life until the final Chapter because questions concerning the practice of my Faith bear directly on my interpretation of Donald's legacy.

As a child the combination of my visual impairment and cerebral palsy, which caused me neither to be able to see very well nor to walk without difficulty, had left me feeling socially marginalized and extremely self-conscious. The strictly segregated residential environment in which I grew up at Perkins School for the Blind did nothing to lessen either of these perceptions. In fact, it exacerbated them. Gaining confidence as a young adult, by virtue of academic success in college and graduate school, I decided to try and do something to make life easier for the generations of disabled young people coming along behind me. If possible, I didn't want any of them to undergo many of the unnecessary hardships and embarrassments which I myself had experienced as a child growing up in the 1950s and the 1960s. As it happened, I was in the right place at the right time to advocate for the beneficial social changes I desired for the younger generation of fellow Americans with disabilities.

One day in the late spring of 1976 I happened to see a story on the local TV news which described a projected "White

House Conference on Handicapped Individuals" to be held in Washington D.C. later on in the year. The newscaster said that local people with disabilities would be recruited to attend this national conference as Rhode Island Delegates. I said to my parents who watched that story with me, "I could do that." My father said, "Why don't you get involved?" So I did. The timing could not have been better.

After graduating Summa Cum Laude from Rhode Island College in 1972 I was accepted into Graduate School, in the History Department, at Brown University in Providence Rhode Island. Receiving my M.A. there in 1973 I then prepared for and passed the qualifying exams for the Ph.D. in History in May 1976. After that, all I had left to do was to find a thesis advisor, determine a research topic and then write a Doctoral Dissertation under the supervision of that person. I was most fortunate that Professor David Underdown readily agreed to be my Dissertation Advisor. He was both an outstanding scholar and an equally fine person, a combination far too rare in the upper reaches of American academic life. It is owing to his unstinting support and encouragement that I earned my Ph.D., at Brown, in 1982. In the course of our long working relationship, we became and remained lifelong friends. His death saddened me deeply but I am profoundly grateful to have known and worked closely with him. His substantial body of scholarly work is a legacy of which any Professor can be justly proud.

Shortly after I passed my Qualifying Exams, the library workers at Brown went on strike for higher wages and better working conditions. I was unwilling, as a matter of principle, to cross their picket line so library research was out of the question until the strike ended in the fall. I had plenty of time on my hands just when the disability community in Rhode Island was organizing itself to take part in the impending White House Conference.

Prior to the Washington D.C. Conference, each state and territory throughout the United States established a local office whose job was to convene preliminary meetings and to screen and recruit representatives to the national gathering. During the summer of 1976 I volunteered some time in the Rhode Island office. I also submitted a letter of interest and a Resume to the screening committee. After being interviewed by them, I was accepted as one of the ten Rhode Island Delegates to the national event which took place at a large hotel in Washington D.C. between May 23 and May 27, 1977.

From my particular point-of-view, the most significant thing about the White House Conference on Handicapped Individuals was that I met my future wife, Kathleen Leonard, there. Kathy, too, was one of Rhode Island's representatives at the Washington Conference who went on to make a significant contribution as a teacher and a Disability Rights advocate on both the state and the national level. Otherwise, the White House Conference was a great disappointment and a missed opportunity. Although it brought together thousands of capable, highly motivated people who represented the entire spectrum of physical disabilities, all we were asked to do was to "vote" on a voluminous set of prepackaged "Recommendations," derived from preliminary

meetings held throughout the country, on a wide variety of issues of importance to "the handicapped community." Within
this rigid format there was no room for free discussion, formal
debate or the spontaneous exchange of ideas among ourselves.
In the event, the shortcomings of the well-intentioned White
House Conference galvanized many of its participants into a
generation of "Disability Rights Activists" who wanted to bring
about real improvement in the quality of our own lives and in
those of the generations of Americans with disabilities who were
to come after us. To some extent we achieved this goal with the
passage by Congress, nearly a full generation after the White
House Conference, of the Americans With Disabilities Act
(A.D.A.), which the elder President Bush signed into law on July
26, 1990. Like the White House Conference before it, however,
the A.D.A. has proven to be a mixed blessing and even something of an outright disappointment. Although most Americans
with disabilities are more fully integrated socially into the larger
society now than they were previously, full equality before the
law—in practice if not in theory—remains illusory. Segregated
residential education—such as that which I experienced at
Perkins School in my youth—is largely, and mercifully, a thing
of the past thanks to the Individuals with Disabilities Education
Act (I.D.E.A.) but the attainment of a high-quality education
for disabled students in integrated public school settings has not
been easy to achieve. Finally, unemployment rates among adults
with disabilities who want to work have remained at about 70%,
almost exactly what they were before the A.D.A. became law.
Our Rehabilitation system has become very good, through no
fault of its own, at turning out well qualified high school and

college graduates who can't find jobs. Small businesses, which constitute the backbone of the American economy, have still not come to realize sufficiently that work-ready people with disabilities represent the last great source of untapped potential employees in this country who can help us to compete successfully in a globalizing marketplace. So, after all this time, the struggle for real equality still goes on.

For me, the White House Conference marked the start of a Disability Rights advocacy career which has continued for more than thirty-five years.[1] My Uncle Donald had exemplified selfless service first in the CCC and later in the United States Army. Disability Rights advocacy—and volunteer participation as a Board Member and Officer in many other non-profit groups without a disability focus—was, for me, a way of "giving something back" to our country, thereby following Donald's good example.

Having always been a person with severe physical disabilities, it should not be surprising that the drive to improve my own prospects and those of other people like me has played a prominent part in my adult life. But, in addition to Donald's abiding influence, other childhood experiences have had an equally profound and continuing effect on me too.

Even before having been exposed in my third grade "Religious Education" class at Perkins to "The Story of Duffy" (see Chapter Two), my mother had given me a clear idea of what it meant to be an Irish-American and how special a gift that particular heritage was. As part of graduation requirements at Perkins we were expected to research and write a Senior Essay. I chose to write about "The Easter Rising of 1916," the Revolutionary Nationalist insurrection, primarily in Dublin, which led ultimately to the independence of most of Ireland from Britain in 1922. In college and Graduate School, between 1968 and 1982, my interest in the systematic study of Irish History continued and increased. At that time, however, courses in that subject as such were not widely available.

Like most historians my age who were interested in Ireland I was trained, primarily and perforce, in British History. Making the best of what seemed, in light of my ethnic background, to be a bad situation I determined to undertake my graduate study of British History from an Irish point of view. Deliberately viewing Britain from an Irish historical perspective was equivalent to turning a telescope around and looking at the world through the wrong end. Doing so made all things British appear uncharacteristically small and gave their worldwide Imperialist pretensions a Lilliputian cast. David Underdown, whose field of particular expertise was 16th and 17th Century Britain, appreciated my professional interest in Irish History and he encouraged me to investigate "The Ormond-Orrery Conflict," the protracted rivalry between the two leading Anglo-Irish soldier-politicians of the 1640-1680 period. The study of the complex relationship between the First Duke of Ormond and the First Earl of Orrery became the subject of my Doctoral Dissertation at Brown University.

For largely demographic reasons, tenure-track teaching positions on the college level were few and far between for many scholars of my generation. Indeed an opportunity to teach permanently on the college level never became available for me. Although accordingly I have long since left formal academic life, the study of Irish History has remained a central professional and personal pursuit.

At a regular meeting in 1988 of the Irish Cultural Association of Rhode Island, a college-based scholarly organization to which I have belonged since its founding, I learned of a fairly obscure statute called "The Irish Nationality and Citizenship Act." This legislation, which dated originally from 1956, granted Irish Citizenship to applicants around the world who had an Irish-born parent or grandparent. My maternal grandfather, Michael Donovan, fell into this latter category and so it was owing to his birth in County Cork in 1869 that I was able to become a Naturalized Irish Citizen in 1988. After completing the application process and being duly recorded in the "Foreign Births Registration Book" kept at the Consulate in Boston, I was able to obtain dual nationality and an Irish/European Union Passport.

My Irish passport says on its inside front cover, in Irish and English,—the country's two official languages—that, "The Minister of Foreign Affairs of Ireland requests all whom it may concern to allow the bearer, a citizen of Ireland, to pass freely and without hindrance and to afford the bearer all necessary assistance and protection."[2] My Irish Naturalization did not require the taking of an oath of allegiance nor did it impact my standing as a native-born American Citizen. Had it in any way done so, I would not have taken this step. For me, then, the acquisition of Irish Citizenship closed a mystic circle. In an instant it linked me, officially, to my ancestors but it also gave me a genuine stake in Ireland's future.

Ireland's history, and the perpetuation and transmission of knowledge about it, was to remain of great personal and professional importance to me. In the spring of 1997 I presented a paper at a meeting of the Irish Cultural Association of Rhode Island entitled, "Soldiers For Peace: Irish Peacekeeping for the United Nations." In the audience that evening was Mr. Raymond J. McKenna. He approached me after the presentation, said he enjoyed it, and asked if I'd be interested in coming to the initial meeting of a new grassroots organization whose purpose was the creation of a Rhode Island Irish Famine Memorial. Since my great-grandparents on both sides of the family were survivors of the Great Famine of 1845-1851, I was eager to become involved in the Rhode Island Irish Famine Memorial project.

I was most fortunate to be one of the two professional historians who became involved with the Rhode Island Irish Famine Memorial undertaking from the beginning. The other was my long time friend and colleague, Dr. Scott Molloy, from the University of Rhode Island.

The impetus for the establishment of a permanent Memorial for the victims and survivors of "the Great Famine" had been provided by the overwhelming public response to an anniversary memorial Mass organized by Ms. Anne M. Burns and celebrated at the Cathedral of Saints Peter and Paul by the Most Reverend Robert E. Mulvee, Bishop of the Roman Catholic Diocese of Providence, in October 1995. This special Mass was intended to commemorate the one hundred fiftieth anniversary of the outbreak of the Famine. The Providence Journal, Rhode Island's leading daily newspaper, covered the event.[3] I was not present on that particular occasion simply because I had not been aware that the event was to take place. Had I known about that Mass beforehand I would have certainly been in attendance at the packed Cathedral.

Following the Memorial Mass, and in light of the enthusiastic public reaction which that event drew, informal discussions among the leaders of Rhode Island's Irish-American community began and continued for a couple of years. The initial formal meeting of the Rhode Island Irish Famine Memorial Committee took place in May 1997.

The Memorial Committee brought together in one place representatives of every major Irish-American organization in the state of Rhode Island. These groups, of which there were about a dozen, ranged from the purely academic and cultural to the overtly political with a large number of social organizations in between. The newly formed Famine Memorial umbrella coalition was from the first primarily a "committee of committees" which otherwise unaffiliated, interested individuals were welcome to join. Its sole purpose, in the words of the Mission Statement which it soon adopted, was:

> To commission, create, and maintain a permanent Monument dedicated to preserving the memory of the one million Irish men, women and children who perished from starvation or disease resulting from the Great Famine which devastated Ireland between 1845-1851. The Memorial is also intended to commemorate the heroic struggle of the one and one half million Irish people who survived the Great Famine and were forced by dire economic, social and political circumstances to leave Ireland during the same period to seek better lives in the United States of America and in other countries around the world. Lastly, the Memorial will celebrate the manifold achievements and contributions of Famine survivors and their descendants who, generation after generation, have so greatly enriched the life of America, in general, and of Rhode Island in particular.[4]

The Committee was incorporated in June 1997 as a nonprofit, tax-exempt educational and charitable organization which soon set about raising the estimated half million dollars which we believed would be necessary to bring our stated purpose to fruition.

In due course, we conducted a nationwide search and competition for an artist to execute our commission. As a group, we were clear from the start what elements we wanted to be included in our Memorial's design. We had three major ideas in mind. First, we wanted the winning artist to provide an accurate sculptural representation of Famine-era Irish people. Second, we insisted that the Memorial should have a substantive narrative and educational component. Lastly, we wanted a mechanism within the design concept to encourage the widest possible community participation in the Memorial project. Six designs were selected for final review by the entire Committee and, in October, 1998, Mr. Robert Shure of Woburn Massachusetts was unanimously selected by secret ballot to execute our commission.

To his credit, Mr. Shure had developed a worldwide portfolio of distinguished artistic work in the course of his forty year professional career. As a world-class sculptor, he had among many other things created the Irish Famine Memorial in Boston and the Korean War Monument already located in downtown Providence. So we had, in concrete and bronze, outstanding examples of some of his previous work close at hand and a clear idea of the breadth of his creative, artistic vision. His selection proved to be an inspired choice.

Bob Shure's design masterfully incorporated the three essential elements which our Committee had identified when laying out the commission. A three-person larger-than-life bronze sculpture group, set on a round granite base, depicted representative victims and survivors of the Great Famine in memorable and moving detail. The sculpture group deliberately had with it no accompanying interpretive commentary. Thus the artist intentionally left each individual viewer free to draw his or her own personal conclusions about the meaning of the imposing figures in front of them. This representational element, then, met the first of our three desired criteria. The second, a means of involving the larger community in the project, was satisfied by the incorporation around the Memorial site of a number of granite benches and walkways paved with bricks and flagstones into which donor-determined inscriptions could be set. By means of this design decision we were able both to raise some of the necessary funds for the project—by encouraging the purchase by individuals of donor-bricks and flagstones and of memorial benches by supportive organizations—and to involve the general public in its completion. Our Committee's decision-making process was always democratic and transparent from its start in 1997 right through to the Dedication of the Memorial on November 17, 2007. Providing a substantive, narrative and educational component—our third and final criterion—was the most complex challenge which we had to meet. Here, too, Mr. Shure provided us with an innovative solution.

The narrative portion of the Rhode Island Irish Famine Memorial contained two distinct but complementary elements: bas-relief sculptures depicting the Famine in Ireland, the Trans-Atlantic crossing of refugees in the so-called "coffin ships," and scenes from Irish-American life here in the United States. Below these bas-reliefs was straightforward, interpretive historical text. Each bronze-faced letter of the text was individually cast and then mounted on the narrative wall.

At a regular meeting of the Memorial Committee held in 2001, I was nominated to compose the Irish portion of the

Famine historical narrative while at the same time Dr. Scott Molloy was asked to write the Rhode Island portion of the piece. Undertaking my part of this task was the most challenging and rewarding experience of my entire professional life. I began work on the Irish portion of the Famine Memorial text in September 2001 and completed my final draft in October 2002 after submitting various versions to peer review by fellow historians during the intervening months. Completing this assignment successfully proved to be far more difficult than researching and writing my Doctoral Dissertation at Brown had been twenty five years earlier.

For me, professionally, the entire creative process in this instance was counterintuitive, fairly unconventional and intellectually stimulating in the extreme.

Before discussing the peculiar creative process which I undertook in crafting my part of the Rhode Island Irish Famine Memorial's historical narrative, perhaps a few words about our usual work methods and professional perspectives might be helpful to general readers of this book so as to enable them more clearly to understand how and why working historians, like me, do what they do when we are engaged in serious research and scholarship.

In doing their chosen work, historians typically identify a particular factual problem which they want to investigate in depth or they pose a specific question or series of questions to be answered. Whatever the undertaking may be, the investigative process usually begins with extensive research into existing "secondary sources," that is, contemporary books, articles and other writings on the subject under consideration which date from the present time or the relatively recent past. Since the time period covered by this book is considerable, and because the topics treated in it are varied, it has been necessary for background purposes to examine published works on Perkins School for the Blind, the Great Famine, the history of Scotland, the growth and transformation of the city of Worcester Massachusetts, the Great Depression, the United States Army both before and during World War II and the Japanese attack on Pearl Harbor. Only by doing such background research into secondary sources has it become possible to create the "context" within which to understand and interpret Donald's particular life experience and legacy.

Once this body of secondary material has been reviewed and digested, the historical researcher next turns to "primary source" materials. In the present instance, these would include documents which were either written by Donald or by people who actually knew him or were, at least, his contemporaries. Since none of his letters and postcards appears to have survived, such things as Donald's Birth, Baptismal and Death Certificates together with his high school transcript, his CCC Discharge Papers, his Army Personnel Record, his IDPF, and his Obituary would represent primary source materials in the context of his "Biography" which forms an important part of this book.

Ordinarily, once secondary and primary source materials had been collected, organized, reviewed and digested, the historian would then construct a new narrative framework based on the information contained in them and upon his or her scholarly interpretation of it. Statements would be made within this new narrative and these would then be supported by referring to prior evidence from secondary or primary sources which would be used to buttress current factual or interpretive conclusions. Assertions on particular historical matters having been made, transitional paragraphs would follow linking the previous topic to the next one to be considered and the narrative would be advanced by making another factual statement or by posing some new particular question to be answered. Eventually, this cumulative, creative process would result in the presentation of a scholarly paper at an academic conference, the submission of a journal article or in the completion of a specific chapter or of an entire book. As a matter of course, the text would be accompanied by footnotes indicating the sources of quotes and references, and, in the case of a book, a full-length bibliography as well.

The crafting of the Rhode Island Irish Famine Memorial narrative text involved a markedly different process in most respects. There would, in the first place, be neither room nor any available format for notes or an attribution of sources in the very limited space provided on the Famine Memorial's narrative wall. This much I knew from the outset.

Although I had to begin, as usual, by familiarizing myself with the considerable body of secondary and primary source material relating to the "Great Famine of 1845-1851," in order to construct my portion of the Rhode Island Memorial's historical narrative, from that point on I was—for me at least—in un-charted creative and professional territory.

As I have said, I began my task in September 2001 by taking a deliberately conventional approach to the project. Having done my research, I decided to write the first draft of the narrative text by including in it all the material which I felt needed to be covered. I touched on the long and complex Anglo-Irish colonial relationship from its beginnings in the early Middle Ages down to the outbreak of the Great Famine in 1845. I then dealt in detail with the varying responses to the Famine on the part of successive British Governments as well as the reaction to the event by different religious groups in Ireland. I dissected interventionist and laissez-faire economic policies bearing on the Famine and went on to assess responsibility for the million deaths associated with it. I concluded by dealing with the twin phenomena of mass eviction and Trans-Atlantic immigration to America in general and to Rhode Island in particular. This original version turned out to be 1425 words long, about the average length of a college undergraduate history term paper.

I sent this version off to our sculptor, Bob Shure, for his review and comment on September 17, 2002. I received his reply on September 20, just before leaving for a ten day vacation with my wife in Ireland. He wrote in part,

> Dear Don:
>
> I received your letter and copy of the narrative for the RIIFM [Rhode Island Irish Famine

Memorial.] The narrative is very well written and (sic) [but?] at first glance, I thought there may be too many words for our space. The minimum letter height for good clarity in bronze is between 1/4" and 3/8". We would need to lay out some of your text at full scale to determine the surface area it requires. Sincerely, Robert Shure [5]

While we were away, Mr. Shure reflected further on the creative challenges inherent in the Irish Famine Memorial project. On October 4, 2002, he wrote again:

Dear Don:

Please see the attached sketch in review of the narrative. The pictorial designs should have an appropriate text under each segment. The designs are from left to right:

1. Dying of hunger

2. Coffin ships

3. Center - shows Irish family and Irish American family

4. Building America

5. Succeeding in American Culture & Politics

Under each design there is an area of about 7" x 30". The bronze has a minimum letter height for casting. With this in mind, I think there can be a maximum of 2000 letters (including spaces between words) in each 7" x 30" area. This is an approximate idea and most of all the text should relate to the picture above.

Please contact me to discuss this.

Sincerely, Robert Shure .[6]

Almost 2,500 years ago, Hippocrates—the ancient Greek father of modern medicine—observed, ""Life is short, the art long…."[7] I had been given a rare opportunity to produce a piece of historical interpretive prose which, as an integral part of a literally monumental public artwork installation, could be expected to last for generations and possibly even for centuries to come. In return for the promise of relative longevity for my work, I would have to accept the very real physical space limitations imposed by the absolute constraints of the larger Memorial project itself. Under the circumstances, this was a bargain I was willing to make and a professional challenge I was ready to accept.

Although the number of individual characters and spaces available to me for my part of the projected narrative wall was eventually increased to a maximum of 5,000 from the original 2,000, the creative challenge was clear. I had to find a way to boil down a description of the Great Famine, with all its historical complexities and profound consequences, into a distillation which would accommodate the absolute spatial parameters laid down by Bob Shure. In doing so, in addition, I would have to construct a factual and interpretive piece which would simultaneously satisfy a number of different audiences over time. In the first place the work in question would have to be meaningful, immediately, to the general public—the vast majority of presumed future readers at the Memorial site—who would have had no prior knowledge either of Irish History in general or of the Great Famine in particular. At the same time, the product of my efforts would have to speak directly and honestly -- for generations to come-- to fellow Irish-Americans and Irish people who would bring varying degrees of awareness and sophistication to their encounter with the Rhode Island Irish Famine Memorial. My final obligation was to write a piece of work intellectually substantive enough to meet the interpretive expectations of fellow Irish historical scholars who might, over time, happen upon our Famine Monument.

Thus I had before me the equally daunting but very different tasks of "counting every word!" and "making every word count!" In addition to meeting the needs of the three distinct potential audiences mentioned above, I had also to take into account the way in which the use of the English language might change over a fairly long period of time. Words in current use today might eventually become obscure or even incomprehensible. But unlike modern students of Shakespeare, for example, who have footnotes and glossaries to help them in understanding what they are reading, both the artistic format and the physical space limitations of the Famine Memorial itself prevented me from providing any such assistance. So I had to choose my words very carefully, selecting them for the general reader while at the same time finding a way to convey within them specialized meanings which would be readily apparent—as necessary—to either knowledgeable Irish-American readers and/or to my fellow scholars.

Having lived with my first extensive narrative draft for a little more than a year I had, by October 2002, attained considerable emotional and intellectual distance from that piece of work. A healthy creative tension, based on mutual respect and affection, had developed between Bob Shure, as an artist, and me, as a historian, in the meantime. I understood very well the nature of the bargain between us; he would give me a "blank canvas" on which to inscribe words and ideas of my own which were likely to survive publicly for a very long time. I, in return, would have to accept and work within the absolute limitations of the relatively small physical parameters which had been provided to me.

So I set to work distilling and shaping my prose to fit into the space provided within Mr. Shure's Memorial concept. On the evening of October 4, 2002 I wrote the following note to him:

> Dear Robert,
>
> I think I've finally done it. My count of the attached document makes it 798 words and 4,996 characters with spaces. What do you

think? Will this do? Please contact me by whatever means, at your convenience, on Sunday to
discuss the latest version.

Thanks again for your patience. If I had not
mistaken your e-mail address in July we would
have had much more time to wrestle with this
thing. As it is, I hope "we done good"!

Sincerely, Don Deignan. [8]

I was under some pressure to complete my revisions because
I had agreed to present the latest draft of the Famine narrative
at a meeting of the Irish Cultural Association of Rhode Island
to be held at Providence College on the evening of October 7,
2002. Accordingly I did so and, in the discussion which followed
my talk, a number of academic colleagues who were present
made several helpful comments and constructive stylistic and
substantive suggestions. Dr. John Quinn, now Chairperson of
the History Department at Salve Regina University in Newport
Rhode Island, asked me to e-mail to him the draft I had just presented. I did so and next day he responded as follows:

Dear Don,

I just read and then re-read your Famine
Memorial draft. I think you've done a very
good job compressing a complicated story into
a brief, understandable narrative. I have several
suggestions, however, most of which are pretty

minor. I know you're under a variety of constraints, so I realize that you may not be able to
act on any of my brilliant ideas! [9]

I replied to Dr. Quinn almost immediately:

Dear John,

Thanks so much for your comments and suggestions. Many of them are, in fact, "brilliant"
and all of them are helpful! I think you have
saved me from making at least two egregious
factual and interpretive errors. [10]

In his response, Professor Quinn was characteristically gracious
and unassuming. He wrote:

Dear Don,

I'm glad to hear that you liked my suggestions.
I know how tricky it is to make any changes
when you're under such a strict word limit.
Good luck with it.... [11]

Final revisions having been made, my portion of the Famine
Memorial narrative amounted to 741 words or 4,595 characters
(individual letters and spaces), totals well under Bob Shure's
strict 5,000 character limit. Actually, Mr. Shure did me a great
favor in this regard by taking it upon himself, wisely, to remove
the following dedicatory paragraph "This memorial is dedicated

to the victims and survivors of the Great Irish Famine of 1845-1851. It also pays tribute to their immigrant descendants who, generation after generation, have so greatly enriched the life of America in general and of Rhode Island in particular" which I had originally written as part of my piece and place it, rather, in the middle of the narrative wall between my work and that of my friend and project partner Dr. Scott Molloy. This aesthetic decision on Bob Shure's part had the beneficial effect of further delineating my work from that of Dr. Molloy and made it less necessary for both of us to be concerned about harmonizing our writing styles and interpretive conclusions within the overall context of the entire historical production.

It was always my intent that the description which I crafted of the Great Famine in Ireland could be read on a number of levels, depending on the point of view and prior knowledge of each individual Memorial visitor who encountered the text. In the first place my narrative could be read literally and superficially as a series of simple, factual statements intended primarily to convey a basic understanding of that event and its importance to the casual reader. Thus, in this vein, I began by declaring that, "The Great Famine was the most important event in Nineteenth Century Ireland." After noting the perennial failure each harvest season between 1845 and 1851 of, ".... the potato crop... on which a large majority of the Irish people depended for their survival,...." I went on to establish that, "The result of this devastating crop failure, caused by a disease commonly called "the Blight," was that at least one million men, women, and children died of outright starvation or of the epidemic diseases which came with it." The foregoing statements are merely historical facts which any casual visitor to the Memorial would need to know in order to appreciate the significance of the installation and its place in Irish and Rhode Island History.

Apart from the standard rehearsal of straightforward "facts," intended to educate the uninitiated reader, the Memorial narrative also required historical interpretation if it was to be of wider, enduring value. To discuss Ireland's Great Famine seriously is to enter deliberately into an ideological and intellectual minefield. No subject is more emotionally charged for Irish-Americans, the diaspora in general, or for people in Ireland itself, than the treatment of Ireland by Britain during the Famine period. Thus it was necessary for me not only to continue constructing a factual framework but also to deal directly and delicately with the long and complex "Anglo-Irish relationship" and its bearing on the terrible events of 1845-1851. So by way of demonstrating the manner in which my narrative technique could accomplish factual, ideological and historically interpretive objectives, simultaneously, I wrote, "Owing to the Famine, the population of Ireland, a northwest European island country slightly smaller than the State of Maine, was reduced by death or emigration from an estimated 8.5 million people to only 6 million." Buried within this seemingly innocuous factual statement was a kind of "coded message" which some fellow Irish-Americans and most professional historians could easily decipher.

Giving Ireland's geographical character, as an island, and its location in northwestern Europe was nothing out of the ordinary. But adding that it was, "slightly smaller than the State of Maine…." was intended, within an innocent, comparative American context, to convey a highly specialized, occult, meaning. During the Famine period the island of Ireland was a single, undivided country which was in fact a little smaller than the state of Maine. In 1922, however, after a period of armed struggle most of Ireland gained its practical independence from Britain, the island was politically "partitioned" into two geographically unequal parts. The larger independent portion roughly the size of West Virginia ultimately became the "Republic of Ireland" in 1949 while the smaller part equivalent to the dimensions of Connecticut remained united with Britain as "the Province of Northern Ireland". Asserting in the Memorial narrative, as I do, that "Ireland…[is]…"slightly smaller than the state of Maine…" is intended to imply, implicitly, that, sometime during the long, projected future life of the Monument, "Partition" will end and Ireland will be reunited as a single state completely independent of Britain. The general public would not need to understand or appreciate this linguistic nuance but I have no doubt that many generations of Irish-Americans and future "scholars" will do so without difficulty.

Dealing appropriately with Ireland's complicated role within the British Imperial framework presented an equally formidable challenge. Ireland's political subordination to Britain during the Famine era had to be acknowledged without "legitimizing" that relationship. So, instead of addressing that vexed and complex question directly, I wrote:

At the time of the Famine, and for centuries before it, Ireland was not an independent country free to determine its own destiny. By virtue of English military conquest, Ireland had become part of what came to be known as the British Empire.

When the Rhode Island Irish Famine Memorial Committee was established in 1997, some people who joined the organization wanted to use the project as yet another "political stick" with which to beat the continuing British "Imperialist presence" in Northern Ireland which was—in their view -- responsible for the latest round of "the Troubles" there. I argued at the time that we should not bring "contemporary Irish politics" into the Memorial project and that finding and telling the factual truth about "the Great Famine," alone, should suffice. This more moderate view ultimately prevailed. We as an organization remained exclusively focused on the creation of the Memorial as a nonpartisan, nonsectarian, nonpolitical site. We completed this endeavor, remarkable for a widely varied group of Irish-American organizations, without having a major disagreement among ourselves from start to finish. [12] This circumstance was owing largely to the superb leadership of Mr. Raymond J. McKenna who served as the Famine Memorial Committee's President from the project's inception through the Monument's dedication. His recent, untimely death has proven to be a great loss for our entire Rhode Island community and, most especially, for me personally. He was my close friend as well as a true "Hibernian Brother."

My part in researching and writing a portion of the Famine Memorial's narrative helped me to think in new and very different ways about my approach to the practice of the historical profession whose discipline I have followed for the last forty years. In the process of doing this work I came to appreciate the wonderful complexity and malleability of the English language. I also experienced for the first time in my long and varied professional career the rigorous joy to be found in squeezing facts and ideas down to their essence by virtue of having to work within radically compressed textual limits. In the strange and uncharacteristic context of the Memorial narrative, I learned that "*Less*" *is indeed "More"!*

Dr. Scott Molloy completed his part of the same work—relating the experiences of Irish Famine immigrants in Rhode Island—under the identically strict 5,000 character editorial constraint within which I had had to work. In his recent groundbreaking book on the life of Joseph Banigan, <u>Irish Titan, Irish Toilers</u>, my old friend and colleague paid me an unlooked for and totally unexpected compliment when, unbeknownst to me beforehand, he wrote:

> For the last twelve years I have also labored on another project; a monument to those Irish Famine survivors who eventually came to Rhode Island like the Banigans… I am especially indebted to Dr. Donald Deignan, another classmate at Rhode Island College in the 1960s, who usually provided the dark context of the Irish Famine in tandem with my lectures on the refugees to Rhode Island. Don's contribution to the effort will never be fully known.[13]

After much soul-searching, I decided to put my full name at the end of my part of the Monument's narrative text. I was reluctant to do so, for a number of reasons. From childhood Irish-American Roman Catholics, like me, have been warned against the sin of "Pride," the first and the worst of all the so-called Seven Deadly Sins. "Don't be too full of yourself," we have always been told. Too much praise from others or immodest self-promotion would inevitably lead to "a swelled head!" All this I knew and believed but, for me, there were equally powerful, countervailing forces at work too.

Being happily married but childless, it is altogether likely that I will have no heirs. So "My Name" will die with me. Under these circumstances I felt that it was especially important to honor the memory of my mother, Margaret Donovan Deignan, who so deeply loved her Irish heritage and me. I also wanted to take lasting, public responsibility—and perhaps some credit too— for what I had written. My part in the Rhode Island Irish Famine Memorial project could be a starting point from which some future journalist or historian could launch an investigation, if he or she ever wished to do so, into what had "made me tick." Lastly, of course, I put my name on the Memorial because I wanted to keep my boyhood promise to "Uncle Donald" to honor his memory in a lasting way. This is only fitting since, after all, we have long shared "our name!" and will continue to do so.

It must finally be admitted that my tribute to Donald J. Deignan on the Famine Memorial wall is a general, obscure and indirect one. He and I will always know what my intention was, as incidental readers of this book will also, but most visitors to the site—especially over time—would have no idea of the dual significance of the name written there. So I also felt the need to honor Donald Joseph in a special, particular way. Accordingly, I purchased a granite flagstone at the Memorial and had inscribed on it: "For my uncle, P.F.C. Donald J. Deignan, 1915-1942, Love Don Deignan."[14] Most people who visit the Rhode Island Irish Famine Memorial in years to come, will have no occasion to visit Donald's grave at the National Memorial Cemetery of the Pacific in Honolulu Hawaii. But, at least by viewing his flagstone at the Providence Irish Memorial site, they will know that there was and is some special connection between us.

Researching and writing Donald's biography, and interpreting his life through the twin prisms of my own childhood attachment and subsequent adult detachment, has proven to be at least as challenging as was the earlier composition of the (Ireland) Irish portion of the Famine Memorial narrative. Individual prisms, by their very nature, tend to distort images, but—as I have discovered after many years of practical experience with powerful, corrective glasses—multiple lenses in appropriate combination can serve to clarify an image and to eliminate distortions as well.

By deliberately dividing this book into three distinct parts, I have provided for myself separate, creative spaces within which to work out particular technical problems and/or psychological challenges in isolation from each other. If I have been successful in crafting this operating model, the end product of my labors should be an integrated and intellectually honest whole.

"How can any treatment of your Uncle Donald, given your deep personal and emotional relationship with him, be "objective?" This is a very fair question and, indeed, an essential one which any reader can be expected to ask of me. In fact, I posed this very question to myself before undertaking my task. All professional historians aim for "objectivity," or claim that they do, in carrying out their work. But as modern people, each of us has long since been forced to admit to ourselves and to our professional colleagues, that the achievement of complete objectivity is impossible. The best we can do is to recognize and to acknowledge our own biases and then, consciously, to correct for them as much is possible. "Peer review," is of course, a helpful and a necessary corrective on those occasions when for whatever reason we fall short of this high, internalized standard.

From the start, when I first conceptualized the outline of this book in 2005 as a straightforward "biography" sandwiched between personal experiences from childhood on the one hand and objective interpretation from the perspective of an adult historian on the other, I realized that I would have to face the same problem which any biographer must confront: how to tell a good story while keeping some emotional and intellectual distance from its principal subject? My solution to this formidable challenge was, in the first instance, "to raise the white flag without firing a single shot in defense of objectivity." I knew that, in the first third of the book, I would have to find a way to reconnect with that anguished child who first encountered Donald Joseph John Deignan, so powerfully, more than fifty years ago. In attempting as a middle-aged man to reconnect with that homesick, forlorn little boy I once was, I decided deliberately to give his emotional responses and childhood perceptions "free rein" without judging or filtering any of them. Thus, through the writing process itself, I was able fairly well to recapture and to evoke once again the deep feelings of pain and loneliness which were so much a part of my early experience at Perkins School. The mature man that I am now was able to travel back in time, mentally, to grieve and to weep, openly and unashamedly, for himself as an erstwhile child and also to mourn profoundly for the lost, heroic uncle who had sustained that same little boy, spiritually and psychologically, throughout his youth. Turning the classical Greek theatrical paradigm on its head, I consciously decided to get the "cathartic element" worked through and out of the way at the start of the book rather than leaving the customary "release" until the end. The child I was fifty years ago knew nothing of the adult concept of "objectivity" and I make no pretense of having achieved it, or of even having tried to do so, in Part I. of this book. The raw feelings and subjective perceptions which I had in December 1959 and for sometime afterwards were and are, in their own place and time, legitimate. I did not, in the first part of the book where they belong, have to justify, qualify or interpret any of them. *They were whatever they were, then, and now, and I felt what I felt!*

This being said, I have been able unapologetically to use the first third of this book for both narrative and cathartic purposes. It was possible there to establish and describe the initial relationship between Donald and me and, at the same time, to surface and to ventilate long suppressed emotions. By first identifying

and then "wringing these long-held but hitherto largely unex-
pressed feelings out of my system," so to speak, the way was
opened for me to finish the remainder of the job before me with
a far greater degree of "objectivity" than would otherwise have
been either likely or even possible under different circumstances.

The initial cathartic exercise apart, the remaining structural elements in the book (the distinct biographical and interpretive
sections) have helped me to attain additional, necessary, scholarly distance from Donald too. Part II., the "biographical" portion of this book, has been as stringently *evidence-based* as I could
make it. The surviving evidence pertaining to Donald's life is
sparse and in many ways inadequate but there has been nothing
I can do to rectify this inherent shortcoming.

When I was writing my Doctoral Dissertation at Brown more
than thirty years ago, I had an abundance of documentary evidence of all kinds with which to deal. Since I wrote about the
long, public relationship between the two leading Anglo-Irish
political figures of the mid-seventeenth century—the Duke of
Ormond and the Earl of Orrery—I had to sift through their
voluminous correspondence with one another and with many
other prominent people besides. In addition, any number of
secondary studies existed to help me in that particular project.
I had almost too much rather than too little evidence to assimilate, interpret and incorporate into my own original work..
While I was grappling with the complex lives of two men at the
top of a vanished society, other currents were flowing within the
historical profession into which I was about to enter.

In the course of my professional life, over the last forty years or so, there has been an interest among many of my colleagues in the historical discipline in the study of "history from the bottom up." They have focused much fine scholarly effort and substantive research on trying to find out how "ordinary people" really lived their daily lives in the past. In trying to do this, they have for the most part been compelled to use surviving official records which deal with groups of people rather than with specific individuals. Such things as land title deeds, household inventories and wills can provide valuable insights into the material circumstances of what the English or Irish would call, "the middling sort of people." The farther down the socio-economic scale an investigator chooses to go, however, the worse the surviving records tend to become at least in the European context with which I am most familiar. In the lower depths of such societies, church records of Baptisms, Marriages and Deaths—especially when they cover several centuries in the same place—can shed much useful light on family and communal relationships. Court records, where they survive, can sometimes show what happened when lowly individuals, illiterate peasants or uneducated industrial workers, fell afoul of the law. All these evidentiary problems in studying the lives of ordinary folk in the past are perforce magnified when emphasis shifts from investigation of a group of people to an analysis of the life of one individual.

In Donald's case, the generic challenge of probing into any individual's life has proven to be particularly daunting. For he was, in almost every respect, an entirely ordinary person; a product of his ethnicity, socio-economic class and historical time period. As such, Donald left virtually nothing of his own behind him in the way of personal information which he himself willfully generated. He could, of course, read and write. What kinds of things he may have read is not now known but he probably confined his interests to the newspapers and the magazines of his own day. It appears that he wrote a good deal to his mother, Anna, and to his Aunt Louise, at least during his Army service between July 1939 and March 1942. But none of these documents have survived, or as yet come down to me, so it is impossible to know much about his "interior landscape" or world view. All that remains are official records from which some useful and valuable inferences may be made. *In the event, we know a good deal about him but almost nothing of him!* The surviving official sources, too, are somewhat flawed and rather fragmentary. His "Discharge Papers" from the CCC constitute the only exception to this rule. The terrible fire at the National Personnel Records Center in Saint Louis, Missouri, in July 1973, destroyed very many U.S. Army veterans' records from World War II. For research purposes this catastrophic documentary loss was compounded by the institutional, bureaucratic intransigence of the United States Army itself. Thus, conclusions about Donald's life and death must be drawn with caution.

I have said earlier in this chapter that I have long recognized the necessity of both differentiating and distancing myself from Donald Joseph Deignan. Writing the middle, or biographical portion, of this book has helped me to do so. I could there simply relate, and to some degree interpret, but not change the known facts of his life. Consideration of these "mere facts" served to turn Donald's life story—little by little—into another conventional historical project for me. *This is not to say that I was dispassionate or disinterested, far from it!* Indeed the clinical task of unearthing and organizing the mundane details of Donald's short life proved to be a fascinating one, made all the more so by its relative, practical difficulty. Apart from various documentary problems, I had yet another obstacle to overcome. Except in the most literal sense, I am not an American Historian. Of course I know something about the broad outlines of American History and my non-academic experiences as a state worker and a non-profit organizational volunteer have given me some insights into the workings of government at the local, state and federal levels. I had to learn, from the ground up, how to navigate my way through a number of unfamiliar administrative bureaucracies including those of the Roman Catholic Diocese of Worcester, the National Archives and Records Administration, various library collections, and the all but impenetrable and incomprehensible labyrinth of the U.S. Army bureaucracy itself.

Virtually every individual and institution or organization which I approached for research assistance and factual information proved to be extremely helpful, and my debts to those many friends and colleagues are detailed in the "Acknowledgements" which precede the main text of this book.

Unfortunately, in terms of helpfulness, the United States Army's massive administrative bureaucracy was, in general, the exception. Even after I sought help from members of Rhode Island's Congressional Delegation and from President Obama, himself, too, in trying to obtain all official records pertinent to P.F.C. Joseph J. Deignan's military service, the Army put obstacles in our way. Brief reference to one exchange of correspondence will illustrate the problem. On May 1, 2007, I wrote to the branch of the Army's Human Resources Command located in Saint Louis Missouri, requesting "…all available information" on P.F.C. Joseph J. Deignan. By way of response, Colonel Wanda L. Good—the Army Officer who received and processed my request—courteously informed me that:

> The following determination is made by the undersigned, under the authority delegated to me by the Commanding General, U.S. Army Human Resources Command. Enclosed are 16 pages of releasable documents concerning your request. Personal information is being withheld under Title 5, U.S. Code, Section 552 (b)(6) of the Freedom of Information Act because release of that information would result in a clearly unwarranted invasion of personal privacy. [15]

As it happened, the "16 pages of releasable documents" to which Colonel Good referred were duplicates of materials which I had already obtained from other sources. So, in reply, I told her, "While I very much appreciate both the cooperative and informative tone of your correspondence, I disagree with your determination to deny me access to additional information, in the possession of the Army, relating to the military service during World War II. of my late uncle Private First Class Joseph J. Deignan." I further pointed out:

> In your correspondence to me, Colonel Good, you denied my access to further informa- tion about my uncle's military record on the grounds that its release would violate Title 5, U.S. Code, Section 552 (b)(6) of the Freedom of Information Act and result in "….a clearly unwarranted invasion of personal privacy." Now my uncle has been dead for more than sixty- five years. His father died in 1940. His mother died in 1956. His eldest brother—my father Francis James Deignan (himself a World War II. Army veteran of the Netherlands East Indies campaign)—died in 1991. And the last of my uncle's remaining siblings died in 2004. I am his last surviving relative. Whose "personal privacy," then, is the Army seeking to protect? Surely not that of my late uncle nor even that of his "family" since I am now, myself, the sum and substance of that entity. I would ask the Army, therefore, to now recognize me, effectively, as my late uncle's "next of kin" so that additional information about him can be released to me in that capacity and so that I can also apply on his behalf for replacements of the medal/ decoration(s) to which he was entitled.[16]

But my "Appeal" did no good and I was eventually advised to withdraw it on the grounds that it would ultimately be denied if I insisted on sending it up the Department of the Army's "chain of command." Eventually, out of a combined sense of frustration and principle, I hired an attorney to represent me in my dealings with the Army. But his success, like mine, proved to be rather limited in spite of his sincere personal interest and best professional efforts. Furthermore, even though my direct, personal appeal to President Obama in his capacity as Commander-in-Chief eventually produced some positive results, their scope was somewhat limited. [17]

False starts, bureaucratic roadblocks and informational dead-ends were commonplace in my research process. But none of these discouraged me and each of them prompted me to rework my questions while trying to find new paths of inquiry. I will deal in much more specific detail with these aforementioned technical challenges when I treat the circumstances of Donald's untimely death in the next chapter.

The opening chapters of this book allowed me to have the deeply cathartic experience I needed so as to be able to approach the remaining parts of my work with a considerable degree of professional detachment. The Biographical chapters in the middle provided a natural "buffer," and a breathing space, between the raw, recaptured emotions of childhood and consideration, finally, of "The Legacy" from an adult's point-of-view. In the final two chapters, I will deal with Donald's death and its consequences for both of us. In doing so, it should be said that terribly difficult and hitherto unanticipated revelations lie ahead. But, by virtue of my own long life experience, I am now able to confront and treat these realities in a vastly different frame-of-mind than that of the small boy who started the present journey with his "Uncle Donald" on December 7, 1959.

CHAPTER EIGHT

THE SHADOW OF SACRIFICE

Anna Cross Deignan and her adult children actually knew very little about the circumstances surrounding the death of her youngest son, P.F.C. Joseph J. Deignan, in Hawaii, during World War II. They never asked questions about that traumatic event and that is, I believe, the way the United States Army wanted it. Not until I, myself, started working on this project in the spring of 2005 did I, in fact, learn much more about how my uncle Donald Joseph actually met his death in March 1942. In retrospect, I am profoundly grateful, from a personal point of view, that his mother, brothers and sisters never knew what I have discovered about his tragic demise. It is to a consideration of that harrowing event, and of the historical context in which it occurred, that this penultimate Chapter must now turn.

Since at least 1920, successive Commanding Generals in the United States Army's Hawaiian Department had anticipated that

American soldiers assigned to that garrison would one day have to confront and repulse a ground invasion of the island of Oahu by Imperial Japanese military forces .[1] So the Hawaiian Division and its successor organizations, the 24th and the 25th Infantry Divisions, respectively, trained continuously for just such an eventuality. As long ago as 1911, Secretary of War Henry L. Stimson had warned that, "the foreign garrison should be prepared to defend itself at an instant's notice against a foe who may command the sea. Unlike the troops in the United States it can not count upon reinforcement or recruitment. It is an outpost on which will fall the brunt of the first attack in case of war."[2] In 1911 Mr. Stimson could not have predicted the important part which airpower would acquire in modern warfare. But otherwise his thirty year old warning about the nature of war between Japan and the United States, at least during its first six months, remained altogether prescient and entirely valid.

When, on the morning of December 7, 1941, Japanese bombs and bullets began falling on the U.S. Navy's Pacific Fleet at Pearl Harbor and on military airfields and other installations all across Oahu it must have seemed to American Army planners on the spot that the opening scene of the long-expected, ground-invasion scenario, with which they were all so familiar, was playing itself out before their very eyes. But they were not caught entirely by surprise by Japan's sudden attack. It will be recalled from Chapter Six that General Wilson, Commander of the 24th Infantry Division, and his Divisional and Departmental colleagues in Hawaii had increased preparedness for the imminent outbreak of hostilities with Japan in the few months just before Pearl Harbor.

Although a devastating, pre-emptive strike at the American Navy's Pacific Fleet based in Pearl Harbor was an integral part of Japan's master plan for its war against the United States, a ground invasion of the Hawaiian Island's was not, initially at least, a Japanese strategic objective. The attack's primary purpose was to sideline the U.S. Navy in the Pacific long enough to allow Japan, unhindered, to complete its vital program of territorial conquests in resource-rich Southeast Asia. After the attack on Pearl Harbor, a follow-up ground invasion of Oahu—which the U.S. Army's Hawaiian Command very much anticipated—was for the Japanese something of a strategic leitmotif; a project periodically discussed but never attempted. Thus, from December 7, 1941 onwards, there was a fundamental divergence in Japanese and American strategic thinking which lasted until the battle of Midway in June 1942, by which time P.F.C. Joseph J. Deignan was long since dead.

In April 1941 when serious planning for the Pearl Harbor onslaught from the air and sea first got underway, the possibility of a ground invasion of the Hawaiian Islands by Japanese troops was raised but, "This idea never progressed beyond informal chitchat…."[3] In September, 1941, as substantive preparations for war with the United States progressed, the Japanese Combined Fleet under the command of Admiral Isoroku Yamamoto held "war games" to test its Pearl Harbor strategy and tactics but, once again, "No serious discussion of an attempt to occupy Hawaii took place" during those exercises.[4] Admiral Yamamoto's Chief of Staff, Rear Admiral Ugaki, thought that the Japanese, "…would have enough problems in executing the aerial strike without adding an amphibious assault. Yamamoto agreed…that Operation Hawaii should include no plan for invasion."[5] As if to emphasize this point, Yamamoto had stressed that the Imperial Japanese Army did not need to be involved in the navy's Pearl Harbor mission.[6] Only after Japan's stunning tactical success on December 7, 1941 did Admiral Yamamoto reconsider his earlier opposition to a Hawaiian ground invasion:

> Less than forty-eight hours after the opening of the Pacific War, Admiral Yamamoto signed orders directing his staff to prepare plans for an invasion of Hawaii. He reasoned that the Hawaii base was the only direct threat to…the Japanese homeland. It contained the headquarters of the U.S. Pacific Fleet and combined the crucial repair and storage facilities for all the American armed forces there.…Hawaii was now the home of communications and intelligence operations for the entire Pacific area and would serve as the launching pad for any U.S. counteroffensive against Japan. The U.S. Pacific Fleet had temporarily lost its battleships, but those American aircraft carriers remained a dangerous fighting force. The loss of facilities on Oahu alone would have required the United States to consider its options in a long-distance war with Japan. The U.S. armed forces would have been compelled to operate from mainland bases on the West Coast. Australia and

> New Zealand, as well as Alaska and the Panama
> Canal, would be exposed and vulnerable....
> Some of the officers on Yamamoto's staff even
> put forth the idea of using Hawaii as the spring-
> board for an invasion of the West Coast of the
> United States.[7]

But for all the significant strategic advantages which the occupation of the Hawaiian Islands would undoubtedly provide to Japan,
the opportunity to mount such an operation was already slip-
ping away even in the immediate aftermath of Pearl Harbor . For
no troop transports had accompanied the Japanese aircraft car-
rier strike force and so Yamamoto vacillated. Ultimately, external
events made up his mind for him. The American island of Guam
fell easily to invading Japanese troops on December 10, 1941 after desultory fighting around Government House in Agana, the
Territorial Capital.[8] But, by contrast, the U.S. Marine garrison on
Wake Island put up a stubborn and effective defense against the
initially small enemy detachment sent to subdue it.[9] Accordingly,
on December 16, two aircraft carriers, two heavy cruisers and
two destroyers—all of which had taken part in the recent Pearl
Harbor operation—were diverted from their homeward voyage
and sent to assist in the attack on Wake Island. This diversion scut-
tled any Hawaiian invasion plan at least for the time being.[10] Less
than ten days later, by the time that the bulk of the Pearl Harbor
strike force had returned to Japanese home waters:

> Yamamoto had already decided that, after some
> crew rest, reprovisioning, and repair, he would

be sending Admiral Nagumo's fleet south to Truk in the Caroline Islands. From there, the First Air Fleet would support landings in the Australian mandated islands of New Guinea, New Britain, and New Ireland. They would assist the Second and Third Fleets in the taking of the Philippines, Borneo, Java, and the… Celebes….Occupying all these islands, along with Malaya and Burma, would complete the conquests that Japan hoped would supply the oil, rice, rubber, tin, and other strategic commodities needed to sustain its war."[11]

Even then, Japan's plan for its "Eastern Operation," the codename given to the eventual invasion of Hawaii, was not shelved entirely. As 1942 began, Rear Admiral Matome Ugaki—Yamamoto's chief of staff—formulated an ambitious attack plan for the new year. Once the remaining American island outposts in the Central Pacific had been captured—and the remnants of the U.S. Navy's Pacific Fleet had been destroyed in a climactic mid-ocean contest with its powerful Japanese counterpart—the Hawaiian archipelago would be Japan's final and most valuable target and prize. Ugaki proposed to Yamamoto that, "After June of this year, we should occupy Midway, Johnston and Palmyra, send our air force forward to these islands and dispatch the combined fleet with an occupying force to occupy Hawaii and at the same time bring the enemy fleet into decisive battle."[12] Ironically, and precisely on schedule, Admirals Yamamoto and Ugaki got the "decisive battle" between the Imperial Japanese Navy and the United States Navy which they eagerly anticipated, but its outcome was far from what they had wished. During the Battle of Midway, which took place between June 3rd and 7th, 1942, the immense opposing fleets of warships never sighted each other. Instead, the pivotal contest which then took place over the middle of the Pacific Ocean was exclusively between airplanes and ships. By the time the battle ended, four of the Japanese aircraft carriers which had launched the Pearl Harbor raid had been sunk by attacking American planes. As those blazing hulks sank they took with them 332 combat aircraft and 1,255 of the highly experienced pilots and sailors who had participated in the Pearl Harbor assault.[13] Japan never recovered from the catastrophic human and materiel losses which its Imperial Navy suffered at Midway. With that defeat, the Japanese invasion threat to Hawaii was effectively over.

In the six months prior to Midway, however, the beleaguered American defenders of Oahu had no way of knowing that strategic events would turn out for the United States as they did. In the interim, they had to prepare for the worst and that preparation in itself took a toll on all of them. During that period—while the Japanese vacillated with regard to their Hawaiian invasion plans—the Americans, P.F.C. Joseph J. Deignan among them, "dug-in" and waited for the next blow to fall.

It had long been an article of faith among U.S. Army planners that, in the event of war with Japan, Oahu would be subjected to an invasion by Japanese ground forces. In the earliest years of the Twentieth Century, American military strategists had drafted elaborate, color-coded plans intended to deal with the eventuality of war in the Pacific between the United States (Blue) and several other powerful nations including Germany, Russia, Britain and Japan, which received the color code designation "Orange." In December 1935, a U.S. Army Intelligence estimate predicted that Japan would probably, "…attack at once with a view to the capture of Hawaii, Alaska, the Philippines and Guam…." The enemy would adopt, "a generally active defensive attitude with the main fleet based on Japan and waging an active submarine war of attrition based on the Hawaiian Islands." Predicated as it was on the element of "surprise," Japan's supposed war plan—in the Army's view—contained, "so many temptations and offers so many inducements which accord so nearly with the Orange character that it is safe to say that the plan has been considered and worked out in all its details and if opportunity beckons too hard Orange will succumb and make the attempt."[14]

Although it is clear that the American military establishment was not altogether surprised by the outbreak of war with Japan in December 1941, the immense geographical scope of the simultaneously coordinated attacks all across the Pacific—together with their amazing initial success—stunned, equally, defense officials in Washington D.C. and those in Hawaii as well. Their strategic outlook was uniformly pessimistic.

In the first few days after Pearl Harbor, Navy planners in Washington suggested that there was a "grave possibility…the Japanese might capture the Hawaiian Islands."[15] At the same time, Army strategists in the War Department concluded gloomily that, "the naval situation in the Pacific is such that a successful defense of Hawaii cannot he absolutely assured."[16] On December 11, 1941, the date on which Germany and Italy declared war on the United States, Admiral Stark—Chief of Naval Operations—told General George C. Marshall—Army Chief of Staff—how bleak the situation in Hawaii was and added:

> This picture…is not over drawn. The Hawaiian Islands are in terrible danger of early capture. Every resource of the United States in ships, troops, aircraft, and material should be considered available for use in this emergency…."[17]

Since no Japanese invasion immediately occurred, however, alarmist sentiments in Washington, at least, soon began to diminish. "By Christmas it was clear that Hawaii was no longer in immediate danger of invasion…and that, while raids and hit-and-run attacks in the eastern Pacific were still possible, a large amphibious operation in that area was most unlikely."[18] In early February, 1942. Secretary of War Henry L. Stimson assured his Navy counterpart, Secretary Frank Knox, that Hawaii was, "the best equipped of all our overseas departments…."[19]

Military authorities in Hawaii—not to mention the large and diverse civilian population of the islands—were far less sanguine about their situation than were the Washington strategists and politicians. In the immediate aftermath of Pearl Harbor, "invasion fever" was high. On December 7th itself:

There were at least a dozen reports of paratroop landings in different places…and Japanese voices were heard constantly on short wave radio. People saw flashing signal lights, flares, swatches cut in sugar cane fields to form arrows pointing at vital installations. Word that the water supply of Honolulu had been poisoned spread rapidly, and Japanese landing parties were observed at various points. The wildest tales were believed. A truck that had been delivering milk for months to Hickam Field became, on the morning of the 7th, a Japanese armored vehicle, complete with troops and machine guns. Japanese cars and trucks were supposed to have deliberately created traffic jams on the roads leading to military installations. Japanese pilots wore civilian clothes, it was thought, so that they could mingle with the civil population if they were shot down. Finally, it was reliably reported that on a specified kilocycle a message "Chopsticks, I don't want to set the world on fire. Why can't it happen again tonight"—was heard, and all preparations were made for another attack on Pearl Harbor.[20]

Civilian and military officials in Hawaii had been preparing since 1939 for the outbreak of war in the Pacific between Japan and the United States of America. During 1941, the planning process gathered headway in preparation for "M Day," the codename given to the date on which hostilities would actually commence. The centerpiece of this planning process was the imposition of Martial Law throughout the Hawaiian Islands as soon as war began. The Territory's elderly civilian Governor, Joseph B. Poindexter—appointed by the Secretary of the Department of the Interior—assumed that he would continue to have administrative functions to perform even after the war started. But the United States Army had long had other ideas.

Late on the morning of December 7, 1941, not long after the second wave of Japanese warplanes had finished their final attack on Pearl Harbor and its supporting military installations on Oahu, Lieutenant General Walter C. Short—Commanding General of the Army's Hawaiian Department—requested a meeting with Governor Poindexter. In the course of that meeting, General Short *requested* that the Governor declare Martial Law, immediately, and, at the same time, that he should turn almost all the functions of the civilian Territorial Government over to the Army until further notice. In itself, the request for a declaration of Martial Law came as no surprise to Poindexter but Short's demand that the civilian authorities should cede day-to-day control of almost all aspects of life in the Islands to the military left Poindexter surprised, deeply shaken and in tears. In the end, Poindexter reluctantly acceded to Short's peremptory demand for absolute power and both men issued simultaneous, parallel declarations of Martial Law.

The reasons given for doing so were equally clear in both documents. In his Declaration, Poindexter stated that:

WHEREAS, the armed forces of the Empire of Japan have this day attacked and invaded the shores of the Hawaiian Islands; and

WHEREAS, it has become necessary to repel such attack and invasion; and

WHEREAS, the public safety requires;

NOW, THEREFORE, I, J. B. POINDEXTER, Governor of the Territory of Hawaii, do hereby announce that … I have called upon the Commanding General, Hawaiian Department, to prevent such invasion;

And,…I do hereby suspend the privilege of the writ of habeas corpus until further notice;

And,…I do hereby place the said territory under martial law;…."[21]

General Short left Poindexter a "fig-leaf" of civilian authority when he allowed the Territorial Governor to declare Martial Law and to ask for the Army's intervention to repel the imminent threat of a Japanese ground invasion of the Hawaiian Islands. But, in the next paragraph of his Declaration, Poindexter's complete capitulation to Army authority was made unmistakably clear. He wrote, "And I do hereby authorize and request the Commanding General, Hawaiian Department, during the present emergency and until the danger of invasion is removed, to exercise all the powers normally exercised by me as Governor…."[22] For good measure, Governor Poindexter further authorized General Short, "…and those subordinate military personnel to whom he may delegate such authority, during the present emergency and until the danger of invasion is removed, to exercise the powers normally exercised by judicial officers and employees of this territory and of the counties and Cities therein, and such other and further powers as the emergency may require…."[23]

Although the Territory's civilian government was never formally abolished by the Martial Law decrees, it was left for more than a year after Pearl Harbor with no real functions to perform. As a practical matter, the United States Army was in complete control. In his parallel Proclamation of Martial Law, General Short—who styled himself from December 7 onwards as "Military Governor" of the Hawaiian Islands—made the Army's new role perfectly clear. Because:

> The military and naval forces of the Empire of Japan have attacked and attempted to invade these islands….I announce to the people of Hawaii, that, in compliance with the above requests of the Governor of Hawaii, I have this day assumed the position of military governor of Hawaii, and have taken charge of the government of the Territory, of the preservation of order therein, and of putting these islands in a proper state of defense. [24]

With impending Japanese invasion in immediate prospect, Short intended to act swiftly and decisively to forestall the threat from the enemy. He declared that, "The troops under my command, in putting down any disorder or rebellion and in preventing any aid to the invader, will act with such firmness and vigor and will use such arms as the accomplishment of their task may require." Even Short, however, recognized the extraordinary nature of the current situation when he admitted that, "The imminence of attack by the enemy and the possibility of invasion make necessary a stricter control of your actions than would be necessary or proper at other times."[25]

Governor General Short bestowed sweeping powers upon himself. He declared to the Hawaiian people:

> I shall therefore shortly publish ordinances governing the conduct of the people of the Territory with respect to the showing of lights, circulation, meetings, censorship, possession of arms, ammunition, and explosives, the sale of intoxicating liquors and other subjects."

> In order to assist in repelling the threatened invasion of our island home, good citizens will cheerfully obey this proclamation and the ordinances to be published; others will be required to do so. Offenders will be severely punished by military tribunals or will be held in custody until such time as the civil courts are able to function.[26]

General Short's tenure as Military Governor of Hawaii was to be brief. Both he and his Naval counterpart—Admiral Husband E. Kimmel, Commander of the Pacific Fleet at Pearl Harbor—were officially "blamed" for not being better prepared to anticipate and to ward off the Japanese attacks from the air and sea on December 7th. Each of them was relieved of duty, reduced in rank and forced to retire from their respective services in professional disgrace. Both Short and Kimmel spent the remainder of their lives trying, unsuccessfully, to vindicate themselves and to restore their professional reputations.

The Martial Law regime which General Short put forcibly into place on the afternoon of Pearl Harbor Day long outlasted him. Some of its more stringent provisions were relaxed slightly in March 1943 but it was not ended entirely until October 1944. Not surprisingly, the Army favored the retention of Martial Law for as long as possible because it allowed the military to retain social and economic control over most aspects of life in the Islands. The business community also tended to favor the system because it controlled working conditions and wages and froze most workers into their current jobs. From the first, however, most of Hawaii's legal community opposed Martial Law both philosophically and practically. As J. Garner Anthony, Hawaii's civilian Attorney General, remarked at the time:

> It was futile to mention what the law was, for
> the Military Governor was the law. The choice
> was clear: obey or be punished, irrespective of

the law, whose force and effect had been supplanted by the force of military control."[27]

Furthermore, ordinary civilians in Hawaii soon found out that the military was prepared to impose rules and regulations on them which it was not equally willing to apply to its own uniformed members or to war workers. Again, to quote Attorney General Anthony who was highly critical of the Martial Law regime:

> One thing particularly irritating to the civilian population was that the blackout and curfew were not applied to Army and Navy posts or to the waterfront in Honolulu. Civilians could look down from their homes in the heights above Honolulu and see the city below in total darkness except for the waterfront, which was ablaze, conducting the busy work of loading and unloading freighters. To the west of the city lay the Army airfield, Hickam Field, and farther on lay Pearl Harbor itself, both illuminated like Christmas trees. The same was true of Schofield Barracks, Bellows Field, and the Kaneohe Naval Air Station.[28]

For all their occasional discontent with certain aspects of Martial Law, in the months between Pearl Harbor in December 1941 and the Battle of Midway in June 1942, most people recognized that stringent regulation of their day-to-day lives was necessary as long as the threat of a Japanese invasion of the Hawaiian Islands was a real possibility. And, as has already been seen, in the days, weeks and months immediately following Pearl Harbor, the threat of an enemy ground invasion of Hawaii seemed to be very real. For, as one historian has cogently observed:

> These were the blackest days of the war for the United States....Guam, Wake Island, Hong Kong, Singapore, and Thailand were in Japanese hands. All of Borneo had been taken. The Philippine Islands were being overrun and Port Darwin in Australia had been bombed. The Japanese seemed invincible, and their easy victories astonished even their own military planners. They were far ahead of their own schedule for conquests."[29]

In this context, the extreme nervousness of many Hawaiian civilians who expected an invasion at any time was entirely understandable. Even if the master strategists in the War and Navy Departments back in Washington D.C. had concluded by Christmas 1941 that a Japanese ground assault on Oahu was increasingly unlikely, their subordinates on the scene in Honolulu did not share that conviction.

The new Army Commander of the Hawaiian Department, Lieutenant General Delos C. Emmons—who had replaced General Short on December 17, 1941—had requested massive reinforcements from the United States Mainland, including two additional Infantry Divisions. The War Department promised him only one of them, the 27th Infantry Division, which had still not arrived in the islands in full strength even by the end of March 1942.[30] General Emmons, who assumed Short's title of Military Governor, mistrusted Hawaii's large population of Japanese-born aliens who might well aid the enemy in the event of an invasion. He was equally unsympathetic to the fervent pleas of patriotism and genuine loyalty of the numerous "Americans of Japanese Ancestry" or "A.J.A's" who inhabited the Islands. They wanted nothing more than to serve the American war effort and to be allowed to fight for the United States, if permitted to do so.[31]

General Emmons, a West Virginian, a West Point graduate and a distinguished Army Air Corps pilot and strategist, was a distant and brusque administrator who had relatively little sympathy for the wartime hardships faced by Hawaii's diverse civilian population. From the time when he assumed his post in December 1941 until he relinquished it at the end of June 1943, Military Governor Emmons was an efficient and busy administrative officer. As will be seen presently, in his role as Commander of the Hawaiian Department, General Emmons would figure prominently in the reporting and investigation of P.F.C. Deignan's mysterious and untimely death on the North Shore of Oahu on March 18, 1942.

In the first six months after Pearl Harbor both the civilian population and the military garrison of the Hawaiian Islands were on edge and anxious about a Japanese invasion. Although unfounded rumors and numerous false alarms were rife, the inhabitants and defenders of Hawaii, alike, had good reason to be uneasy.

On the nights of December 15th, 30th, and 31st, 1941, Japanese submarines surfaced and shelled various locations on Hawaii's outer islands with their deck guns.[32] But instead of being the prelude to invasion, the shelling of various Hawaiian targets by Japanese submarines were, in effect, "parting shots." For, "Prior to returning to their Marshall Islands bases for refueling and resupply, the Japanese boats were supposed to surface and fire their deck guns at onshore targets if conditions were favorable for such action."[33]

In the early weeks of March 1942, the Japanese hatched an even more ambitious plan to rattle the nerves of Oahu's civilian residents and military defenders. The enemy determined, once again, to bomb Pearl Harbor. Late on the night of March 4, 1942—exactly two weeks before Donald's sudden death by gunshot—a pair of long-range Japanese Navy seaplanes took off from their base in the Marshall Islands and, after refueling from a submarine at sea, dropped a number of 550- pound bombs on suburban Honolulu. Their target, Pearl Harbor, was obscured by heavy clouds and darkness so their bombs fell harmlessly either into the ocean or onto the slopes of a sparsely populated mountain just outside Honolulu. Japanese propaganda claimed that heavy damage and casualties had once again been inflicted at Pearl Harbor but this assertion was entirely false.[34] If Donald— stationed as he then was on the other side of Oahu—was even aware of this attack, he could not share his reactions to it or his feelings about it with his family because, "All servicemen in Hawaii had been warned not to include any information about military operations in their correspondence."[35]

Further island-wide air-raid alerts for the civilian population and the military installations on Oahu followed on March 7 when enemy planes were supposedly detected over the northern-most point of the island, close to Donald's actual location. On March 14, 1942, just four days before P.F.C. Deignan's death, air-raid alarms sounded once again throughout Oahu.[36] The effect was that American nerves, throughout the island, were seriously frayed.

By mid-March 1942, then, Donald and all his military comrades had been under constant, severe physical and psychological stress for three and one-half months, ever since the attack on Pearl Harbor. The devastating impact of this cumulative stress and strain upon Donald, individually, will be considered in detail later in this Chapter. First, however, the "internal narrative" in Donald's IDPF must now be considered.

In Chapter Six, I examined in detail the "public version" or perhaps more accurately "the Public Relations Version," from the United States Army's point of view, of the events surrounding Donald's death, initial burial and final reburial. The relevant pages from his IDPF (Individual Deceased Personnel File) cited there portrayed him, generically at least, as one hero among many other heroes, all of whom had "given their lives for our country." That particular narrative, based largely as it was on official letters which passed between the Army and Donald's parents from mid 1942 until early 1953, was intended to comfort his family and to validate his "supreme sacrifice" on behalf of the American people. With the exception of the discordant

"Coombs incident," recounted in Chapter Six, the tone of the "public narrative" was gentle, reassuring and even sentimental.

But, in effect, that same IDPF contained within its pages a second, parallel, confidential narrative of events which was never intended either for public disclosure or consumption. This portion of the IDPF, created exclusively for the Army's own internal, institutional use, told a radically different and a much darker story about the circumstances of Donald's death than did the alternate information supplied by the Army to his mother over the course of the decade and more between 1942 and 1953.

From the start the IDPF's "confidential narrative," whose compilation began within a few hours after P.F.C. Joseph J. Deignan's sudden, violent demise, was vague, fragmentary and even contradictory. The Telegram from the War Department addressed, unfortunately, to Donald's late father but received by his mother on March 20, 1942 informed his parents that their youngest son had "died in service in Hawaii yesterday...," according to the caption under the headline **"Dies In Hawaii"** which appeared on Page One of **The Worcester Evening Gazette** that same night. This newspaper piece served as Donald's Obituary.

Ironically, like the accidental death of his father, Bernard, almost two and one half years earlier, P.F.C. Deignan's passing was front page news in one of his home town's newspapers. This partial coverage is probably owing to the fact that The Worcester Telegram was the morning paper and so it would have not received word of Donald's death before it went to press early on March 20, 1942.

Within the body of the news story, it was stated that, "Pvt. First Class Joseph J. Deignan, 25, died yesterday in Schofield Barracks, Hawaii, of a gunshot wound." Rather surprisingly, since a reporter had evidently spoken with his mother before writing the story, **The Evening Gazette** got Donald's age wrong twice. In two places the paper listed his age as 25 but in fact Joseph J. Deignan was actually 27 years old at the time of his death. [37]

The same day his "Obituary" appeared in the **Worcester Evening Gazette**, the United States Army had taken official notice of the death of Private First Class Joseph J. Deignan. Very early on the morning of March 20, 1942, a radio-telegrapher at Fort Shafter—Headquarters of the Army's Hawaiian Department—had informed the Adjutant General's Office in Washington, DC of P.F.C. Deignan's death. The tone of this particular, official document was deliberately emphatic and almost clinical in character. It read, in part:

> P 12 WTJ LF 192 WD 1 EX PRTY
>
> FTSHAFTER TH 0155 CST MAR TWENTY 1942
>
> THE ADJUTANT GENERAL
>
> WASHINGTON DC
>
> REMYRAD NINETEEN MARCH FORTY TWO REPORTING DEATH OF JOSEPH J DEIGNAN SIX ONE FOUR ONE FOUR

EIGHT ONE PFC SPECIALIST FOURTH CLASS FA FOLLOWING COMPLETE AND CORRECTED REPORT IS SUBMITTED STOP DIED ELEVEN EIGHTEEN PM EIGHTEEN MARCH FORTY TWO REPEAT EIGHTEEN MARCH FORTY TWO ONE FOURTH MILE EAST OF WAIMEAOAHU TH STOP.[38]

Here the variance between the "Public" and the "Internal" Army Records and IDPF "narratives" began. Donald's mother, Anna, had been informed in the March 20 War Department Telegram notifying her of his death that her son had died at "Schofield Barracks," where he had been stationed since September 14th, 1939, when he officially joined Battery C of the 13th Field Artillery Battalion of the Army's old "Hawaiian Division." What Donald's disconsolate mother did not know, for perfectly good Army Intelligence reasons, was that he and his entire Battalion had been moved shortly after the attack on Pearl Harbor into defensive positions, several miles from Schofield Barracks, along the North Shore of the island of Oahu, at Waimea Bay.

During and immediately after the Japanese Air and Naval attacks on the United States Navy's Pacific Fleet at Pearl Harbor, authorities in the Army's Hawaiian Department anticipated a follow-up ground invasion of the archipelago by enemy forces. Accordingly, the Twenty Fifth Infantry Division was dispatched to take up defensive positions around Honolulu Harbor and its vicinity while the Twenty Fourth Infantry Division, its sister organization, was tasked with defending the Northern Sector of Oahu against the like eventuality. Thus, Donald and his comrades in Battery C. of the 13th F.A., were assigned to support their 24th Infantry colleagues in defending the northern half of the island of Oahu against an expected, imminent ground onslaught by the Japanese.

At 11:18 p.m. on Wednesday, March 18, 1942, one fourth of a mile east of Waimea Bay, a single gunshot shattered the almost perfect but terribly tense silence of that wartime Hawaiian night. The degree to which the troops guarding northern Oahu's beaches observed "black-out" conditions is not clear. Weather conditions that night are also unknown. But it is quite likely that the farther away from his defensive position a soldier wandered, for what ever reason, the darker his surroundings became. The direction from which the sound of the gunshot came was some distance uphill from the beach where "C" Battery of the 13th F.A. had been dug-in since the evening of December 7, 1941. Soldiers from Battery C who ran in the direction of the firearm's discharge to see what had just happened had to cross the "Kam Highway," a paved two-lane road, which paralleled their defensive positions strung out along the shore of nearby Waimea Bay. Once across the road, which linked them with Schofield Barracks and the City of Honolulu beyond it, the running men had to clamber in almost complete darkness up a steep hill covered by thick underbrush, jutting rocks, tangled bushes and increasingly dense stands of tropical trees. After some time, amid this difficult, jumbled terrain, the impromptu search party found the lifeless body of P.F.C. Joseph J. Deignan contorted on the ground and soaked in a widening pool of his own blood. It would be determined later that the single '45 Caliber Pistol bullet wound to his upper left chest had caused catastrophic internal injuries from which he died all but immediately after they were received.

Donald's bloody body was then picked up and placed either on a litter—if one was available—or more likely wrapped in an Army blanket and carried down the hill by several of his comrades. He weighed only 116 pounds, so handling him would not in itself have been a problem. But the combination of darkness and thick undergrowth would have made the transport of his body somewhat difficult. When the retrieval party reached the Kam Highway at the bottom of the hill his remains would have been placed in an ambulance or perhaps in the back of an Army truck and driven to the Battery C Dispensary at Schofield Barracks. Given the narrowness of the road and the "black-out" conditions being observed along its length, the trip would have taken some time to complete.

By 2:30 a.m. on the morning of March 19, 1942, however, Donald's body had arrived at Schofield Barracks and been examined at the Dispensary by a member of the Army Medical Corps who declared P.F.C. Deignan "Dead On Arrival."[39] The Battery C "Morning Report" for March 19 contained only one entry, "Pvt. First Class Deignan...Died..."[40] At 7:50 PM on Friday evening, March 20, Lieutenant General Emmons—Military Governor of Hawaii—sent the following, terse, telegraphic message to the Office of the Quartermaster General at the War Department in Washington D.C., **"REMAINS PFC JOSEPH J DEIGNAN SIX ONE FOUR ONE FOUR EIGHT ONE INTERRED MARCH TWENTY NINETEEN FORTY TWO IN POST CEMETERY SCHOFIELD BARRACKS TH PLOT TWO ROW L GRAVE SIXTEEN STOP A FOUR TWENTY P EMMONS 750 PM"**[41] Since the weekend was already well underway on the east coast of the United States, it was not until Monday, March 23, 1942 at 11:09 PM that the Telegraphic Section of the Quartermaster General's Office recorded receipt of General Emmons' message of the previous Friday.[42] General Emmons also reported Donald's death to the Office of the Adjutant General in Washington to whom he gave a fuller account of the circumstances of that event. For the moment it is only necessary to focus on the report which Emmons made to the Quartermaster General, not for what little it actually said but for the great deal which it did not say.

General Emmons's report to the Quartermaster General merely noted when and where Donald was buried. Pointedly, even for internal Army purposes, it said almost nothing either about the circumstances of Private First Class Deignan's death or about the particulars of his burial. As will be recalled from Chapter Six, on July 21, 1942, E.A. Stommel, Special Assistant to the Quartermaster General of the Army, had officially informed Bernard Deignan of the exact location of his son's final resting place. Mr. Stommel had then gone on to assert, "You may have the assurance that the burial was reverently and properly conducted…"[43] But Stommel's "assurance" about the manner in which Donald's initial interment was carried out was at least partially inaccurate. It is true that P.F.C. Deignan received the military honors due a fallen soldier prior to and at the time of his burial. General Emmons ordered his subordinate in command at Schofield Barracks to provide armed honor guards so as at all times, "…to insure that no bodies are ever left unattended prior to interment."[44] Ceremonial rifle volleys were indeed fired over Donald's grave by members of the 34th Infantry Regiment and "Taps" was also doubtless played at the time of his burial in the Schofield Barracks Post Cemetery.[45] But, for reasons which will be discussed shortly, no religious service of any kind was conducted on that occasion. In fact, on the March 1942 **"Report of Interment "** the spaces for "Type of Religious Ceremony" and "Person Conducting Burial Rites" were each left conspicuously blank.[46] At the top of this particular document the word **"RESTRICTED"** appears in black letters all capitalized type. Since this piece of information was contained within the confidential portion of the IDPF, Anna Deignan never knew that no Roman Catholic priest ever prayed over or even blessed her youngest son's body. *She was always merely allowed by the Army, for its own purposes, to believe otherwise.*

The lack of any religious ceremony at his March 1942 funeral was particular to Donald. But in the years immediately following World War II, additional generic indignities—equally unknown to his mother—were to be visited upon Donald's earthly remains. During the Pacific Campaign, American soldiers who died overseas were buried, initially, near the place where they had fallen. After the War their remains were removed from these temporary locations and, in accordance with the express wishes of "Next Of Kin," either eventually buried in American Military Cemeteries overseas or returned to the Mainland United States for final interment near home. From Chapter Six it will be recalled that Donald's mother had requested that her son should be buried in Hawaii at the newly established National Memorial Cemetery of the Pacific in Honolulu. In meeting her wishes, and those of tens of thousands of other bereaved survivors of World War II casualties, the Army had a huge administrative and logistical task to perform. Thus, between 1947 and 1949, the remains of thousands upon thousands of military personnel were disinterred, warehoused, processed and reburied on an almost industrial scale. Specifically, in Donald's case, on September 26, 1947, authorities at the Schofield Barracks Post Cemetery in Hawaii received a "Disinterment Directive" from the Memorial Division of the Quartermaster General's Office at the War Department in Washington D.C. ordering them to exhume Donald's body and prepare it for removal, in due course, to the Memorial Cemetery of the Pacific for final re-interment there. Accordingly, on October 6, 1947, Donald—in his **"Temp. Casket"**—was removed from Plot 2, Row L, Grave 16 and examined. Next to the entry **"Condition of Remains"**, on the **REPORT OF INTERMENT**, the notation **"Skeleton Incomplete"** was made. After its exhumation, Donald's body was brought to a warehouse elsewhere at Schofield Barracks to await final **"Disposition"** of his remains. There his flag-draped "box" resided—placed in ranks among many others on tiers of metal shelves—for almost five full months.[47] Finally, on February 2, 1948, Donald's remains were placed in a permanent casket by William J. Williams—a civilian Embalmer—and on the same date the casket was sealed, marked and boxed for shipment by J.N. Robinson. After that, however, Donald would have to wait for more than a year before being finally laid to rest in Section B., Grave 100 at the National Memorial Cemetery of the Pacific in Honolulu on February 4, 1949. As in 1942, the 1947 "Disinterment Directive" in the space provided for "Religion" was marked "Not Ind."

During her entire adult life, Anna Deignan had had a difficult time of it. She lost several children, abruptly, in infancy. She lived in real poverty throughout her married life. She had to cope for thirty-five years with a drinking husband and all that that behavior implied for her large family. Finally, she experienced the traumatic and unexpected death of her youngest son during wartime. If Anna Deignan had known how her youngest boy was, for the most part, to be treated for the seven years between the time of his death in 1942 and the date of his final burial in Hawaii in 1949, she would have been well and truly heartbroken. But if Anna had known the rest of the real story surrounding her son's sudden death, she would have been utterly devastated. Had she actually known the supposed "facts," according to the Army, Donald's name would never after have been mentioned at all in family gatherings, let alone in the reverential and sentimental tones in which it was occasionally invoked. But, of course, Anna Deignan never knew anything about the actual circumstances of her youngest son's death or its aftermath because the Army intended that she should not know them.

Internal Army documents contained within the IDPF, itself, are central to understanding how Donald actually met his death on the night of March 18, 1942, but they are not the only surviving pieces of official information which serve to illuminate that event. Shortly after 2:30 A.M. on the morning of March 19, 1942 a member of the United States Army Medical Corps, unidentifiable because his signature is illegible, completed and signed a **"STANDARD CERTIFICATE OF DEATH"** for Joseph J. Deignan. It listed the time of death as 2:30 A.M. (March 19) but the date of death as March 18. This discrepancy can be accounted for by the fact, noted earlier, that Donald actually died some miles away from the place where he was eventually seen by the attending Army physician who signed his Death Certificate. Donald's "Immediate cause of death" was given as "1. Wound, penetrating, gunshot, upper abdomen." Item #22. on the Death Certificate instructed that "If death was due to external causes, fill in the following; *(a)* Accident, suicide, or homicide (Specify)......" The Army clerk filling out the Death Certificate for the Army Doctor who signed it dutifully typed "Suicide" in the space provided to account for a death "due to external causes..."[48] According to the Army, then, Donald deliberately ended his own life with a single pistol shot to his "upper left chest."

Mention has already been made, earlier in this Chapter, of the Battery C "Morning Report" for the entire month of March 1942. The only notation for March 19 was, "Pvt. First Class Deignan...Died...". Next to that entry, on the same line and between parentheses, was the single, handwritten word "Suicide."

This stark notation, in itself, explains completely why no Roman Catholic priest would officiate at Donald's Schofield Barracks funeral the next afternoon. For "Suicide" was, at the time, regarded by the Roman Catholic Church as a grievous or "Mortal Sin" sufficiently serious to condemn the person committing such an act to damnation in Hell for eternity. Paradoxically, the Army honored Donald as a fallen comrade but the priests in uniform and on duty at Schofield Barracks in 1942 Hawaii considered Donald's Immortal Soul "lost forever" as the result of his evidently self-destructive act. Fortunately, the Church's understanding of the psychological complexities inherent in suicidal behavior has changed markedly and compassionately in recent decades. This profound theological and attitudinal change on the part of our Church has enabled me, as will be seen in the next and last Chapter, to provide Donald with some significant spiritual help even at this very late date. For the present, however, our focus must return to the events of March 18-20, 1942 and their aftermath.

Even as early as mid-morning on March 19, 1942, the Army's Hawaiian bureaucracy had already begun constructing and compiling its "internal narrative" pertaining to Donald's death. It already had in hand the Death Certificate signed by a member of its own Medical Corps who had attributed P.F.C. Deignan's demise to "Suicide" and described the fatal injuries which he had sustained thereby in clinical and graphic detail. The "Morning Report" from Battery C was the next piece of evidence added to the Army's lengthening documentary chain. There was still more official material to come.

Around 2:25 P.M. (14:25 in Military parlance), on March 19th, Governor General Emmons drafted the following message to the Adjutant General—the Army's chief administrative officer— in Washington, DC. Emmons wrote:

JOSEPH J DEIGNAN SIX ONE FOUR ONE EIGHT FOUR ONE

PVT FIRST CLASS FIELD ARTY SCOBKS TH FOUND DEAD TWO THIRTY AM NINETEENTH MAR NINETEEN FORTY TWO AT SCOBKS.... CAUSE OF DEATH GUN SHOT WOUND LEFT CHEST APPARENTLY SELF INFLICTED.... NEAREST RELATIVE MR BERNARD DEIGNAN FATHER ONE NINE FIVE LINCOLN ST WORCESTER MASS....

The Lieutenant General and Military Governor of the Hawaiian Islands tantalizingly concluded this particular piece of correspondence with, **"FURTHER DETAILS LATER... EMMONS."** His message was sent to the Adjutant General at 3:23P.M. local time on the afternoon of March 19, 1942.[49] The Army Telegrapher in Hawaii who sent the message from General Emmons, just quoted above, made a simple but significant mistake in its transmission. He transposed one of the digits in Donald's Army Serial Number: Instead of sending the correct number "6141481" he sent "6141841." This routine error was to have important and beneficial consequences for Donald's story in years to come.

In promising **"FURTHER DETAILS LATER..."** General Emmons was as good as his word. At 12:26 A.M., local time, on the morning of March Twentieth 1942, his staff at Fort Shafter—Headquarters of the Hawaiian Department—completed drafting the following message to the Adjutant General in Washington D.C. Emmons characterized this document as a **"... COMPLETE AND CORRECTED REPORT..."** of Donald's death. P.F.C. Deignan of the Field Artillery had died at 11:18 P.M. on March 18, 1942 **" ONE FOURTH MILE EAST OF WAIMEA OAHU TH"** (Territory of Hawaii). Emmons went on to confirm that the direct cause of Donald's death was indeed **"...GUNSHOT WOUNDS LEFT CHEST...APPARENTLY SELF INFLICTED...."** This sentence is in itself intriguing in that it speaks of "gunshot wounds" rather than of a single "gunshot wound" as had been the case in earlier correspondence on the subject. Within this same "Corrected and Complete Report of Death" Emmons described the clinical details of the immense damage which the bullet(s) had done to Donald's liver and other internal organs when the 45 Caliber Pistol he was supposedly holding discharged into his chest. The use here of the plural **"GUNSHOT WOUNDS"** may—like the earlier digital transposition in his serial number—have been nothing more than a telegraphic error. But, on the other hand, the next sentence in Emmons's "Corrected and Complete Report" did nothing to dispel the confusion which the use of the word **"WOUNDS"** had just created. It referenced the **"QUESTION"** of Donald's death was in the **"LINE OF DUTY AND MISCONDUCT"** as still **"BEING DETERMINED BY BOARD OF OFFICERS."** If Donald did in fact deliberately take his own life did he also

fire more than one bullet into his chest at that terribly dark mo-
ment? General Emmons had nothing more to say on that matter
or any other pertaining to the death of P.F.C. Deignan. What
Emmons did add, however, was that Donald's **"NEAREST
RELATIVE AND DESIGNATED BENEFICIARY'** was **"MR
BERNARD DEIGNAN...FATHER...ONE NINETY FIVE
LINCOLN STREET WORCESTER MASS WHO HAS NOT
BEEN NOTIFIED BY THIS HEADQUARTERS."** Even if
Donald had not changed his beneficiary from his deceased father
to his loving mother, he had allowed three dollars and forty cents
per month to be deducted from his pay which entitled his "desig-
nated beneficiary" to receive **" FIVE THOUSAND DOLLARS
NATIONAL SERVICE LIFE INSURANCE."** Governor
General Emmons concluded his Corrected and Complete
Report by informing the Adjutant General that Donald's re-
mains **"...WILL BE INTERRED AT POST CEMETERY
SCHOFIELD BARRACKS TH."** Per standard procedure, the
document was signed simply **"EMMONS".**[50]

This then, according to the Army, was the "complete" internal
narrative record of Donald's death contained within his IDPF.
But that entire document said nothing whatsoever about his
state of mind in March 1942 nor did it identify, or much less
speculate upon, any possible motive for his supposedly "suicidal"
action at that time.

Superficially, at least, it appears that the Army "went by the book"
in its handling of P.F.C. Deignan's sudden death. Army Regulation
(AR 600-550), which dealt with "PERSONNEL DECEASED,"

covered such matters thoroughly. Paragraph 19 of that document stated that "W.D.A.G.O. [War Department Adjutant General's Office] Form No. 52 (Report of Death) was to be used. AR 600-550 required that "in the case of every person subject to military law as defined in the second article of war [a Report of Death] will be prepared in triplicate, immediately subsequent to the date of death, by the surgeon or by the immediate commanding officer of the deceased..."[51] As we have already seen, this procedure was carried out promptly and routinely in Donald's case. Furthermore, reference was made in two of the three messages sent over General Emmons' signature to the War Department, in the hours immediately following Donald death, to an investigation into the matter being made by a "Board of Officers." This action, too, was mandated by AR 600-550 under certain circumstances.

Paragraph 21, subparagraph (a) of that Regulation entitled "Investigation and report by board of officers..." required that, "(1) Under the conditions stated in (2) and (8) below, the commanding officer of the post, camp, station, or transport where a death has occurred will convene a board of officers, at least one of whom shall be a medical officer, when such officer is available, to investigate the circumstances and report the facts leading up to and connected with the death, and to determine as a result of such investigation whether death occurred in line of duty and whether it was or was not the result of the deceased's own misconduct. Procedure and report of the board are prescribed in 5, o, 4, a, f, g h and 4 below.[52] The Army Medical Corps Doctor who examined Donald's body in the early morning hours of March 19, 1942 concluded that his death was attributable to "Suicide."

The Battery C "Morning Report" later that same day *merely noted that finding without explanation or comment*. But the "Complete and Corrected" Report by General Emmons, transmitted to the Adjutant General's Office in Washington on March 20, 1942 was much more cautious since it still described Donald's fatal injuries only as **"APPARENTLY SELF INFLICTED."**[53]

Thus, from the first, there was a material discrepancy in the surviving record between the "Suicide" finding of the attending Army physician and the final, official and more circumspect version of events sent by Emmons to Washington. Nowhere in the IDPF is there any evidence that the Board of Officers actually investigated either "… the circumstances" or "the facts leading up to and connected with the death…," as they were clearly required by Army Regulations to do.[54] Beyond any doubt, a Board of Officers was required to investigate Donald's death because "Investigation" was specifically called for, "in case death is due or is suspected to be due to foul play, violence or unnatural causes, or when death is sudden from unknown causes, except death from wounds or injuries received in action."[55]

Since no evidence concerning either "… the circumstances" or "the facts leading up to and connected with the death…" was included in Donald's record, it appears that his Board of Officers was at least partially derelict in the performance of its duty. They seem simply to have accepted the "Suicide" finding of the Medical Corps Doctor as sufficient explanation and let the matter rest there. Why was the Board of Officers not more thorough in making its mandatory investigation? I will return to a consideration of this question, in its particular historical context, in due course.

Leaving aside for the moment the evident procedural flaws in the official investigation of Donald's demise, it should be said that the version of AR 600-550 in effect at the time of his death had been issued as long ago as March 6, 1936. For its time, that Regulation's view of "Suicide" within the ranks was, theoretically at least, remarkably forward-looking and compassionate. Its primary purpose was to determine whether soldiers who committed suicide had died "in the line of duty" or as a result of their own deliberate "misconduct." The Regulation delineated two types of "Suicidal" behavior in instructing Boards of Officers to make such determinations:

> If. (1) Suicide is the deliberate and Intentional destruction of his own life by a person of years of discretion and of sound mind. In such case death is due to the misconduct of the deceased, and therefore, if he was in the military service, not in line of duty.

> (2) The taking of his own life by a person who, at the time of the act, is so mentally unsound as to be unable to realize the direct physical or moral consequences of the act, or by one who, having such realization, nevertheless, because of derangement of the reasoning or volitionary faculties, Is-unable to refrain from the act, may be properly termed "self- destruction

while mentally unsound." This does not constitute misconduct, and does not in itself alone, in cases arising in the military service, justify the finding "not in line of duty." In such cases the questions whether or not death was due to the misconduct of the deceased, and whether or not it occurred in line of duty, are determined with relation to the origin and cause of the mental unsoundness. If his mental unsoundness was due to misconduct of the deceased, then his death was due to such misconduct and was not in line of duty. If his mental unsoundness was not due to his own misconduct, then his death was not due to such misconduct, but nevertheless in such case, if his mental unsoundness was not Incurred in line of duty, his death also was not in line of duty. On the other hand, If the mental unsoundness was incurred In line of duty, and was not due to misconduct on the part of the deceased, his death should be regarded as having occurred in line of duty.[56]

Sub-paragraph (4) of Paragraph 21 of Army Regulation 600-550 established a number of grounds upon which the act of "Suicide" could be construed as, "misconduct" rather than as evidence of "mental unsoundness" on the part of a deceased soldier:

> The mere fact of self-destruction, or bona fide suicide attempt thereat, is not alone sufficient

to justify a finding of such mental unsoundness. Nor is such a finding justified where there is evidence of a reasonable or natural though normally Insufficient motive, such as desire to escape punishment or shame, grief over the death of someone beloved, disappointment in love, discouragement due to ill health or financial difficulties, or loss of self-respect due to bad habits or failures in undertakings, etc., unless there is further proof of actual mental unsoundness.[57]

By themselves, grief, shame, fear of punishment, disappointment in love, financial difficulties or a sense of personal inadequacy were not sufficient causes to allow Boards of Officers to conclude that soldiers who took their own lives while laboring under such burdens had died "in line of duty." But then the authors of AR 600-550 moved from the consideration of lesser motives for suicide into the realm of metaphysics and psychology. In the end, they came down on the side of compassion and common sense when evaluating suicide:

On the other hand, in view of the powerful instinct of self-preservation Inherent in human nature, and the natural repugnance of any sane man against taking his own life, it should ordinarily require very little definite proof of actual unsoundness of mind, in addition to the fact of actual or attempted self- destruction, to justify

a finding of mental Irresponsibility. Each case
should be decided upon its own merits In the
light of common sense, with a view to substantial justice both to the Government and to others concerned.[58]

Not surprisingly, AR 600-550—which had been drafted in
peacetime—did not consider the extreme, prolonged, chronic
and acute stresses to which soldiers were subjected during wartime as factors which could lead to the occurrence of "Suicide"
within the ranks.

In 1936, when the version of AR 600-550 which was still in
force at the time of Donald's death in 1942, had first been issued, America was at peace. In the mid 1930s, the United States
Army was a small and thoroughly professional force. Boards of
Officers who were tasked with looking into unexpected military deaths were supposed to deliver their findings only "…after
thorough Investigation and a consideration of all available evidence."[59] But in 1942 wartime Hawaii the United States Army
had neither the time, inclination nor resources to observe such
laudable peacetime niceties.

Even though the last sentence of Paragraph 21 of AR 600-550
required that, "The original report of the board with the action thereon of the commanding officer will be forwarded in
duplicate through military channels to The Adjutant General,"
that document never made its way into Donald's IDPF. It is owing only to the happy accident that a radio-telegrapher at Fort
Shafter inadvertently transposed a digit in Private First Class

Deignan's Army Serial Number on March 20, 1942—when his demise was reported to the War Department by General Emmons—that we know that even a pro-forma official investigation of Donald's death actually took place. A series of internal Army documents dealing with the error in the recording and reporting of Donald's death serve to confirm this conclusion.

As early as December 17, 1946, the Office of the Quartermaster General at the War Department in Washington D.C. had already begun tying up administrative loose ends from World War II. On that date an Assistant to the Quartermaster General wrote to the "Commanding General U.S. Army Forces, Middle Pacific" to "Request a duplicate Report of Burial be forwarded this office for the following decedent: Name: Deignan, Joseph J...Rank: Private First Class...Serial Number: 6141481...". This particular communication was directed to the "Attention" of "MIDPAC Sector Graves Registration Officer."[60] The Quartermaster General's Assistant did not indicate why he wanted a duplicate copy of Donald's 1942 "Report of Burial" but it is clear, in retrospect, that the Army was then trying to rectify the error in its official records which stemmed from the radiogram mistake made on the date of its original transmission. The original Serial Number transmission error was to be compounded over time by the Army's failure to correct it. The original "Report of Death" sent from Hawaii to Washington on March 20, 1942 had listed Private First Class Deignan's Serial Number, erroneously, as "6141841". The original "Report of Burial", on the same date, reproduced that mistake. Even though the Quartermaster General's December 17, 1946 correspondence to the "MIDPAC

Sector Graves Registration Officer" listed the correct Serial Number: "6141481", the rest of the Army's vast administrative bureaucracy still had not "gotten the Memo" by April 22, 1947. On that date the Army's **"REQUEST FOR DISPOSITION OF REMAINS"** Form, addressed to Bernard Deignan rather than to his long-time widow, Anna, continued to record Donald's Serial Number inaccurately with the 1942 transposed digit. In responding to the War Department's various pieces of official correspondence generated over the next two years, the Deignan family, in reply, continued to cite the same, wrong number because that is what they had been given by military authorities. Ironically, even the Quartermaster General himself perpetuated the historic clerical error when he wrote to Anna Deignan on April 27, 1949, to inform her that Donald's remains "…have been permanently interred…" at the National Memorial Cemetery of the Pacific in Honolulu. In that same letter, the Quartermaster General further carefully pointed out that, "Customary military services were conducted over the grave at the time of burial."[61] Once again the Army implied that "customary military servic-es" meant that proper Roman Catholic religious rites had also been conducted when Donald was finally laid to rest at the new National Memorial Cemetery of the Pacific. But the Army's own internal documents, also contained in the IDPF, give the lie to any such false if comforting implication. Of course, Donald's unsuspecting mother had no way of knowing the truth of the matter.

Despite the fact that the Quartermaster General's Office in Washington had written to the Commanding General of

"MIDPAC" as long ago as December 1946, it was not until February 27, 1950 that the Army finally took effective concrete steps to correct the 1942 Serial Number error for the official record of P.F.C. Joseph J. Deignan. On the latter date, and more than a year after Donald had been finally buried in Hawaii, Major Sharpe of the "Repatriation Branch" of the Quartermaster General's Memorial Division wrote to his opposite number, Major Sekowski, the Quartermaster General's "Liaison" officer at the Pentagon, to request a <u>"CLARIFICATION IN DISCREPANCY OF SERIAL NO"</u>. Sharpe asked, "1….that a clarification be furnished this Office concerning the correct serial number of the following decedent: Deignan, Joseph, J., pfc., 6141481, whose serial number appears on records (sic) this Office as follows:…". Major Sharpe then went on to list all the dates between March 1942 and April 1947 on which Donald's serial number had been misconstrued in official correspondence. He then asked Major Sekowski, "…that a corrected Report of Death be furnished this Office if present one is found to be in error."[62] On April 6, 1950 Major Sekowski responded to Major Sharpe's request by informing him that, "Attached herewith Corrected Report of Death for Deignan, Joseph J., 6141481, pfc, as per request dated 27 Feb 1950."[63]

Even though the "Corrected report of Death", dated March 21, 1950, was ostensibly concerned only with rectification of the Serial Number error from the original "Report of Death" made on March 20, 1942, it is, in itself, a remarkable and interesting historical document. This War Department Form, issued by the Adjutant General's Office in Washington, D.C., consists of a number of boxes in each of which particular pieces of information are entered. Thus, in the top row, from left to right, Donald's full legal name "Deignan, Joseph J.", his correct Army Serial Number "6141481" and rank "pfc" are given. On the next line down, his Home Address is entered simply as "Worcester, Massachusetts". His "Arm of Service" is recorded as "Field Artillery" and his date of birth is given as "March 15, 1915." These first two lines contain familiar and standard information but as the document continues, it deviates significantly from the norm. The third line simply gives "Place of Death" as "Territory of Hawaii." The "Cause of Death" is listed, without comment or explanation, as "Gunshot wound" and the "Date of Death" is noted as "March 18, 1942." Gone altogether are the earlier, contradictory references—found elsewhere in the IDPF or on the Death Certificate—to "Place of Death" as either "Schofield Barracks" or "Waimea, Oahu." Equally, there is here no mention made of the "Gunshot wound" being either **"APPARENTLY SELF INFLICTED"** or resulting from **"Suicide."** The fourth line lists P.F.C. Deignan's "Station" broadly as "Territory of Hawaii" and his "Date of Entry on Current Active Service" as "6 July 1939." Spaces pertaining to "Pay" are understandably left blank. The fifth line on the Form, labeled "Emergency Address," lists "Mrs. Bernard Deignan, mother, 195 Lincoln Street, Worcester, Massachusetts." The sixth line, entitled "Beneficiary" records "Mrs. Bernard Deignan, mother, same as above."

But the heart of the matter of the "Investigation" into Donald's death, which would have appeared to have been called for in Paragraph 21 of AR 600-550, is addressed—obliquely at least—on the seventh line of the Corrected Report of Death. Earlier portions of that same Form allowed for the entry of typewritten, narrative information in block spaces provided for that purpose. Line seven, however, consists of a series of **"YES"/"NO"** categorical check boxes in which a typewritten **"X"** can be entered as required by way of response. Thus, under the heading **"INVESTIGATION MADE,"** the **"YES"** box is checked. Next to it, under **"IN LINE OF DUTY,"** **"YES"** is also indicated. But the next box to the right, **"OWN MISCONDUCT"** features an **"X"** in the **"NO"** box. Donald is found, affirmatively, to have been in **"ON DUTY STATUS"** at the time of his death. And his death was marked with yet another **"X"** as being a **"NON-BATTLE"** casualty. Below the various rows of narrative and "check mark boxes" on the Corrected Report of Death, ample blank space was provided for additional typed comments. But, apart from noting that the reason for the 1950 "Report" was to correct the 1942 digital error in Donald's Serial Number, none were made.[64]

When I had the opportunity in October 2009 both to speak to and correspond with a civilian representative of the Department of the Army, she suggested to me that the "check box" information on the Corrected Report of Death was included there so as merely to allow my grandmother, Mrs. Bernard Deignan, to receive Donald's life insurance payout as his intended beneficiary. She further said that she believed that the Corrected Report of Death from 1950 did not alter the Army's "Suicide" finding in March 1942.[65]

Why, then, did the Army's 1950 Corrected Report of Death make no mention either of the place or of the "Suicidal" circumstances of Private First Class Deignan's death in 1942? Furthermore, why was no reference made, either in the IDPF or in the Corrected Report of Death from March 1950, to the formal findings of Donald's Board of Officers which were supposed to have been forwarded in duplicate to the Office of the Adjutant General in Washington? Answers to both of these compelling questions have not yet come to light after nearly seven years of systematic, scholarly research. So all we know, even now, is only *what* Donald is alleged to have done but not *why* he may have done it.

Although Donald's "Board of Officers" may indeed have made a formal "Investigation" into his death, no copy of any such document was included in the IDPF. A scant day and a half after his demise, Donald was buried. No forensic investigation into the facts and circumstances of his death appears to have been conducted at the time. Several retired police officers, at opposite ends of the country, who have reviewed the IDPF for me have all concluded that proper, basic investigative procedures were not followed. One of them—a criminal justice and forensics professor—referring to the IDPF and its treatment of Donald's case, declared:

It does not really shed any more light on this. There has to be an investigative report somewhere that tells in detail what took place, ie how they found him, gun position, etc. , who the investigating officer was, who attended the funeral etc…. There are too many details missing from what I have at my disposal to make a decision.[66]

But if no thorough investigation was made in March 1942, why was this so? On March 18, 1942—the date of Donald's untimely death—the Japanese were still credibly believed to be lurking in force, just over the horizon, somewhere off Oahu's North Shore. A ground invasion of Oahu was still thought to be a real possibility. One Pearl Harbor Army veteran told me that, in the weeks after the Japanese attack, "We were all nervous. Especially at night, we shot at anything that moved for the first few days."[67] Under such conditions, the Army had no time to waste precious resources by thoroughly investigating the death of a single American soldier who, for whatever reason, appeared to have taken his own life. The Army's institutional inclination was to regard the death of Private First Class Deignan as "an open and shut case" of Suicide; a matter to be resolved quickly and officially forgotten as soon as possible. So, bureaucratically, the Army took the easy way out. Publicly, the War Department let Donald's family believe that he had died "a hero." Internally, however, its officials simply "blamed the victim" for his own death and moved on. Such a choice of action was far less involved and time-consuming than any alternative procedure would have been, even though there was one available to military officials if they had wished to avail themselves of it.

Paragraph 22 of AR 600-550 headed "Report of inquest by summary court In case of a person who dies, or Is found, dead, under circumstances which require Investigation" would seem to have mandated Army Officers on the spot to have conducted a more probing investigation of Donald's case than they seem to have done. Sub-paragraph (a) of Paragraph 22 required that:

When a person dies or is found dead at any post, camp, or station under the exclusive jurisdiction of the United States and the death is due or is suspected to be due to foul play, violent or unnatural causes, or death is sudden from unknown causes, except deaths from wounds or injuries received in action, the commanding officer will immediately designate and direct the summary court to investigate the circumstances attending death, to the end that the cause thereof may be determined and the person criminally responsible therefore may be brought to justice. The summary court will with the least practicable delay view the body of the deceased and summon and examine upon oath or affirmation, such witnesses as may have knowledge of the cause and circumstances of the death.[68]

If Donald's death had been nothing more than an isolated event, it is just possible that Army officials in Hawaii might have mounted the kind of systematic investigation clearly called for in such circumstances as those described in Paragraph 22 (a.) of AR 600-550. But the fact is that the sudden and violent manner in which P.F.C. Joseph Deignan's life ended was far from an isolated incident. Between December 8, 1941 and April 16, 1942, alone, at least 39 soldiers with "gunshot wounds" were admitted to NORTH SECTOR GENERAL HOSPITAL at Schofield Barracks for treatment. In addition, during the month of March

1942, by itself, 3 more soldiers who can be identified as belonging specifically to the 24th Infantry Division died of gunshot wounds. P.F.C. Joseph J. Deignan, himself, was one of those three soldiers. Thus, altogether, no fewer than 42 men were treated or examined post mortem for gunshot wounds between early December 1941 and mid April 1942 in Oahu's North Sector. In 30 of the 39 cases admitted to NORTH SECTOR GENERAL HOSPITAL during this period, injuries were listed as being **"ACCIDENTAL."** in character. Of the remaining 9 cases, 1 was listed as **"SUICIDAL"** while 2 more were attributed to **"ATTEMPTED SUICIDE"**; 3 were the responsibility of **"OTHER MAN"** and causation of a further three was recorded as **"UNDETERMINED."**[69] Of the total number of 42 soldiers treated for gunshot wounds between December 1941 and April 1942 in Oahu's North Sector General Hospital, 11 died.

Among the 39 cases reported by Colonel Canning to his superior, 3 were listed as **"UNDETERMINED"** and **"Pending LOD (Line Of Duty) Board** findings."** Thus, fully 1/7 of Oahu's North Sector gunshot casualties were subject to investigation by Boards of Officers who were supposedly expected to determine the circumstances under which deaths or injuries occurred. It is a melancholy fact, and much more than a mere coincidence, that the soldiers buried immediately to Donald's right and left in the Post Cemetery at Schofield Barracks both died of "gunshot wounds" at about the same time as he did. Row L. in Plot 2 at the Schofield Barracks Cemetery may well have been "Suicide Row" from the Army's point of view.[70]

In March 1942, the Army's resources in Hawaii—forensic and otherwise—were stretched thin. As has been seen, a strict Martial Law regime, under which the Army controlled every aspect of Hawaiian life, had been in place since the afternoon of December 7, 1941. Since that date, almost all civilian courts in the Territory had been summarily suspended and supplanted by barely competent military "Provost Courts" and "military tribunals." Under such circumstances, although "LOD Boards" were undoubtedly convened, it is very likely that their investigations, in general, were as cursory and ephemeral as the one presumably conducted in Donald's particular case. Even during wartime, deaths caused by "Accident" or "Murder" would have to have been "Investigated" thoroughly, but military fatalities attributable to "Suicide" need not have received such time and resource-consuming legal or administrative attention. In short, perhaps it is true that dead men tell no tales but they can be made to incriminate themselves if it is convenient for the living that they should do so. By "blaming the victim" and then moving on, this is what the Army seems to have done to Donald and, quite possibly, to far too many of his unfortunate comrades as well.

It continues to be my firm belief that Donald's family never had an inkling of the actual circumstances surrounding his death. This conviction on my part is bolstered by an incident which took place in 1983. In the summer of that year, both to celebrate the relatively recent receipt of my Ph.D. in history and the launch of what would prove to be an attenuated and ill-starred academic career, my parents and I took a trip to New York City. Our intent was to take in a couple of Broadway Shows, to have dinner at their favorite French restaurant, and to buy books to augment my professional library. My father had long been an avid reader of The New York Times and, in preparation for our upcoming visit, he perused the dining section of that paper. There he found positive reviews of a famous old bar called Gallagher's and of a new Japanese restaurant.

At that time, I was still walking everywhere instead of using a wheelchair as I now often do. To spare my mother with her heart condition and me with my cerebral palsy from the physical difficulty of walking long distances in the mid-summer New York City heat, my father undertook to reconnoiter both places in advance of our excursion. Accordingly, in the early afternoon, he headed off for Gallagher's where evidently he downed a couple of good quality shots of Scotch in quick succession on an empty stomach.

In light of Bernard Deignan's alcoholism and the tensions and problems which it had caused within his family, my father had never been much of a drinker. "One drink, one drunk," he used to say and indeed I almost never saw him over indulge. But on this particular occasion he did so.

Thus fortified he made his way to the new Japanese restaurant, about which he had read, where trouble soon ensued. At some point, as he subsequently told us, he said to "the Japs" there present, "You bastards killed my brother!" whereupon he was unceremoniously thrown out of the place. Needless to say, our dinner plans for that evening changed abruptly. For me, this anecdote conclusively establishes that, even late in his life, my father continued to accept without question the well-established family belief that his youngest brother had been killed at Pearl Harbor. Even in 1983, however, my acceptance of this piece of "received truth" had been more qualified than was the attitude of my father and his siblings towards this version of events. My unearthing in 1984 of Donald's obituary in one of the Worcester papers turned the questions which had first arisen for me at his grave in August 1970 into real doubts about the factual circumstances of his death in March 1942. Even as long ago as 1984, things just didn't add up for me. My old doubts were both dispelled and supplanted by an entirely new set of questions which stemmed from my receipt and critical reading of P.F.C. Joseph J. Deignan's IDPF in June 2006.

Entirely absent either from the public or internal narrative portions of that all-important document is any indication of a "Motive" for Donald's supposed suicidal action on the night of March 18, 1942. Because none of his personal correspondence has survived and since the IDPF contains no information whatsoever about his psychological state of mind prior to the event—although the LOD Board of Officers findings should have spoken to that matter—it is impossible to know with any degree of certainty why Donald did what he is alleged to have done to himself in a desperate instant. Nonetheless, on the basis of such circumstantial evidence as has survived and come thus far to light, I can and do advance the hypothesis which follows. In brief, it is this: Donald's suicide in March 1942 was directly attributable to the traumatic events which he experienced during the Pearl Harbor

Day aerial attack on Schofield Barracks, the harmful effects of which were greatly exacerbated both by a heightened sense of personal vulnerability and by the prolonged, constant strain of waiting for an invasion which never came.

To place Donald's deadly psychiatric distress in a broader World War II medical context, it may be well to consider the opinion of the author of the Army's volume on the provision of "Medical Services In The War Against Japan." She wrote, "For reasons that went deep into contemporary medical beliefs and assumptions, neuropsychiatric casualties—the nation's leading cause of non-battle disability separations—might almost be called the definitive American military medical problem of World War II."[71]

Beyond any doubt, P.F.C. Joseph J. Deignan was present in Battery C of the 13th Field Artillery Battalion adjacent to the Headquarters of the 24th Infantry Division at Schofield Barracks on the Island of Oahu on Sunday morning December 7, 1941. During the first wave of the attack on Pearl Harbor which began at 7:55 A.M. on that morning, Japanese warplanes bombed and strafed Wheeler Field, the large U.S. Army Air-Corps Pursuit Squadron base abutting Schofield Barracks. Before then returning to their aircraft carriers, the Japanese planes flew low over Schofield Barracks and strafed it indiscriminately, almost casually, so as to use up their remaining machinegun ammunition before landing back onboard their ships. As it happened, the enemy flew directly over the heads of the men of the 24th Infantry Division's four supporting Field Artillery Battalions lined up side-by-side and housed in a neat row of massive buildings.[72]

Initially they struck the 63rd F.A. It is instructive to note that two of the three men from the 24th Infantry Division who were killed on Pearl Harbor Day came from this organization. The Japanese attackers then flew on, in turn, over the 52nd, 13th and 11th Field Artillery Battalions' locations before "climbing-out" and heading home to their waiting warships. Thus, Donald almost certainly saw hostile aircraft flying low and directly over his head, machineguns blazing, and firing—it must have seemed—right at him, personally.

From the Japanese point of view, the strafing of Schofield Barracks was nothing more than a mere strategic afterthought. As Gordon Prange cogently wrote:

> Actually the Japanese paid much less attention to the Hawaiian Department's ground forces than to the Navy or to the Hawaiian Air Force. They made no attempt to knock out Army installations except those concerned with air power. Anyone in an analytical mood might have reflected that this neglect quite clearly indicated that the Japanese did not have immediate invasion on their minds.[73]

But the nuances of Japan's grand strategy were lost on Donald at that terrible moment. He realized with a sudden shock that strange men flying unfamiliar-looking warplanes were trying to kill him with their machineguns at very close range. Although he was not wounded himself on December 7th, and even though he appears not to have lost any close friends to violence either on Pearl Harbor Day or afterwards, Donald must have reflected later on the random chance which had allowed him to escape death or serious injury on that momentous occasion.

His "near-death experience" at the hands of anonymous Japanese fighter pilots on the morning of December 7, 1941 must certainly have been traumatic for Donald Joseph. In light of what happened to P.F.C. Deignan just three and one-half months later, it is reasonable to assume that simply witnessing the strafing of Schofield Barracks—at close quarters as he did—was enough to trigger in Donald the beginning of the progressive process of mental deterioration which eventually led to his "suicide." As a result of the Japanese attack on December 7th, 1941 the seeds of what would today be called "Post Traumatic Stress Disorder"— or P.T.S.D. for short—were evidently sown in Donald's psyche.

Lieutenant Colonel Dave Grossman, a retired professional soldier and a practicing psychologist, has written extensively about the onset of P.T.S.D. among military combat veterans and police officers. He has noted aptly that:

> To be at risk for PTSD, you must be exposed to a traumatic incident in which two things occur. First, the incident must be a life and death event that involves actual or threatened death or serious injury to you or to others…. The second element that must occur is for you to respond to the exposure with intense fear, helplessness or horror.[74]

Lacking any countervailing evidence to the contrary—of which there seems to be none—it would appear that Donald's personal experience on December 7th fits perfectly with Grossman's criteria for being at risk of developing P.T.S.D. Donald would have been a fool not to be "afraid" as machinegun bullets fell around or at least fairly near him. He would doubtless have felt entirely "helpless" while death-dealing planes flew just overhead and seemed to be shooting directly at him for long minutes together. Lastly, if he happened to see dead or seriously wounded soldiers scattered on the ground around him he would have been truly "horrified" both at their condition and at the awful suddenness with which violent death or grievous, life-threatening injury had come upon them.

Having almost certainly witnessed traumatic events on Pearl Harbor Day and having additionally dealt with feelings of fear, helplessness and horror in their aftermath, it is surely more than reasonable to conclude—as I do—that Donald was then and there initially and thoroughly traumatized. If this was indeed so, much worse lay in store for him, personally, in the difficult months to come.

It has already been noted, in Chapter Six above, that—even before the bombs and bullets stopped falling on Pearl Harbor— the 24th Infantry Division had begun moving out in good order to take up its assigned combat position on the North Shore of Oahu to forestall an expected ground invasion by the Japanese. There are several extant "Histories" dealing with the various campaigns of the 24th Infantry Division during World War II.

For the present purpose, knowing precisely where Private First Class Joseph J. Deignan was and exactly what he was doing between December 7, 1941 and March 18, 1942, all of them are equally inadequate. Most of them are extremely vague and very brief in their treatment of the Division's defensive activities in Hawaii between December 1941 and August 1943 when the so-called "Victory Division" actually left for combat in the South Pacific. The best of these "Histories" is an official one which was prepared by the War Department after the end of the conflict. "The Twenty-Fourth Infantry Division: A Brief History" sets the scene nicely, and dramatically, from the outset:

> That was the situation on the sunny morning of 7 December 1941. It was the closing day of a week end, and many men had not yet returned to Schofield Barracks. Those present were fascinated by what appeared to be a tremendous air show, and it was not until machine gun bullets began to rip into buildings, and spurt geysers of dust from the ground, that they noted the markings of the Japanese air force on the planes.
>
> Within minutes after the full realization of what was happening struck home, machine guns of 2 Division units were in action, firing at the Japanese attack planes.... These men were the first to fight back.[75]

A little further along, this same document goes on to inform us helpfully that:

> The Division was assigned to defend the northern half of Oahu, where extensive coastal defenses were built. The rocky, cliff terrain of the east and west sections of the Island formed good natural barriers but the extreme northern area, with its excellent beach was admirably suited for landing parties should the Japanese attempt a land strike….This included the area of Waimea Bay, which is in the intermediate section between Kahuku Point on the east and Kaena Point on the west.[76]

We know, from the "internal narrative" portion of Donald's IDPF, that his body was indeed found, **"ONE FOURTH MILE EAST OF WAIMEA OAHU TH"** late on the evening of March 18, 1942.[77] In the meantime, Donald's personal situation and psychological condition had progressively gone from bad to worse.

Long before the start of the War, Hawaii's idyllic physical setting had been deceptive. Private First Class Deignan's considerable peacetime experience in the ranks of the old "Pacific Army"—during its twilight years—has already been discussed in detail in Chapter Six. Even in those supposedly tranquil prewar days, the Hawaiian Department had not been an easy locale in which to serve. Speaking of the underlying stress inherent in that tropical posting—even in peacetime—the pre-eminent historian of America's Pacific Army wrote that:

> On Hawaii, soldiers coined the term "rock happy" or "gone pineapple" to refer to comrades' depressed, moody, or erratic behavior. One private wrote of two suicides in his company: "It happens quite often here as it is a tough post to pull. The time drags away if you don't have anything to do."[78]

In November 1941, P.F.C. Deignan had re-enlisted in the Army for another hitch in Hawaii. So he knew for certain that he would be there for the next several years at a minimum. Whether or not he had already become depressed and started to go "rock happy" or "pineapple," even then, is not known. But, after December 7th he realized that he would have to remain in the service for the duration of the war and that the only way he would leave Hawaii at all would be to go into combat with C Battery of the 13th F.A. within the 24th Infantry Division. Whatever the cause of its onset may have been, it is well known in psychological circles that Depression almost always precedes and accompanies P.T.S.D. such as that which Donald probably experienced after the Pearl Harbor attack. According to one leading authority on the subject, veterans suffering from severe P.TS.D. sometimes entertain suicidal thoughts on a daily basis. [79]

In any case, after Pearl Harbor, P.F.C. Deignan's problem was not that he had too little to do within his "outfit" then at Waimea Bay. On the contrary, he was probably constantly busy there, and therefore still further stressed, during the remaining months of his life. He had survived the aerial attack on Schofield Barracks physically unscathed. But even if he reflected on that fact, and the implications of his chance escape from sudden, violent death, Donald had very probably had nobody with whom he could discuss his complex feelings and emotions even if he had wished to do so. Strict military censorship prevented him from sharing what he had seen and felt with his family back in Worcester. Even if he had been able to do so, they would probably not have comprehended what he might have had to say. For there always has been and remains a gulf of understanding and experience between military personnel and the civilian population which they serve.

So, within the human confines of Battery C, Donald was probably left psychically alone with his innermost thoughts and recent, graphic war experiences with no good way either to ventilate or to process them. What was worse, having escaped death on December 7th, he now found himself, almost literally, back in "the bull's-eye" again. General Emmons and his subordinates in the Hawaiian Department believed that a Japanese invasion of Oahu was imminent and they further supposed that—when it came—it would come at Waimea Bay; precisely where Donald and the 24th Division were positioned and waiting for it.

As soon as they had arrived at Waimea Bay, the men of the 24th Infantry Division had set up machinegun positions, with fields of interlocking fire, right along the beach.[80] A short distance behind them, the heavy guns of the Division's several Field

Artillery Battalions were emplaced. The author of one of the United States Army's many official volumes dealing with the history of World War II, quoted an Army surgeon in the aftermath of the New Georgia campaign as finding that, "War neurosis... was not frequent in field artillery, engineer, quartermaster, signal and reconnaissance units of the divisions..."[81] This may have been true because, oftentimes, many such Field Artillerymen found themselves removed to some degree from the front lines of combat which infantrymen typically occupied. But, in the case of the 13th F.A. and its sister Battalions at Waimea Bay that insulating phenomenon did not apply. P.F.C. Deignan would not now be able to enjoy the relative safety of Field Artillerymen well behind the frontlines. If "the Japs" came back this time, there would not be hundreds of them flying overhead for short and terrible moments. Instead, the enemy would materialize before the waiting American defenders in the form of thousands of hardened combat troops determined to storm ashore directly in front of them.

In researching this book, I made a point of visiting Oahu and the particular places where Donald had been. As I told my wife before I left the hotel in Honolulu, I wanted "to get the geography into my head." On one afternoon, after a research visit to the U.S. Army Hawaii Museum, I happen to have returned to our hotel in the company of Mr. Marshall Uchida—a Japanese-American cabdriver, U.S. Air-Force veteran, and resident of Hawaii's capital city. When he gave me his business card, I noticed with interest that—among other things—he conducted "sightseeing tours" of Oahu. Accordingly, I asked him if he would drive me to Waimea Bay so I could see the place where my uncle, a Pearl Harbor survivor, had actually died. Marshall readily agreed to my request, and at 10:00 A.M. on Saturday, February 6, 2010, we set out on our journey. Along the way, he described the local economy and geography of places we were passing through in detail. When we reached Waimea Bay, itself, we took a number of pictures of the beach and of the landscape immediately behind it. Marshall then volunteered to see if he could find any locals at the Waimea Bay State Park who might be able to talk with me about the place and its bearing on my research project. Indeed, I met and spoke with two local gentlemen thoroughly familiar with the area about my uncle's defense position and the determination of the place of his death. One of them said, "…he would have been right about here! … Just about a quarter mile [from the beach].[82] Then we got back into the car and I asked Marshall to drive me "1/4 mile east of Waimea," where, according to his IDPF, Donald's body had been found by his Battery C comrades. In doing so, we crossed the two-lane Kam Highway and proceeded along a side-road up an increasingly steep and wooded hill. Mr. Uchida meticulously measured the exact distance traveled on his cab's odometer. When we reached the "1/4 mile" mark, we got out of the cab and Marshall kindly took several pictures of me leaning against a large rock. This location is very close, in all likelihood, to the exact spot at which P.F.C. Joseph J. Deignan died. I do not know if it was as overgrown and wooded in March 1942 as the place is today, but I do know that it is within sight of the beach on which the enemy was expected to land in tens of thousands at that earlier date.[83]

In anticipation of that dire event, General Emmons had developed two defensive plans. The first of these envisioned that the Americans would be able to repel Japanese landings in force right on the beach. If this measure failed, however, the soldiers of the Twenty-Fourth Infantry Division would have to mount a defense in depth in the rough inland terrain beyond the coastal zone. Either tactical contingency might well include close quarters if not hand-to-hand fighting between American and Japanese troops on Oahu's North Shore. If Donald considered this dire prospect in the months between Pearl Harbor and his death, such thoughts would have done nothing to decrease his level of anxiety and stress.

Then, too, just interminably "waiting for action to begin" must in itself have taken a real , further toll on Donald's interior resource reserves. As Colonel Dave Grossman has pointed out, prolonged combat stress will eventually debilitate almost all otherwise well-adjusted soldiers. Grossman has reminded us that, "In every war in which American soldiers have fought in this…century, the chances of becoming a psychiatric casualty—of being debilitated for some period of time as a consequence of the stresses of military life—were greater than the chances of being killed by enemy fire."[84]

That P.F.C. Joseph J. Deignan ambled in the dark up a steep hill behind Waimea Bay and then died of a gunshot wound on the evening of March 18, 1942 is certain. But why that tragic event happened is unknown and unknowable. Equally certain, however, is the fact that the Japanese invasion of Oahu—which Donald and his thousands of comrades were sent into the Hawaiian jungle to prevent—never happened. In any case, "…it is most likely that had the Japanese invaded Oahu—and even had their aviation been able to secure command of the sky—they would have been slaughtered on the beaches in truly catastrophic numbers."[85]

But P.F.C. Joseph J. Deignan would have taken no consolation from this retrospective historical conclusion. In fact, for nearly seventy years after his sudden and violent death on the evening of March 18, 1942, Donald was destined to occupy in turn two unquiet and unblessed graves; the first in the Post Cemetery at Schofield Barracks and the second in the National Memorial Cemetery of the Pacific in Honolulu. How Donald came at last to gain a measure of spiritual peace and reconciliation is the subject, fittingly, of the final chapter of this book.

CHAPTER NINE

"ONE SWORD, AT LEAST,"

Nearly a decade before his untimely death during World War II, it will be recalled that Donald had completed two successful "hitches" in the Civilian Conservation Corps. There he had gone from being a hapless, drifting teenager to become a mature, responsible young man. Within the ranks of the CCC, in Maine, Massachusetts and Oregon he had thrived both physically and psychologically. Within the context of this successful service, a rather odd and interesting thing happened.

Apart from asking general questions to obtain necessary background information, CCC intake interviewers sometimes made personal observations about prospective enrollees. In Donald's case, one such instance occurred in July, 1934 when, next to the rather peculiar entry **"Talent for furnishing public entertainment"**, his interviewer wrote *"None."* [1] Superficially, at least, this judgment should not be surprising. What little we know about Donald's personality comes down to us from his childhood and early adolescence. Small in stature and self-conscious about his physical appearance, Donald was quiet, shy and introverted. Perhaps little had changed when he underwent his first CCC intake interview in the summer of 1934.

A century or so before Donald's birth, an Irish Catholic poet and musician, Thomas Moore, had written a famous poem and ballad entitled "The Minstrel- Boy" which celebrated, equally, Ireland's long and distinguished military and musical traditions which were often closely intertwined throughout Irish History:

> The Minstrel-Boy to the war is gone,
> In the ranks of death you'll find him;
> His father's sword he hath girded on,
> And his wild harp slung behind him. [2]

Leaving aside the harp , and substituting a .45 Caliber Pistol— the preferred personal weapon of Field Artillerymen—for the Sword, and taking into account his evident inability to entertain in public, Donald, in other respects, had much in common with "The Minstrel-Boy." Like the subject and hero of Moore's poem, Donald was a young man of Irish extraction who willingly went off to war and never came back. Like Moore's young Irish soldier who bequeathed his legacy to the poem's narrator, Donald has left me behind to honor him and to reflect on his life and its meaning. Here the similarity between Moore's metaphorical protagonist and my very real uncle seemingly ends. For The Minstrel-Boy "fell," in the company of many of Moore's own friends, in the Rebellion of 1798 against Ireland's historic enemy, Britain. But Donald died alone, the only casualty in some terrible conflict with himself.

Whatever the actual circumstances of Donald's sudden and violent death on the evening of March 18, 1942 at Waimea Bay on the North Shore of Oahu may have been, the Army's presumption that—for whatever reason—he took his own life has here to be accepted completely, if only because of its inevitable theological consequences at that time. That presumption of "suicide" has had profoundly important consequences both for Donald himself and for me too. Paradoxically, even in death, as a contemporary photograph from March 20, 1942 attests, his comrades honored P.F.C. Deignan. He was still a soldier among soldiers and for them no taint of cowardice or dishonor surrounded his final conduct. His colleagues in the United States Army paid him the final respects which were due to one of their own who had fallen in battle. From the few moments after his death, when he was "found" at 11:18 PM on March 18th until his burial nearly two days later in the Post Cemetery at Schofield Barracks at 4:20 PM on the afternoon of March 20, 1942, his body was never left unattended. One or more members of the 34th Infantry Regiment was always close by to mount "an honor guard" over him. A vigil must be kept, and tradition dictated that, as Donald prepared to make the journey from this world to the next, he should never be left unprotected and alone. By contrast, the post-mortem treatment which Donald received at the hands of the Roman Catholic Church in which he was raised was of a radically different character. At the time, his Church appears to have condemned and disowned him completely. This final Chapter will deal with the disparate treatment accorded to Donald, in death, by the Army and the Church and with the process by which these discrepancies were at long last rectified and reconciled.

It will be recalled, in Chapter Six above, that even in 1942 the Army took great pains to assure the Deignan family that, "the burial was reverently and properly conducted…."[3] This statement was naturally intended to comfort and to reassure Donald's mother, particularly, that her son had been treated with dignity and propriety by the military authorities under whom he had served. But this was only half true. While the Army rendered customary ceremonial honors over Donald's Grave, the Church almost certainly did not do so. Mr. Stommel's letter of July 1942 implied that some sort of religious services had been conducted on the occasion of the 1942 interment but it did not directly say so. The internal document portion of the IDPF, as opposed to the public or family correspondence part of that File, confirmed the theological reality of the situation.

On a Form entitled **"REPORT OF INTERMENT"** which bore the black letter legend **"RESTRICTED"** at the top, the Army gave much detailed information about the physical circumstances of Donald's death and burial which, of course, his family neither ever knew of nor was ever intended to know about. In Section 1. "Identification," it described in very general terms where Donald's body was found. In addition, it attributed his "Cause of Death" to a "Gunshot Wound, left chest apparently self-inflicted." Within the adjoining space provided for "Religion," however, the word

"Unknown" was simply typed in. In Section 2. of the same Form entitled "Burial," the spaces provided, respectively, for "Type of Religious Ceremony" and "Person Conducting Burial Rites" were left conspicuously blank. It is thus almost certain that no Roman Catholic Military Chaplain participated in Donald's funeral late on the afternoon of March 20, 1942.[4]

For in Twentieth Century war-time Hawaii, just as much as in the earliest years of the Christian Church or for that matter in Medieval Denmark, too, "suicide" was for Roman Catholics a "Mortal Sin"! It was grounds for automatic Excommunication and a guarantee of eternal damnation and torment in the un-quenchable fires of Hell for any person who *presumed* to take his or her own life.

In his 1st Letter to the Corinthians, Chapter 3, Verse 16, Paul wrote:

> Do you not know that you are God's temple and that God's Spirit dwells in you? If anyone de-stroys God's temple, God will destroy him. For God's temple is holy, and that temple you are.[5]

In a more secular vein, recall, for example, Hamlet's agonized lament early in the play,

> Oh, that this too solid flesh would melt,
> Thaw, and resolve itself into a dew!
> Or that the Everlasting had not fixed
> His canon 'gainst self-slaughter![6]

Later on in the same work, consider the Priest's injunction after Ophelia's probable suicide,

> She should in ground unsanctified have lodged
> Till the last trumpet…
> We should profane the service of the dead
> To sing a requiem and such rest to her
> As to peace-parted souls.[7]

What happened from a religious point of view on February 4, 1949, when Donald was finally laid to rest in the National Memorial Cemetery of the Pacific, is less certain. Teams of Military Chaplains representing the Jewish, Buddhist, and Roman Catholic Faiths routinely blessed the graves of deceased service members who belonged to one or another of those three denominations. Apart from saying that:

> Customary military services were conducted over the grave at the time of burial….You may be assured that this final interment was conducted with fitting dignity and solemnity and that the gravesite will be carefully and conscientiously maintained in perpetuity by the United. States Government.[8]

For the rest, the IDPF was ambiguously and indeed deliberately silent with regard to any specific Roman Catholic religious services having been performed over Donald's Grave. Again, by indirection, the Army created the reassuring impression that spiritual matters had been handled properly but its officials did not actually say so. Thus Donald's family was left to draw its own reasonable conclusions, based on the official evidence provided, about the nature of his second and final burial. Equally, for reasons of kindness and expediency, the Army kept "the awful truth" about the reality of P.F.C. Deignan's death from his patriotic and unsuspecting family. The "Coombs incident," discussed in Chapter Six, showed that Anna Deignan, when provoked, could be a formidable person. If the Army had given the least indication that Donald's death during World War II had been anything other than tragically "honorable," she and her sons Francis and Robert—Army veterans both—would have demanded an explanation and perhaps even an official investigation of the circumstances. But, of course, they were given no reason to do so by the Army. Many years passed, and Donald's nephew and namesake grew to manhood, becoming in the process a professional historian who intended to get to the bottom of things just as he had promised his "Uncle Donald" he would do when that young man first visited his boyhood hero's grave on August 30, 1970.

When I received a copy of the IDPF on June 12, 2006—which I had requested under provisions of the Freedom of Information Act—I read with interest the following sentence in the cover letter which accompanied that File, "Please be advised that we do not specialize in historical information and cannot speculate, evaluate documents or circumstances, or draw conclusions in order to answer any questions you may have about the IDPF."[9] By that date, forty years of specialized academic training and prior experience had prepared me precisely to "evaluate documents...

(and) circumstances (and to) draw conclusions…about the IDPF."
I recognized immediately the nature of the "double and parallel
narratives" within its pages and I was of course surprised—to
say the least—at the Army's internal conclusion that Donald had
probably taken his own life with a firearm in March 1942.

Fortunately I knew in a general way that, between those dark
days at the start of World War II and the present time, the
Church's attitude toward "Suicide" had become much more enlightened and compassionate. Under the heading of **"Suicide"**,
the CATECHISM OF THE CATHOLIC CHURCH, (Second
Edition), in use today, says, in part;

> Everyone is responsible for his life before God
> who has given it to him. It is God who remains
> the sovereign Master of life.
>
> We are obliged to accept life gratefully and pre-
> serve it for his honor and the salvation of our
> souls. We are stewards, not owners, of the life
> God has entrusted to us. It is not ours to dis-
> pose of.[10]

But the CATECHISM goes on to recognize, in language strik-
ingly reminiscent of Army Regulation 600-550 discussed extensively in the previous Chapter, that, "Grave psychological
disturbances, anguish, or grave fear of hardship, suffering, or
torture can diminish the responsibility of the one committing
suicide."[11] And the same passage concludes compassionately by
saying:

> We should not despair of the eternal salvation
> of persons who have taken their own lives. By
> ways known to him alone, God can provide
> the opportunity for salutary repentance. The
> Church prays for persons who have taken their
> own lives.[12]

Throughout the Summer of 2006, I mulled over the disturbing implications in the "internal portion" of the IDPF's "double narrative" pages. In December 1959, spiritual consolation had lifted me out of my original childhood despair. The same thing happened, once again, in August 2006 although this time I recognized the process at work far more quickly and clearly than I had first done nearly fifty years earlier. On that second more recent occasion, I knew that I needed spiritual help and so I sought it.

On August 15, the Feast of the Assumption, a "Holy Day of Obligation," I went to Confession at the St. Francis Chapel in downtown Providence so as to be able to attend Mass and to receive Holy Communion on one of the Principal Feast Days of the Roman Catholic Church. In Chapter Four I have earlier discussed Donald's probable experience with old-style "Confession" in the Worcester of the 1920s. Its character is vastly different and much more enlightened and healing today than it was back then. "Confession," now often called "The Sacrament of Reconciliation," gives penitents the opportunity to be absolved from their sins by confessing them to a priest who, by virtue of the power given to him by Jesus Christ himself, is able to forgive and remove them. Confession also affords the chance for a layperson to discuss troublesome moral or spiritual matters with the priest who is administering the Sacrament of Reconciliation to him or her in strict and absolute confidence. So, on this occasion, after revealing my various sins, I finally said: "Father, there is one more thing which troubles me. I have just recently learned that the man I was named after—my uncle who died during World War II while serving in the U.S. Army—may have committed suicide."

The Franciscan Priest, who was sitting directly opposite me in his office, handed me the kleenex box at his elbow, as the tears welled up in my eyes, and said, "Anyone in such desperate distress, in so much need of God's love, would have been forgiven almost immediately!"

Strengthened by such a reassuring theological opinion, I continued my research and writing. But that conversation remained at the back of my mind for the next several years. Finally, one morning in the fall of 2009, I said to my wife, Kathy, "It's pretty clear to me that Donald probably committed suicide in March 1942. Under the circumstances, as his namesake and last living male relative, I think that I have to do all I can to make sure, before I die, that his grave is finally blessed officially by the Church. I suggest that we spend our winter vacation in Hawaii in 2010 to make sure that this is done."

My wife readily agreed with that idea. Accordingly, I set the wheels in motion to make it so. On December 31, 2009, I wrote to the staff of the National Memorial Cemetery of the Pacific in Honolulu, in part, as follows:

Dear Sir/Madam:

My name is Donald Deignan and I live in Providence Rhode Island. My late uncle, P.F.C. Joseph J. Deignan, SN/SSN: 6141481, is buried in Grave 100 B. at your facility. My wife and I plan to be in Honolulu during the week of February 1-5, 2010 and we would like to visit my uncle's grave. Here is why I am asking in advance for your advice and assistance with our visit....I have reason to know, by virtue of my extensive historical research, that my uncle was born and raised as a Roman Catholic but I also know from his I.D.P.F. (Individual Deceased Personnel File), a copy of which I have obtained from the Army, that no denominational affiliation was listed at the time of his death and that no religious service was recorded as having been conducted either in 1942 or in 1949. The cause of his death was evidently "suicide" and in those days such an act automatically precluded a Roman Catholic priest from officiating at his funeral. Since then, however, the Church's attitude toward "suicide" has changed sufficiently to allow for prayers to be said over the graves of Catholics who, for whatever reason, take their own lives. My uncle was a Pearl Harbor Attack survivor, and I theorize that that event, or something else equally traumatic, caused him to take his own life in March 1942. His family, of course, never knew anything about the real circumstances of his death and I have only learned them recently…. During my impending visit to Honolulu, I would like to arrange to meet at the National Memorial Cemetery of the Pacific with a Roman Catholic Military Chaplain, or a civilian priest, and ask him to pray with me so as belatedly and certainly to bless my uncle and his final, earthly resting place. My question to you is how would I go about making such an arrangement and can any member of your staff assist in fulfilling my request? Please advise….I am myself a practicing Roman Catholic and my uncle's last living male relative and namesake. His legal name was Joseph J. Deignan but his Baptismal Name was "Donald" and I was named for him. Family honor and religious duty, equally, compel me to strive to have his grave blessed by the Church in which both of us were raised. I hope that the staff of the Cemetery can help me to accomplish this important task….Achieving some "closure" would mean a great deal to me and to my wife as well.[13]

Two weeks later, I received the following letter from Mr. James Messner, a Public Relations Specialist, at the Cemetery:

Dear Mr. Deignan:

I am writing in response to your letter requesting that a Catholic Priest be available the first
week of February 2010 to say a prayer over the
gravesite of your uncle, the late PFC Joseph H.
Deignan, who is interred in Section "B", Grave
Number 100.

You indicated in your letter that no clergy was
present when your uncle was interred in the
National Memorial Cemetery of the Pacific
on February 4, 1949, and that there was no
religious preference listed in his Individual
Deceased Personnel File. However, our record shows that the Latin or Christian Cross
was placed on his marker. As far as clergy being
available at the time of burial, all interments
were done with a Catholic Priest, Jewish Rabbi
and Buddhist Priest present who conducted
services over those being interred.

We can, if you still desire, ask a Catholic Priest
to be available when you visit the gravesite.
However, I will need a good date and time that
you will be at the cemetery....We will let you
know when we have confirmation on a Priest
being available to bless the gravesite. Any hono-
rarium would be between you and the Priest.[14]

The next day, I replied to Mr. Messner, by e-mail, as follows:

Dear Mr. Messner:

Thank you very much for both your e-mail and letter to me of January 14, 2010, regarding my visit to your cemetery and an individual blessing for my late uncle's grave there. I am gratified to learn that a Catholic priest may have said a prayer over him in 1949 but, given the particular circumstances of my uncle's death, I cannot be sure that this then if (sic) fact happened. The "Latin Cross" on his grave marker was requested by my grandmother on a form supplied to her by the U.S. Army. She had no real idea of the circumstances surrounding her son's death.… The primary purpose of my impending visit to Hawaii is to insure that a Roman Catholic priest says a prayer, in my presence, at my uncle's grave. I would welcome your help in securing a clergyman to perform this rite. I will of course be happy to compensate him for doing so for me.… As regards the timing of this event, my wife and I will be entirely at your disposal as well as that of the priest in question.… So, if you can find a priest for me, my wife and I will be glad to meet him at the cemetery at a time convenient to him and you too. I will call your office on Monday morning, February 1st,

> to discuss final arrangements personally with you....If you have trouble finding a priest, for any reason, kindly let me know and I will myself contact the Diocese of Honolulu directly for this purpose if necessary.[15]

Happily, it turned out that it was not necessary for me to contact the Diocese of Honolulu to obtain the services of a Catholic priest to officiate at my uncle's grave. Early on the afternoon of January 19, 2010, Mr. Messner asked me, upon my arrival in Honolulu to:

> Please call Mr. Duane Vachon in this office. He is the one talking to the Priest to see if he will be available to assist you.[16]

Later that same afternoon, I heard from Jim Messner again. This time he informed me that:

> Father Dave Travers has agreed to do your service at 10 a.m., February 3, 2010, at the gravesite. Circumstances surrounding the death was not mentioned as far as I know.[17]

I then wrote to Mr. Messner and said:

> That's wonderful news! Thanks so much for your great help. I can't tell you how important this is to me.[18]

It turned out that Dr. Duane Vachon, himself a practicing Roman Catholic, had asked his parish priest, Father Dave Travers—a Massachusetts native and a retired U.S. Navy Chaplain—if he would assist me, and Father Dave gladly agreed to do so. Accordingly, my wife and I met Dr. Vachon and Father Travers at the Office of the National Memorial Cemetery of the Pacific at 10:00 a.m. on Wednesday February 3, 2010. My wife, Kathy, and I together with Father Dave and Duane Vachon piled into a golf cart for the short trip to my uncle's already flag-bedecked grave. On the way there, I explained briefly to Father Travers the circumstances of Donald's death—supposedly by suicide—in March 1942. He took it all in and said nothing.

When I had initially sought to secure the services of a priest, in advance of our visit to Hawaii in February 2010, I had expected—even if I was able to do so—that he would say a brief prayer over Donald and be done with it. But there, by Donald's grave, overshadowed by a huge Chinese Banyan tree on that bright Hawaiian morning, something wonderful happened. Father Travers read the entire Interment Service for my uncle by his grave. What is more, Father Dave made the entire ceremony deeply personal and particular to Donald. He said:

> We cannot undo what has been done in the past but we can come here to rectify a wrongful situation which occurred many years ago. We gather here today, after many years of sorrow, to remember Donald and to pay him at last the proper respect he deserved to receive in March

> 1942. May he sleep here in peace until Christ awakens him to Eternal Life in Heaven.

Father Dave continued:

> "It is appropriate that we read here today from the Gospel of John where Jesus said, "For I have come down from Heaven not to do my own will but the will of him who sent me; and this is the will of him who sent me, that I should lose nothing of all that he has given me, but raise it up at the last day."[19]

Then Father Travers continued,

> Christ promised Paradise to the penitent thief. May he also receive Donald into Paradise to be with Him forever. For, in his heart, O Lord, Donald longed to do your will.

After we all then said the Lord's Prayer, Father Travers blessed Donald's grave and said, "Eternal rest grant unto him, O Lord." And my wife, Kathy, and I, acting as the congregation, responded, "And may perpetual light shine upon him." Then Father Dave concluded,

> May his soul, and all the souls of the Faithful Departed, through the Mercy of God, rest in peace. Amen. Go in peace in the Name of the Father and of the Son and of the Holy Spirit, Amen.

Beforehand, I had expected much less. In the event, I could have asked for nothing more! For me, the Service was profoundly moving and deeply cathartic. As I wrote sometime later in a note of thanks to Jim Messner and Duane Vachon:

> My wife and I can't thank you and Father Dave Travers enough for your kindness, patience, sensitivity and practical help during our visit to the National Memorial Cemetery of the Pacific on February 3, 2010. For me, the service at my uncle's grave was a deeply moving and a profoundly healing spiritual experience. It brought me "closure" and a sense of personal peace I can hardly describe.[20]

The treatment which we received from all the staff at the Cemetery was in every respect, from first to last, nothing less than outstanding. It was also, apparently, altogether typical. This spectacularly beautiful final resting place of more than 35,000 American war dead is maintained with meticulous attention to detail and in a compassionate and dignified manner which should reassure all of us whose loved ones rest there that they are being well cared for by the conscientious representatives of a grateful nation.

After the graveside service concluded, I thanked Father Dave warmly for his words which had given me great peace of mind. He said, "I think what we have done here today may have been more important for all of us than for Donald." In saying this, Father Dave was reaffirming the theological conviction that

Almighty God Himself had long since forgiven Donald for any sins he may have committed, including suicide, and that God had already received him into the peace of His Eternal Kingdom.

Then, after Father Travers had departed, I asked for "a few minutes alone" with Donald. My wife and Dr. Vachon thereupon withdrew to a respectful distance.

For the second time in forty years I was, again, alone with Donald. So then and there, in part, I said to him aloud:

> I came here first almost exactly forty years ago with my parents, as you well know. At that time I was unaware of the circumstances that led to your death. I have at this point lived my life for perhaps twice as long and more as you did yours. And if I, as a mature man, could talk to you as a younger man I would have told you that, "Everything will be all right." That there was no harm, or wrong, or problem so grievous that you could not have overcome it and not…have taken the course of action that you did. But,…as Father Dave said, in his remarks a few minutes ago, "We cannot undo the past. But we can rectify situations that should have been dealt with better, more appropriately, more completely in 1942."… And so, I hope this gives you peace. I hope this gives you rest. I hope this gives you…the closure and the honor…that you deserve.[21]

I then went on to say:

> You need to know that...I am here, not only
> in my own name, but... in the name of your
> entire family Your father,...your mother,...
> your brothers,...and your sisters,...and...your
> niece, Kathy,...my first cousin, the last other
> surviving member of our family; and for her
> husband,...and their children....I will convey
> to them what we did here today and I will teach
> them to honor your memory as I have done.[22]

Then I told Donald something which he doubtless already
knows. But it is something which I, myself, firmly believe:

> When next we meet, it will not be in this
> place. And, as Father Dave said,... God prom-
> ised Paradise to the penitent thief and I know
> that equally He has promised Paradise...to you.
> And I hope and trust we will meet there, face
> to face, in God's own good time.[23]

Finally, I said:

> Thank you for being in my life. Thank you for
> allowing me to come here and honor you and
> do the best I could...to set things right. It is
> the least that any dutiful nephew and namesake
> could do...and I am pleased to have done it.[24]

So now, more than fifty years after it started, my intellectual and spiritual journey with my Uncle Donald—which began on a bleak December day in 1959 when I was but a forlorn ten year old boy at Perkins School for the Blind—is all but over. During the intervening decades I have learned a good deal about him both as a myth and as a man. Sadly, I know now that he was never "The Pearl Harbor Hero" of my youthful imaginings. Private First Class Joseph J. Deignan simply happened to be in the right place at the wrong time. His "heroism" was at best incidental and generic; for he was merely one of tens of thousands of young American Soldiers, Sailors and Marines who risked wounds or death just because they chanced to be stationed on the island of Oahu on a fateful Sunday morning in December 1941. Many of them indeed acted heroically during the Pearl Harbor Attack and its aftermath but there is no surviving evidence to suggest that Donald actually did so.

My uncle was, in fact, in almost every respect an entirely ordinary and decent young man. His very "ordinariness" and "decency" are things worth celebrating. For Donald loved his family and he tried to take care of his impoverished mother and sisters, as best he could, during very difficult economic times in the Great Depression. His decision to join the United States Army in July 1939 was probably motivated far more by pragmatism than by patriotism. Nonetheless, he was a good soldier who served our country faithfully until he finally broke-down under the unrelenting psychological strain of the difficult wartime service in which he found himself after the attack on Pearl Harbor. In the end, Donald was thus, tragically, not so much "a hero" as he was "a harbinger." Donald's wounds, save for the very final ones, were invisible. But they were no less real than were those physical injuries sustained by some of his comrades in conventional battle. During World War II and ever since, tens of thousands of U.S. service members, having seen combat as Donald did, have suffered in varying degrees from Post Traumatic Stress Disorder. Like Donald, himself, they all deserve to be honored and cherished for the unstinting devotion they have given to our country at no small cost to themselves. Our gratitude to each and every one of them—to those whose lives were lost and to those whose lives were forever changed—should be unbounded.

Personally, I wish finally and unequivocally to say here that the apparently tragic manner in which Donald's life ended in no way diminishes either the love and respect which I have for him as a person or my appreciation of the many sacrifices which he made for others during his lifetime. As our Church would rightly have it now, "Hate the Sin but love the Sinner," and so I do.

For my part, having grown up and long lived in "The Shadow of Sacrifice", it is now more than time for me to move beyond its ambiguous shade and to take up new challenges of a different kind. After many years in Donald's psychological and spiritual company, the time has come for me to heed Isaiah's ancient injunction:

> Remember not the events of the past,
> the things of long ago consider not;
> see, I am doing something new![25]

As for Donald, himself, I hope and believe that I have done my duty by him to the best of my ability. Much earlier in this Chapter I compared Donald's military career and his ultimate fate with that of "The Minstrel Boy," the heroic Irish soldier of Thomas Moore's famous poem. Sitting alone beside Donald's newly blessed and peaceful Hawaiian grave in February 2010, I quoted aloud to my uncle later lines from that same moving poem so as to sum up what I had tried to do for Donald; in bearing his name, honoring his memory, gaining for him a measure of spiritual peace and reconciliation and in striving to live a life of which he would be proud. To set the seal on our long and complex relationship, I said aloud to Donald Joseph John Deignan:

> "Tho' all the world betrays thee,
> "*One* sword, at least, thy rights shall guard,
> "*One* faithful harp shall praise thee!"[26]

Five thousand miles of physical distance and an unknown number of remaining years will henceforth again separate me from my uncle. We will, however, continue to be bound together—as we always have been—by real, unbreakable bonds of mutual love and loyalty. When I was a boy, he helped and sustained me both spiritually and psychologically. As a man I believe that I have been able, in some measure, to repay that youthful debt and to aid him in that same way too by gaining for him at long last the respect and reconciliation which he deserves. More than fifty years ago, I tearfully promised my "Uncle Donald" that I would live my own life so as to honor his. Someday in the not too distant future—when we meet, at last, face-to-face in Paradise—we will both finally know how well I have kept that earnest promise made to him so long ago.

Don Deignan [author] at age 9 with his
mother, Margaret, (standing) and her parents,
Michael and Mary Donovan, Barrington
Rhode Island, June 1959. Photograph by
Dr. Frank J. Deignan. (Author's Archives.)

"Old Francis Deignan" (1837-1914) with
two of his sons. Worcester Massachusetts.
No date. Photographer unknown. (Author's
Archives.)

Bernard and Anna (Cross) Deignan on their
wedding day, June 21, 1905. Worcester
Massachusetts. Photographer unknown.
(Author's Archives.)

Donald Joseph as a little boy. Keefe
Place, Worcester Massachusetts, 1918.
Photographer unknown. (Author's Archives.)

Donald Joseph as a young teenager. Keefe
Place. Worcester Massachusetts. June, 1926.
Photographer unknown. (Author's Archives.)

Donald Joseph taking a break from "Forestry work" in the CCC. Alfred Maine. Summer 1934. Photographer unknown. (Author's archives.)

Donald J. J. Deignan, age 21, in CCC work
uniform. Pittsfield Massachusetts, June 1936.
Photographer unknown. (Author's Archives.)

Private Joseph J. Deignan (left), with an unidentified buddy, Fort Slocum New York, July 1939. Photographer unknown. (Author's Archives.)

Donald and fellow soldiers "sight-seeing" in a
"Panama City Horse Taxi." Panama Canal
Zone, August 22, 1939. Photographer un-
known. (Author's Archives.)

Private First Class Joseph J. Deignan poses in his "Dress Uniform" shortly after his promotion. Schofield Barracks, Territory of Hawaii, May 1940. Photographer unknown. (Author's Archives.)

Donald (right) and an unidentified fellow soldier on a day's leave, both dressed in civilian clothes, strolling along a downtown Honolulu street, October 8, 1941, just two months before the Pearl Harbor Attack. Photographer unknown. (Author's Archives.)

The Officers and Men of C. Battery, 13th F.A.,
November 1941. Donald Joseph is in the
center of the fourth row down from the top
among the Privates First Class. Photograph
courtesy of Schofield Studios. (Author's
Archives.)

View, from a distance, of the Schofield
Barracks Post Cemetery where P.F.C.
Deignan was buried on March 20, 1942.
Photographer unknown. (Author's Archives.)

Private First Class Deignan's Army Funeral,
March 20, 1942. Schofield Barracks Post
Cemetery. Photographer unknown. (Author's
Archives.)

Soldiers from the U.S. Army's 34th Infantry Regiment fire ceremonial volleys over Donald's grave at Schofield Barracks at his initial interment in March 1942. Photographer unknown. (Author's Archives.)

One of Donald Joseph's comrades-in-arms
poses for a picture kneeling by Private First
Class Deignan's grave at Schofield Barracks
Cemetery. No date. Photographer unknown.
(Author's Archives.)

Grave Marker of Private First Class Joseph
J. Deignan, National Memorial Cemetery of
the Pacific, Honolulu Hawaii. Photograph by
Pamela Dahlberg. October 2008. (Author's
Archives.)

The author with Father Dave Travers after the
Memorial Service and Blessing of Donald's
Grave in the National Memorial Cemetery of
the Pacific, February 3, 2010. Photograph by
Kathleen P. Leonard. (Author's Archives.)

Dr. Duane Vachon and Dr. Don Deignan pose
for a picture outside the Cemetery Office
after the conclusion of Donald's Memorial
Service, February 3, 2010. Photograph by
Kathleen P. Leonard. (Author's Archives.)

The author stands on the spot "ONE
FOURTH MILE EAST OF WAIMEA OAHU
TH" where Donald's body was found at 11:18
P.M. on March 18, 1942. Photograph by
Marshall Uchida, February 6, 2010. (Author's
Archives.)

A panoramic view of Waimea Bay today.
Here, in March 1942, Donald and his 24th
Infantry Division comrades awaited an ex-
pected "Japanese Invasion" which never came.
Photograph by Marshall Uchida. (Author's
Archives.)

Donald's brothers, Frank (right) and Robert
(left), in later life. Photograph by Cecile
Deignan. (Author's Archives.)

The Rhode Island Irish Famine Memorial
Narrative Wall, Providence Rhode Island,
Dedicated November 17, 2007. Robert
Shure, Sculptor. Famine text by Dr. Donald
D. Deignan. Immigrant text by Dr. D. Scott
Molloy. Photograph by Richard McCaffrey,
2016.

EASTER RISING

This plaque commemorates the one-hundredth anniversary of Ireland's 1916 Easter Rising. During that armed insurrection in Dublin and other parts of the country, against British colonial rule, Ireland was proclaimed a sovereign, independent Republic. The Rising failed and, in its aftermath, sixteen of its leaders were executed by the British. Those deaths inspired resistance which eventually secured independence for twenty-six counties in 1922. In 2016, six counties in the north of Ireland still remained under British rule.

Here we pay tribute to the Martyrs of 1916. We also honor all those people who have suffered persecution, exile, imprisonment, and death for the cause of a free, united Irish Republic.

Dedicated April 24, 2016

1916 "Easter Rising Monument," Rhode Island Irish Famine Memorial site, Dedicated April 24, 2016. Text by Dr. Donald D. Deignan. Photograph by Richard McCaffrey, 2016.

Flagstone honoring P.F.C. Donald J. Deignan
at the Rhode Island Irish Famine Memorial
site. Photograph by Richard McCaffrey, 2016.

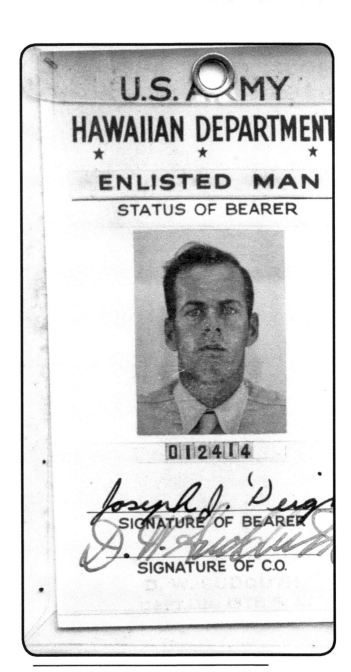

[Donald] Joseph J. Deignan's Hawaiian
Department Military ID, September 1939.
Photographer unknown. (Author's Archives.)

NOTES

✱ ✱ ✱

CHAPTER ONE: DECEMBER 7, 1959

1. 1959 *"Christmas Music"* Program of Perkins School for the Blind. Perkins School for the Blind, Watertown Massachusetts, Research Library Archives.

2. *Kentucky Folk Carol*, "Jesus, Jesus Rest Your Head", Ibid., p. 3.

3. United States Catholic Conference, Inc. <u>CATECHISM of the CATHOLIC CHURCH</u>. SECOND EDITION: revised in accordance with the official Latin text promulgated by Pope John Paul II. Vatican City: LIBRERIA EDITRICE VATICANA, 1997, pp. 249-250.

4. Ibid., pp. 665, 643-644, 364, respectively.

5. 1959 *"Christmas Music"* Program, p. 8.

6. Fyodor Dostoevsky, <u>The Brothers Karamazov</u>, Translated by Andrew R. MacAndrew. Introductory Essay by Konstantin Mochlusky. Bantam Books: New York, 1981, p. 934.

★ ★ ★

CHAPTER TWO: "NEITHER FISH NOR FOWL"

1. Records of Donald Donovan Deignan at Rhode Island State Services for the Blind and Visually Impaired, Providence Rhode Island, File No. R-884, "Environment" in Case notes, [2/13/52] p. 1. (Hereafter referred to as "Don Deignan, S.B.V.I. Records".

2. Robert Barlow, M.D., Editor-in-Chief. THE MERCK MANUAL OF DIAGNOSIS AND TREATMENT, Fourteenth Edition, Rahway, New Jersey: Merck Sharp & Dohmer Research Laboratories, 1982, Chapter 214, Paragraph 2004.

3. Mrs. Bertha Mitchell to Miss Elenor Kelly, March 26, 1957, Don Deignan, S.B.V.I.. Records, p. 8.

4. Barlow, THE MERCK MANUAL OF DIAGNOSIS AND TREATMENT, Chapter 133, Paragraphs 1366-1367.

5. Mrs. John Langdon to Mrs. Leonore Gay, January 24 1952. Don Deignan's S.B.V.I. Records, p. 1.

6. Ibid.

7. Ibid.

8. Bureau for the Blind, Providence Rhode Island, "Annual Report 1951-1952", p. 2.

9. Don Deignan, S.B.V.I. Records, p. 1.

10. Miss Lydia Fletcher, March 10, 1954, "Case Notes", Ibid. p. 4.

11. Bureau for the Blind, "Annual Report 1954-1955", p. 6.

12. March 21, 1957, Mrs. Bertha Mitchell, "Case Notes" Don Deignan S.B.V.I. Records, p. 8.

13. Mrs. Bertha Mitchell to Miss Eleanor Kelly, March 26, 1957. Don Deignan, S.B.V.I. Records, p. 9.

14. Ibid., September 9, 1957.

15. Ibid., Carl J. Davis to Mr. Frank J. Deignan, May 31, 1957, p. 10.

16. Carl Seaburg and Stanley Paterson, **Merchant Prince of Boston: Colonel T. H. Perkins, 1764-1854**, Cambridge, Massachusetts: Harvard University Press, 1971, pp. 378-386.

17. Kimberly French, **HISTORY OF PERKINS SCHOOL FOR THE BLIND,** The Campus History Series. Charleston, South Carolina: Arcadia Publishing, 2004, pp. 41-42.

18. Ibid. p. 23. Dr. Howe had participated in the Greek War of Independence in the late 1820s and his emotional

attachment to Greece remained a life-long one. On a return visit there in 1866 Howe met a young journalist named Michael Anagnos who returned with him to Perkins and in due course became the School's second Director. Mr. Anagnos founded the first kindergarten for blind children in the United states in 1887 and one of the institution's Lower School Cottages is named for him.

19. Evelyn C. Prince, August 8, 1959, "Case Notes", Don Deignan, S.B.V.I. Records, p. 26. See also Photograph #1.

20. Miss Lydia Fletcher, December 8, 1959, "Case Notes", Don Deignan, S.B.V.I. Records, p.11.

21. Perkins School for the Blind, "Student Records of Donald Donovan Deignan" (1957-1968), February 16, 1960, pp. 18-19.

22. Ibid., December 1963, p. 24.

23. Ibid., June 30, 1968, p. 31.

★ ★ ★

CHAPTER THREE: "HE WAS JUST A KID!"

1. August 30, 1970, from "Japan", audiotape transcript, p. 5. (Author's Archives.)

2. Gordon W. Prange, Donald M. Goldstein and Katherine V. Dillon. AT DAWN WE SLEPT: The Untold Story of Pearl

Harbor. New York: McGraw-Hill Book Company, 1981, p. 11.

3. Film, "Wake Island', (1942), copy in Author's Archives. See also Lawrence H. Suid, Dolores A. Haverstick. Stars and Stripes on Screen: A Comprehensive Guide to Portrayals of American Military on Film. Lanham, Maryland: The Scarecrow Press, Inc., 2005, p. 261.

4. Film, "Bataan", (1943), copy in Author's Archives. Suid, Stars and Stripes on Screen, p. 17.

5. The Roman Way 1961, Volume III., June 1961, Rome, Italy: Published by The Students of Notre Dame International School, Fifth Grade class photo. (Copy in Author's Archives.)

6. Ms. Jan Seymour-Ford to Don Deignan, March 29, 2006. (E-mail copy in Author's Archives.)

7. We arrived in Japan on August 3, 1970 and disembarked the next day. See "United States of America PASSPORT of Donald Donovan Deignan", #j:164448, p. 14., (Author's Archives.)

8. Mark H. Goldberg, "CAVIAR AND CARGO": The C 3 Type Passenger Cargo Ships. Volume 2 of The American Merchant Marine History Series. The American Merchant Marine Museum Foundation, 1992, pp. 231-263. I am deeply indebted to Mr. Barry Eager for this reference.

9. "Japan", audiotape transcript, August 6, 1970, p. 1. (Author's Archives.)

10. Ibid., p. 4.

11. Ibid., p. 2.

12. Ibid.

13. Ibid.

14. Ibid., p. 3.

15. Ibid.

16. Ibid.

17. Ibid.

18. Ibid., p. 4.

19. Ibid., p. 5.

20. Ibid.

★ ★ ★

CHAPTER FOUR:
AT THE BOTTOM OF THE HEAP

1. 1900 United States Census. Worcester County Massachusetts. City of Worcester, Ward 3, Block 27.

2. Leitrim Genealogy Centre. Our Leitrim Ancestors: GENEALOGY OF THE DUIGNAN FAMILY OF KILTUBRID CO. LEITRIM. BALINAMORE, CO. LEITRIM, IRELAND, 2008, pp. 1-2. Irish vital records from the mid- nineteenth century are generally fragmentary and of poor quality. This is so for a number of reasons. Between 1690 and 1829, the practice of Roman Catholicism, both in Ireland and throughout the rest of the British Empire, was prohibited by a body of laws called "The Penal Code." Active persecution of the Roman Catholic Faith in Ireland had ceased long before the repeal of the Penal Code in 1829 but the Church—after several centuries of existence as a rudimentary, underground organization--was still not fully functional as a public institution until the 1840s. Baptismal Records were not kept in the Parish of Kiltubrid until 1841 and Civil Records of Births, Marriages and Deaths were not systematized, nationally, until the early 1860s. Add to this the fact that the Duignan family, like the vast majority of their neighbors, were illiterate, Irish-speaking, landless laborers, and it is easy to understand why dates of birth and the ages of people both at the time of marriage and death can only be approximated before 1864 when vital records were centralized.

3. T.W. Freeman, PRE-FAMINE IRELAND: A STUDY IN HISTORICAL GEOGRAPHY, Manchester: Manchester University Press, 1957, p. 250.

4. Brian Mitchell, <u>a new geographical atlas of ireland.</u> Baltimore, Maryland: GENEALOGICAL PUBLISHING Co., Inc., 1986, p. 5.

5. <u>GENEALOGY OF THE DUIGNAN FAMILY</u>, p. 8.

6. Freeman, <u>Pre-Famine Ireland</u>, pp. 148-149.

7. <u>GENEALOGY OF THE DUIGNAN FAMILY</u>, p. 20.

8. Freeman, <u>Pre-Famine Ireland</u>, p. 247.

9. James S. Donnelly, Jr., <u>The Great Irish Potato Famine</u>, Sutton Publishing Limited, Gloucestershire, England, 2001, p.171.

10. Ibid., p. 176.

11. <u>GENEALOGY OF THE DUIGNAN FAMILY</u>, p. 1.

12. F.S.L. Lyons, <u>Ireland Since The Famine</u>. Suffolk, England: The Chaucer Press, Ltd., Collins/Fontana. Eighth Edition, 1982, pp.51-52.

13. <u>GENEALOGY OF THE DUIGNAN FAMILY,</u> p. 26.

14. Ibid. p. 20.

15. Ibid. p. 21.

16. Freeman, <u>Pre-Famine Ireland</u>, p. 254.

17.   Quoted in Kerby A. Miller, <u>Emigrants And Exiles: Ireland and the Irish Exodus to North America</u>, New York: Oxford University Press, 1985, p.105.

18.   Ibid., p. 106.

19.   Lyons, <u>Ireland Since The Famine</u>, p. 44.

20.   Francis Degnan's "Marriage Certificate". (Copy in Author's Archives.)

21.   1861 Scottish National Census. Found at <u>www.scotlandspeople.gov-uk.</u> Website. Hereafter cited as "scotlandspeople".

22.   1881 Ibid.

23.   Donnelly, <u>The Great Irish Potato Famine</u>, pp. 141-144.

24.   Tim Pat Coogan, <u>WHEREVER GREEN IS WORN: The Story of the Irish Diaspora</u>, New York: Palgrave, 2001, p. 237.

25.   <u>The Holy Bible containing the Old and New Testaments</u>. Standard Revised Version. Catholic Edition. Princeton, New Jersey: SCEPTER, 1966. Zephania: 3:12-13.

26.   Brenda Collins, "The Origins of Irish Immigration to Scotland in the Nineteenth and Twentieth Centuries", <u>Irish Immigrants and Scottish Society in the Nineteenth</u>

and Twentieth Centuries Proceedings of the Scottish Historical Studies Seminar Strathclyde University 1989-90. Edited by T.M. Devine, Edinburgh, Scotland: John Donald Publishers, Ltd., 1991, p. 1. .

27.   C. T. Atkinson, Old West Linton, Catrine, Ayrshire, Scotland: Stenlake Publishing, 2002, p. 3.

28.   Quoted in The Irish In Modern Scotland by James Edmund Handley, Cork, Ireland: Cork University Press, 1947, p. 168.

29.   Ibid.

30.   Mr. Chris Atkinson to Donald D. Deignan, September 7, 2010. (E-mail copy in Author's Archives.)

31.   Ibid.

32.   1881 Scottish National Census. "scotlandspeople".

33.   Bernard Degnan's Birth Certificate, August 8, 1877. (Author's Archives.)

34.   Bernard Degnan, Baptismal Certificate", "Scottish Catholic Archives 1877." "scotlandspeople".

35.   Atkinson, Old West Linton, p. 1.

36.   Ibid., pp. 3, 6.

37. Tom Gallagher, <u>Glasgow The Uneasy Peace: Religious tension in modern Scotland, 1819-1914</u>. Manchester, England: Manchester University Press, 1987, p. 4.

38. *Imperial Gazetteer of Scotland*, edited by John Marius Wilson, 1868.

39. Atkinson, <u>Old West Linton</u>, p. 45.

40. Gallagher, <u>Glasgow The Uneasy Peace</u> , p. 71.

41. 1881 Scottish National Census. "scotlandspeople".

42. Edward J. Cowan & Richard Finlay, <u>SCOTLAND SINCE 1688: Struggle For A Nation</u>, London: Cima Books, 2000, p. 81.

43. David Armitage, "The Scottish Diaspora" in <u>Scotland: A History</u>, (Edited by Jenny Wormald), Oxford, England,Oxford University Press, 2005, p. 294..

44. Ibid., p. 279.

45. Malcom Gray,"The Course of Scottish Emigration, 1750—1914": Enduring Influences and Changing Circumstances" in <u>Scottish Emigration and Scottish Society</u>, <u>Proceedings of the Scottish Historical Studies Seminar Strathclyde University 1990-91.</u> Edited by T.M. Devine, Edinburgh, Scotland: John Donald Publishers, Ltd., 1992, p. 34.

46. Handley, The Irish In Modern Scotland , p. 243.

47. S.S. Corean "LIST OF PASSENGERS, DISTRICT OF BOSTON AND CHARLESTOWN, PORT OF BOSTON", Passengers #45 through #51., October 18, 1888.

48. Ibid.

49. Background information about the S.S. Corean has been derived from the "Norway Heritage.com" website.

50. Gallagher, Glasgow The Uneasy Peace , p. 5.

51. Francis Degnan, *The Worcester Directory*. Worcester, MA: Drew, Allis & Co., 1889, p. 129.

52. Timothy J. Meagher, Inventing Irish America: Generation, Class, and Ethnic Identity in a New England City, 1880-1928, Notre Dame, Indiana: University of Notre Dame Press, 2001, p. 24.

53. Ibid., pp. 26-28.

54. Thomas Francis O'Flynn, The Story of Worcester Massachusetts, Boston, Little, Brown and Company, 1910, pp. 14, 24.

55. Charles Grenfill Washburn, <u>Industrial Worcester</u>. Burgeonville, Pennsylvania: General Books, LLC, 2009, pp. 1-15.

56. O'Flynn, <u>Story of Worcester</u>, pp. 115-117.

57. Washburn, <u>Industrial Worcester</u>, p. 177.

58. Ibid., p. 168.

59. Meagher, <u>Inventing Irish America</u>, p. 20.

60. Ibid., p. 21.

61. Ibid., pp. 273-274.

62. Ibid., p. 45.

63. Washburn, <u>Industrial Worcester</u>, p. 89.

64. Ibid., pp. 80, 83, 87, 88.

65. Francis Degnan, <u>*The Worcester Directory*</u>. Worcester, MA :Drew, Allis & Co., 1892, p. 147.

66. Charles J. Deignan, <u>Worcester Daily Telegram</u>, September 23, 1916, (no page).

67. Peter Deignan, <u>Worcester Evening Gazette</u>, September 8, 1936, p. 21.

68.   James Deignan, <u>Worcester Evening Gazette</u>, September 8, 1939, p. 25.

69.   William F. Deignan, <u>Worcester Daily Telegram</u>, October 1, 1941, p. 14.

70.   Francis J. Deignan, <u>Worcester Evening Gazette</u>, November 30, 1942, p. 23.

71.   Miss Mary C. Deignan, <u>Worcester Evening Gazette</u>, September 3, 1938, p. 16.

72.   Agnes T. Deignan, <u>Worcester Evening Gazette</u>, February 15, 1947, p. 16. The statement of her age and birthplace are directly contradictory. If Agnes was indeed 57 at the time of her death in February 1947, she could not have been born in Scotland, as her Obituary claimed, because her year of birth would have been 1890. By that time, the entire Deignan family had been in Worcester for more than a year. On the other hand, there is no mention of Agnes in the 1881 Scottish National Census nor for that matter on the S.S. Corean's 1888 Passenger List. So she was certainly born sometime well after 1881. But she may have been an infant in 1888, too young to be listed separately on the ship's Manifest.

73.   Bernard Deignan, *The Worcester Directory*. Worcester, MA: Drew, Allis & Co., 1902, p. 391.

74. Original and later corrected copy of Bernard Deignan's "Naturalization Certificate", Central District Court of Worcester. (Author's Archives.)

75. Meagher, <u>Inventing Irish America</u>, p. 59.

76. Washburn, <u>Industrial Worcester</u>, p. 89.

77. Meagher, <u>Inventing Irish America</u>, p. 47.

78. Washburn, <u>Industrial Worcester</u>, p. 89.

79. David Armitage, "The Scottish Diaspora" in <u>Scotland: A History</u>, p.297.

80. Charles A. Nutt, <u>History of Worcester and Its People</u>, (4 volumes), (New York: Lewis Historical Publishing Company, 1919) Volume I., p. 348.

81. Ibid.

82. Meagher, <u>Inventing Irish America</u>, p. 71.

83. Washburn, <u>Industrial Worcester</u>, p. 177.

84. David Brody, <u>*Steelworkers in America*: The Nonunion Era</u>. Cambridge Massachusetts: Harvard University Press, 1960, p. 93.

85. Washburn, <u>Industrial Worcester</u>, p. 93.

86. American Steel & Wire Company, *"The Story of Wire*: FROM IRON ORE TO FINISHED PRODUCTS"*. New Jersey: American Steel & Wire Company, 1948, p. 1.

87. Ibid.

88. Washburn, <u>Industrial Worcester</u>, p. 80.

89. *"The Story of Wire"*, pp. 24-25.

90. Ibid., p. 31.

91. Ibid.

92. Bernard Deignan, <u>*The Worcester House Directory*</u>. Worcester, MA: Drew, Allis & Co., 1904, p. 370.

93. Bernard Deignan, <u>*The Worcester Directory*</u>. Worcester, MA: Drew, Allis & Company, 1905, p. 197.

94. Meagher, <u>Inventing Irish America</u>, p. 58.

95. "Copy of Record of Marriage", June 21, 1905. Office of the City Clerk, City of Worcester, MA.

96. See Photograph #3. Bernard and Anna's Wedding Picture. (Author's Archives.)

97. Meagher, <u>Inventing Irish America</u>, p. 52.

98. Bernard Deignan, *The Worcester House Directory*. Worcester, MA: Drew, Allis & Co.,1906, p. 249.

99. Marilyn W. Spear, WORCESTER'S THREE-DECKERS, WORCESTER PEOPLE AND PLACES, VI. WORCESTER, MASSACHUSETTS: WORCESTER BICENTENNIAL COMMISSION, 1977, p. 7.

100. Ibid., p. 5.

101. Ibid., p. 30.

102. Ibid., p. 12.

103. Ibid., p. 26.

104. Meagher, Inventing Irish America, p. 72.

105. Joseph Deignan, "Copy of Record of Birth", March 15, 1915. Office of the City Clerk, City of Worcester, Massachusetts.

106. Bernard Deignan, *The Worcester Directory*. Worcester, MA: Drew, Allis & Co., 1915, p. 218.

107. Francis Deignan, "Copy of Record of Death", August 12, 1914, Office of the City Clerk, City of Worcester, Massachusetts.

108. Francis Deignan with sons. See Photograph #2. (Author's Archives.)

109. Francis Deignan, <u>Worcester Evening Post</u>, August 13, 1914, p. 3.

110. Sanborn Insurance Co. <u>Insurance Maps of Worcester, Massachusetts, 1910.</u> New York: Sanborn Map Company, c.1911, 3 volumes.

111. Bernard Deignan, <u>The Worcester House Directory</u>. Worcester, MA: Drew, Allis & Co., 1916, p.448.

112. Washburn, <u>Industrial Worcester</u>, p. 92.

113. Meagher, <u>Inventing Irish America</u>, p. 280.

114. Ibid.

115. Brody, <u>Steelworkers in America</u>, p.270.

116. <u>The Worcester House Directory</u>. Worcester, MA: Drew, Allis & Company, 1898, p. 220; <u>Polk's Worcester House Directory</u>. Boston, MA: R. L. Polk & Company, 1973-74, p. 182.

117. Speare, "Worcester's Three-deckers", p. 8.

118. See Photographs #4. and #5. (Author's Archives.)

119. Coogan, <u>Wherever Green Is Worn</u>, p. 236.

120. Brody, <u>Steelworkers in America</u>, p. 90.

121. Town Clerk of West Linton to Bernard Deignan, November 15, 1932. (Letter in Author's Archives.)

122. Atkinson, <u>Old West Linton</u> , p. 10.

123. Meagher, <u>Inventing Irish America</u>, pp. 50-51.

124. Ibid., pp. 34-35.

125. Gallagher, <u>Glasgow The Uneasy Peace,</u> p. 12.

126. Meagher, <u>Inventing Irish America</u>, p. 55.

127. Ibid., p. 271.

128. Ibid., p. 219.

129. Ibid., p. 282.

130. Quoted in Meagher, <u>Inventing Irish America</u>, pp. 345-346.

131. Ibid., p. 97.

132. Letter from Kathy Morrissey to Donald Deignan, August 25, 2010. (Author's Archives.) I wish to thank Ms. Morrissey, Secretary of Our Lady of Providence Parish, Worcester, for establishing for me the dates on which Donald made his "First Holy Communion" and "Confirmation" at Saint Bernard's Church in Worcester.

133. <u>Catechism of the Catholic Church</u>, pp. 261-262, 269.

134. Letter from Kathy Morrissey to Donald Deignan, August 25, 2010. (Author's Archives.)

135. <u>Catechism of the Catholic Church</u>, pp. 332-333.

136. Copy of Donald J. Deignan's North High School academic records. (Author's Archives.)

137. Coogan, <u>WHEREVER GREEN IS WORN</u>, p. 246.

138. Meagher, <u>Inventing Irish America</u>, p. 104.

139. Leslie Alexander Lacy, <u>The Soil Soldiers: The Civilian Conservation Corps in the Great Depression</u>. Radnor, Pennsylvania: Chilton Book Company, 1976, pp. 42- 43.

140. Meagher, <u>Inventing Irish America</u>, p. 105.

★　★　★

CHAPTER FIVE:
IN THE "CCC" AND AFTERWARDS

1. John Salmond, <u>The Civilian Conservation Corps, 1933-1942: A New Deal Case Study</u>. (Durham, North Carolina: Duke University Press, 1967) , p. 135,(hereafter cited as "The CCC").

2. Both sets of Donald's "Discharge Papers" from the Civilian Conservation Corp were received from the National Archives and Records Administration, National Personnel Records Center (CPR), St. Louis, MO, (hereafter cited as

"Discharge Papers, 1935" or "Discharge Papers, 1937"), "Discharge Papers, 1935", p. 3.

3.   Stan Cohen, <u>THE TREE ARMY: A PICTORIAL HISTORY OF THE CIVILIAN CONSERVATION CORPS 1933-1942</u>. (Missoula, Montana: Pictorial Histories Publishing Company, 1980), p. 54, (hereafter cited as "Tree Army").

4.   "Emergency Conservation Work Act", quoted in Alexandra Lacey, <u>The Soil Soldiers</u>, p. 212, (hereafter cited as <u>"SOIL SOLDIERS"</u>).

5.   Ibid.

6.   Ibid., pp. 212-213.

7.   Ibid., p. 16.

8.   Ibid., p. 213.

9.   Ibid., p. 215.

10.   Ibid., p. 16.

11.   Ibid., pp. 214-221.

12.   "The CCC", p. 30.

13.   "Discharge Papers, 1935", p. 2.

14.   Ibid.

15. Ibid.

16. Ibid.

17. Ibid., pp. 5-6.

18. "The CCC", p.141.

19. Ibid., p. 64.

20. Usher Parsons, <u>A CENTENIAL HISTORY OF ALFRED, YORK COUNTY, MAINE</u>. (Philadelphia, Pennsylvania: Sanford, Everts & Co. 1872) (hereafter cited as "History of Alfred"),

21. John P. Cook, <u>History of Alfred's Second Century 1894-1994</u>, (no publisher listed),p. 1., (hereafter cited as <u>"Alfred's Second Century"</u>.

22. Mary Carpenter Kelly, (two untitled pieces) April 4, and April 9,1944, held in Parsons Memorial Library, Alfred Maine, "CCC Folder", (hereafter cited as "Alfred Library CCC Folder".

23. <u>Alfred's Second Century</u>, p. 6.

24. Ibid.

25. Ibid.

26. "Discharge Papers, 1935", p. 9.

27. Mary Carpenter Kelly, "Officers and Men of the C.C.C. at Alfred Hear Talk on Nursery Culture and Reforestation.", July 13, 1933, "Alfred Library CCC Folder".

28. Mary Carpenter Kelly, (untitled piece), April 9, 1944, "Alfred Library CCC Folder".

29. Ibid.

30. Mary Carpenter Kelly (untitled piece), January 24, 1936. "Alfred Library CCC Folder".

31. Mary Carpenter Kelly (untitled piece), January 24, 1936. "Alfred Library CCC Folder".

32. Ibid.

33. Mary Carpenter Kelley, (untitled piece), April 4, 1944, "Alfred Library CCC Folder".

34. [Mary Carpenter Kelley, (untitled piece), May 11, 1936, "Alfred Library CCC Folder."

35. Ibid.

36. Mary Carpenter Kelley, (untitled piece), March 27, 1934, "Alfred Library CCC Folder".

37. Mary Carpenter Kelley, (untitled piece), February 17, 1936. "Alfred Library CCC Folder".

38. Mary Carpenter Kelly, (untitled piece), April 4, 1944; and, Mary Carpenter Kelley, "Massachusetts Members of 13oth C.C.C. Company Get a Revere Beach Sunburn Shoveling Snow in Maine", March 15, 1934."Alfred Library CCC Folder".

39. "Discharge Papers, 1935", p. 9. See also Photograph #6. (Author's Archives.)

40. Mary Carpenter Kelley, (untitled piece), April 16, 1934, "Alfred Library CCC Folder".

41. Mary Carpenter Kelley, (untitled piece), December 27, 1933. "Alfred Library CCC Folder".

42. Ibid.

43. Mary Carpenter Kelly, November 26, 1933."Thanksgiving at the C.C.C., Alfred.", in "Alfred Library CCC Folder".

44. Mary Carpenter Kelley, (untitled piece), April 9, 1944, "Alfred Library CCC Folder".

45. Mary Carpenter Kelley, (untitled piece), March 27, 1934. "Alfred Library CCC Folder".

46. Mary Carpenter Kelly, "Thanksgiving at the C.C.C., Alfred.", November 26, 1933. "Alfred Library CCC Folder".

47. Mary Carpenter Kelley, March 27, 1934, (untitled piece), [Alfred Library CCC Folder".

48. See "Discharge Papers, 1935".

49. Ibid.

50. "The CCC", p. 138.

51. Ibid., pp. 40-41, 43, 45.

52. Ibid., p. 31.

53. Ibid., p. 137.

55. Ibid., pp. 40-41.

56. Ibid. p. 34.

57. Ibid., pp. 137-141.

58. "Discharge Papers, 1935", p. 9.

59. "The CCC", p. 59.

60. Ibid. pp. 63-68.

61. Exactly when the Deignans moved to 53 Lincoln Street is unclear but it was probably in March 1936.

62. "Discharge Papers, 1937", p. 2.

63. "Discharge Papers, 1935", p. 4.

64. "Discharge Papers, 1937", p. 2.

65. Ibid.

66. "Donald J.J. Deignan, age 21", in CCC work uniform. Pittsfield Massachusetts, June 1936. [Photograph #7.] (Author's Archives.)

67. "Discharge Papers, 1937", p. 8.

68. George E. O'Hearn, "Narrative Report", December 11, 1935, p. 1, in NARA, "Mt. Greylock Camp Report", (hereafter cited as "Greylock Camp Report".

69. "Narrative Report", February-March 1936, p. 2., "Greylock Camp Report".

70. Ross Abore to the Office of the Emergency Conservation Work Director, November 28, 1934, "Greylock Camp Report".

71. January 30, 1934, "Greylock Camp Report".

72. "Relative to SP-7, Pittsfield, Massachusetts, July 2, 1937", "Greylock Camp Report", p. 1.

73. Superintendent George E. O'Hearn to United States Department of the Interior, Office of National Parks,

Buildings and Reservations, "Narrative Report", August 31, 1934, p.1., "Greylock Camp Report."

74. Andrew B. Jones to George E. O'Hearn, December 24, 1935, "Greylock Camp Report".

75. February 23, 1936 photograph, "Greylock Camp Report".

76. "Discharge Papers, 1937", p. 8.

77. "Narrative Report", (February—March), 1936, "Greylock Camp Report", p. 1.

78. Ibid., pp. 1-2.

79. "Discharge Papers 1937", pp.6-7.

80. Ibid., p. 8.

81. Susan Shea, "Final Report Research relating to Donald Joseph John Deignan 2009", p. 1., hereafter cited as "Shea Final Report".

82. "Discharge Papers, 1937", p. 8.

83. "Greylock Camp Report", [no author or date.]

84. George E. O'Hearn, "Narrative Report", August 31, 1934, p. 4., "Greylock Camp Report".

85. "Narrative Report", April 1, 1935, p. 7, "Greylock Camp Report."

86. "Narrative Report", August 16, 1935, p.1., "Greylock Camp Report".

87. "Narrative Report", April-May, 1935, pp.6-7, "Greylock Camp Report".

88. Quoted in "Shea Final Report", p. 5.

89. Ibid.

90. "Commanding Officer, 107th Co, CCC to Commanding Officer, Third CCC District, July 18, 1934", "Greylock Camp Report".

91. Ross Ware to Office Of The Director, Emergency Conservation Work, July 6, 1937, "Greylock Camp Report".

92. Mr. P.J. King to (CCC Acting Director) J.J. McEntee, SUPPLEMENTARY REPORT, July 24, 1939, p. 1., "Greylock Camp Report"

93. The Tree Army, p. 31.

94. "Discharge Papers, 1937", p. 8.

95. Alan D.St. John, OREGON'S DRY SIDE: Exploring East of the Cascade Crest. (Portland, Oregon: Timber Press, 2007), p. 24.

96. Ibid., p. 50.

97. Richard H. Engeman, <u>The Oregon Companion: An Historical Gazetteer OF The Useful, The Curious, And The Arcane</u>. Portland Oregon: Timber Press, Inc., 2009) p. 161.

98. Ibid., pp.194-195, 67-68.

99. "Discharge Papers, 1937", p. 9.

100. Ibid.

101. Ibid., p. 8.

102. <u>The Soil Soldiers</u>, p. 52.

103. Ibid., pp. 47-48.

104. Ibid., p. 51.

105. Ibid., p. 70.

106. Ibid., pp.140-141.

107. Ibid., p. 53.

108. Maurice F. Whalen to George O'Hearn, June 12, 1935, "Greylock Camp Report".

109. <u>The Soil Soldiers</u>, p. 42.

110. Ibid., pp. 48-49.

111. Report of Educational Advisor, Company 107, November 30, 1934, "Greylock Camp Report".

112. "Discharge Papers 1937", p. 10.

113. The Soil Soldiers, p. 38.

114. "Discharge Papers, 1937", p. 9.

115. Quoted in The Soil Soldiers, p.44.

116. Ibid., pp.134-135.

117. "The CCC", pp. 85-87.

118. Ibid., p. 114.

119. "Narrative Report, October 7, 1935", p. 1., "Greylock Camp Report".

120. The Tree Army, p. 31.

★ ★ ★

CHAPTER SIX: LIFE IN "C." Battery, 13th F.A: 1939-1942

1. Brian McAllister Linn, Guardians of Empire: The U.S. Army and the Pacific, 1902-1940. Chapel Hill, North Carolina: The University of North Carolina Press, 1994, p. 66.

2. Joseph's "Enlistment Record", as such, has not survived. In 2002 the National Archives and Records Administration (NARA) scanned and digitized "Army Enlistment Records", originally contained on computer "punch-cards", for the period from 1938 through 1946. The searchable electronic file which resulted contained nearly nine million records of men and women who served in the United States Army during World War II. But a significant percentage of the punchcards could not be successfully scanned and read so the information on them was lost. Joseph's Enlistment Record was among those which could not be reproduced and preserved electronically. So much about his Army service remains, like his life in general, elusive, unknown and unrecoverable.

3. "LeBrun Interviews Transcript ," p. 16. (Author's Archives.)

4. Linn, <u>Guardians of Empire</u>, p. 63.

5. Ibid., p. 65.

6. "Donald and an unidentified Buddy at Fort Slocum, New York, July 1939. Photograph #8. (Author's Archives.)

7. Charles Wardlow. THE UNITED STATES ARMY IN WORLD WAR II, The Technical Services, <u>THE TRANSPORTATION CORPS: RESPONSIBILITIES, ORGANIZATION, AND OPERATIONS</u>, WASHINGTON,

D.C., OFFICE OF THE CHIEF OF MILITARY HISTORY, 1951, pp. 136-137.

8.   Stephan Gemlin, "**S.S. Republic** Passenger Ship Transport Hospital Ship". THE MARINE NEWS, MAY, 1946, pp. 60-62, 143. As previously noted, I am grateful to my friend and colleague, Mr. Barry Eager, for providing me with a copy of his material on the *Republic.*

9.   "The Canal Record 1939", (no. 2. vol. 33, p. 30.) I am indebted for this information to Mr. Charles Dinsmore and his colleagues in the Smathers Library at the University of Florida, Gainsville.

10.   Norman J. Padelford, THE PANAMA CANAL IN PEACE AND WAR. New York: The MacMillan Company, 1942, pp. 111-112. During peacetime, at least, toll charges or "tariffs" were lower on ships which went through the Panama Canal without passengers.

11.   "Panama City Horse Taxi". Donald and several of the men who sailed with him from New York to Hawaii on the U.S.A.T. Republic in late August 1939 had a few hours to see the local sights while their ship transited the Panama Canal without them. See Photograph #9. (Author's Archives.)

12.   Bluhm, Raymond K. Jr. Editor-in-Chief, Dale Andrade, Bruce Jacobs, John Lengellier, Clayton R. Newell, Matthew Seelinger, U.S. ARMY: A COMPLETE

HISTORY, Arlington, Virginia: The Army Historical Foundation, Hugh Lauter Levin Associates, Inc., 2004, , p. 619.

13. Ibid.

14. Honolulu Advertiser, Friday, September 15, 1939, p. 9. The Republic docked at 7:00 a.m. at pier 9, the previous morning.

15. Linn, Guardians of Empire, p. 65.

16. Ibid., p. 63.

17. Donald B. Connelly, John M. Schofield & the Politics of Generalship, Chapel Hill, North Carolina: The University of North Carolina Press, 2006, p. 326.

18. Tropic Lightning Museum. "Historic Guide Schofield Barracks Hawaii". Waihiawa Hawaii. Tropic Lightning Museum, (no date). The Post "Theater," where Donald probably attended 8:00 A.M. Mass on December 7, 1941, had 1400 seats and was the largest such structure of its kind on Oahu at that time. Apparently Private First Class Deignan and his fellow Field Artillerymen in the 24th Infantry Division lived in their own Quadrangle separate from those of the Infantry Regiments which they were assigned to support. I wish to thank Mr. Pierre Moulin for providing me with copies of two very useful pamphlets on

the history of Schofield Barracks from which the information in this paragraph is drawn.

19.   Ron Chernow, <u>Alexander Hamilton</u>, New York: Penguin Books, 2005. pp. 84-85. Given the United States Army's keen interest in the "Lineage" of its various units, the treatment of the origins of the "13th F.A." Regiment and Battalion are, equally, ambiguous to say the least. Janice E. McKenney in her work <u>FIELD ARTILLERY REGULAR ARMY AND ARMY RESERVE</u>, Army Lineage Series, Washington D.C.: OFFICE OF THE CHIEF OF MILITARY HISTORY, THE UNITED STATES ARMY, 1985 says in one place that "The regiment was organized in 1917 from personnel of the 5th Field Artillery, represented in the canton." [p. 207.] But elsewhere in the same volume, in her treatment of the 5th Field Artillery Regiment itself, [pp. 67-83], she makes no mention at all of this connection. Furthermore, even though direct successor organizations of Alexander Hamilton's original "Battery" served in every American conflict from the Revolutionary War through Vietnam and other Batteries of the Fifth Field Artillery Battalion served at least until the end of World War II, Herbert Phillips declared flatly 1947 that, "Thirty years ago today, in the hot desert near El Paso, Texas, Sergeant James A. Regan brought his sixty man platoon to a halt in front of Lt. Benjamin B. Carter. He saluted and reported. He was the first of a group to comply with telegraphic instructions, General Orders 9, 10, and 11 from the adjutant General of the Army;

to physically dissolve the Fifth Field Artillery Regiment and to create in its stead a new unit." Herbert P. Phillips, "THE CLAN": ORGANIZATION DAY BOOKLET of the THIRTEENTH FIELD ARTILLERY BATALLION, Washington, D.C: Adjutant General's Office, Historical Records Section, 1947, p. 3.

20. Phillips, "THE CLAN", p. 5.

21. Quoted by Linn, Guardians of Empire, p. 51.

22. RG 407, Entry 427, Box 6839, WWII Operations Reports, 24th Inf. Div., After Action Report of the 13th F.A. Battalion, "Blacklist" (Occupation of Japan), NARA, College Park Maryland, [hereafter, "NARA, College Park".

23. Mark E. Grotelueschen, DOCTRINE UNDER TRIAL: American Artillery Employment in World War I. Westport Connecticut: Greenwood Press, 2001, pp. 138-139, 151-152.

24. **War Department, FM 100-5 "Field Service Regulations, Operations"**, (May 22, 1941), pp. 8-9.

25. May 1940 "C." Battery Unit Roster, National Personnel Records Center, (Military Branch), Saint Louis, MO.

26. See Photograph #10. (Author's Archives.)

27.   Obituary of Bernard L. Deignan, <u>Worcester Telegram</u>
        <u>September 2, 1940</u>, p. 12.

28.   The history and "Lineages" of the 13th Field Artillery
        Regiment, and of its successor Organization the 13th Field
        Artillery Battalion, are detailed by Janice E. McKenney
        in <u>FIELD ARTILLERY REGULAR ARMY AND ARMY</u>
        <u>RESERVE</u>, Army Lineage Series, Washington D.C.:
        OFFICE OF THE CHIEF OF MILITARY HISTORY, THE
        UNITED STATES ARMY, 1985, pp. 207-220. For "C."
        Battery, in particular, see especially pp. 212-213 and 217.
        Much additional information in this paragraph is derived
        from the surviving "C." Battery "Unit Rosters" in the files of
        the National Personnel Records Center (Military Branch)
        in Saint Louis Missouri. These documents, which were
        prepared at the end of every month, list the name, rank,
        serial number, sub-unit, duty code and date of enlistment
        of each soldier on the roster during a specific month. Unit
        Rosters covering the months from October 1941 through
        March 1942 were used in compiling aggregate informa-
        tion about Donald's Unit. Additional information about
        individual members of the Battery has been obtained by
        mining the online Archival Databases "Electronic Army
        Serial Number Merged File, ca. 1938 – 1946 (Enlistment
        Records) maintained by the National Archives and
        Records Administration or "N.A.R.A." In general, these
        files give a soldier's full name, Army serial number, state
        of residence, home county, place of enlistment, includ-
        ing day, month and year, education, civilian occupation,

citizenship and marital status. There are, however, gaps
in these electronic holdings for technological reasons
involving the nature of data transfer from one informational format to another. Ironically, Joseph J. Deignan's
"Enlistment Record" is one of those which did not survive
the transfer from one system to the other. After the information transfer process was completed the original documents on which it was based were deliberately destroyed.
Finally, I made extensive use of a composite photograph
taken by "Schofield Studios", probably in November 1941.
Donald sent a copy of this group picture home to his family shortly before the Pearl Harbor attack. At the top it
shows the Battery's two Commissioned Officers, Captain
D.W Hiester and Lieutenant W.G. Stevenson, together
with 109 soldiers organized in descending order, by rank,
from 1st Sergeant down to Private. It appears that each soldier's picture was taken individually and then transferred
onto a single sheet of paper so as to produce the finished
collective black-and-white photograph. Interestingly, although there is considerable overlap between the young
men shown in this picture and the corresponding names
on "C" Battery's Unit Roster for November 1941 the two
documents are far from identical. There are a good number of soldiers who are listed on the Unit Roster who do
not appear in the picture. And, equally, there are 19 men
who are shown in the photo but are not recorded as being on the Unit's November 1941 monthly Roster. All the
men in the composite photograph appear serious. Many
of them seem shy and the entire group looks very young

if not altogether innocent. Taken together, these various sources combine to provide a compelling and fairly complete "official record " of the men of "C. Battery" of the 13th Field Artillery Battalion on the eve of World War II.

29.   Linn, <u>Guardians of Empire</u>, p. 72.

30.   Ibid., p. 116.

31.   Ibid., p. 117.

32.   Quoted by Phillips in "The Clan", p. 22.

33.   Linn, <u>Guardians of Empire</u>, p. 134.

34.   Ibid. p. 125.

35.   Ibid., p. 128.

36.   Ibid., pp. 128-136.

37.   "October 8, 1941". Donald and a Buddy, in civilian clothes, strolling along in downtown Honolulu, almost exactly two months before the Japanese attack on Pearl Harbor and Schofield Barracks. See Photograph #11. (Author's Archives.)

38.   MacKinnon Simpson, <u>HAWAII HOMEFRONT: LIFE IN THE ISLANDS DURING WORLD WAR II</u>, Honolulu, Hawaii: Bess Press, 2008, pp. 136, 140, 142-145.

39. Rudyard Kipling, "Tommy" in <u>RUDYARD KIPLING'S VERSE: INCLUSIVE EDITION 1885-1918,</u> New York: Doubleday, Page & Company, 1922, pp. 453-454.

40. Linn, <u>Guardians of Empire</u>, p. 201.

41. The Hawaiian Division was activated on February 25, 1921. Bluhm, et al, <u>U .S. ARMY: A COMPLETE HISTORY</u>, p. 601.

42. In the words of one of the 24th Infantry Division's earliest historians, the "Shoulder patch is a green taro leaf bordered in yellow, superimposed on a red circle which is bordered in black. This was the shoulder patch of the old Hawaiian Division which was reorganized and redesignated the 24th shortly before war broke out. It was natural for the division to choose a patch symbolic of the Hawaiian Islands. The taro is a native plant of Hawaii and from it is extracted certain food concoctions and a drink (*sic*) called poi." Edmund F. Henry, **"FACT SHEET ON THE 24TH INFANTRY DIVISION"**, (no date), RG 407, Entry 427, Box 6611, WWII Operations Reports, 24th Inf. Div., "AGF Fact Sheet, 24th Infantry Division. NARA, College Park.

43. RG 407, Entry 427, Box 6615, WWII Operations Reports, 24th Inf. Div., Gen. Order #1, "Brigadier General D.S. Wilson Assumes Command." October 1, 1941. Ibid.

44. RG 407, Entry 427, Box 6615, WWII Operations Reports, 24th Inf. Div., " New Division Commander at Schofield," October, 1941. Ibid.

45. RG 407, Entry 427, Box 6615, WWII Operations Reports, 24th Inf. Div., Gen. Order #2, "Announcement of Division Staff Officers," October 1, 1941. Ibid.

46. RG 407, Entry 427, Box 6615, WWII Operations Reports, 24th Inf. Div., Staff Memo. #1, "Administrative Procedure," October 10, 1941. Ibid.

47. Ibid.

48. Ibid.

49. RG 407, Entry 427, Box 6615, WWII Operations Reports, 24th Inf. Div., "Roster of Officers," October 21, 1941. Ibid.

50. Glen Willford, RACING THE SUNRISE: Reinforcing America's Pacific Outposts, 1941-1942. Annapolis, Maryland: Naval Institute Press, 2010, p. 285.

51. Quoted in "After Action Report of the 13th F.A. Battalion, RG 407, Entry 427, Box 6839, WWII Operations Reports, 24th Inf. Div., "Blacklist" (Occupation of Japan), NARA, College Park.

52. RG 407, Entry 427, Box 6615, WWII Operations Reports, 24th Inf. Div., "Principal Training Activities," 6-11 October 1941. Ibid.

53. RG 407, Entry 427, Box 6615, WWII Operations Reports, 24th Inf. Div., "Principal Training Activities," 13-18 October 1941. Ibid.

54. RG 407, Entry 427, Box 6615, WWII Operations Reports, 24th Inf. Div., "Principal Training Activities", 20-25 October, 1941. Ibid.

55. RG 407, Entry 427, Box 6839, WWII Operations Reports, 24th Inf. Div., "Battalion History, October 1941, (Page 2., e. Marches), Ibid.

56. Ibid. The term "Road March" is something of a misnomer since the men of the 13th F.A. rode in trucks while conducting these exercises. This fact accounts for the long distances covered in relatively short periods of time. When the troops reached their destination on such occasions, they would unhitch their artillery pieces from the trucks towing them, deploy the weapons in formation and then break down the equipment, stow it, and prepare to return to Schofield Barracks for the night. See **"FM 6-5, Field Artillery Field Manual, Organization and Drill"**, (October 1, 1939), pp. 64-65.

57. RG 407, Entry 427, Box 6615, WWII Operations Reports, 24th Inf. Div., Memorandum: "24th Infantry

Division—Communication Exercise November 4, 1941",
p. 1., Ibid.

58.   RG 338, Entry 37042, Box 3461, Unit Histories, 24th
Infantry, Training Memo. #5, "Training Program" Nov. 1,
1941 to May 23, 1942. p. 1. Ibid.

59.   Ibid.

60.   Ibid., p. 2.

61.   Ibid., pp. 2-3.

62.   Ibid., p. 3.

63.   Ibid., p. 4.

64.   Linn, <u>Guardians of Empire</u>, p. 65.

65.   Battery "C" Unit Roster for November 1941, (NPRC,
Saint Louis), p. 1. See also Photograph #12. (Author's
Archives.)

66.   RG 407, Entry 427, Box 6615, WWII Operations Reports,
24th Inf. Div., "Roster of Officers," October 21, 1941, p.
7. NARA, College Park. Captain Hiester was listed as being with Battery "B" of the 63rd F.A. in October but he was
literally "pictured" as Battery "C"'s Commanding Officer
in the "composite Unit Photograph" referred to extensively in Foot-note #28 above. This happy coincidence

helps to date that photograph from November 1941 as previously suggested.

67.   Stetson Conn, Rose C. Engelman, Byron Fairchild. UNITED STATES ARMY IN WORLD WAR II. <u>GUARDING THE UNITED STATES AND ITS OUTPOSTS</u>. Washington, D.C. CENTER OF MILITARY HISTORY, 2000, p. 192.

68.   Eugene P. Broderick, <u>24th Infantry Division: "The Victory Division"</u>. Paducah, Kentucky: Turner Publishing Company, 1997, pp. 12-13.

69.   U.S. Army Human Resources Command, Alexandria, Virginia, "Individual Deceased Personnel File" of Joseph J. Deignan, hereafter referred to as "IDPF", p. 17.

70.   Ibid., p. 7.

71.   Donald's Obituary, <u>Worcester Evening Gazette</u>, March 20, 1942, Page 1.

72.   Quoted in "PERSONNEL, DECEASED", ARMY REGULATIONS No. 600-550, U.S. Army Heritage & Education Center, U.S. Army Military History Institute, Carlisle, Pennsylvania, 1936, p. 11. [Hereafter cited as (AR 600-550.]

73.   E.A. Stommel to Bernard Deignan, July 21, 1942, IDPF, p. 25.

74. G.A. Horon to Bernard Deignan, February 26, 1947, Ibid., p. 21.

75. Ibid.

76. Major Thomas B. Larkin to Mr. Bernard Deignan, April 22, 1947, Ibid., p. 20.

77. Major Richard B. Coombs to Mr. Bernard Deignan, June 13, 1947, Ibid.,. p.17.

78. Mrs. Anna C. Deignan to the Quartermaster General of the Army of the United States, June 14, 1947, Ibid., p.16.

79. Lt. Colonel B.M. Baukhight to Mrs. Anna C. Deignan, August 21, 1947, Ibid., p. 15.

80. Mrs. Anna C. Deignan to the Quartermaster General of the Army of the United States, June 14, 1947, Ibid., p. 16.

81. "REQUEST FOR DISPOSITION OF REMAINS", April 22, 1947, Ibid., p. 12.

82. On Friday, September 2, 1949, "...the fourth anniversary of VJ Day...", the *Honolulu Advertiser* announced, on Page 1, **"Punchbowl To Be Dedicated At 2 Today".** Approximately 10,000 people attended the solemn dedication ceremony. In point of fact, however, Ernie Pyle— the famous World War II newspaper correspondent whose life had been taken by a Japanese sniper during the Iwo

Jima Campaign—was publicly buried in the Punchbowl on July 19, 1949. His interment thus actually "Opened" the National Memorial Cemetery of the Pacific to the general public even before its official dedication some months later. "Pyle Rites Today To Open Punchbowl", *Honolulu Advertiser*, Tuesday, July 19, 1949, p. 1.

83.   IDPF, p. 5.

84.   Ibid.

85.   Major General H. Feilmaan to Mrs. Anna C. Deignan, April 27, 1949, Ibid., p. 11. In fact, burials began at the National Memorial Cemetery of the Pacific on January 4, 1949 long before the new facility was dedicated or even opened to the public. On January 3, 1949, the *Honolulu Star-Bulletin* carried a front page story under the headline "Burials Start Tuesday in Punchbowl". Over the next two month, the story said, the Army planned to inter 200 bodies each day until 8,000 initial World War II casualties had been laid to rest. The same article went on to assure readers that **"SERVICES WILL BE READ**. Each day a joint army- navy air force burial service will be read over the remains to be buried that day. Military chaplains of each of the major religions professed by the decedents will lead the burial rites....The religious service will be followed by the traditional firing of three volleys from a rifle squad and the sounding of taps." Thus, Donald's final burial on February 4, 1949 was clearly only a very small, impersonal part of a mass and formulaic event.

86. Colonel James B. Clearwater to Mrs. Anna C. Deignan, January 9, 1953, IDPF., p. 3.

★ ★ ★

CHAPTER SEVEN: "A CITIZEN OF IRELAND"

1. The following partial list will give some idea of the variety of my volunteer work and interests over the last thirty-five years locally and nationally. An * indicates a term as President or Chairperson of an organization.

   1976-1977: White House Conference on Handicapped Individuals

   1977-1986: Meeting Street School Board of Directors

   1978-1984: Rhode Island Developmental Disabilities Council*

   1983-1986: Rhode Island Association for Retarded Citizens

   1983-1988: Rhode Island Committee for the Humanities

   1990-1996: United Cerebral Palsy of Rhode Island*

   1988-2011: PARI Independent Living Center Board of Directors*

   1988-2018: Governor's Advisory Council for the Blind*

   1992-2003: Governor's Commission on Disabilities

1996-: Kent House/Bridgemark, Inc. (Addiction recovery services)

1985-2010: Irish Cultural Association of Rhode Island

1997-: Rhode Island Irish Famine Memorial Committee, Inc.*

1998-2003: Library Board of Rhode Island

2001-2015: Heritage Harbor Museum Board of Directors

2003-2006: Secretary, "Special House Commission on Vision Services"

2009-2016: Ancient Order of Hibernians R.I. State Board Historian

2014-2016: 1916 Anniversary Memorial Committee

2008: Friendly Sons of St. Patrick, Providence, "Man of the Year".

2.　"European Community (Ireland) Passport issued to Deignan, Donald Donovan, May 24, 1988" (Author's Archives.)

3.　"Mass to mark 150 years since famine began", The Providence Journal, October 10, 1995, p. F-2; and, "Irish-Americans recall the Famine of 1845- 49", The Providence Journal, October 21, 1995, p. C-7.

4.   "Mission Statement" of the Rhode Island Irish Famine Memorial Committee, Inc., (Author's Archives.)

5.   Robert Shure to Don Deignan, September 20, 2002, (e-mail copy in Author's Archives.)

6.   Robert Shure to Don Deignan, October 4, 2002, (e-mail copy in Author's Archives.)

7.   Hippocrates, <u>Aphorisms</u>, quoted in John Bartlett, <u>Familiar Quotations: *A collection of passages, phrases and proverbs traced to their sources in ancient and modern literature*</u>. SIXTEENTH EDITION. JUSTIN KAPLAN, GENERAL EDITOR. Boston: Little, Brown and Company, 1992, p. 71.

8.   Don Deignan to Robert Shure, October 4, 2002, (e-mail copy in Author's Archives.)

9.   Dr. John Quinn to Don Deignan, October 8, 2002, (e-mail copy in Author's Archives.)

10.   Don Deignan to Dr. John Quinn, October 10, 2002, (e-mail copy in Author's Archives.)

11.   Dr. John Quinn to Don Deignan, October 11, 2002, (e-mail copy in Author's Archives.)

12.   The complete text of my portion of the Rhode Island Irish Famine Memorial narrative is as follows:

"The Great Famine was the most important event in Nineteenth Century Ireland. In the seven terrible years between 1845 and 1851, the potato crop, on which a large majority of the Irish people depended for their survival, failed completely or partially during each harvest season. The result of this devastating crop failure, caused by a disease commonly called "the Blight," was that at least one million men, women, and children died of outright starvation or of the epidemic diseases which came with it. Owing to the Famine, the population of Ireland, a northwest European island country slightly smaller than the State of Maine, was reduced by death or emigration from an estimated 8.5 million people to only 6 million.

At the time of the Famine, and for centuries before it, Ireland was not an independent country free to determine its own destiny. By virtue of English military conquest, Ireland had become part of what came to be known as the British Empire. In the process, many Irish Catholics were forced to become tenant farmers or landless laborers who survived by growing their potatoes on small, poor quality plots of land.

When the potato crop first failed late in 1845 Britain's Conservative Prime Minister, Sir Robert Peel, ordered food supplies sent to Ireland for distribution to the hungry at low cost. Peel believed that he had some moral obligation to help Ireland in the time of its supposed temporary distress. But this conviction was not altogether shared by the

Liberal Lord John Russell, who succeeded Peel as British Prime Minister in 1846. Russell and Sir Charles Trevelyan, his chief economic advisor for Ireland, believed that their government should take only a limited part in relieving disasters like the Great Famine. They thought that the private charity of individuals and philanthropic organizations should shoulder the burden of Famine relief. Accordingly, religious groups such as the Society of Friends (the Quakers) came forward to offer unconditional aid to Ireland.

Above all, Russell believed in protecting the rights of private property owners and in the promotion of a free market economy in both Britain and Ireland. In fact the Government believed so strongly in the economic principle of noninterference in trade that it allowed the export from Ireland of abundant supplies of meat and grain during all the Famine years. Policies such as these outraged public opinion around the world and forced the British Government, eventually, to provide direct Famine relief.

Early in 1847, "Black '47" as this year is known in Irish history, the British Government reluctantly established soup kitchens throughout Ireland to feed people at public expense. Remarkably, these soup kitchens provided food for three million people per day during the months of their operation. Thus Britain demonstrated that it could deal effectively with the Famine when it was forced by undeniable circumstances and world public opinion to do so. But at the first opportunity, Russell and Trevelyan closed the soup

kitchens and left Ireland to look after itself during the remainder of the Famine. The subsequent deaths of hundreds
of thousands of Irish people were the responsibility of the
British Government and the direct result of its callous in-
difference to Ireland's plight, especially between 1847 and
1851.

During the later years of the Famine many survivors
were too weak or sick to work and so they could not pay the
rent which they owed to their landlords. It is estimated that
nearly fifty thousand entire families were evicted from their
homes for nonpayment of rent between 1849 and 1851
alone. For most of these people, emigration was the only
alternative to death from starvation or disease on the roads
or in the grim and deadly government- sponsored "work-
houses" in Ireland.

So it was that many thousands of sick, hungry, dispos-
sessed people -- often bringing with them little more than
the clothes on their backs -- boarded ships bound for the
United States or other countries. These vessels, often called
"coffin ships," were sometimes small, unseaworthy, un-
sanitary and greatly overcrowded. Numerous deaths from
malnutrition and disease were not uncommon among the
Irish passengers bound for America in the wake of the Great
Famine. It is not surprising that an Irish poet, John Boyle
O'Reilly, called the Atlantic Ocean "The Bowl of Tears." A
new and uncertain life awaited the survivors of this difficult

voyage. To our benefit, many of them chose to make that life here in Rhode Island.

By Donald Donovan Deignan, Ph.D."

My interest in "The Easter Rising", which began on its fiftieth Anniversary in 1966, has remained constant. In 2014, I welcomed Ireland's Prime Minister, Enda Kenny, to the Famine Memorial site. Then I helped to found the 1916 Centenary Anniversary Committee. On April 24, 2016, we dedicated a Monument to the "Martyrs of 1916" at the Famine Memorial. I drafted its final text which reads as follows:

"Easter Rising

This plaque commemorates the one-hundredth anniversary of Ireland's 1916 Easter Rising. During that armed insurrection in Dublin and other parts of the country, against British colonial rule, Ireland was proclaimed a sovereign, independent Republic. The Rising failed and, in its aftermath, sixteen of its leaders were executed by the British. Those deaths inspired resistance which eventually secured independence for twenty-six counties in 1922. In 2016, six counties in the north of Ireland still remained under British rule.

Here we pay tribute to the Martyrs of 1916. We also honor all those people who have suffered

persecution, exile, imprisonment, and death for the cause of a free, united Irish Republic.

Dedicated April 24, 2016"

13. Scott Molloy, <u>Irish Titan, Irish Toilers: Joseph Banigan and Nineteenth-Century New England Labor (Revisiting New England)</u>, Hanover, New Hampshire, New England University Press, 2008, pp. xiii-xiv.

14. Flagstone inscribed in honor of P.F.C. Donald J. Deignan, at the Rhode Island Irish Famine Memorial, Providence Rhode Island. See also Photograph #25. (Author's Archives.)

15. Colonel Wanda L. Good to Mr. Donald D. Deignan, Ph.D., February 14, 2008, (copy in Author's Archives.)

16. Donald D. Deignan to Colonel Wanda L. Good, March 11, 2008, pp. 1-3, (copy in Author's Archives.)

17. Donald D. Deignan, Ph.D. to President Barrack H. Obama, June 22, 2012, and Scott A. Levins to Donald Deignan, September 3, 2012. (Copies in Author's Archives.) My former student and long-time personal friend, Congressman James R. Langevin (D-2 RI) generously arranged for me to meet and speak personally about my project with the President when Mr. Obama visited Providence in October 2010. After discussing my work briefly with him at that time, the President invited me to

contact him, through Congressman Langevin's Office, if I needed further assistance. Accordingly, in due course, I wrote to President Obama and asked Mr. Langevin for his help in transmitting my letter. At the President's request, Mr. Scott A. Levins, Director of the National Personnel Records Center, sent a substantive response to my correspondence. I am deeply grateful to President Obama, Congressman Langevin and Director Levins for their help in completing this project. Even with their collective help, it appears that many aspects of P.F.C. Deignan's military service and sudden, violent death will remain unknown and unknowable.

CHAPTER EIGHT: THE SHADOW OF SACRIFICE

1.   Linn, <u>Guardians of Empire</u>, p. 195.

2.   Ibid., p. 62.

3.   Prange, <u>AT DAWN WE SLEPT</u>, p. 101.

4.   Ibid., p. 230.

5.   Ibid.

6.   Steve Horn, <u>THE SECOND ATTACK ON PEARL HARBOR: OPERATION K. AND OTHER JAPANESE ATTEMPTS TO BOMB AMERICA IN WORLD WAR II.</u> Annapolis, Maryland: Naval Institute Press, 2005, p. 50.

7. Ibid., pp. 61-62.

8. Robert F. Rogers, <u>DESTINY'S LANDFALL: A HISTORY OF GUAM</u>, Honolulu, Hawaii: University of Hawaii Press, 1995, pp. 163-168.

9. Gregory J. W. Urwin, <u>Victory in defeat: THE WAKE ISLAND DEFENDERS IN CAPTIVITY 1941-1945</u> (Annapolis, Maryland: Naval Institute Press, 2010)_pp. 3-21.

10. Prange, <u>AT DAWN WE SLEPT</u>, pp. 575-577.

11. Horn, <u>THE SECOND ATTACK ON PEARL HARBOR</u>, pp. 57-58.

12. Ibid., p. 130.

13. Prange, Gordon W., Donald M. Goldstein and Katherine V. Dillon. <u>Miracle at Midway</u>. New York: MUF Books, 1982. , p. 327.

14. Quoted by Gordon W. Prange, Donald M. Goldstein and Katherine V. Dillon in <u>PEARL HARBOR: The Verdict of History</u>. New York: Penguin Books, 1991, p. 506.

15. Louis Morton, THE UNITED STATES ARMY IN WORLD WAR II, The War in the Pacific, <u>STRATEGY AND COMMAND: THE FIRST TWO YEARS</u>, Washington,

D.C.: CENTER OF MILITARY HISTORY, THE UNITED STATES ARMY, 2000, p. 143.

16.   Ibid., p. 146.

17.   Ibid., p. 147.

18.   Ibid.

19.   Quoted by Carl C. Dod in UNITED STATES ARMY IN WORLD WAR II, The Technical Services, THE CORPS OF ENGINEERS IN THE WAR AGAINST JAPAN, Washington, D.C.: THE CENTER OF MILITARY HISTORY, UNITED STATES ARMY, 1987, p. 27.

20.   Morton, STRATEGY AND COMMAND, p. 141.

21.   J. Garner Anthony, Hawaii Under Army Rule, Honolulu, Hawaii: The University Press of Hawaii, 1975, p. 127.

22.   Ibid.

23.   Ibid.

24.   Ibid., pp. 127-128.

25.   Ibid., p. 128.

26.   Ibid.

27.   Ibid., p. 42.

28. Ibid., p. 59.

29. Horn, <u>THE SECOND ATTACK ON PEARL HARBOR</u>, p. 104.

30. Morton, <u>STRATEGY AND COMMAND</u>, p. 207.

31. Ruth A. Tarbah,, <u>HAWAII: A History</u>, New York: W.W. Norton & Company, 1984, p. 167.

32. Ibid., p. 166. See also, Brown, DeSoto, Anne Ellett, <u>HAWAII GOES TO WAR: LIFE IN HAWAII FROM PEARL HARBOR TO PEACE</u>, Honolulu, Hawaii: Editions Limited, 1989, p. 62.

33. Horn, <u>THE SECOND ATTACK ON PEARL HARBOR</u>, pp. 41-42.

34. Ibid., pp. 92-99.

35. Ibid., p. 106.

36. Ibid., pp. 123-127.

37. Worcester Evening Gazette, March 20, 1942, p. 1.

38. IDPF. p. 26.

39. Hawaii Department of Commerce, "Standard Certificate of Death", for Joseph J. Deignan, March 19, 1942, (Copy in Author's Archives.)

40. "Morning Report for March 1942 for Battery C. of the 13th Field Artillery Battalion", (NPRC, Saint Louis), (Copy in Author's Archives.)

41. IDPF, p. 26.

42. Ibid.

43. Ibid., p. 25.

44. Major F.A. Stacy to Commanding Officer, Schofield Barracks, T.H., April 19, 1942, RG 494, Entry 44 (UD-UP), Box 252, Adjutant General Gen. Correspondence 1917-44, Decimal 293.1, Honors, "Funeral Firing Squads." NARA, College Park.

45. See Photographs #13. and #14. (Author's Archives.)

46. IDPF. p. 29.

47. Brown, <u>HAWAII GOES TO WAR</u>, p. 155.

48. "Death Certificate" of Deignan, Joseph J. (Copy in Author's Archives.)

49. IDPF, p.27.

50. Ibid., p. 28.

51. AR 600-550, Paragraph 21 (a).(4.), p. 11.

52. Ibid.

53. IDPF, p. 28.

54. AR 600-550, Paragraph 21 (a) (1.), p. 9.

55. Ibid., Paragraph 21 (3.), p. 9.

56. Ibid., Paragraph 21 (h)(2) pp. 10-11.

57. Ibid.,, Paragraph 21 (4.), p. 11.

58. Ibid.

59. Ibid.

60. IDPF, p. 23.

61. Major General H. Feilman, The Quartermaster General, to Mrs. Anna C. Deignan, April 27, 1949, Ibid., p. 11.

62. Ibid., p. 8.

63. Ibid., p. 9.

64. Ibid., p. 32.

65. Ms. Kathleen Vaughn-Burford to Don Deignan, October 7, 2009, (e-mail in Author's Archives.)

66.   Richard Hauzinger to Don Deignan, January 29, 2010, (e-mail in Author's Archives.)

67.   "LeBrun Interviews Transcript", pp. 3, 44. (Author's Archives.)

68.   AR 600-550, Paragraph 22 (a), p. 12.

69.   Colonel A.J. Canning, Medical Corps, to Chief of Staff, Hawaiian Department, "INFORMAL MEMORANDUM", RG 494, Entry 44 (UD-UP), Box 433, Adjutant General Gen. Correspondence 1917-44, Decimal 704, Casualties, "List of gunshot wounds admitted to this hospital," April 17, 1942. NARA, College Park. See also, RG 494, Entry 44 (UD-UP), Box 433, Adjutant General Gen. Correspondence 1917-44, Decimal 704, Casualties, "Reports of Separation," April 1, 1942. Ibid.

70.   IDPF, p. 29.

71.   Condon-Rall, Mary Ellen, Albert E. Courdrey. UNITED STATES ARMY IN WORLD WAR II. The Technical Services. THE MEDICAL DEPARTMENT. MEDICAL SERVICES IN THE WAR AGAINST JAPAN. Washington, D.C.: CENTER OF MILITARY HISTORY, UNITED STATES ARMY, 1998, p. 264. If Donald had in fact survived World War II, traumatized as he evidently was by his Pearl Harbor experience and its immediate aftermath, he would probably have been one of the very large number of "N.P. Cases" from that conflict. What distinguished

Donald from the million other American service members who suffered from psychiatric difficulty during and after the War was the fact that his "breaking-point" merely came sooner and had more catastrophic consequences than theirs did. See Thomas Childers, <u>SOLDIER FROM THE WAR RETURNING The Greatest Generation's Troubled Homecoming from World War II</u>. Boston: Houghton Mifflin Harcourt, 2009, passim.

72. RG 407, Entry 427, Box 6615, WWII Operations Reports, 24th Inf. Div., "Organization of the 24th Infantry Division," Dec. 7, 1941. NARA, College Park.

73. Prange, <u>AT DAWN WE SLEPT</u>, p. 526.

74. Grossman, Dave, Loren W. Christensen. <u>ON COMBAT: The Psychology and Physiology of Deadly Conflict in War and in Peace</u>, Third Edition, Warrior Science Publications, 2008, p. 278.

75. RG 407, Entry 427, Box 6611, WWII Operations Reports, 24th Inf. Div., "The Twenty-Fourth Infantry Division: A Brief History" (no date), p. 6. N.A.R.A., College Park.

76. Ibid.

77. IDPF, p. 26.

78. Linn, <u>Guardians of Empire</u>, p. 74. n. 102. See also Edward Coffman, <u>THE REGULARS</u>, p 320 for Army suicide problems in the 1920s and the 1930s.

79. Shay, Jonathan. <u>ODYSSEUS IN AMERICA: COMBAT TRAUMA AND THE TRIALS OF HOMECOMING</u>, New York; Scribner, 2002, p. 54.

80. Simpson, <u>HAWAII HOMEFRONT: LIFE IN THE ISLANDS DURING WORLD WAR II</u>, p. 36.

81. Quoted by Robert R. Palmer in UNITED STATES ARMY IN WORLD WAR II, The Army Ground Forces, <u>THE PROCUREMENT AND TRAINING OF GROUND COMBAT TROOPS</u>, by Robert R. Palmer, Bell I. Wiley and William R.I. Kast, Washington, D.C.: HISTORICAL DIVISION, DEPARTMENT OF THE ARMY, 1948, p. 50.

82. "Transcript of Interview at Waimea Bay", February 6, 2010, p. 8. (Author's Archives.)

83. Photographs #19. and #20. taken by Marshall Uchida at Waimea Bay, February 6, 2010. (Author's Archives)

84. Grossman, <u>ON COMBAT,</u> p. 11.

85. Linn, <u>GUARDIANS OF EMPIRE</u>, p. 246.

★ ★ ★

CHAPTER NINE: "*ONE* SWORD, AT LEAST"

1.   "Discharge Papers, 1935", p. 8.

2.   Thomas Moore, "The Minstrel-Boy", quoted in <u>Moore's</u>
     <u>Irish Melodies The Illustrated 1846 Edition</u> By Thomas Moore,
     Mineola, New York: Dover Publications, Inc. 2000, p. 99.

3.   Major General H. Feilman, The Quartermaster General,
     to Mrs. Anna C. Deignan, April 27, 1949, IDPF, p. 11.

4.   Ibid., p. 29. The Catholic Priests on duty at Schofield
     Barracks on March 20, 1942, in considering Donald's
     death by "Suicide" would doubtless have agreed with the
     verdict that, "He dies for lack of discipline, and because of
     his great folly he is lost." <u>The Holy Bible</u>: (Proverbs. 5:23.)

5.   Ibid., (1. Cor. 3:16.)

6.   "Hamlet", Act I, sc. ii, p. 889. Quoted in <u>SHAKESPEARE</u>
     <u>THE COMPLETE WORKS.</u> Edited By G. B. Harrison.
     New York: Harcourt, Brace & World, Inc. 1968.

7.   "Hamlet, Act V, sc. i, Ibid., p. 928.

8.   Major General H. Fielmaan, Quartermaster General, to
     Mrs. Anna C. Deignan, April 27, 1949, IDPF, p. 11.

9.   Thomas M. Jones to Mr. Donald D. Deignan, June 6,
     2006, IDPF Cover Letter, p. 1.

10.   <u>CATECHISM OF THE CATHOLIC CHURCH,</u> p. 550.

11.   Ibid.

12.   Ibid.

13.   Donald D. Deignan, Ph.D. to the Staff of the National Memorial Cemetery of the Pacific, December 31, 2009, (Author's Archives.)

14.   Mr. James Messner to Donald Deignan, Thursday, January 14, 2010, (e-mail in Author's Archives.)

15.   Don Deignan to Mr. James Messner, Friday, January 15, 2010, (e-mail in Author's Archives.)

16.   Mr. James Messner to Don Deignan, Tuesday, January 19, 2010, (e-mail in Author's Archives.)

17.   Mr. James Messner to Don Deignan, Tuesday, January 19, 2010, (e-mail in Author's Archives.)

18.   Don Deignan to Mr. James Messner, Tuesday, January 19, 2010, (e-mail in Author's Archives.)

19.   <u>The Holy Bible</u>: (John 6:38-39.)

20.   Don Deignan to James Messner, Monday, March 8, 2010, (e-mail in Author's Archives.)

21. "Second Visit to Hawaii", Transcript, February 3, 2010, p. 1., (Author's Archives.)

22. Ibid.

23. Ibid.

24. Ibid.

25. The Holy Bible: (Is. 43:16-21.)

26. Thomas Moore, Moore's *Irish Melodies*, p. 99.

SELECT BIBLIOGRAPHY

Agawa, Hyrouki. <u>THE RELUCTANT ADMIRAL: Yamamoto and the Imperial Navy</u>. Translated by John Bester. New York: Kodanshia International, Ltd. First trade paperback edition, 2000.

"ALL ABOUT WORCESTER". Worcester, Massachusetts: The League of Worcester Voters, 1988.

Allen, Gwenfread. <u>PACIFIC WAR CLASICS HAWAII'S WAR YEARS 1941-1945</u>. Kailua, Hawaii: Pacific Monograph, 1999.

American Steel & Wire Company, *"The Story of Wire*: FROM IRON ORE TO FINISHED PRODUCTS". New Jersey: American Steel & Wire Company, 1948.

Anthony, J. Garner. <u>HAWAII UNDER ARMY RULE</u>. Honolulu, Hawaii: The University Press of Hawaii, 1975.

Armitage, David . "The Scottish Diaspora" in <u>Scotland: A History</u>. Edited by Jenny Wormald. Oxford, England: Oxford University Press, 2005.

ARMY REGULATIONS No. 600-550. "PERSONNEL, DECEASED". U.S. Army Heritage & Education Center, U.S. Army Military History Institute. Carlisle, Pennsylvania, 1936.

Atkinson, T.C. <u>OLD WEST LINTON</u>. Catrine, Ayreshire, Scotland: Stenlake Publishing, 2002.

"Attack stunned area vets: Pearl Harbor survivors recall horror of December 7, 1941". Herb Weiss in "SENIOR DIGEST", Volume 3, No. 8, December 2006. Seekonk, Massachusetts: Olivia Publications, 2000.

Austin, Paul. <u>BULLETS AND BAYONETS: 34TH INFANTRY REGIMENT WORLD WAR II Infantry in Action</u>. Fort Worth, Texas: River Oaks Printing Company, Inc. Second Edition, 1996.

Bailey, Beth, David Farber. <u>THE FIRST STRANGE PLACE: Race and Sex in World War II Hawaii</u>. Baltimore: The Johns Hopkins University Press, 1994.

Barlow, Robert. Editor-in-Chief. <u>THE MERCK MANUAL OF DIAGNOSIS AND TREATMENT</u>. Fourteenth Edition. Rahway, New Jersey: Merck Sharp & Dohmer Research Laboratories, 1982.

Bartlett, John. <u>Familiar Quotations: *A collection of passages, phrases and proverbs traced to their sources in ancient and modern literature*</u>. SIXTEENTH EDITION. JUSTIN KAPLAN,

GENERAL EDITOR. Boston: Little, Brown and Company, 1992.

Beckett, J.C. THE MAKING OF MODERN IRELAND, 1603-1923. New York: Alfred A. Knopf, 1973.

Beevor, Antony. THE SECOND WORLD WAR. New York: Little, Brown and Company, 2012.

Benedict, Ruth. THE CHRYSANTHEMUM AND THE SWORD: PATTERNS OF JAPANESE CULTURE. Boston: Houghton Mifflin, 1946.

Bernstein, Michael A. THE GREAT DEPRESSION: Delayed Recovery and Economic Change in America, 1929-1939. New York: Cambridge University Press, 1987.

Bix, Herbert P. HIROHITO AND THE MAKING OF MODERN JAPAN. New York: Harper Collins Publishers, Inc., 2000.

Bluhm, Raymond K. Jr. Editor-in-Chief. Dale Andrade. Bruce Jacobs. John Lengellier. Clayton R. Newell. Matthew Seelinger. U.S. ARMY: A COMPLETE HISTORY. Arlington, Virginia: The Army Historical Foundation. Hugh Lauter Levin Associates, Inc., 2004.

Broderick, Eugene P. 24th Infantry Division: "The Victory Division". Paducah, Kentucky: Turner Publishing Company, 1997.

Brody, David. _Steelworkers in America_: The Nonunion Era. Cambridge Massachusetts: Harvard University Press, 1960.

Brown, DeSoto, Anne Ellett. HAWAII GOES TO WAR: LIFE IN HAWAII FROM PEARL HARBOR TO PEACE. Honolulu, Hawaii: Editions Limited, 1989.

Budnick, Rich. Hawaii's Forgotten History 1900-1999: the good…the bad…the embarrassing. Honolulu, Hawaii: Aloha Press, 2005.

Bureau for the Blind, Providence Rhode Island, "Annual Report of the Bureau for the Blind 1951-1952".

Providence: RHODE ISLAND STATE SERVICES FOR THE BLIND AND VISUALLY IMPAIRED ARCHIVES, 1952.

Bureau for the Blind, Providence Rhode Island, "Annual Report of the Bureau for the Blind 1954-1955". Providence: RHODE ISLAND STATE SERVICES FOR THE BLIND AND VISUALLY IMPAIRED ARCHIVES, 1955.

Bykofsky, Joseph, and Harold Larsen. THE UNITED STATES ARMY IN WORLD WAR II. OPERATIONS OF THE TRANSPORTATION CORPS OVERSEAS. Washington, D.C.: OFFICE OF THE CHIEF OF MILITARY HISTORY. DEPARTMENT OF THE ARMY, 1957.

"CCC Folder". Parsons Memorial Library. Alfred, Maine.

Chernow, Ron. ALEXANDER HAMILTON. New York: Penguin Books, 2005.

Childers, Thomas. SOLDIER FROM THE WAR RETURNING The Greatest Generation's Troubled Homecoming from World War II. Boston: Houghton Mifflin Harcourt, 2009.

Coffman, Edward M. THE REGULARS: The American Army, 1898-1941. Cambridge, Massachusetts: Belknap Press of Harvard University Press, 2004.

Cohen, Stan. THE TREE ARMY: A PICTORIAL HISTORY OF THE CIVILIAN CONSERVATION CORPS 1933-1942. Missoula, Montana: Pictorial Histories Publishing Company, 1980.

Condon-Rall, Albert E. Courdrey. UNITED STATES ARMY IN WORLD WAR II. The Technical Services. THE MEDICAL DEPARTMENT. MEDICAL SERVICES IN THE WAR AGAINST JAPAN. Washington, D.C.: CENTER OF MILITARY HISTORY. UNITED STATES ARMY, 1998.

Comparato, Frank E. AGE of GREAT GUNS: CANNON KINGS AND CANNONIERS WHO FORGED THE FIREPOWER OF ARTILLERY. Harrisburg, Pennsylvania: The Stackpole Company, 1965.

Conn, Stetson, Rose C. Engelman, Byron Fairchild. UNITED STATES ARMY IN WORLD WAR II. GUARDING THE

UNITED STATES AND ITS OUTPOSTSTS. Washington, D.C. CENTER OF MILITARY HISTORY, 2000.

Connelly, Donald B. John M. Schofield & the Politics of Generalship. Chapel Hill, North Carolina: The University of North Carolina Press, 2006.

Coogan, Tim Pat. WHEREVER GREEN IS WORN: The Story of the Irish Diaspora. New York: Palgrave, 2001.

Cook, John P. History of Alfred's Second Century: 1894 to 1994. No Publisher listed, 1994.

Cornwell, John. The Dark Box: A Secret History of Confession. New York: Basic Books, c.2014

Cowan, Edward J. & Richard Finlay. SCOTLAND SINCE 1688 Struggle For A Nation. London: Cima Books, 2000.

Crane, Dick. A Wonderful Journey: the Autobiography of Dick Crane. Peggy O'Keefe, & Susan Ryan. (Editors). Middletown, Rhode Island: WIM Publishing, 1995.

Crane, Ellery Bicknell, E. Melvin Williams. HISTORY OF WORCESTER COUNTY MASSACHUSETTS. 3 Volumes. New York: Lewis Historical Publishing Company, 1924.

Cullen, Karen J. Famine in Scotland: The "Ill Years" of the 1690s. Edinburgh, Scotland: Edinburgh University Press, 2010.

Deignan, Donald D. "The Ormond-Orrery Conflict, 1640-1680: A Study in Mid-Seventeenth Century Irish Society and Politics". (Unpublished Doctoral Dissertation). Brown University. Providence Rhode Island, 1982.

Deignan, Donald D. "Seventy-Five Years of Service and Partnership: A Brief History of Services for the Blind and Visually Impaired (1930-2005". [Second Edition.] Providence, Rhode Island: Department of Human Services, 2005.

Deignan, Francis James. "THE EFFECT OF MOTIVATIONAL FACTORS UPON GRADES EARNED AT CLARK COLLEGE BY VETERANS OF WORLD WAR II". (Unpublished Master's Thesis). Clark University, Worcester Massachusetts, 1947.

Devine, T.M. Editor. Irish Immigrants and Scottish Society in the Nineteenth and Twentieth Centuries: Proceedings of the Scottish Historical Studies Seminar Strathclyde University 1989-90. Edinburgh, Scotland: John Donald Publishers, Ltd., 1991.

Devine, T.M. Editor. Scottish Emigration and Scottish Society, Proceedings of the Scottish Historical Studies Seminar Strathclyde University 1990-91. Edinburgh, Scotland: John Donald Publishers, Ltd., 1992.

Dod, Carl C. UNITED STATES ARMY IN WORLD WAR II. The Technical Services. THE CORPS OF ENGINEERS IN THE

WAR AGAINST JAPAN. Washington, D.C.: THE CENTER OF MILITARY HISTORY. UNITED STATES ARMY. 1987.

Doerr, Anthony. *Four Seasons in Rome:* ON TWINS, INSOMNIA, AND THE BIGGEST FUNERAL IN THE HISTORY OF THE WORLD. New York: Scribner, 2007.

Dolan, Jay P. The Irish Americans A History. New York: Bloomsbury Press, 2008.

Donnelly, James S. Jr. The Great Irish Potato Famine. Gloucestershire, England: Sutton Publishing Limited, 2001.

Dostoevsky, Fyodor. The Brothers Karamazov. Translated by Andrew R. MacAndrew. Introductory Essay by Konstantin Mochlusky. Bantam Books: New York, 1981.

Dye, Bob. Editor. HAWAII CHRONICLES III: World War Two in Hawaii, from the pages of Paradise of the Pacific. Honolulu, Hawaii: University of Hawaii Press, 2000.

Engeman, Richard H. THE OREGON COMPANION: An Historical Gazetteer OF The Useful, The Curious, And The Arcane. Portland Oregon: Timber Press, Inc., 2009.

Farnsworth, Albert, George B. O'Flynn. THE STORY OF WORCESTER MASSACHUSETTS. Worcester, Massachusetts: The Davis Press, Inc., 1934.

FILMS VIEWED IN AUTHOR'S ARCHIVES:

"Wake Island", (Paramount) 1942.

"Bataan", (MGM) 1943.

"They Were Expendable", (MGM) 1945.

"From Here to Eternity", (Columbia Pictures) 1953.

"Run Silent, Run Deep", (United Artists) 1958.

Fitzgerald, Patrick, Brian Lambkin. Migration in Irish History, 1607-2007. Basingstoke, Hampshire, England: Palgrave, 2008.

Frank, Richard B. DOWNFALL The End Of The Imperial Japanese Empire. New York: Random House, 1999.

Freeberg, Ernest. The Education of Laura Bridgman: First Deaf and Blind Person to Learn Language. Cambridge, Massachusetts: Harvard University Press, 2001.

Freeman, T.W. PRE-FAMINE IRELAND: A STUDY IN HISTORICAL GEOGRAPHY, Manchester, England: Manchester University Press, 1957.

French, Kimberly. PERKINS SCHOOL FOR THE BLIND. The Campus History Series. Charleston, South Carolina: Arcadia Publishing, 2004.

Friend, Jason. PORTRAIT OF THE BORDERS. Wellington, Somerset, England: Halsgrave, 2008.

Gailey, Harry A. MACARTHUR'S VICTORY The War in New Guinea, 1943-1944. New York: Ballentine Books, 2004.

Gallagher, Tom. Glasgow The Uneasy Peace: Religious tension in modern Scotland, 1819-1914. Manchester, England: Manchester University Press, 1987.

Gaujac, Paul. THE EQUIPMENT OF THE US ARMY AMERICAN FIELD ARTILLERY 1941-45. [Colour plates by Nicholas Cohn. Translated from the French by Roger Branfill-Cox.] Paris, France: Histoire & Collections, 2009.

Gaultney, Bruce. Worcester Memories Celebrating 325 Years. Battle Ground, Washington: Pediment Publishing, 2009.

Gawne, Jonathan. Finding Your Father's War: A Practical Guide to Researching and Understanding Service in the World War II U.S. Army. Philadelphia: Casemate, 2006.

Gemlin, Stephan. "**S.S. Republic** Passenger Ship Transport Hospital Ship". THE MARINE NEWS, MAY, 1946.

Giangreco, D.M. HELL TO PAY: Operation DOWNFALL and the Invasion of Japan, 1945-1947. Annapolis, Maryland: Naval Institute Press, 2009.

Gillon, Steven M. PEARL HARBOR: FDR LEADS THE NATION INTO WAR. New York: Basic Books, 2011.

Gitter, Elizabeth. The Imprisoned Guest: Samuel Howe and Laura Bridgman, The Original Deaf-Blind Girl. New York: Farrar, Straus and Giroux, 2001.

Goldberg, Mark H. "CAVIAR AND CARGO": The C 3 Type Passenger Cargo Ships. Volume 2 of The American Merchant Marine History Series. Kings Point, New York: The American Merchant Marine Museum Foundation, 1992.

Grandchamp, Robert, Jane Lancaster and Cynthia Ferguson. Forward by Col. Howard E. Brown. "Rhody Redlegs": A History of the Providence Marine Corps of Artillery and the 103rd Field Artillery, Rhode Island Army National Guard, 1801-2010. Jefferson, North Carolina: McFarland & Company Publishers, Inc., 2011.

Greenfield, Roberts, Ken, Robert R. Palmer and Bell I. Wiley. THE UNITED STATES ARMY IN WORLD WAR II. The Army Ground Forces. THE ORGANIZATION OF GROUND COMBAT TROOPS. Washington, D.C.: HISTORICAL DIVISION UNITED STATES ARMY, 1947.

Groom, Winston. 1942 The Year that Tried Men's Souls. New York: Atlantic Monthly Press, 2005.

Grossman, Dave, Loren W. Christensen. ON COMBAT: The Psychology and Physiology of Deadly Conflict in War and in Peace. Third Edition. Warrior Science Publications, 2008.

Grotelueschen, Mark E. DOCTRINE UNDER TRIAL: American Artillery Employment in World War I. Westport Connecticut: Greenwood Press, 2001.

Grotelueschen, Mark E. The AEF Way of War The American Army and Combat in World War I. New York: Cambridge University Press, 2007.

Gudmundsson, Bruce I. On Artillery. Westport, Connecticut: Praeger Publishers, 1993.

Handley, James Edmund. The Irish In Modern Scotland. Cork, Ireland: Cork University Press, 1947.

Hastings, Max. RETRIBUTION THE BATTLE FOR JAPAN, 1944-45. New York: Alfred A. Knof, 2008.

Hawaii Department of Commerce. Honolulu, Hawaii. "Standard Certificate of Death for Joseph J. Deignan, March 19, 1942".

Her Majesty's Stationery Office. CENSUS OF IRELAND. GENERAL ALPHABETICAL INDEX TO THE TOWNLANDS AND TOWNS, PARISHES AND BARONIES of IRELAND, 1861. Baltimore, Maryland:

Genealogical Publishing Co., Inc. Reprinted 1986.

Hillstrom, Laurie Collier. DEFINING MOMENTS: THE ATTACK ON PEARL HARBOR. Chicago, Illinois: The University of Chicago Press, 2009.

Horn, Steve. THE SECOND ATTACK ON PEARL HARBOR: OPERATION K AND OTHER JAPANESE ATTEMPTS TO BOMB AMERICA IN WORLD WAR II. Annapolis, Maryland: Naval Institute Press, 2005.

Hornfischer, James D. SHIP OF GHOSTS: The Story of the U.S.S. Houston, FDR's Legendary Lost Cruiser, and the Epic Saga of Her Survivors. New York: Bantam Books, 2006.

Howes, Craig & Jon Osorio. (Editors). The Value of Hawaii: Knowing the Past, Shaping the Future. Honolulu, Hawaii: University of Hawaii Press, 2010.

Hoyt, Edwin P. YAMAMOTO: The Man Who Planned The Attack on Pearl Harbor. Guildford, Connecticut: THE LYONS PRESS, 2001.

"Individual Deceased Personnel File of Joseph J. Deignan". U.S. Army Human Resources Command. Alexandria, Virginia.

Jones, James. WW II: A CHRONICLE OF SOLDIERING. New York: Grosset & Dunlap, 1975.

Jones, James. FROM HERE TO ETERNITY. New York: Dell Publishing, 1998.

Junger, Sebastian. TRIBE: On Homecoming and Belonging. New York: Hachette Book Group Inc., 2016.

Keneally, Thomas. THE GREAT SHAME: and the Triumph of the Irish in the English-Speaking World. New York: NAN. A. TALESE, 1999.

Kennedy, David M. FREEDOM FROM FEAR The American People in Depression and War, 1929-1945. New York: Oxford University Press, 2005.

Kheriaty, Aaron and John Cihak. The Catholic Guide to Depression. Manchester, NH: Sophia Institute Press, c. 2012

Killigrew, John W. THE IMPACT OF THE GREAT DEPRESSION ON THE ARMY. New York: Garland Publishing, 1979.

Kipling, Rudyard. RUDYARD KIPLING'S VERSE INCLUSIVE EDITION 1885-1918. New York: Doubleday, Page & Company, 1922.

Lacy, Alexander Leslie. The Soil Soldiers: The Civilian Conservation Corps in the Great Depression. Radnor Pennsylvania: Chilton Book Company, 1976.

Leitrim Genealogy Centre. Our Leitrim Ancestors: GENEALOGY OF THE DUIGNAN FAMILY OF KILTUBRID CO. LEITRIM. BALINAMORE, CO. LEITRIM, IRELAND, 2008.

Linn, Brian McAllister. Guardians of Empire: The U.S. Army and the Pacific, 1902-1940. Chapel Hill, North Carolina: The University of North Carolina Press, 1994.

Lyons, F.S.L. Ireland Since The Famine. Suffolk, England: The Chaucer Press, Ltd. Collins/Fontana. Eighth Edition, 1982.

Maher, Neil. M. NATURE'S NEW DEAL: The Civilian Conservation Corps and the Roots of the Environmental Movement. New York: Oxford University Press, 2008.

Marshall, Rosalind K. John Knox. Edinburgh Scotland: Berlinn Limited, 2008.

Martin, James, S.J. THE JESUIT GUIDE TO (ALMOST) EVERYTHING: A Spirituality for Real Life. New York: Harper/Collins Publishers, 2010.

Mayo, Lida. THE UNITED STATES ARMY IN WORLD WAR II. The Technical Services. THE ORDNANCE DEPARTMENT: ON BEACHHEAD AND BATTLEFRONT. Washington, D.C.: OFFICE OF THE CHIEF OF MILITARY HISTORY. THE UNITED STATES ARMY, 1968.

McKenney, Janice E. (Compiler). FIELD ARTILLERY REGULAR ARMY AND ARMY RESERVE. Army Lineage Series. Washington D.C.: OFFICE OF THE CHIEF OF MILITARY HISTORY. THE UNITED STATES ARMY, 1985.

Meagher, Timothy J. INVENTING *IRISH* AMERICA: Generation, Class, and Ethnic Identity in a New England City, 1880-1928, Notre Dame, Indiana: University Of Notre Dame Press, 2001.

Miller, Kerby A. Emigrants And Exiles: Ireland and the Irish Exodus to North America. New York: Oxford University Press, 1985.

Mitchell, Brian. a new geographical atlas of ireland. Baltimore, Maryland: GENEALOGICAL PUBLISHING Co., Inc., 1986.

Molloy, Scott. Irish Titan, Irish Toilers: Joseph Banigan and Nineteenth-Century New England Labor (Revisiting New England). Hanover, New Hampshire. University Press of New England, 2008.

Moore, Thomas. Moore's *Irish Melodies The Illustrated 1846 Edition.* Mineola, New York: Dover Publications, Inc., 2000.

"Morning Report for March 1942 for Battery C. of the 13th Field Artillery Battalion". National Archives and Records Administration. National Personnel Records Center. Military Branch. Saint Louis Missouri.

Morton, Louis. THE UNITED STATES ARMY IN WORLD WAR II. The War in the Pacific. STRATEGY AND COMMAND: THE FIRST TWO YEARS. Washington, D.C.: CENTER OF MILITARY HISTORY. THE UNITED STATES ARMY, 2000.

Morton, Louis. THE UNITED STATES ARMY IN WORLD WAR II. The War in the Pacific. THE FALL OF THE PHILIPPINES. Washington, D.C.: CENTER OF MILITARY HISTORY. THE UNITED STATES ARMY, 1989.

Morrill, Frank J., William O. Hultgren and Eric J. Salmonsson. WORCESTER 1880-1920: Images of America. Charleston, South Carolina: Arcadia Publishing, 2003.

Morrill, Frank J., William O. Hultgren and Eric J. Salmonsson. WORCESTER: POSTCARD HISTORY SERIES. Charleston, South Carolina: Arcadia Publishing, 2005.

Moulin, Pierre. A History of Fort DeRussy: U.S. Army Museum of Hawaii. Honolulu, Hawaii: Mutual Publishing, LLC., 2008.

"Mt. Greylock Camp Report". National Archives and Records Administration. College Park, Maryland. Record Group 79, Boxes 62 and 63.

National Archives and Records Administration. College Park Maryland. Textual Archives.

Record Group 338, Entry 37042, Box 3461, Unit Histories, 24th Infantry, Training Memo. #5, "Training Program" Nov. 1, 1941 to May 23, 1942.

Record Group 407, Entry 427, Box 6839, WWII Operations Reports, 24th Inf. Div., After Action Report of the 13th F.A. Battalion, "Blacklist" (Occupation of Japan).

Record Group 407, Entry 427, Box 6611, WWII Operations Reports, 24th Inf. Div., "AGF Fact Sheet, 24th Infantry Division."

Record Group 407, Entry 427, Box 6615, WWII Operations Reports, 24th Inf. Div., Gen. Order #1, "Brigadier General D.S. Wilson Assumes Command." October 1, 1941.

Record Group 407, Entry 427, Box 6615, WWII Operations Reports, 24th Inf. Div., "New Division Commander at Schofield," October, 1941.

Record Group 407, Entry 427, Box 6615, WWII Operations Reports, 24th Inf. Div., Gen. Order #2, "Announcement of Division Staff Officers," October 1, 1941.

Record Group 407, Entry 427, Box 6615, WWII Operations Reports, 24th Inf. Div., Staff Memo. #1, "Administrative Procedure," October 10, 1941.

Record Group 407, Entry 427, Box 6615, WWII Operations Reports, 24th Inf. Div., "Roster of Officers," October 21, 1941.

Record Group 407, Entry 427, Box 6615, WWII Operations Reports, 24th Inf. Div., "Principal Training Activities," 6-11 October 1941.

Record Group 407, Entry 427, Box 6839, WWII Operations Reports, 24th Inf. Div., "Battalion History, October 1941".

Record Group 407, Entry 427, Box 6615, WWII Operations Reports, 24th Inf. Div., Memorandum: "24th Infantry Division—Communication Exercise November 4, 1941".

Record Group 407, Entry 427, Box 6615, WWII Operations Reports, 24th Inf. Div., "Organization of the 24th Infantry Division," Dec. 7, 1941.

Record Group 407, Entry 427, Box 6611, WWII Operations Reports, 24th Inf. Div., "The Twenty-Fourth Infantry Division: A Brief History".

Record Group 494, Entry 44 (UD-UP), Box 252, Adjutant General Gen. Correspondence 1917-44, Decimal 293.1. Major F.A. Stacy to Commanding Officer, Schofield Barracks, T.H., April 19, 1942, Honors, "Funeral Firing Squads".

Record Group 494, Entry 44 (UD-UP), Box 433, Adjutant General Gen. Correspondence 1917-44, Decimal 704. Colonel A.J. Canning, Medical Corps, to Chief of Staff, Hawaiian Department, "INFORMAL MEMORANDUM", Casualties, "List of gunshot wounds admitted to this hospital," April 17, 1942.

Record Group 494, Entry 44 (UD-UP), Box 433, Adjutant General Gen. Correspondence 1917-44, Decimal 704. Casualties, "Reports of Separation," April 1, 1942.

National Archives and Records Administration. National Personnel Records Center. Civilian Personnel Records. Saint Louis, Missouri, "Discharge Papers of Donald J.J. Deignan", 1935 and 1937.

Nelson, Harold W. Editor-in-Chief. Bruce Jacobs. Editor. Raymond K. Blum, Jr. Graphics Editor. THE ARMY. Arlington Virginia: The Army Historical Foundation, 2001.

Norton, Desmond. LANDLORDS, TENANTS, FAMINE: _The Business of an Irish Land Agency in the 1840s_. Dublin: University College Dublin Press, 2006.

Nutt, Charles. HISTORY OF WORCESTER AND ITS PEOPLE. (4 Volumes.) New York: Lewis Historical Publishing Company, 1919.

O'Clery, Helen. (Compiler). THE IRELAND READER. New York: Franklin Watts, Inc. 1963.

O'Flynn, Francis Thomas. The Story of Worcester Massachusetts. Boston: Little, Brown and Company, 1910.

O'Grada, Cormac. Ireland before and after the Famine Explorations in economic history, 1800-1925. New York: Manchester University Press. Paperback edition, 1996.

Okrent, Daniel. LAST CALL: The Rise and Fall of Prohibition. New York: Scribner, 2010.

Padelford, Norman J. THE PANAMA CANAL IN PEACE AND WAR. New York: The MacMillan Company, 1942.

Palmer, Robert R., Bell I. Wiley and William R.I. Kast. UNITED STATES ARMY IN WORLD WAR II, The Army Ground Forces, THE PROCUREMENT AND TRAINING OF GROUND COMBAT TROOPS, Washington, D.C.: HISTORICAL DIVISION, DEPARTMENT OF THE ARMY, 1948.

Panama Canal Office of Public Affairs. "THE PANAMA CANAL". Miami Florida, 1985.

Parsons, Usher. A CENTENIAL HISTORY OF ALFRED, YORK COUNTY, MAINE. Philadelphia, Pennsylvania: Sanford, Everts & Co. 1872.

Perkins School for the Blind. *"Christmas Music"* Program of Perkins School for the Blind. Watertown Massachusetts: Research Library Archives, 1959.

Perkins School for the Blind. Watertown, Massachusetts. "Student Records of Donald Donovan Deignan, September, 1957 - June, 1968".

Phillips, Herbert P. "THE CLAN": ORGANIZATION DAY BOOKLET of the THIRTEENTH FIELD ARTILLERY BATALLION. Washington, D.C: Adjutant General's Office. Historical Records Section, 1947.

Prange, Gordon W., Donald M. Goldstein and Katherine V. Dillon. <u>AT DAWN WE SLEPT: The Untold Story of Pearl Harbor</u>. New York: McGraw-Hill Book Company, 1981.

Prange, Gordon W., Donald M. Goldstein and Katherine V. Dillon. <u>Miracle at Midway</u>. New York: MUF Books, 1982.

Prange, Gordon W., Donald M. Goldstein and Katherine V. Dillon. <u>PEARL HARBOR: The Verdict of History</u>. New York: Penguin Books, 1991.

Prange, Gordon W., Donald M. Goldstein and Katherine V. Dillon. <u>DEC. 7 1941: THE DAY THE JAPANESE ATTACKED PEARL HARBOR.</u> New York: Warner Books, 1989.

Rogers, Robert F. <u>DESTINY'S LANDFALL: A HISTORY OF GUAM</u>. Honolulu, Hawaii: University of Hawaii Press, 1995.

Rosenzweig, Roy. <u>Eight hours for what you will Workers and leisure in an industrial city, 1870-1920</u>. New York: Cambridge University Press. Paperback, 1985.

Rottman, Gordon L. <u>FUBAR SOLDIER SLANG OF WORLD WAR II.</u> Oxford, England: Osprey Publishing, Paperback Edition, 2009.

St. John, Alan D. <u>OREGON'S DRY SIDE: Exploring East of the Cascade Crest</u>. Portland Oregon: Timber Press, 2007.

Salmond, John A. The Civilian Conservation Corps, 1933-1942: A New Deal Case Study. Durham, North Carolina: Duke University Press, 1967.

Salvatore, Nick. WE ALL GOT HISTORY: THE MEMORY BOOKS OF AMOS WEBBER. New York: Times Books, 1996.

Seaburg, Carl and Stanley Paterson, Merchant Prince of Boston: Colonel T. H. Perkins, 1764-1854. Cambridge, Massachusetts: Harvard University Press, 1971.

Sewell, Dennis. Catholics: Britain's Largest Minority. London: Penguin Books, 2002.

Shakespeare, William. The Complete Works. Edited By G. B. Harrison. New York: Harcourt, Brace & World, Inc. 1968.

Shay, Jonathan. ODYSSEUS IN AMERICA: COMBAT TRAUMA AND THE TRIALS OF HOMECOMING. New York: Scribner, 2002.

Shea, Susan, "Final Research Report". Typescript, 2009.

Simpson, MacKinnon. HAWAII HOMEFRONT: LIFE IN THE ISLANDS DURING WORLD WAR II. Honolulu, Hawaii: Bess Press, 2008.

Smith, Henry M. THE CITY OF WORCESTER MASSACHUSETTS: ITS PUBLIC BUILDINGS AND

BUSINESS. Worcester, Massachusetts: Sanford & Davis, 1886.

Southwick, Albert B. *Once Told Tales of Worcester County*. Worcester, Massachusetts: DATABOOKS, 1994.

Southwick, Albert B. *More Once Told Tales of Worcester County*. Worcester, Massachusetts: DATABOOKS, 1994.

Southwick, Albert B. *150 Years of Worcester: 1848-1898*. Worcester, Massachusetts: Chandler House Press, 1998.

Spear, Marilyn W. "WORCESTER'S THREE-DECKERS". WORCESTER PEOPLE AND PLACES, VI. WORCESTER MASSACHUSETTS: WORCESTER BICENTENNIAL COMMISSION, 1977.

Stanton, Shelby L. WORLD WAR II ORDER OF BATTLE: U.S. ARMY (GROUND FORCE UNITS). Mechanicsburg Pennsylvania: Stackpole Books, 2000.

State of Rhode Island and Providence Plantations. Department of Human Services. Office of Rehabilitation Services. State Services for the Blind and Visually Impaired. Providence, Rhode Island. "Records of *Donald Donovan Deignan*": *File No. R-884, 1952-1982.*

Stauffer, Alvin P. THE UNITED STATES ARMY IN WORLD WAR II. The Technical Services. THE QUARTERMASTER CORPS: OPERATIONS IN THE WAR AGAINST JAPAN.

Washington, D.C.: CENTER OF MILITARY HISTORY. UNITED STATES ARMY, 1990.

Stone, Scott C.S. PEARL HARBOR The Way It Was— December 7, 1941. Waipahu, Hawaii: ISLAND HERITAGE PUBLISHING, Fourth Edition, 2009.

Strong, L.A.G. *The Minstrel Boy*: A Portrait of Tom Moore. New York: Alfred A. Knopf, 1937.

Suid, Lawrence H. Dolores A. Haverstick. Stars and Stripes on Screen: A Comprehensive Guide to Portrayals of American Military on Film. Lanham, Maryland: The Scarecrow Press, Inc., 2005.

Tarbah, Ruth M. Hawaii: A History. New York: W.W. Norton & Company, 1984.

The American Battle Monuments Commission. "Honolulu Memorial National Memorial Cemetery of the Pacific Honolulu, Hawaii". Arlington Virginia: The American Battle Monuments Commission, (no date).

"The Canal Record 1939", (no. 2. vol. 33). Smathers Archives, University of Florida, Gainesville.

The Holy Bible containing the Old and New Testaments. Standard Revised Version. Catholic Edition. Princeton, New Jersey: SCEPTER, 1966.

The Honolulu Advertiser, Honolulu, Hawaii.

The Honolulu Star-Bulletin, Honolulu, Hawaii.

The New York Times, New York, New York.

The Providence Journal-Bulletin, Providence, Rhode Island.

The San Francisco Chronicle, San Francisco, California.

The San Francisco Examiner, San Francisco, California.

The Worcester Evening Gazette, Worcester Massachusetts.

The Worcester Evening Post, Worcester, Massachusetts.

The Worcester Telegram, Worcester, Massachusetts.

The Roman Way 1961. Volume III., June 1961. Rome, Italy: Published by The Students of Notre Dame International School.

"THE WOODEN CROSS ISSUE". (Typescript). National Memorial Cemetery of the Pacific, Honolulu, Hawaii.

Toland, John. THE RISING SUN The Decline and Fall of the Japanese Empire 1936-1945. Barnsley, South Yorkshire, England: Pen & Sword Books, Ltd., 2011.

Tropic Lightning Museum. "Historic Guide Schofield Barracks Hawaii". Waihiawa Hawaii. Tropic Lightning Museum, (no date).

Tropic Lightning Museum. "Schofield Barracks". Waihiawa Hawaii. Tropic Lightning Museum, 1996.

"Unit Rosters for Battery C. 13th Field Artillery Battalion 1939-1942". National Personnel Records Center. Military Branch. Saint Louis Missouri.

United States Catholic Conference, Inc. CATECHISM of the CATHOLIC CHURCH. SECOND EDITION: revised in accordance with the official Latin text promulgated by Pope John Paul II. Vatican City: LIBRERIA EDITRICE VATICANA, 1997.

Urwin, Gregory J. W. Victory in defeat: THE WAKE ISLAND DEFENDERS IN CAPTIVITY 1941-1945. Annapolis, Maryland: Naval Institute Press, 2010.

Valtin, Jan. CHILDREN of YESTERDAY: The Twenty-Fourth Infantry Division in World War II. Nashville, Tennessee: The Battery Press, 2004.

Vaughan, W.E., A.J. Fitzpatrick. Editors. IRISH HISTORICAL STATISTICS: POPULATION, 1821-1971. Dublin: Royal Irish Academy, 1978.

Wainright, Jonathan M. GENERAL WAINRIGHT'S STORY. Edited by Robert Considine. New York: Bantam Books, 1986.

War Department. FM 6-50 "FIELD ARTILLERY FIELD MANUAL SERVICE OF THE PIECE 75MM GUN, M1897 AND M1897 A4, HORSE-DRAWN AND TRUCK-DRAWN." Washington D.C.: Government Printing Office 1939.

War Department. FM 100-5 "Field Service Regulations, Operations". Washington, D.C.: Government Printing Office, 1941.

Wardlow, Charles. THE UNITED STATES ARMY IN WORLD WAR II. The Technical Services. THE TRANSPORTATION CORPS: RESPONSIBILITIES, ORGANIZATION, AND OPERATIONS. WASHINGTON, D.C. OFFICE OF THE CHIEF OF MILITARY HISTORY, 1951.

Warren, Kenneth. BIG STEEL: The First Century of the United States Steel Corporation 1901-2001. Pittsburg, Pennsylvania: University of Pittsburg Press, 2001.

Washburn, Charles Grenfill. Industrial Worcester. Burgeonvill, Pennsylvania: General Books, LLC, 2009.

Weintraub, Stanley. Pearl Harbor Christmas: A World at War, December 1941. Cambridge, MA: Da Capo Press, c. 2011.

Wels, Susan. DECEMBER 7, 1941 PEARL HARBOR AMERICA'S DARKEST DAY. [Foreword By Senator Daniel K. Inouye. Introduction By Sir John Keagan.] San Diego, California: Tehabi Books, 2001.

Willford, Glen. RACING THE SUNRISE: Reinforcing America's Pacific Outposts, 1941-1942. Annapolis, Maryland: Naval Institute Press, 2010.

Williams, Mary H. (Compiler.) THE UNITED STATES ARMY IN WORLD WAR II. Special Studies. CHRONOLOGY 1941-1945. Washington, D.C. CENTER OF MILITARY HISTORY. THE UNITED STATES ARMY, 1989.

Yeulenski, Lois R. (Compiler) WORCESTER IMAGES of America . Charleston, South Carolina: Arcadia Publishing, 1999.

Zimm, Alan D., Matt Baughman. ATTACK ON PEARL HARBOR: STRATEGY, COMBAT, MYTHS, DECEPTIONS. Havertown, Pennsylvania: Casemate Publishers, 2011.

INDEX

Italicized page numbers indicate illustrations.

CPSIA information can be obtained
at www.ICGtesting.com
Printed in the USA
FFHW021053020619
52775266-58316FF

9 781478 778400